Nationalism on the Internet

In this timely book, critical theorist Christian Fuchs asks: What is nationalism and what is the role of social media in the communication of nationalist ideology?

Advancing an applied Marxist theory of nationalism, Fuchs explores nationalist discourse in the world of contemporary digital capitalism that is shaped by social media, big data, fake news, targeted advertising, bots, algorithmic politics, and a high-speed online attention economy. Through two case studies of the German and Austrian 2017 federal elections, the book goes on to develop a critical theory of nationalism that is grounded in the works of Karl Marx, Rosa Luxemburg, and Eric J. Hobsbawm.

Advanced students and scholars of Marxism, nationalism, media, and politics won't want to miss Fuchs' latest in-depth study of social media and politics that uncovers the causes, structures, and consequences of nationalism in the age of social media and fake news.

Christian Fuchs is a professor of media and communication studies and a critical theorist of communication and society. He is a co-editor of the journal *tripleC: Communication, Capitalism & Critique* (www.triple-c.at) and the author of many books, including *Social Media: A Critical Introduction, Digital Demagogue: Authoritarian Capitalism in the Age of Trump and Twitter, Digital Labour and Karl Marx*, and *Internet and Society: Social Theory in the Information Age*.

Nationalism on the Internet
Critical Theory and Ideology in the Age of Social Media and Fake News

Christian Fuchs

Routledge
Taylor & Francis Group
NEW YORK AND LONDON

First published 2020
by Routledge
52 Vanderbilt Avenue, New York, NY 10017

and by Routledge
2 Park Square, Milton Park, Abingdon, Oxon, OX14 4RN

Routledge is an imprint of the Taylor & Francis Group, an informa business

© 2020 Taylor & Francis

The right of Christian Fuchs to be identified as author of this work has been asserted by him in accordance with sections 77 and 78 of the Copyright, Designs and Patents Act 1988.

All rights reserved. No part of this book may be reprinted or reproduced or utilized in any form or by any electronic, mechanical, or other means, now known or hereafter invented, including photocopying and recording, or in any information storage or retrieval system, without permission in writing from the publishers.

Trademark notice: Product or corporate names may be trademarks or registered trademarks, and are used only for identification and explanation without intent to infringe.

Library of Congress Cataloging-in-Publication Data
A catalog record for this title has been requested

ISBN: 978-0-367-36038-2 (hbk)
ISBN: 978-0-367-35766-5 (pbk)
ISBN: 978-0-429-34347-6 (ebk)

Typeset in Univers
by Swales & Willis, Exeter, Devon, UK

"I feel at home in the entire world wherever there are clouds and birds and human tears."

— Rosa Luxemburg

"Those who do not move, do not notice their chains."

— Quote attributed to Rosa Luxemburg

This book is dedicated to the socialists, humanists, anti-authoritarians, anti-fascists, and anti-nationalists of the world. If they unite, they can save humanity from the dangers of barbarism and war that are immanent to capitalism.

Contents

List of Figures	ix
List of Tables	xi
Chapter One – Introduction: Nationalism Today	1
PART I – Foundations of a Marxist Theory of Nationalism	**19**
Chapter Two – Bourgeois Theories of Nationalism	21
Chapter Three – Marx's Concept of Nationalism	33
Chapter Four – Otto Bauer's and Rosa Luxemburg's Opposing Theories of the Nation and Nationalism	43
Chapter Five – Contemporary Marxist Theories of Nationalism	79
PART II – Nationalism on Social Media	**123**
Chapter Six – German Nationalism on Social Media in the 2017 Elections to the Bundestag	125
Chapter Seven – Online Nationalism and Social Media Authoritarianism in the Context of the ÖVP/FPÖ Government in Austria	179
Chapter Eight – Conclusion: Towards a Society of the Commons beyond Authoritarianism and Nationalism	245
References	285
Index	303

Figures

1.1	A model of right-wing politics	3
5.1	Five types of communications/mediated communication	114
5.2	@RoyalFamiliy's tweet about the Queen's Christmas Message 2017	120
6.1	Right-wing politics	160
7.1	The FPÖ's results in Austrian federal elections	184
7.2	Facebook posting by Heinz-Christian Strache	199
7.3	Facebook posting by Herbert Kickl	200
7.4	Facebook posting by Sebastian Kurz	201
7.5	Development of the wage share in Austria and the EU-15 countries	209
8.1	The antagonism between the capitalist empire and the multitude	278
8.2	Political convergence of movements for the commons	280

Tables

1.1	Number of Twitter and Facebook followers in far-right politics, accessed on 29 January 2018 and 2 May 2019	14
2.1	Five theories of nationalism, based on Smith (1998) and Özkirimli (2010)	22
4.1	A comparison of Otto Bauer's and Rosa Luxemburg's concepts of the nation and nationalism	71
5.1	Number of empires and nation-states with more than 1 million inhabitants	97
5.2	Types of nationalism's ideological discourse structures	110
5.3	Social forms of nationalism (media types, entities, social relations/practices, events)	116
6.1	Composite indicator for a country's reasonable share of asylum permits in the EU	126
6.2	Results of the 2017 Bundestag elections	128
6.3	Overview of collected social media data	131
6.4	Most frequently mentioned words in the Twitter dataset	133
6.5	The political Twitter accounts posting most frequently about Germany, the nation, refugees, migrants, the EU, and Islam	134
6.6	The ten most frequently mentioned users in politicians' tweets about Germany, the nation, refugees, migrants, the EU and Islam in the Twitter-politician dataset	135
6.7	Users mentioning Alice Weidel in the Twitter-politician dataset	136
6.8	Users mentioning Martin Schulz in the Twitter-politician dataset	136
6.9	Users mentioned most frequently in the Twitter-television debate dataset	136
6.10	The users with the largest number of postings made in the Twitter-television debate dataset	137
6.11	Selected spending items of the German federal budget	148
6.12	The development of the share of the members of specific religions in the total German population	151
6.13	Age groups in Germany	152
6.14	ISIS supporters' terror attacks in Germany	157
6.15	A typology of racism's friend/enemy logic along societal dimensions	163
6.16	Twitter profiles used in the analysis	167

6.17	Facebook pages used in the analysis	168
6.18	YouTube channels used in the analysis	168
7.1	Results of the 2017 Austrian federal elections	180
7.2	Voting behaviour of various groups in the 2017 and 2013 Austrian federal elections (per cent of total voters)	181
7.3	FPÖ parliamentarians and ministers who are members of organisations that belong to the milieu of the Burschenschaften	187
7.4	Main donors of the ÖVP's 2017 election campaign	190
7.5	Audience rates of main television debates in the 2017 Austrian federal elections that involved Sebastian Kurz and/or Heinz-Christian Strache	197
7.6	Facebook postings and online newspaper articles selected for analysis	198
7.7	Nationalist discourse topics used in the analysis	202
7.8	The development of the share of the members of specific religions in the total Austrian population (in per cent)	207
7.9	Analysis of reactions to Facebook postings of the frontrunners in the 2017 Austrian federal elections	211
7.10	Share of specific types of postings in the analysed dataset, $N = 2,367$	213
7.11	Dimensions of authoritarianism in the analysed dataset among postings supporting the ÖVP/FPÖ government, $N = 1,607$	214
7.12	The mentioning of specific enemies in the analysed dataset	219
7.13	Asylum seekers in Austria	222
7.14	Asylum applications in the EU	223
7.15	Reported crimes in Austria	224
7.16	Number of intentional homicides per hundred thousand inhabitants	226
7.17	Share of population aged 65/75 or older, in per cent	227
7.18	Share of pensioners in total population, in per cent	227

Chapter One
Introduction: Nationalism Today

1.1 Nationalism Today

1.2 Studying Nationalism

1.3 This Book's Structure

1.1 Nationalism Today

Right-wing politicians and parties have in recent years had success in a significant number of countries. Examples include:

- the Alliance of Patriots of Georgia;
- the Alternative for Germany;
- the Bharatiya Janata Party under Narendra Modi in India;
- Boris Kollár's We Are Family, Marian Kotleba's People's Party Our Slovakia, and Andrej Danko's Slovak National Party in Slovakia;
- Brexit, UKIP, the Brexit Party, and Nigel Farage in the UK;
- the Conservative People's Party of Estonia in Estonia;
- the Croatian Party of Rights in Croatia;
- the Danish People's Party in Denmark;
- the Democratic Centre in Colombia;
- Donald J. Trump in the USA;
- the Finns Party in Finland;
- the Freedom Party, Heinz-Christian Strache, Norbert Hofer, and Sebastian Kurz in Austria;
- Geert Wilders and the Party for Freedom in the Netherlands;
- the Golden Dawn in Greece;
- the Great Indonesia Movement Party in Indonesia;
- Jair Bolsonaro and the Social Liberal Party in Brazil;
- Jarosław Kaczyński's Law and Justice party in Poland;

Introduction

- Jobbik and Viktor Orbán's Fidesz in Hungary;
- the Liberal Democratic Party in Japan;
- Marine Le Pen and the National Front in France;
- Matteo Salvini's Northern League, Giorgia Meloni's Brothers of Italy, and Beppe Grillo's Five Star Movement in Italy;
- the National Alliance in Latvia;
- the National Popular Front in Cyprus;
- One Nation in Australia;
- Prayut Chan-o-cha's military junta governing Thailand;
- the Progress Party in Norway;
- Recep Tayyip Erdoğan's rule of Turkey;
- Rodrigo Duterte in the Philippines;
- Santiago Abascal's Vox in Spain;
- the Serbian Radical Party in Serbia;
- the Slovenian National Party in Slovenia;
- Svoboda in the Ukraine;
- the Sweden Democrats in Sweden;
- the Swiss People's Party in Switzerland;
- Tomio Okumura's Freedom and Direct Democracy party and Andrej Babiš' Action of Dissatisfied Citizens in the Czech Republic;
- the United Patriots, Attack, Bulgarian National Movement, and Volya in Bulgaria;
- the United Romania Party in Romania;
- United Russia, Vladimir Putin's All-Russia People's Front, and the Liberal Democratic Party in Russia; and
- Vlaams Belang in Belgium.

This list is not complete, but shows that right-wing politics plays a role in many countries and parts of the world. Many of these parties are characterised by top-down leadership, nationalism, the use of the friend/enemy scheme for scapegoating minorities and political opponents, and law and order politics. These four elements interact and together constitute right-wing politics (Fuchs 2018a). Figure 1.1 visualises a model of right-wing politics. In right-wing politics that operates based on and accepts the democratic state, the elements of patriarchy and militarism take on the

FIGURE 1.1 A model of right-wing politics

form of law and order politics (the belief that crime and social problems can be solved by policing, surveillance, and tough prison sentences) as well as material investments and an ideological stress on the importance of repressive state apparatuses (the police, the army, the judicial system, the prison system). Such politics can also be termed conservative politics. In contrast, fascist forms of right-wing politics oppose and want to abolish the democratic state. They want to organise society as a dictatorship that is built on and uses means of terror. Terror is used against political opponents and other identified enemies and scapegoats in order to try to annihilate them. Far-right politics operates based on the democratic state, but its boundaries to fascism are more fluid than in the case of conventional right-wing politics. In far-right politics, violent political rhetoric and communication that can imply and lead to physical violence against opponents is fairly common. In right-wing extremist politics, the boundary to fascism is even more crossed than in far-right politics. This means that in right-wing extremist political groups, parties, ideology, and practices, there are individuals who advocate the use of physical violence against opponents.

All right-wing politics has in common that it sees inequality between humans as a natural feature of society and therefore considers an egalitarian society as utopian and unrealistic (Bobbio 1996). In contrast, the political left sees inequality as a result of social contradictions and therefore argues that equality between humans can and should be established politically. Right-wing practices always contain various degrees of the four dimensions of right-wing politics. These elements define a group identity (nationalism), a method for organising the relationship between leaders and followers in the political group itself and society (leadership principle), an antagonistic relationship between citizens of the nation and enemies that is built on hatred (friend/enemy scheme), and methods of dealing with enemies (law and order politics, militarism). All right-wing politics denies the class conflict and advances the ruling class' interests. It reifies and fetishises private property of the means of production and the existence of class society and class relations, which means that the economy is based on the leadership principle so that a small minority owns, controls, and governs the economy, whereas others are compelled to produce goods they do not own. Right-wing politics favours undemocratic models of the economy, where one class exploits the labour of another class.

Let us have a look at some political quotes:

- Donald Trump on Twitter: "The only way to stop drugs, gangs, human trafficking, criminal elements and much else from coming into our Country is with a Wall or Barrier."[1]
- Jair Bolsonaro: "The scum of the earth is showing up in Brazil, as if we didn't have enough problems of our own to sort out."[2]
- Heinz Christian Strache in a newspaper interview: "That's why we consequently continue our path for our home country of Austria, the fight against

population exchange, just like the people expect it from us. [...] We do not want to become a minority in our own homeland."[3]

- Marine Le Pen on Twitter: "By attacking the idea of the Nation and the control of immigration you let communitarianism, Islamism and terrorism grow."[4]
- Recep Erdoğan on Twitter: "One nation. One flag. One fatherland. One state."[5]
- Viktor Orbán on Facebook: "Nowadays, Hungary and the Hungarian people represent order in an increasingly disorderly Europe. Many of the leaders of Europe do not undertake the fight against modern mass migration and the incoming flood of illegal and law violating migrants."[6]
- Nigel Farage on Twitter: "NHS should be a National, not International Health Service. £181,000 bill for one illegal migrant is madness."[7]
- Matteo Salvini on Facebook: "While the Pope calls for welcoming all the migrants, 700 illegal immigrants have landed in Calabria and another 3,000 will arrive in Italy in the next few hours. Immigration? No, INVASION organized and financed by the new slavers."[8]

Nationalism is a common element of all of these examples. Protecting a unitary nation is presented as important. Nationalism ideologically constructs a collective cultural and political identity by referring to "our Country", "our home country", "our homeland", "the idea of the Nation", "one nation", "one flag", "one fatherland", "one state", "Hungary and the Hungarian people", or the National Health Service. Right-wing ideology understands the nation as a cultural and/or biological community that it presents as a people. Nationalism not just wants to establish a nation-state, where the imagined members of the nation live, but also strives for purity of the nation. In reality, societies are never homogeneous because there are different ways of life and nation-states are the outcome of conflicts, wars, imperialism, and colonialism.

All nationalism presents the nation as being threatened by aliens and as needing to be protected in order to secure purity that needs to be protected from aliens. In the examples, immigrants, refugees, Muslims, drug dealers, and organised criminals are presented as enemies of the nation. The cultural and biological nation is an ideological construct that serves to distract attention from actual exploitation and domination. In the age of digital capitalism, nationalist ideology is frequently communicated over social media platforms such as Facebook, Twitter, or YouTube.

1.2 Studying Nationalism

This book asks: What is nationalism? What is the role of social media in the communication of nationalist ideology?

This work advances an applied Marxist theory of nationalism that revives classical critical theories of nationalism by using them as tools for studying nationalism in contemporary digital capitalism that is shaped by social media, big data, fake news, targeted advertising, bots, algorithmic politics, and a high-speed online attention economy. The book develops a critical theory of nationalism that is grounded in the works of Karl Marx, Rosa Luxemburg, and Eric J. Hobsbawm. Their theories are applied to two case studies that analyse how nationalism was in the year 2017 communicated on social media in the context of the German and Austrian federal elections.

Critical studies that compare nationalism in different countries, analyse how nationalism is communicated, and apply Marxist theory for understanding nationalism are needed. The reason why I have chosen Austria and Germany as two case studies is that I know these two countries well and speak German, which allows me to understand social media content posted in these nation-states. Austria and Germany are interesting cases because both countries together gave under Hitler rise to Nazi-fascism and are today again haunted by the rise of the far-right – the Alternative for Germany (AfD) and the far-right ÖVP/FPÖ coalition government led by Sebastian Kurz and Heinz-Christian Strache in Austria.

We certainly need more international comparative studies of nationalism and how it is communicated. Given the diversity of the world's languages and the lack of diversity of funding sources, conducting comparative social research based on projects that provide funding to scholars in different countries located not just in Europe or North America is a difficult but nonetheless important task. National funding agendas are mostly nationalist in character, which means that they want to advance scientific progress, which is often seen as a foundation of economic growth and innovation, in just one country or region (such as the European Union). There is a lack of true internationalisation of research and international funding.

Marxist Theories of Nationalism

Many thought that the increasing levels of economic, political, and cultural globalisation since the 1970s would bring an end to nationalism. Marxist historian Eric

J. Hobsbawm (1992b), who was a political optimist, argued, for example, that the "owl of Minerva which brings wisdom, said Hegel, flies out at dusk. It is a good sign that it is now circling round nations and nationalism" (192). Writing in 1996, Jürgen Habermas (1998) was confident that "the catastrophes of two world wars have taught Europeans that they must abandon the mind-sets on which nationalistic, exclusionary mechanisms feed. Why should a sense of belonging together culturally and politically not grow out of these experiences" (152). Such assessments have unfortunately proven historically false. More than 100 years after the First World War, nationalism has returned.

Writing about the owl of Minerva, Hegel (1820/2008) stresses that philosophy can only interpret history ex post:

> When philosophy paints its grey in grey, then has a shape of life grown old.
> By philosophy's grey in grey it cannot be rejuvenated but only understood.
> The owl of Minerva begins its flight only with the falling of dusk.
>
> (16)

In Roman mythology, Minerva was the goddess of wisdom, who was equated with the Greek goddess Athena. Athena was often either imagined and pictured as an owl or portrayed together with an owl. The owl of Minerva is therefore a symbol of wisdom.

Hegel (1820/2008) stresses that philosophy cannot give

> instructions as to what the world ought to be. Philosophy in any case always comes on the scene too late to give to it. As the *thought* of the world, it appears only when actuality has completed its process of formation and attained its finished state.
>
> (16)[9]

On the one hand, Hegel is right in stressing that thought alone is not a political force. At the same time, we of course have to see, especially today, in an age we can describe as digital and communicative capitalism, that intellectual strategies are key aspects of politics and the realm of intellectual production has become a key site of class struggle. But also in the digital age, it holds true that thinking the world is not sufficient for changing it. Marx (1845) said that the "philosophers have only *interpreted* the world in various ways, the point is to *change* it" (5). Politics also needs to be put into action through social praxis conducted in social relations.

On the other hand, one should also be quite cautious about Hegel's assessment of philosophy in the preface to his *Philosophy of Right*. Herbert Marcuse (1941/1955) argues in this context that Hegel's preface "renounces critical theory", assumes that society "as actually constituted" had already "brought to fruition the material conditions for its change" so that the "truth that philosophy contained at its core" had already been realised (183). The *Philosophy of Right* would "mark the resignation of a man who knows that the truth he represents", i.e. "the philosophy of middle-class society", had "drawn to its close and that it can no longer invigorate the world" (Marcuse 1941/1955, 183). In contrast to Hegel, Marx saw a clear political role of theory, namely its task as critical theory to help guiding praxis and social struggles. Marx (1844a) argued that critical theory

> becomes a material force as soon as it has gripped the masses. Theory is capable of gripping the masses as soon as it demonstrates *ad hominem*, and it demonstrates *ad hominem* as soon as it becomes radical. To be radical is to grasp the root of the matter. But for man the root is man himself. [...] The criticism of religion ends with the teaching that *man is the highest being for man*, hence with the *categorical imperative to overthrow all relations* in which man is a debased, enslaved, forsaken, despicable being.
> (182)

Critical theory analyses the structures and status of power, and by doing so illuminates potentials for praxis, social struggles, and alternatives.

A critical theory of contemporary nationalism has two tasks: (a) it needs to analyse what nationalism is, in what political-economic contexts it stands, and why it exists; and (b) it needs to analyse how the ideological structure of contemporary nationalism is communicated. This book contributes to both tasks by: (a) elaborating foundations of a Marxian theory of nationalism based on the works of Karl Marx, Rosa Luxemburg, and Eric J. Hobsbawm; and (b) presenting the results of two empirical case studies that analyse how nationalism was communicated on social media in the context of federal elections in Germany and Austria.

Nationalism is an ideological, dominative class project. Nationalism, racism, and xenophobia are closely related. Nationalism defines the inner ideological identity of a nationalist collective. Racism and xenophobia present certain groups and cultures as outsiders who are said to threaten the national collective: "Racism is constantly emerging out of nationalism. [...] And nationalism emerges out of racism. [Racism is] *a supplement internal to nationalism*" (Balibar and Wallerstein 1991, 53, 54).

At the time of Nazi-Germany, nationalism was predominantly defined biologically. The Nazis saw the German nation and the German people as a purist project of white, Aryan blood that aimed at annihilating those who were defined as non-Aryans. White supremacism and nationalism have taken on new forms today. Often, nationalism is today defined culturally. The enemies of the nation are presented as having a different culture, religion, lifestyle, language, worldview, different morals, etc. This is why critical theories of nationalism and racism speak of new racism (Balibar and Wallerstein 1991; Barker 1981), racism type 2/differentialist racism (Taguieff 2001), or neo-nationalism (Banks and Gingrich 2006).

The book at hand takes a Marxist-humanist approach for understanding nationalism. In doing so, it especially builds on the works by Karl Marx, Rosa Luxemburg, C.L.R. James, and Eric Hobsbawm. These approaches share the insight that nationalism is not an inherent feature of humanity and society, but is an ideological construct arising in the context of class, capitalism, colonialism, and imperialism. In understanding nationalism, critical humanism challenges the fetishism of the nation. It stresses that the nation as cultural or biological community is artificial and that societies are never unitary, but that humans living in society have commonalities as well as differences. Marxism adds to this understanding that nationalism as an ideology tries to distract attention from actual power differentials between the capitalist class and the working class, as well as the powerful and the powerless, by constructing an illusionary common national interest of these groups. Nationalism presents outsiders as enemies of the nation in order to legitimate class, capitalism, exploitation, and domination. Rosa Luxemburg stressed how nationalism operated in the late nineteenth and early twentieth centuries as the ideology of imperialism that advanced hatred that led to the First World War. For her, the struggle for the creation and defence of nations is always ideological and only the working class has a right to self-determination (Luxemburg 1976, 108). The book at hand takes a Luxemburgist position on nationalism, which implies that it is critical of approaches such as left populism and left-wing nationalism. In classical Marxism, Luxemburg's approach to nationalism is quite distinct. As part of its discussion of Marxism and nationalism, the book at hand shows that Luxemburg's understanding of nationalism differs especially from her contemporaries Otto Bauer and Lenin. Whereas Bauer reified nationalism, Lenin saw it as a necessary complementary tool of class struggles and anti-imperialist struggles. Luxemburg reminds us today that left nationalist strategies such as a left Brexit ("Lexit") are confronted with the dangers of supporting the same agenda as the far-right. C.L.R. James stresses that anti-colonial struggles often did not result in democratic socialism, but privileged nationalist and militarist agendas so that "military dictatorship after military dictatorship has succeeded to power" (James 2012, 116). Pitting one nation against another and demanding the establishment of new nations faces the danger of overlooking the fundamental character of class antagonisms. Transnational capitalism and national capital are the sources of exploitation of workers in different countries, regions, cultures, and societies. Capital has nothing in common with workers, but workers in different parts of the world have in common that they are exploited by capital and have a universal objective interest in overcoming capitalism. The contemporary rise of new nationalisms shows how the fetishism of the nation and the scapegoating of migrant workers, refugees, and certain cultures serves ideological purposes.

So, for example, the Leave campaigns in the Brexit referendum were entirely focused on creating fears of immigrants, presenting the EU as a cause of immigration and immigrants as a financial burden for the social system who undercut wages and destroy jobs. So, for example, UKIP created a poster showing a migrant caravan together with the following text: "BREAKING POINT: The EU has failed us. We must break free of the EU and take back control of our borders. Leave the European Union. ON 23rd JUNE." The poster works with the symbol of the mass in order to try to create fear. Speaking of a "breaking point" shall create negative feelings and associations of a fragile society whose cohesion and social system is under threat. This example shows exactly how racism and nationalism work: they create fear by scapegoating weak groups or minorities who are blamed for society's problems so that attention is distracted from the political-economic causes of social problems. Far-right demagogues do not speak about the exploitation of labour by capital, class relations, or capitalism's contradictions, but construct an imaginary conflict between immigrants (or other scapegoats) and the citizens of a nation-state. While being silent on the class antagonism between capital and labour and often favouring and advancing politics that deepen the gap between capital and labour and between the rich and the rest, the far-right ideologically nationalises social conflicts. It claims that there is a common national interest of capital and labour that are imagined and presented to be both under threat by foreigners. That capital often exploits both workers in its home country and abroad is concealed. The far-right claims to speak for the common interest of everyone, but in reality advances partial interests and conceals actual class antagonism by artificially creating imaginary antagonisms between "the people" and foreigners.

Right-wing ideology pretends to represent the interest of the working class by ideologically "nationalising" the class conflict so that the latter is presented as an antagonism between workers and the nation on the one side and immigrants on the other side. So, for example, in her 2016 Conservative Party conference, Theresa May[10] claimed:

> And if you're one of those people who lost their job, who stayed in work but on reduced hours, took a pay cut as household bills rocketed, or — and I know a lot of people don't like to admit this — someone who finds themselves out of work or on lower wages because of low-skilled immigration, life simply doesn't seem fair.

She presented the Tories as "the party of the workers" and a party that has the responsibility to "represent and govern for the whole nation". Workers and capital are seen as part of a national collective that is under threat by foreign forces — the EU and immigrants. The foreign threat to the nation is not just presented in the form of immigrants, but also by linking and associating multiculturalism, internationalism, and global capital and arguing that these phenomena are unrooted: "But if you believe you're a citizen of the world, you're a citizen of nowhere. You don't understand what the very word 'citizenship' means."[11] "Citizenship" is here used as a word appealing to nationalist sentiments and claiming that there is an antagonism between national and international life (not between human life and capital).

The rise of imperialism as a phase of capitalist development was a reaction to the Long Depression, an economic crisis of capitalism that started in 1873. Nationalism intensified as an ideology and political practice of imperialism. Rosa Luxemburg points out the connection of nationalism and imperialism and that nationalist logic fosters the potential for warfare. She stresses that class struggles are not just struggles for democracy and socialism, but require international solidary and are also struggles for an international socialist democracy without borders, states, and nationalism. She reminds us that socialism is either international or cannot be at all. Luxemburg's humanist-socialist position on nationalism is summarised by the following words:

> Imperialism in all countries has no "understanding", it knows only one right: capital profit, only one language: the sword, only one means:

violence. [...] Socialism alone can accomplish the great work of lasting peace, to heal the thousand bleeding wounds of mankind, to transform the fields [...] that have been stamped down by the Apocalyptic Horsemen of War into flourishing gardens, to conjure up tenfold new productive forces instead of the destroyed ones, to awaken all physical and moral energies of mankind and to replace hatred and discord with fraternal solidarity, harmony and respect for everything that bears human dignity. If representatives of the proletarians of all countries join hands under the banner of socialism to make peace, then peace is made in a few hours. [...] The International will be humanity! Long live the world revolution of the proletariat! Proletarians of all countries, unite!

(Liebknecht et al. 1918)

Rosa Luxemburg's works tell us that we should never forget that an increase of nationalism in a phase of capitalist crisis can unfold into major wars. We can learn from her that democratic socialism is the only viable alternative to nationalism, imperialism, war, and capitalism. "The consistent internationalism of her life and work" (Geras 1976/2015, 45) is a role model for the contemporary critique of nationalism. "She remains the most important representative of a libertarian socialist tradition inspired by internationalism, economic justice, and a radical belief in democracy" (Bronner 2013a, 12). "Her internationalist and cosmopolitan convictions are also important for interpreting globalization and confronting narrow forms of identity politics" (Bronner 2013b, 187).

Nationalism 2.0

Social media platforms such as Facebook, Twitter, and YouTube have become important spheres of political communication that have added a new level of communication to traditional media of the public sphere such as newspapers and television. Social media feature:

- user-generated content;
- the convergence of the production, consumption, and circulation of information in one technology;
- the convergence of self-, interpersonal, group, organisational, and mass communication on one platform;

- the convergence of communication (traditionally the realm of the media) and cooperation (traditionally the realm of labour and production) in one social system;
- the convergence of social roles on profiles and platforms;
- opportunities for the fast spreading of information through networks of contacts;
- the collection, processing, storage, assessment, and monitoring of big data;
- the convergence of cognition, communication, and cooperation in one system;
- the algorithmic control of information flows; and
- the algorithmic creation of attention and visibility (that has in recent times resulted in the critique of fake news and its threats to democracy), etc. (Fuchs 2017b).

In the 1990s and early 2000s, many observers assumed that the far-right hated digital technologies, was a digital Luddite and bad at adopting new technologies, and that the left, because of its affinity to grassroots politics, was at the forefront of adopting digital media. Twenty years later, these assumptions have been proven wrong. Far-right movements, groups, parties, and individuals are among the most widely followed social media profiles (for some examples, see Table 1.1).

This book is structured into two parts, each dealing with one of the two main questions (see p. 6). First, foundations of a Marxian theory of nationalism are elaborated. Second, two case studies are presented that are based on the theory foundations and make use of them in empirical analysis. Austria and Germany are suited case studies for the study of nationalism on social media because these two countries have together given rise to Nazi-fascism, have been confronted with post-fascist conditions, and have in recent years seen significant electoral gains of far-right parties.

The Rise of New Nationalisms

How can we explain the recent rise of new nationalisms? A Marxist theory of nationalism situates nationalism in the context of capitalism. This does not mean an economic reductionist approach, but rather a materialist and dialectical theory of society, in which various societal realms are grounded in the material phenomenon of social production and have their own relative autonomy. Any society consists of

TABLE 1.1 Number of Twitter and Facebook followers in far-right politics, accessed on 29 January 2018 and 2 May 2019

Name	Country	Twitter (29 January 2018)	Facebook (29 January 2018)	Twitter (2 May 2019)	Facebook (2 May 2019)
Donald Trump	USA	47mn	24.5mn	59.9mn	25.3mn
Narendra Modi	India	40mn	43mn	47.1mn	43mn
Recep Erdoğan	Turkey	12.52mn	9mn	13.7mn	9mn
Rodrigo Duterte	Philippines	170k	4.3mn	183k	4.3mn
Marine Le Pen	France	2mn	1.5mn	2.23mn	1.5mn
Geert Wilders	Netherlands	950k	260k	811k	321k
Nigel Farage	UK	1.1mn	790k	1.3mn	850k
Boris Johnson	UK	400k	535k	551k	550k
Viktor Orbán	Hungary	-	550k	-	653k
Heinz-Christian Strache	Austria	40k	750k	57.5k	780k
Sebastian Kurz	Austria	280k	740k	334k	802k
Alternative for Germany (AfD)	Germany	105k	400k	134k	470k

the realms of the economy, politics, and culture as distinct spheres of the production of use-values, collectively binding decisions and meanings. Capitalism is not just a general economic realm of commodity production, the exploitation of surplus-value generating labour, and the accumulation of monetary capital. It is a societal formation (*Gesellschaftsformation*) that is based on the logic of accumulation. The economic feature of all societal realms under capitalist rule is that they are shaped by the instrumental logic of accumulation. But accumulation takes on different logics in the various realms of society. Capitalist society is a society that is based on the logic of the accumulation of monetary capital, political influence, and cultural visibility/reputation. Competing collective and individual actors struggle for the accumulation of these resources. Accumulation tends to result in inequalities and crises.

Capitalism is based on antagonisms between capital and labour in the economy, political elites and citizens in the political economy, and celebrities and the invisible in the cultural system. In recent decades, capitalist development has intensified the gaps between the two sides of these contradictions, which has resulted in deepening socio-economic inequality (a gap between the shares of wealth controlled by the rich and the non-rich), increasing political alienation (the degree of political influence of a small number of people on the one side, and the feeling of not being able to have political influence, to have a political voice, and to be politically recognised on the other side), and deepening cultural alienation (the fragmentation of life that is based on a culture of individualisation that gives visibility and attention to a small number of celebrities and renders large groups of people isolated, ignored, and on their own).

Economic accumulation has in the past decades advanced the global outsourcing of labour, wage repression (the decline and stagnation of the share of wages in total economic value), an increasing organic composition of capital (increasing investments into new technologies that substitute and automate labour), and the financialisation of the economy. In 2008, these changes resulted in a large economic crisis. The globalisation of politics has resulted in fast changes that have increased the polarisation of society and have given many individuals the feeling they are not in control of society and do not have influence on it. It became difficult for everyday people to understand the dynamics of global capitalism. Neoliberalism advanced the individualisation of social risks, the privatisation of commodification of (almost) everything, and the tendential collapse of traditional collective milieus of socialisation that have been replaced by consumer and celebrity culture, mobile privatisation, mediated isolation, and the tendency of the colonisation and collapse of the public sphere. The crisis of politics has expressed itself as the declining trust in political institutions and declining participation in elections and political life. After the start of the new world economic crisis, a new phase of hyper-neoliberalism followed that bailed out banks and corporations by taxes and at the same time advanced social cuts to finance these measures. Established parties, politics, and state institutions' reputation thereby suffered, which intensified the political crisis. Finally, an ideological crisis emerged in the context of the rise of new nationalisms and authoritarianism that threaten to undermine democracy and the rule of law.

The rise of new nationalisms and authoritarian capitalism emerged from widespread economic, political, and cultural alienation. Far-right demagogues seized the phase of crisis and widespread socio-economic, political, and cultural discontent for constructing immigrants, refugees, Muslims, and other minorities as scapegoats that are blamed for the crises and associated problems. They have promised top-down leadership, law and order politics, and defending the nation against the constructed enemies who are blamed for society's problems. They have also instrumentalised the fear of Islamist terrorism that has emerged in the context of 9/11, al-Qaida, and the Islamic State by constructing the image that all Muslims are potential terrorists and claiming there is a cultural conflict between Western culture and Arab culture. The far-right has also used the refugee crisis that has emerged in the context of the political crisis of the Middle East as an opportunity for creating fears of refugees and presenting refugees as terrorists, criminals, extremists, social parasites, and cultural aliens.

1.3 This Book's Structure

Part I focuses on the "Foundations of a Marxist Theory of Nationalism". Chapter 2 discusses bourgeois concepts of nationalism by engaging with the approaches of Ernest Gellner and Benedict Anderson. These two theories have often been considered as being part of critical theories of nationalism. I argue that Gellner and Anderson have not properly analysed the role of nationalism in capitalism. Chapter 3 focuses on foundations of establishing an alternative critical theoretical approach for the analysis of nationalism by engaging with Marx's concept of nationalism. Chapter 4 compares two specific classical Marxist theories of the nation, the ones by Otto Bauer and Rosa Luxemburg. Chapter 5 engages with newer Marxist theories of nationalism and stresses the connections of anti-nationalist Marxist thought that exists between the approaches of Karl Marx, Rosa Luxemburg, and Eric J. Hobsbawm.

Part II, "Nationalism on Social Media", applies the theoretical foundations to two case studies in the context of social media. On the one hand, it analyses, in the first case study (Chapter 6), how Twitter, Facebook, and YouTube were used for communicating nationalism in the context of the German federal elections in 2017. On the other hand, it focuses, in Chapter 7, on how nationalism was communicated on social media in the context of the new right-wing coalition government formed by the Austrian People's Party (ÖVP) and the Freedom Party of Austria (FPÖ) after the Austrian federal elections in 2017. In Chapter 8, broader conclusions about nationalism, nationalism 2.0, and fake news are drawn.

Notes

1 Twitter, @RealDonaldTrump, 23 December 2018, https://twitter.com/realdonaldtrump/status/1076844349860823042

2 Who is Jair Bolsonaro? Brazil's Far-Right President in his Own Words. The Guardian Online, 29 October 2018, www.theguardian.com/world/2018/sep/06/jair-bolsonaro-brazil-tropical-trump-who-hankers-for-days-of-dictatorship

3 Translation from German: „Deshalb gehen wir den Weg für unser Heimatland Österreich, den Kampf gegen den Bevölkerungsaustausch, konsequent weiter, wie es die Menschen von uns auch erwarten. [...] Wir wollen nicht zur Minderheit in der eigenen Heimat werden." Interview mit Heinz-Christian Strache. *Kronen Zeitung Online*, 28 April 2019.

4 Translation from French: "En attaquant l'idée de Nation et la maîtrise de l'immigration vous laissez grandir le communautarisme, l'islamisme et le terrorisme." Twitter, @MLP_officiel, 11 March 2018, https://twitter.com/mlp_officiel/status/972856348319731713

5 Translation from Turkish: "Tek Millet. Tek Bayrak. Tek Vatan. Tek Devlet." Twitter, @RTErdogan, 10 March 2019, https://twitter.com/rterdogan/status/1105007951109148672

6 Viktor Orbán, 26 June 2016, www.facebook.com/orbanviktor/videos/10154194245626093/

7 Twitter, @Nigel_Farage, 21 March 2016, https://twitter.com/nigel_farage/status/711873806395019264

8 Translation from Italian: "Mentre il Papa invita ad accogliere tutti i migranti, 700 clandestini sono sbarcati in Calabria e altri 3.000 arriveranno in Italia nelle prossime ore. Immigrazione? No, INVASIONE organizzata e finanziata dai nuovi schiavisti." Matteo Salvini, 16 April 2017, www.facebook.com/salviniofficial/posts/10154691216098155?comment_tracking=%7B%22tn%22%3A%22O%22%7Da

9 Italic emphasis in all quotes throughout the book taken from original sources.

10 Theresa May, Conservative Party conference speech, 5 October 2016, www.telegraph.co.uk /news/2016/10/05/theresa-mays-conference-speech-in-full (accessed 2 May 2019).

11 Theresa May's Conservative Party Conference Speech 2016, transcript: https://blogs.specta tor.co.uk/2016/10/full-text-theresa-mays-conference-speech/

Part I

Foundations of a Marxist Theory of Nationalism

Chapter Two
Bourgeois Theories of Nationalism

2.1 Introduction

2.2 Ernest Gellner's *Nations and Nationalism*

2.3 Benedict Anderson's *Imagined Communities*

2.4 Conclusion

2.1 Introduction

Five Types of Theories

Anthony D. Smith (1998) and Umut Özkirimli (2010) identify five types of theories of nationalism: primordialism, perennialism, ethno-symbolism, modernism, and postmodernism. Table 2.1 gives an overview of features of these approaches.

Fetishist Theories of Nationalism

An important way of distinguishing theories of nationalism is to ask the question whether they see nationalism and the nation as immanent in human existence and society as such, or as historical phenomena that only exist in particular societies that are shaped by certain class distinctions and forms of domination. Depending on whether the first or second answer is given, we can distinguish between fetishist and critical theories of nationalism. Fetishist theories reify nationalism, whereas critical theories stress the ideological, constructed, invented, fabricated, and illusionary character of nationalism.

For Marx, ideology is a form of practice, experience, discourse, and consciousness that distorts reality by presenting it in false ways. He therefore speaks of ideology as "a *camera obscura*" that makes "men and their relations appear upside-down" (Marx and Engels 1845/46b, 36). Marx characterises ideologies as "phantoms" (Marx and Engels 1845/46b, 36) — he uses the term *Nebelbildungen* (Marx and Engels 1845/46a, 26) in the German original, which can literally be translated as "misty creatures". In *Capital Volume 1*, Marx introduces the notion of commodity fetishism, by which he indicates that the commodity and capital advance a commodity ideology, in which social relations

TABLE 2.1 Five theories of nationalism, based on Smith (1998) and Özkirimli (2010)

Approach	Basic understanding of the nation and nationalism	Example representatives
Primordialism	Nation and nationalism are immanent in human biology or culture and expressions of language, religion, territory, or kinship.	Clifford Geertz, Steven Grosby, Adrian Hastings, Edward Shils, Pierre van den Berghe
Perennialism	Nations and nationalism are perennial, persistent, recurrent, and continuous features of humankind that develop historically over long periods of time and derive from myths, language, and ethnic ties.	John Armstrong, Walker Connor, Joshua Fishman, Donald Horowitz, Hugh Seton-Watson
Ethno-Symbolism	Myths, symbols, memories, values, and traditions produce ethnic communities that can turn into nations and whose nationalism refers to their ethnic past and ethnic authenticity.	John Armstrong, Frederic Barth, John Hutchinson, Anthony D. Smith
Modernism	Nations and nationalism are distinct modern phenomena that are created together with the formation of nation-states, capitalism, industrialism, bureaucracy, and modern communication technologies.	Benedict Anderson, Paul Brass, John Breuilly, Karl Deutsch, Ernest Gellner, Anthony Giddens, Michael Hechter, Eric J. Hobsbawm, Miroslav Hroch, Elie Kedourie, Hans Kohn, Daniel Lerner, Michael Mann, Tom Nairn, Charles Tilly
Postmodernism	Nations and nationalism are social constructs serving dominant purposes. Their existence is challenged by migrant labour, globalisation, multiculturalism, global communication, and entertainment. National identities are fragmented, diverse, hybrid, ambivalent, fluid, constructed, and shaped by cultural differences.	Homi Bhabha, Michael Billig, Rogers Brubaker, Partha Chatterjee, Stuart Hall, Deniz Kandiyoti, George Mosse, Nira Yuval-Davis

assume "the fantastic form of a relation between things" (Marx 1867, 165). The commodity hides the social relations producing it and makes things (commodities and money) appear as natural and eternal properties of society.

In the realm of modern politics, we find forms of fetishism such as nationalism, anti-Semitism, and racism. These are specific types of political fetishism. Rosa Luxemburg (1976) stresses in her critique of nationalism that the latter is a "misty veil" that "conceals in every case a definite historical content" (135). Nationalism fetishises the nation in the form of a "we"-identity (a national people) that is distinguished from enemies (outsiders, other nations, immigrants, refugees, etc.) who are presented as intruders, aliens, subhumans, uncivilised, parasites, criminals, terrorists, etc. in order to deflect attention from class contradictions and power inequalities.

Primordialism, perennialism and ethno-symbolism in different ways reify the nation, and thereby also nationalism, by assuming that the nation is part of human essence. They advance a "retrospective nationalism" (Özkirimli 2010, 69; Puri 2004, 44; Smith 1998, 196) that is "projecting back onto earlier social formations the features peculiar to nations and nationalism" (Smith 1998, 196). The nation and nationalism always define an alien and enemy outside, from which national identity differs and against which it has to be defended. The problem of essentialist theories of the nation and nationalism is that they imply that in the last instance, war is a central and unavoidable feature of all societies. They advance a negative picture of the human being and cannot imagine a peaceful society. Fetishising the nation and nationalism means fetishising warfare and militarism. The argument that armament is necessary for national defence has historically resulted in arms races that have created the possibility of nuclear extinction of life on Earth.

Let us consider an example. Anthony D. Smith, in his ethno-symbolist approach, defines the nation as "a group of human beings, possessing common and distinctive elements of culture, a unified economy system, citizenship rights for all members, a sentiment of solidarity arising out of common experiences, and occupying a common territory" (Smith 1998, 188). All societies and all human groups have a culture, an economy, a system of decision-making, membership rules, common experiences, some cohesion, and common space. Smith's definition of the nation is a definition of society. And as a consequence, he reifies the nation by equalising the nation and society. Smith's concept of the nation is expansive: he expands the concept in time and space so that he cannot adequately distinguish between society and the nation. But declaring particular phenomena as natural properties of society is precisely the definition of fetishism. In fetishism and reified consciousness, isolated parts of society appear "as a timeless law valid for every human society" (Lukács 1971, 9) and take on the "fetishistic semblance of autonomy" (Lukács 1971, 231). Smith advances a fetishist theory of the nation and nationalism.

The distinction between fetishist and critical theories of nationalism does not imply that all modern and postmodern approaches are critical. Some of them fetishise the nation and nationalism as being necessary for and immanent in *all* modern societies or they fetishise subaltern nations and nationalisms.

I will in the following sections discuss some of the most influential theories of nationalism, and will in this analysis use the distinction between fetishist and critical theories of nationalism. A search on Google Scholar for the keyword "nationalism" shows that Ernest Gellner's *Nations and Nationalism* (18,166 citations), Benedict Anderson's *Imagined Communities: Reflections on the Origin and Spread of Nationalism* (82,172 citations), and Eric J. Hobsbawm's *Nations and Nationalism since 1780: Programme, Myth, Reality* (11,652 citations) are among the most well-known and cited books analysing nationalism.[1] Section 2.2 focuses on Gellner's approach and Section 2.3 on Anderson's.

2.2 Ernest Gellner's Nations and Nationalism

Defining Nationalism

For Ernest Gellner (2006), nationalism is the "political principle, which holds that the political and the national unit should be congruent", that "ethnic boundaries should not cut across political ones" (1). It is "the striving to make culture and polity congruent" (42). For Gellner, language is the central aspect of culture (42). The principle of nationalism is expressed in national sentiments and nationalist movements. Gellner considers both the definition of the nation as: (a) shared culture; and (b) shared consciousness of belonging to a nation as inappropriate (6–7). The territorial unit can only become "ethnically homogeneous [...] if it either kills, or expels, or assimilates all non-nationals" (2).

Gellner argues that life in agricultural society was too differentiated, inward-turned, isolated, dispersed, and locally contained for nationalism and national consciousness to emerge. There was hardly lateral communication between communities (11). He stresses that bureaucracy, entrepreneurial spirit, the rationality of orderliness and efficiency, and the ideas of perpetual growth and progress are characteristic for industrialism. Gellner bases his understanding of industrialism on Max Weber. Nationalism would be a central feature of modernity and industrialism. "Nationalism, the organization of human groups into large, centrally educated, culturally homogeneous units", is for Gellner a "distinctive structural requirement of industrial society" (34). Modern organisations (corporations, bureaucracies) are according to this argument based on a division of labour that requires cooperation, specialisation, standardisation, and communication enabled by cultural homogeneity that is achieved by universal, compulsory, formalised, codifiable education. General education and the school system guarantee the "employability, dignity, security and self-respect of individuals" (35). Nationalism is "the general imposition of a high culture on society" that replaces the reproduction of detached "local groups" by "folk cultures" and "low cultures" (56). "Homogeneity, literacy, anonymity are the key traits" (132) of nationalism.

The Missing Link: Nationalism and Class Society

Gellner advances a liberal theory of nationalism, in which nationalism is independent of capitalism and class structures and a positive and necessary feature of modernity and industrialism. Class societies require violence in order to guarantee their existence. In slave-holding societies and feudal societies, labour-power and the products of labour are fully or partly owned by the slave-master and feudal lord, respectively. Such a class structure can only be upheld by direct violence, i.e. the whip, the sword, the noose, and the gun. In capitalism, violence in addition to direct violence takes on the form of structural and ideological violence. Structural violence means that the dull compulsion of the labour-market forces the "double free" wage-worker into exploitation. The wage-worker is "free" in the

> double sense that as a free individual he can dispose of his labour-power as his own commodity, and that, on the other hand, he has no other commodity for sale, i.e. he is rid of them, he is free of all the objects needed for the realization of his labour-power.

> (Marx 1867, 272–273)

The gender division of labour is an older structural form of violence that continues to exist in capitalism, where it takes on new forms. Ideological violence tries to naturalise class relations and exploitation, and tries to "convince" workers and other subalterns that their exploitation and domination is natural and without alternative and that social problems have other roots than the class structure. Nationalism is one of the ideologies that tries to construct a feeling of unity between the subaltern classes and the capitalist class in order to distract attention from class differences, the class structure, and the power inequalities entailed in the class structure. Ernest Gellner presents a unitary concept of the nation that overlooks that within modern nations, there are class differences that create power imbalances that also, but not exclusively, have to do with the access to culture and education.

So, ideology, violence, difference, conflict, and classes are rather absent from Gellner's concept of nationalism. Nationalism constructs a unity that is opposed to an outside. This outside can be constructed as inner and/or outer enemies of the nation. Whereas the inner enemies typically are foreigners, immigrants, minorities, and socialists, the outer enemies tend to be other nations and groups at the international level. Nationalism as ideology not just justifies a national society's (i.e. a society bound by national borders) class structure, but also its imperialist, colonial, or neo-colonial expansion and wars, which tend to be justified by the ideology of the "national interest" and "national security" that claim that the nation needs to be defended against foreign enemies and by the ideology of "national superiority" that claims that the superior nation must "civilise" and thereby "help" the world's "primitive", "underdeveloped", and "backward" regions. War is an inherent potential and implication of nationalism. Gellner largely leaves out aspects of imperialism in his theory of nationalism.

Those making arguments similar to Gellner can respond to my criticism that, for example, the Soviet system and Maoist China were also nationalist, and that therefore nationalism is not limited to capitalism. But by doing so, they fall into the Stalinist trap, namely the argument that Stalinism and Maoism were non-capitalist societies and forms of socialism. The 1936 Constitution of the USSR that was drafted under Stalin claimed in article 4 that the Soviet Union had abolished capitalism:

> The socialist system of economy and the socialist ownership of the means and instruments of production, firmly established as a result of the abolition of the capitalist system of economy, the abrogation of private ownership of the means and instruments of production and the abolition of the exploitation of man by man, constitute the economic foundation of the U.S.S.R.

> (Stalin 1936)

Liberal theories of nationalism that see nationalism as a necessary feature of both capitalist and socialist modernity overlook that Stalinist society, Maoist society, and comparable systems are specific forms of capitalism. Marxist critics of Stalinism stress that the Soviet system was a form of state capitalism in which the bureaucracy acted as collective capitalist (James 2013b).

Nationalism and the Media

Gellner (2006) argues that the media are not systems that distribute nationalist ideology, but that the "most important and persistent [nationalist] message is generated by the medium itself", i.e. by the media's structure of "abstract, centralized, standardized, one to many communication" that uses the nation's formal, national language so that "only he who can understand" the transmitted language is included in the national community (122). Gellner is political theory's Marshall McLuhan. He applies McLuhan's dictum that the "medium is the message" because "it is the medium that shapes and controls the scale and form of human association and action" (McLuhan 1997, 149) to the theory of nationalism and argues that national media are nationalism's message. If this were true, then the emergence of global communication systems, such as the Internet, would have to bring about an end of nationalism that is, however, nowhere in sight. Global, digital media use a global networked system of communication that combines one-to-one, one-to-many, and many-to-many communication. Nationalism continues to be expressed and challenged in novel ways through such means of communication, which shows that nationalism is a political-economic and ideological phenomenon, and not one implicated by the technical structure of media systems.

2.3 Benedict Anderson's Imagined Communities

The Nation as Imagined Community

For Anderson (2006), the nation "is an imagined political community" (6). It is imagined because "the members of even the smallest nation will never know most of their fellow-members, meet them, or even hear of them, yet in the minds of each lives the image of their communion" (6). He explicitly opposes "imagining" and "creation" to "fabrication" and "falsity" (6), which implies that the nation for Anderson does not have an ideological character. For Anderson, the nation is limited by boundaries and has cultural roots (7). Anderson shares with Gellner the assumption that nationalism is a modern phenomenon. Nationalism is for Anderson a secular form of religion. It is for him not ideological in character, but a quasi-religion (12).

For Anderson, nationalism arose together with the rise of print capitalism, i.e. the invention and diffusion of "the novel and the newspaper" that allowed "the technical means for 're-presenting' the *kind* of imagined community that is the nation" (25). Modern media would allow the national aggregation of media consumption "in silent privacy", a "ceremony" that is repeated day by day by the media consumer and "simultaneously by thousands (or millions) of others of whose existence he is confident, yet of whose identity he has not the slightest notion" (35). Together, these anonymous individuals who perform the same media practice form for Anderson the nation as imagined community by imagining each other as the nation without knowing and experiencing each other. According to Anderson, print capitalism that is based on "print-as-commodity" (37) has made the nation and nationalism possible. Print capitalism "gave a new fixity to language, which in the long run helped to build that image of antiquity so central to the subjective idea of the nation" (44). Print capitalism required the standardisation of language into a national literary language that could be written, printed, read, and communicated in formal contexts. For Anderson, "the convergence of capitalism and print technology" (46) created the nation. The national print language became the "[l]anguage-of-state", "the language of business, of the sciences, of the press, or of literature" (78). Not just the media, but also other institutions and structures such as the census, the map, and the museum, would help to construct the nation (163).

Anderson argues that nationalism is not necessarily racist, pathological, and rooted "in fear and hatred of the Other" (141). His argument is directed against Marxist theories of nationalism, as represented by Rosa Luxemburg and Eric Hobsbawm, that stress the ideological and therefore manipulative character of nationalism. Anderson makes this point because he believes in the power and importance of anti-colonial and anti-imperialist nationalism that he terms "popular nationalism" (161) and that he sees emerging from self-defence. He dismisses Eric Hobsbawm's (1977) argument that "Marxists as such are not nationalists" (9) as "fiction" (Anderson 2006, 16). Anderson claims that "nations inspire love" in the form of "poetry, prose fiction, music, plastic arts" (141), "political love" of the homeland (143), etc. He also doubts that nationalism is a cause of racism and anti-Semitism (148).

The Missing Link: Nationalism and Ideology

By focusing on the construction of community, Anderson only looks at the inner dynamic of nationalism. He overlooks the dialectic of inner identity and outer context, from which identities differ and against which they define themselves. He leaves open the question why exactly there is a need for nationalism. In doing so, he, just like Gellner, ignores the fundamental role of class structures in the emergence and reproduction of nationalism. Modern class society *requires* nationalism as ideology in order to justify the exploitation of workers, the domination of consumers, and the geographic expansion of capitalist production and markets. In capitalist society, love for the nation comes along with the exclusion of those who are not seen as members of the nation and are presented as opponents, competitors, foreigners, aliens, scapegoats, enemies, etc. Other than Anderson, Étienne Balibar points out that there is a necessary dialectic of racism and nationalism: "Racism is constantly emerging out of nationalism [...] and nationalism emerges out of racism" (Balibar and Wallerstein 1991, 53). Racism calls for the preservation of the nation's fictive ethnicity, its proclaimed cultural and/or biological origin and purity (59). Racism "constantly induces an excess of 'purism' as far as the nation is concerned: for the nation to be itself, it has to be racially or culturally pure" (59–60).

When Anderson (2006) argues that "from the start the nation was conceived in language, not in blood" (145), he overlooks that nationalist language is war by other means, intellectual warfare that often aims at denigrating the foreign by the nation's positive self-presentation or negative othering. Anthony W. Marx (2003) argues that Anderson's imagined community approach incorrectly assumes that printing's "spreading communication brings inclusive solidarity" (16) and ignores that "amid religious, elite, and economic conflicts this was not possible [...]. Indeed, the content or messages so spread were often divisive rather than necessary unifying" (16), so that exclusion was the basis of nationalist unity.

Nationalism and Print Capitalism

Anderson's account creates the impression that technology and the economy develop independently, which becomes evident when he says that nations emerged as a result of the interaction and convergence of capitalism and print technology (Anderson 2006, 42–43, 46). He does not ask why printing developed.

Printing first served the purpose of communicating religious rule, which is why it is no accident that the first woodblock-printed book was *The Diamond Sutra*, an important Buddhist text, and the Gutenberg Bible became the first major book printed in Europe with the help of the metal movable-type printing press. Newspapers emerged in the context of the transformation of the class structure from feudalism to capitalism, i.e. the emergence of the bourgeoisie and the modern working class and the decline of aristocratic and religious rule. Marx (1857/58, 160–161) argues that the publication of lists of current prices was an early role of the newspapers in emerging capitalism.

The nineteenth-century newspaper played the role of an instrument of communication that helped inform and organise the bourgeois class and the working class. The bourgeois public sphere (Habermas 1991) and the proletarian or radical public sphere (Curran 1991; Negt and Kluge 1993) emerged along with the emergence and consolidation of capitalism. Modern information and communication technologies and capitalism did not develop independently, as technological determinists claim. Rather, new technologies assert themselves because there is a political-economic

30 A Marxist Theory of Nationalism

intention and a need for them that has to do with the transformation of political economy and class structure and associated contradictions and struggles.

Raymond Williams (2003a) describes the emergence of the press as standing in the context of the rise of capitalism and its contradictions and struggles:

> The development of the press gives us the evidence for our first major instance. It was at once a response to the development of an extended social, economic and political system and a response to crisis within that system. The centralisation of political power led to a need for messages from that centre along other than official lines. Early newspapers were a combination of that kind of message – political and social information – and the specific messages – classified advertising and general commercial news – of an expanding system of trade. [...] But for the transmission of news and background – the whole orienting, predictive and updating process which the fully developed press represented – there was an evident need for a new form, which the largely traditional institutions of church and school could not meet. And to the large extent that the crises of general change provoked both anxiety and controversy, this flexible and competitive form met social needs of a new kind. As the struggle for a share in decision and control became sharper, in campaigns for the vote and then in competition for the vote, the press became not only a new communications system but, centrally, a new social institution. [...] New relations between men, and between men and things, were being intensely experienced, and in this area, especially, the traditional institutions of church and school, or of settled community and persisting family, had very little to say.
>
> (14–15)

Benedict Anderson: Nationalism Theory's Marshall McLuhan?

Anderson, in contrast to Williams, gives the impression that printing became a popular technology by accident and by chance co-joined with capitalism. Anderson's position is much closer to Marshall McLuhan (1997), who claims that "print fostered nationalism" (55), "print causes nationalism" (141), print "created individualism and nationalism" (157), or that "nationalism and industrialism [...] both derived directly from the explosion of print technology in the 16th Century" (233). Williams (2003a) criticises that in

McLuhan's approach, "intention [...] is irrelevant" (130) and that McLuhan ideologically represents "technology as a cause" (131).

2.4 Conclusion

This chapter showed that Ernest Gellner and Benedict Anderson's theories conceive nationalism as a modern project, but do not adequately relate it to class structures and ideology.

Ernest Gellner presents a unitary concept of the nation that overlooks that within modern nations, there are class differences that create power imbalances that also, but not exclusively, exist in regard to the access to culture and education. Ideology, violence, difference, conflict, and classes are rather absent from Gellner's concept of nationalism.

Benedict Anderson, like McLuhan, overestimates technological development and sees it as an independent, accidental factor that is autonomous from political economy, social and class structures, and ideology. Print technology proliferated and became a mass phenomenon in the context of the rise of capitalism and its contradictory public sphere, in which class struggle manifested in the form of the antagonism between the bourgeois and the proletarian public spheres. Nationalism in this context arose as an ideology and movement that aimed at creating the unity and reproduction of the nation-state, the stabilisation of class structure, and the enablement of imperialism.

Chapters 3, 4, and 5 aim to show that Marxist theory poses a viable alternative to bourgeois theories of nationalism.

Note

1 Data source: Google Scholar, accessed on 25 December 2017.

Chapter Three
Marx's Concept of Nationalism

3.1 Marx's Concept of Nationalism

3.2 Edward Said's Critique of Marx

3.3 Key Aspects of Nationalist Ideology

This chapter focuses on foundations of a critical theory of nationalism in Marx's works.

Mike Davis (2018) argues that too many Marxist analyses of nationalism have incorrectly assumed "the autonomy of the discursive, the cultural, or the ethnic" and have not put nationalism into the context of "property relations" (178). We "need *more* economic interpretation, not less" (178). The point of this chapter is that we can gain much for a dialectical and materialist analysis of nationalism by engaging with Marx's writings on the nation and nationalism. Kevin Anderson (2016) writes in his book *Marx at the Margins: On Nationalism, Ethnicity, and Non-Western Societies* that Marx's analyses of nationalism and non-Western society have often been neglected or misinterpreted, including in radical scholarship:

> Marx's life exemplified his ideal of internationalism, for by the end he was neither German nor British, but a European or even a global intellectual. [...] Marx's lifelong intellectual project centered on the critique of political economy – on the elaboration of a model of the structure of modern capitalist society and of the potential for its positive transformation through the movement for self-emancipation of the modern working class. [...] his writings on nationalism, ethnicity, and non-Western societies constituted an important, albeit neglected, part of that effort.
>
> (4)

Anderson (2016) argues that much can be gained for critical theory by engaging with Marx's writings on nationalism:

> Marx's critique of capital, it has been shown, was far broader than is usually supposed. To be sure, he concentrated on the labor-capital relation within Western Europe and North America, but at the same time, he expended considerable time and energy on the analysis of non-Western societies, as well as that of race, ethnicity, and nationalism.

34 A Marxist Theory of Nationalism

> [...] I argue for a move toward a 21st century notion of Marx as a global theorist whose social critique included notions of capital and class that were open and broad enough to encompass the particularities of nationalism, race, and ethnicity, as well as the varieties of human social and historical development, from Europe to Asia and from the Americas to Africa.
>
> (237, 6)

The chapter first discusses some key aspects of Marx's concept of nationalism (Section 3.1). Second, it engages with Edward Said's criticism of Marx (Section 3.2). Third, some conclusions are drawn (Section 3.3).

3.1 Marx's Concept of Nationalism

Internationalism Instead of Nationalism

For Marx, the working class has to take an internationalist perspective in its struggles in order to succeed:

> The Communists are further reproached with desiring to abolish countries and nationality. The working men have no country [*Vaterland* in the German original]. We cannot take from them what they have not got. Since the proletariat must first of all acquire political supremacy, must rise to be the leading class of the nation, must constitute itself *the* nation, it is so far, itself national, though not in the bourgeois sense of the word.
>
> (Marx and Engels 1848, 502–503)

Erica Benner (1995, 53–56) argues that this passage should not be interpreted as meaning that the working class shall only fight internationally and globally because it has no national interest, but rather as meaning that conservative patriotism and belief in the fatherland (*Vaterland*) form an ideology alien to the working class' interests and that the working class also has to struggle at the level of the nation state in combination with struggles at the international level. The working class has no true interest in "ethnic nationality" (Benner 1995, 54), but in struggles at the level of the nation-state. Marx "pointed out in his writings on populist nationalism, intense feelings of physical or material insecurity furnish an important set of prudential reasons for supporting nationalist leaders" (Benner 1995, 234).

Marx played a key role in the founding of the International Workingmen's Association, also known as the First International. In the International's Inaugural Address, he stresses that working-class politics needs to oppose nationalist warfare and conquest:

> If the emancipation of the working classes requires their fraternal concurrence, how are they to fulfil that great mission with a foreign policy in pursuit of criminal designs, playing upon national prejudices, and squandering in piratical wars the people's blood and treasure? [Nationalist wars and conflicts] [...] have taught the working classes the duty to master themselves the mysteries of international politics; to watch the diplomatic acts of their respective Governments; to counteract them, if necessary, by all means in their power; when unable to prevent, to combine in simultaneous denunciations, and to vindicate the simple laws of morals and justice, which ought to govern the relations of private individuals, as the rules paramount of the intercourse of nations. The fight for such a foreign policy forms part of the general struggle for the emancipation of the working classes. Proletarians of all countries, Unite!
>
> (Marx 1864, 13)

Marx here argues that nationalism ("national prejudices") tends to be used as an ideology for justifying wars and conquest. Counteracting it requires internationalist politics. In 1864, Marx had not changed his position on internationalism in comparison to 1848, when the *Manifesto* was published.

Benner, in her detailed study of Marx and Engels' writings on the nation and nationalism, challenges the often repeated claim that the two favoured colonialism as a means of advancing modernisation, industrialisation, and the formation of a proletariat. Marx encouraged "the emergence in India of indigenous social movements opposed at once to colonial exploitation *and* to the traditional 'despotism'" (Benner 1995, 176).

> According to this analysis, self-determination for a colonized people cannot be achieved simply through the obdurate assertion of what has been suppressed by the colonizers. The real work of building a self-determining society must go beyond a separatist politics of identity, and concern itself with advancing the freedom and material welfare of people who, before the colonial era, had been demeaned and exploited by their own rulers.
>
> (179)

Marx's Critical Concept of Ideology

Marx critically theorised ideology and practised the ideology critique of religion, bourgeois thought, and capitalism. In his very early works, he stressed that ideologies create illusions and deceive, and criticised religion as ideology:

> Religion is the sigh of the oppressed creature, the heart of a heartless world, just as it is the spirit of spiritless conditions. It is the *opium* of the people. To abolish religion as the *illusory* happiness of the people is to demand their *real* happiness. The demand to give up illusions about the existing state of affairs is the *demand to give up a state of affairs which needs illusions*.
>
> (Marx 1844a, 175–176)

For Marx, the belief in religion is an ideological expression of a dominative society. He criticised left-wing thinkers such as Bruno Bauer and Ludwig Feuerbach for stopping at the critique of religion and not seeing how it is related to capitalism and necessitates the critique of capitalism. For Marx, "the criticism of heaven" has to turn "into the criticism of the earth, the *criticism of religion* into the *criticism of law* and the *criticism of theology* into the *criticism of politics*" (Marx 1844a, 176).

The German Ideology is a draft book that Marx and Engels wrote for gaining self-understanding of contemporary German philosophy and left-wing critique of their time. In *The German Ideology*, Marx argues that in "all ideology men and their relations appear upside-down as in a *camera obscura*" and that "this phenomenon arises just as much from their historical life-process as the inversion of objects on the retina does from their physical life-process" (Marx and Engels 1845/46b, 36). Ideology constructs illusions and tries to make them appear as the true status of reality. It here becomes evident that Marx conceives ideology based on Hegel's dialectic of essence and appearance: ideologies make existence appear different from how it really is. It hides the true essence and state of the world behind false appearances and communicates these false appearances as truths and nature. Ideology makes being appear as immediate, but illusionary reality whose simplicity hides the underlying complexity of the world that cannot always be experienced directly. Hegel (1991) argues that the "immediate being of things is [...] represented as a sort of rind or curtain behind which the essence is concealed" (addition to §112). For Hegel, the truths hidden behind appearances are part of the world's logic. In contrast, for Marx, the process of hiding, naturalising, concealing, and making truth disappear is an immanent expression of and practice in class societies.

Economic and Political Fetishism

With his notion of commodity fetishism, Marx (1867), in *Capital*, shows that capitalism has an inherent ideological tendency to reify capitalist phenomena by making them appear as natural features of all societies. One cannot see the social relations of production behind the commodity. As a consequence, the commodity "stands on its head" and produces "grotesque ideas" (163). Marx (1867, 163–177) developed the insight that ideology hides power relations and naturalises domination into the concept of commodity fetishism. The commodity is a "mysterious" and "a very strange thing" (Marx 1867, 163).

> The mysterious character of the commodity-form consists therefore simply in the fact that the commodity reflects the social characteristics of men's own labour as objective characteristics of the products of labour themselves, as the socio-natural properties of these things. Hence it also reflects the social relation of the producers to the sum total of labour as a social relation between objects, a relation which exists apart from and outside the producers. Through this substitution, the products of labour become commodities, sensuous things which are at the same time supra-sensible or social.
>
> (Marx 1867, 164–165)

The very structure of capitalism makes commodities, capital, money, classes, etc. appear as natural properties of society. Because of the division of labour and the mediated character of capitalism, producers and consumers do not directly experience the whole production process of the commodity. In everyday capitalist life, we are primarily confronted with commodities and money as things, whereas the production process and its class relations remain hidden. Capitalism is thereby in itself ideological in the very practices of capitalist production. Fetishism is ideological just like ideology is fetishist: ideology fetishises certain changeable social relations as static, unchangeable, natural, thing-like entities.

Social relations between humans appear as a "relation between physical things" (Marx 1867, 165). All ideology tries to naturalise domination or exploitation. Fetishism also takes on the form of political fetishism. Nationalism naturalises and fetishises the existence of nations. It is a form of political fetishism. Nationalism fetishises the nation in the form of a "we"-identity (a national people) that is distinguished from enemies (outsiders, other nations, immigrants, refugees, etc.) that are presented as intruders, aliens, subhumans, uncivilised, parasites, etc. in order to deflect attention from class contradictions and power inequalities.

Marx on Nationalism

Marx did not limit the analysis of ideology and fetishism to the economy, but also criticised political fetishisms such as nationalism. He did not explicitly speak of political fetishism, but he discussed the role of ideology in distracting attention from class struggle and benefiting the ruling class. For example, in 1870, he analysed the role of nationalism in distracting attention from class struggle and benefiting the ruling class. He analysed the creation of false consciousness among the working class in one country so that it hates immigrant workers and workers in the colonies. He specifically addresses this issue in respect to Ireland as a British colony and gives a precise analysis of the role of nationalism and xenophobia that is also valid in the context of today's new nationalisms:

> Ireland is the BULWARK of the *English landed aristocracy*. The exploitation of this country is not simply one of the main sources of their material wealth; it is their greatest *moral* power. [...] And most important of all! All industrial and commercial centres in England now have a working class *divided* into two *hostile* camps, English PROLETARIANS and Irish PROLETARIANS. The ordinary English worker hates the Irish worker as a competitor who forces down the STANDARD OF LIFE. In relation to the Irish worker, he feels himself to be a member of the *ruling nation* and, therefore, makes himself a tool of his aristocrats and capitalists *against Ireland*, thus strengthening their domination *over himself*. He harbours religious, social and national prejudices against him. [...] This antagonism is kept artificially alive and intensified by the press, the pulpit, the comic papers, in short by all the means at the disposal of the ruling class. *This antagonism* is the *secret of the English working class's impotence*, despite its organisation. It is the secret of the maintenance of power by the capitalist class. And the latter is fully aware of this.
>
> (Marx 1870, 473, 474, 475)

A similar passage can be found in a piece from 1869:

> The "English bourgeoisie has not only exploited Irish poverty to keep down the working class in England by *forced immigration* of poor Irishmen, but it has also divided the proletariat into two hostile camps. [...] The average English worker hates the Irish worker as a competitor who lowers wages and the *STANDARD OF LIFE*. He feels national and religious antipathies for him. He regards him somewhat like the *POOR WHITES* of the Southern States of

North America regarded black slaves. This antagonism among the proletarians of England is artificially nourished and kept up by the bourgeoisie. It knows that this scission is the true secret of maintaining its power".

(Marx 1869, 88)

Bonapartism and Nationalism

Marx (1852) introduced the term Bonapartism for analysing Napoleon III's dictatorial rule in France. Napoleon III staged a *coup d'état* and gained power in 1851. A feature of Bonapartism is that "the state seem[s] to have made itself completely independent" (Marx 1852, 186). Nationalism is an important ideological feature of Bonapartism:

[Bonapartism] professed to save the working class by breaking down Parliamentarism, and, with it, the undisguised subserviency of Government to the propertied classes. It professed to save the propertied classes by upholding their economic supremacy over the working class; and, finally, it professed to unite all classes by reviving for all the chimera of national glory.

(Marx 1871, 330)

Marx stresses the role of nationalism as ideology that constructs fictive ethnicity of a people and the nation in order to deflect political attention from the class contradiction.

Internationalist Socialist Politics

But what should be done in a situation where nationalism, racism, xenophobia, or other ideologies divide dominated groups? Marx argues that it is the task of the political left to draw attention to how ideology works and to undermine its foundations in order to advance solidarity and alternatives. Internationalist socialist politics is the best answer to nationalism. At the time when Marx wrote the cited passages about Ireland, the First International had been formed. Marx saw practical ideology critique as one of its tasks:

Thus, to hasten the social revolution in England is the most important object of the International Working Men's Association. The sole means of doing so is to make Ireland independent. It is, therefore, the task of the "INTERNATIONAL" to bring the conflict between England and Ireland to the forefront everywhere, and to side with Ireland publicly everywhere. The special task of the Central Council in London is to awaken the consciousness of the English working class that, *for them, the national emancipation of Ireland* is not a QUESTION OF ABSTRACT JUSTICE OR HUMANITARIAN SENTIMENT, but *THE FIRST CONDITION OF THEIR OWN SOCIAL EMANCIPATION.*

(Marx 1870, 475)

In *Capital Volume I*, Marx argues that emancipation requires solidarity between the exploited workers in different contexts, including issues of colour and geography: "Labour in a white skin cannot emancipate itself where it is branded in a black skin" (Marx 1867, 414). He points out that the formal abolishment of slavery in the USA helped advance more radical demands of the US working class movement, specifically the demand for the eight-hour working day. The point is that class solidarity that emancipates one group in one context is an impetus for class struggles and radical demands in other contexts. Different struggles can enrich each other through solidary action. This requires unity in diversity of social struggles.

3.2 Edward Said's Critique of Marx

Edward Said: "Marx's Economic Analyses are [...] a Standard Orientalist Undertaking"

Edward Said (1979) claims that Marx "returned with increasing conviction to the idea that even in destroying Asia, Britain was making possible there a real social revolution" (153). "Marx's economic analyses are perfectly fitted thus to a standard Orientalist undertaking, even though Marx's humanity, his sympathy for the misery of people, are clearly engaged. Yet in the end it is the Romantic Orientalist vision that wins out" (154).

Kevin B. Anderson (2016) acknowledges that there are certain problems in Marx's concept of development, but argues that this "in no way implies a lack of sympathy for the human beings suffering" (20). Marx (1853), in his articles on India, indeed wrote that "the English interference" destroyed Indian communities and their economy. It thereby brought about "the only social revolution ever heard of in Asia" (131–132). Marx said that "England has to fulfil a double mission in India: one destructive, the other regenerating the annihilation of old Asiatic society, and the laying the material foundations of Western society in Asia" (217).

In his 1853 articles on India, Marx also writes that in India and other places of the world, the bourgeoisie is "dragging individuals and people through blood and dirt, through misery and degradation" (221). In very clear terms, Marx argues that colonialism is a form of barbarism: "The profound hypocrisy and inherent barbarism of bourgeois civilization lies unveiled before our eyes, turning from its home, where it assumes respectable forms, to the colonies, where it goes naked" (222). As a consequence, radical social change would be needed both in India and Britain:

> The Indians will not reap the fruits of the new elements of society scattered among them by the British bourgeoisie, till in Great Britain itself the now ruling classes shall have been supplanted by the industrial proletariat, or till the Hindus themselves shall have grown strong enough to throw off the English yoke altogether.
>
> (221)

Kevin B. Anderson's Defence of Marx in Response to Edward Said

This passage shows that Marx anticipated and supported the "rise of an Indian liberation movement" (Anderson 2016, 24). He sympathised with the idea of anti-imperialist liberation movements. At the same time, he stresses that ideally radical social change works best when there is international solidarity in class struggle. Marx did not see the Indian people as passive and did not think they were incapable of conducting a revolution. He rather stresses that all bourgeois rule brings about misery, violence, degradation, and murder, and that the Indian case verifies this assumption. He argues that the Indians did not benefit from capitalist and colonial rule. Given capitalism's exploitative character, only radical social transformations can establish a humane society. For Marx, this is true for India, Britain, and the rest of the world. The need for revolution is the ultimate conclusion of Marx's writings on India.

That Marx (1853) speaks of colonialism as creating "blood and dirt, [...] misery and degradation" (221) shows how wrong postmodernists and post-Marxists are when they claim that Marx assumed "that the capitalist penetration would lead directly to positive economic development in what are now known as Third World countries" (Jameson 1990, 47). Anderson (2016), in a detailed study of all of Marx's writings on nationalism, ethnicity, non-Western and colonised societies (including Algeria, China, Egypt, India, Indonesia, Ireland, Latin America, Poland, and Russia), colonialism, slavery, and racism (including rather unknown works such as the *Ethnographical Notebooks*), shows that Marx saw different development paths of different societies, including the possible development from village communities to modern communism under specific circumstances, analysed "the complexities and differences of non-Western societies", and showed "the intersectionality of class with ethnicity, race, and nationalism" (237) without taking a postmodern perspective, as is so common today.

3.3 Conclusion: Key Aspects of Nationalist Ideology

Marx stresses key aspects of nationalist ideology that one can still observe in contemporary capitalism:

- *Division*: Nationalism is an ideology that divides subordinated classes and groups and benefits the ruling class.
- *Distraction*: Nationalism distracts attention from class conflict and the class foundation of social problems by constructing scapegoats who are blamed for these problems and about whom prejudices and false claims are spread.
- *Hegemony*: By falling into the nationalist ideological trap of nationalism, subordinated classes advance not just the exploitation and domination of other classes, but also their own exploitation and domination. The dominated class agrees to its own domination and exploitation.
- *The media*: The tabloid press often advances and keeps alive nationalism and ideologies in general.
- *Reproduction of capitalism*: Via nationalism and other ideologies, the power of the capitalist class is maintained and its effects are hidden.

Chapter Four
Otto Bauer's and Rosa Luxemburg's Opposing Theories of the Nation and Nationalism

4.1 Introduction

4.2 Otto Bauer's Concept of the Nation

4.3 The Political Impacts of Austro-Marxism and Otto Bauer's Theory

4.4 Rosa Luxemburg's Critical Theory of Nationalism

4.5 Conclusion

4.1 Introduction

Otto Bauer (1881–1938) was a leading theorist of Austro-Marxism and in the years 1918–1934 deputy chairman of the Austrian Social Democratic Workers Party. His most well-known work and only book translated into English is *The Question of Nationalities and Social Democracy*. Rosa Luxemburg (1871–1919) was a co-founder of the party Social Democracy of the Kingdom of Poland and Lithuania. She became one of the leaders of the left-wing faction of the Social Democratic Party of Germany that she left because of the party's support of the First World War. She, together with Karl Liebknecht, founded the Spartacus League, which later became the Communist Party of Germany. Luxemburg also theorised nationalism and the nation from a Marxian perspective.

This chapter asks: What are the differences between Otto Bauer's and Rosa Luxemburg's theories of the nation and nationalism? What are the foundations of a Marxist theory of nationalism?

We today experience a surge of new nationalisms. Donald Trump, Brexit, Recep Tayyip Erdoğan, Marine Le Pen, Viktor Orbán, Heinz Christian Strache, Geert Wilders, the Alternative for Germany (AfD), Narendra Modi, Rodrigo Duterte, or Vladimir Putin are some of the symbols of contemporary nationalisms. One hundred years ago, the combination of imperialism and nationalism led to the First World War. Bauer and Luxemburg lived, wrote, and struggled at that time.

If one wants to contain nationalism, then an adequate understanding of how it works is needed. Looking at aspects of the history of theorising nationalism may provide historical and theoretical insights that are still relevant today. If it is true that nationalism stands in a complex relation to capitalism, then Marxist theories of nationalism can help produce such insights. Based on this assumption, it is therefore feasible to look at Bauer's and Luxemburg's approaches because both advanced influential understandings of the nation and nationalism. It is also interesting to compare these two approaches because they advance fairly different, opposing understandings of the nation and nationalism that have in common that Marx is the main reference and starting point.

The chapter has the following structure: Section 4.2 discusses and reflects on Otto Bauer's concept of the nation; Section 4.3 analyses the political implications of Bauer's approach; Section 4.4 builds on Marx and focuses on Rosa Luxemburg's theory of nationalism; and Section 4.5 draws some conclusions.

4.2 Otto Bauer's Concept of the Nation

Marxist Affirmations of Bauer's Approach

Quite some Marxist literature has either neutrally discussed or uncritically supported Bauer's theory of nationalism. Forman (1998) argues that "Bauer thought socialism intimately linked with the national community" and "rejected the proposition that the socialist project was inherently at odds with a properly conceived program of national cultural development" (106). Ephraim Nimni (1991), who translated Bauer's book *The Question of Nationalities and Social Democracy* into English, argues, "The characteristics of the phenomenon described by Bauer as community of fate are useful in understanding the national community both as a multidimensional and as a developmental process" (194). For Nimni, Bauer's approach is "a useful initial step in the process of deconstructing the relationship between nation and state" (194). Avineri (1991) calls Bauer's approach to nationalism "a sophisticated historical approach" (652). Ronald Munck (2000), based on Bauer, reifies nationalism: "As with Gramsci's much more influential work on the national-popular, we find with Bauer a welcome move beyond most Marxists' continuous understanding of nation and nationalism as 'problems' and not just an integral element of the human condition" (133). Michael Löwy (1998) also views Bauer's concept positively when he speaks of the latter's "original concepts and lucid analyses that he developed in order to make the national phenomenon intelligible and do justice to its socio-historical nature" (46). For Löwy, Bauer's work on nationalism is "a monument of critical intelligence and humanist rationalism" (46).

Such analyses mostly ignore that Bauer, from 1918 onwards, propagated pan-Germanism and the *Anschluss* of Austria to Germany (unification of Austria and Germany). The chapter at hand argues that this move was not an accident, but was based on Bauer's nationalist views and his theory of nationalism.

Otto Bauer established an Austro-Marxist theory of the nation that stood in the context of the Austro-Hungarian Empire's specific structure. In 1910, the Austro-Hungarian Empire consisted of 18 countries. According to the 1910 Census, 23.4 per cent of the Empire's population spoke German, 19.6 per cent Hungarian, 12.5 per cent Czech, 9.7 per cent Polish, 8.6 per cent Serbian and Croatian, 7.8 per cent Ukrainian, 6.3 per cent Romanian, 3.8 per cent Slovakian, 2.4 per cent Slovenian, and 1.5 per cent Italian.[1]

Karl Renner's Theory of the Nation

Bauer built his theory on Karl Renner's approach. Renner (1899) argued for minority rights on the territories of the Austro-Hungarian Empire. A nationality is "determined by a spiritual and cultural community with an appreciable national literature that expresses this cultural community" (Renner 1899, 376). The nation is, for Renner, "a spiritual and cultural community" (377), "a community of thinking and feeling life" that holds a "national and ethnic-community consciousness", "the feeling of belongingness" (376), and has common "expressions of *thought and feeling*" that are expressed "in the national literature" (380).

Renner's definition is quite unitary and disregards that modern society is a class and stratified society, in which experiences, thought, feelings, and culture are not unified, but diverge and are shaped by differentiations and conflicts of attitudes, tastes, and political opinions. So, for example, we, to varying degrees, find communists, socialists, conservatives, liberals, fascists, apolitical citizens, etc. within one and the same local community, region, and nation-state.

The Nation as Community of Character

Bauer (1924/2000), based on Renner, defines the nation as "a community of character that has grown out of a community of fate" (7). "*The nation is the totality of human beings bound together by a community of fate into a community of character*" (117). We "will call the complex of physical and intellectual characteristics that distinguishes one nation from another its national character" (20). A "range of corresponding characteristics can be observed among the great majority of the nation's members" (22). "The fact of national character, the commonality of character among the members of a nation, is obvious from experience" (26). Bauer argues for seeing "the nation as a community of culture or, in other words, considering how the national character is determined by the shared tradition of cultural elements passed down from earlier generations" (36). He suggests one should see "common history as the [nation's] effective cause, common culture and common descent as the means by which this cause becomes operative, common language as the mediator of the common culture, simultaneously its product and its producer" (114).

Bauer never explains why he uses the term "fate" for defining the nation. The notions of fate and destiny have the religious connotation of a predetermined future and history that is external to and independent of human beings. It is not clear why Bauer uses such a problematic term as part of his of definition of the nation as "community of fate". The deterministic aspect of this nation concept is that it assumes that a person born into a specific nation necessarily shares specific forms of thought and behaviour. Bauer's concept of the nation is fetishist because it sees the nation as immanent to all societies, even socialist societies. It disregards the inherent connection of the modern state and the nation.

Alfred Klahr's Critique of Bauer

The Austrian communist Alfred Klahr (1937) argues that Bauer's concept of the nation is idealist and unhistorical:

> Otto Bauer's notion is idealist because he explains the ideological feature of the national community of character as the nation's decisive feature without setting it in relation to other features, the community of territory and economic life, from which it emerges.[2]

Bauer holds "the idea that the Germans already in the age of kinship communism and the feudal society of the Middle Ages formed a nation and thereby anticipates curious modern theories of the Nazis!"[3] (Klahr 1937). Writing in 1937, Klahr argues that Austrians and Germans never formed a nation because they lived under different political and economic conditions of life. Klahr and the Communist Party of Austria (KPÖ) rejected Bauer's and the Social Democrats' German nationalist idea of a unification of Germany and Austria. They argued for Austria's independence as part of the anti-fascist struggle against the Nazis.

Klahr (1937) argues that the Austrian nation is a bounded unity consisting of an economic system, a political territory (the state), a language community, and a national cultural character, which was Stalin's (1913, 307)[4] definition of the nation. He argues that language, Austrian literature, and art constitute the "Austrian national culture"[5] (Klahr 1937). In the context of anti-fascism, the struggle for an Austrian democratic, anti-fascist nation-state was certainly appropriate. But for doing so, one does not need the notion of an Austrian nation, but only of an Austrian political nation-state that is built on an anti-fascist constitution and does not see itself as part of the German nation and the political project of German nationalism.

The problem is that the stress on the Austrian nation can turn into chauvinism and xenophobia. In its party programme, the Freedom Party of Austria defines itself as a "patriotic Austrian force" (FPÖ 2011, 2) and defines "our homeland of Austria as part of the German-speaking linguistic and cultural community" (2). The ideology of the Austrian cultural nation is used for the political demand "Austria First" (2), which means for the FPÖ that "Austria is not a country of immigration" (5) and that it rejects "forced multiculturalism, globalisation and mass immigration" (17). The conclusion is that Austria has a unitary language and culture and that immigrants, Muslims, and other minorities have to assimilate or be kept out because it is assumed that multiculturalism destroys the Austrian nation. The example shows that the combination of German language and Austrian-German culture as definition criterion of the nation can turn into chauvinist understandings of the nation. Klahr would probably answer to such claims that anti-fascism is part of the political culture of his own understanding of the Austrian nation. One, however, needs to add that Austrian culture and the languages spoken in Austria have never been unitary, but always diverse. Multiculturalism has always been an immanent aspect of Austrian culture. It makes sense to speak of a diverse Austrian culture. Speaking of a unitary Austrian *national* culture in contrast opens up possibilities for abuse. The nation consists in the form of a nation-state and people living in it, which inevitably results in diverse ways of life that have some minimal common core (such as a common educational system, media system, etc.) that constitutes a unity in diversity. But the nation is first and foremost a political concept. Overstressing the level of culture poses the danger of chauvinist understandings of the nation.

Nationality as Radical Cultural Difference

In the last instance, Bauer (1924/2000) propagates that there are radical cultural differences between different cultures:

Over and above these differences, all peoples share certain characteristics that identify us as human beings. On the other hand, classes, professions, and individuals within each nation exhibit distinctive qualities, particular features that distinguish them from one another. But the fact remains that the average German is different from the average Englishman, although they may well have much in common as human beings and as members of the same class or profession, and that the English share with one another a range of characteristics, however much they are distinguished from one another by individual and social differences.

(20)

Thus, community of fate does not refer to subjection to the same fate, but to the common experience of the same fate in the context of constant relations, of continual interaction. The English and the Germans both experienced capitalist development, but at different times, in different places, and in the context of only a loose relationship to each other.

(100–101)

Bauer underestimates the cultural opening that modernity has enabled and that has given everyday people more access to education, universities, museums, culture, etc. This opening came along with the expansion of commodity culture, mass production, and consumer culture. Generalised commodity culture requires general education for skills development of the workforce and culture as realm of commodity consumption. In many countries, most people have access to culture and education today, but there are qualitative differences between classes in terms of the education they get, educational success, and cultural tastes. Culture is in capitalism, as Bourdieu (1984) says, a culture of class distinction.

"Non-Historical Nations"

Bauer (1924/2000, Chapter 4) speaks of "non-historical nations" as language groups that consist of peasants and workers in a society, where the aristocratic or bourgeois ruling class do not speak the mother tongue of the peasants and workers. As examples, he mentions the Slovenes in Austria from the ninth century onwards (158, 159) and the Czechs between 1620 and 1740 (171, 177). Bauer distinguishes between historical nations that he sees as "civilised" because they have a developed economy and a ruling class, and "uncivilised" nations that he considers as backwards and undeveloped. He therefore characterises the "non-historical nations" as being "devoid of culture" (159) and having no "living culture" (159). In what Bauer terms the non-historical Czech nation, "Czech became the language of the despised and the exploited classes" (172). But any group having a common language has some common aspects of life, at least in production and culture. Production, language, and culture evolve historically. The distinction between historical and non-historical nations is certainly a political-moral judgement. It is no wonder that Bauer's unitary concept of culture and the nation also resulted in prejudices and racist stereotypes: "The beautiful women of Italy might attract me for the moment with their unusual charms, but I will soon yearn again for the blonde beauties of my own land" (122). The "difference in anthropological features is accompanied by a difference in psychological features" (100).

Modern culture and the nation-state are not unified and unitary, but contradictory and class-stratified. There are conflicting centrifugal and centripetal cultural forces. Centrifugal cultural forces are sources of cultural differentiation in modern society. They include class differentiation/conflict, political conflict/struggles, ideological conflict/struggles, local life, local culture, local media, local entertainment, urban/rural differentials, educational differences, gender relations, flexible accumulation that produces a diversity of commodities and commodity cultures and therefore niche tastes, etc. Centripetal cultural forces provide common experiences and references. They include the nation-state, citizenship, wage-labour, shared experiences of exploitation, general education, the political and legal system, global culture, global media, global entertainment, consumer culture, legal rights, dominant religion, public service media, the monopolisation of private media, the teaching of language, literature, philosophy, history, politics, art, culture, and science in schools and universities, state-sponsored and award-winning art and culture, healthcare systems, national sports teams, dominant parties and ideologies, the public transport system, etc. Modern culture consists of a dialectic of attraction and repulsion that has to do with the stratified, contradictory, and class character of modern society.

Let us take an example from Austria, the country Bauer predominantly writes about. People living in Austria's very west, in Vorarlberg, speak a dialect that is close to Swiss German. In contrast, many people living in Austria's most eastern region, Burgenland, speak a dialect called Hianzisch that originated in East-Central Bavaria. An Austrian speaking heavy Vorarlbergian dialect and one speaking heavy Burgenlandian dialect will first hardly be able to understand each other. The person from Burgenland is likely to be unfamiliar with the habit of eating *Hafaloab* in parts of Vorarlberg (a dumpling made out of corn, potatoes, and eggs, often filled with bacon,

50 A Marxist Theory of Nationalism

smoked meat, or sausage), just like the person from Vorarlberg may be unfamiliar with eating *Umurkensuppe*, a soup typical in Burgenland made from cucumbers, chicken, mint, sour cream, yoghurt, and paprika. Both individuals may have fairly different eating habits and dialectics, but both of them are by many considered to be Austrians. What unites them is Austrian citizenship and Austrian institutions such as public education and the media. But they are not really part of a German or Austrian community of fate or a German or Austrian community of culture or an Austrian or German language community, but part of an imaginary political community that was created as a result of the First World War when Burgenland became part of the Austrian state. The nation is not a metaphysical category, but exists only in the form of the nation-state and nationalist and patriotic consciousness. It is tied to politics and ideology.

Karl Kautsky's Review of Bauer's Book

Kautsky (1908) critically reviewed Bauer's book on the nationality question:

> Every entity in society is a community of fate. Each society has its own common fates and traditions. This is true of the gens, the municipality, the state, the guild, the party, and even the joint stock company. And many of these entities are also cultural communities that build on the common culture of its member to whom they convey a common culture. [...] On the other hand a human group's commonality of fates and culture does not strictly distinguish one nation from another one. Despite the difference of their nationality, the German and the French Swiss are united by a much closer community of fate and culture than the German Swiss, the Viennese or someone from Holstein. And where large class differences emerge within a nation, cultural differences also arise that go much deeper than many cultural differences between nations, while the commonality of class often also produces a cultural community among the members of the same class who belong to different nations. The German and the Danish peasant in Schleswig in any case stand in a closer cultural community than the German peasant and the German journalist and artist from Western Berlin, while the two latter stand in a closer cultural community with journalists and artists from Paris.[6]

(3)

Bauer (1924/2000) argues that the feudal nation was defined by knights' and aristocrats' culture and the capitalist nation is defined by the bourgeois class' culture

(107). Everyday people would be excluded from defining the nation and would only in socialism be able to collectively define the nation: "The human beings of the future will thus create their own culture [...] Only socialism can integrate the broad mass of working people into the national community of culture" (94).

Ruling Culture and Lived Culture

Culture is, for Bauer, limited to the ruling class. However, all subordinate classes also communicate in everyday life and develop traditions, habits, tastes, and ways of life. Culture is not the realm of the privileged few, but exists wherever humans interact in society and thereby produce meanings of the world in everyday life. Given that Bauer does not tie the notion of the nation to the nation-state, but to culture, he ends up idealising the role of the bourgeoisie and ruling classes in general in the formation of culture. For E.P. Thompson (1978), culture is the lived experience of a class or group. Experience includes culture, ideas, instincts, feelings, norms, obligations, values, beliefs, affects, morals (171), needs, interests, consciousness (164), myth, science, law, ideology (9), and thought (98). Experience in relation to class has to do with class consciousness expressed in a class' culture, traditions, values, ideas, and institutions (Thompson 1963, 10). Popular culture derives from common experience and customs in common (Thompson 1993).

Language and the Nation

Language is, for Bauer (1924/2000), not a foundational aspect of the nation, but an epiphenomenon:

> The nation can thus be defined as a community of character that has grown not out of a similarity of fate, but out of a community of fate. This fact also constitutes the significance of language for the nation. I create a common language together with those individuals with whom I most closely interact; and I interact most closely with those individuals with whom I share a common language.
>
> (101)

> The nation is a community of language, says Kautsky. This is undoubtedly true. But can we be satisfied with this statement? [...] We want to understand the community of language itself as a historical phenomenon, language itself as within the flow of historical development. We must

therefore comprehend the linguistic community as emerging from the community of culture and fate, the specificity of the individual linguistic community as emerging from the specificity of the community of culture and character. This is why it seems to me inadequate to regard the nation as a community of language, and why I have attempted to derive the linguistic community itself from the community of fate, culture, and character.

(16–17)

Nationalism and the Nation-State

Bauer (1924/2000) is certainly right when he argues that the "modern state was born as a child of commodity production" (139) and that capitalism requires "a large, populous, economically unified region; the necessity of capitalist development therefore argued against the political fragmentation of the nation" (148). The capitalist state helps with organising a territory for the control of labour-markets, commodity markets, and the exploitation of labour. It supports the organisation of capital with the help of property laws, the army, the police, and the judicial and penalty systems that enforce private property and class relations. It also supports capital by building and maintaining infrastructures (transport, science and technology, utilities, communications, cities, etc.) and institutions that support the development and reproduction of labour-power (schools, universities, state support for families, healthcare system, pension system, etc.).

There is no doubt that social institutions have been established as a result of the working class' struggles. But that the bourgeois state accepted the establishment of these institutions also has to do with the insight that they benefit capital. The modern state is a bureaucratic state that organises citizenship and the rule of political groups. The capitalist state is also a bureaucratic state that interrelates the interests of factions of the capitalist class, subordinated classes, dominant political groups, and subordinated political groups. The nation-state needs an ideology that justifies its existence. The modern nation has an objective existence in the form of the nation-state and a subjective existence in the form of national consciousness and nationalism. Nationalism is an ideology that propagates pride in the cultural, political, and economic belonging to a constructed nation in order to justify the existence of the actual or prospective nation-state and class relations organised within (and beyond) the nation-state. The nation is an objective (the nation-state) and subjective (nationalist ideology and consciousness) aspect of class societies. Bauer's fetishisation of the nation risks fetishising the violence, imperialism, exclusion, warfare, and genocides that have come along with the existence of actual existing nation-states.

Otto Bauer's German Nationalism

Bauer's culturally essentialist and unitary concept of the nation was the underlying reason why he saw Austria as part of the German nation. This means that he saw Austrian and German culture as unitary. As a consequence, he argued for the political unification of Austria and Germany. Bauer saw peasants as too silly to be German nationalists, whereas he argued that workers were more developed and therefore more inclined to take on the ideology of German nationalism:

> Today, the Tyrolean peasant is closely tied to his compatriots by the particular peasant culture of the region and clearly distinguished from the Germans outside the region. This fact of national being is reflected in the national consciousness. The Tyrolean peasant feels himself in the first instance to be a Tyrolean and seldom recalls his Germanness. For the Tyrolean worker the situation is already quite different; he shares less in the particularity of the Tyrolean peasant and is tied to the German nation by far stronger bonds. By making every German a product of German culture and providing all Germans with the possibility of enjoying the progress of German culture, socialist society alone will eliminate the particularism within the nation. Without doubt, this development will strengthen the power of the political principle of nationality.
>
> (Bauer 1924/2000, 406)

> The [Austrian] workers are not good Germans, but we are struggling to make them into good Germans!
>
> (420)

Bauer and the Demand for Austria's Anschluss *to Germany*

In 1919, Bauer argued for the unification of Austria and Germany. He thought that the *Anschluss* of Austria to Germany would create a large working class that would be so powerful that it would be able to create socialism:

> Our prospects are completely different if German-Austria becomes a limb of the great German republic. The great German republic will not be a loose

federation of states, but a tight-knit federal state with a strong unified government and a common legislative parliament [...] That this state power will be governed by the will to socialism is guaranteed by the German workers' quantity, the spiritual maturity and the revolutionary determinedness. The *Anschluss* to Germany thus initiates the way to socialism. It is the first precondition for socialism's realisation. Therefore the struggle for socialism must in this country at first be carried out as the *Anschluss* to Germany.[7]

(Bauer 1919/2017, 34)

Bauer overlooks that socialism is not simply a matter of the quantitative size of territory and the total number of workers, but one of the quality of class struggle, political tactics and strategies, the role of ideologies and their deconstruction, public discourse, the interaction of crises and political agency, the development of the productive forces, etc. (Bauer 1919/2017, 54).

In the eighth century, wide parts of today's Austria belonged to the Bavarian duchy. In 1156, Austria became a duchy independent from Bavaria. It was first ruled by the House of Babenberger, and from 1246 onwards until the end of the Austro-Hungarian Empire in 1918 by the House of Habsburg. The territory of today's Germany was not ruled by the House of Habsburg, but by royal houses such as the House of Wittelsbach, the House of Luxembourg, and the House of Hohenzollern. Given that Austria became independent from Bavaria in 1156 and has ever since had its own history as a state relatively independent from the rule on the territory of today's Germany (with the exception of the years between 1938 and 1945 under Hitler), Bauer's claim that Austria is German is somewhat odd. What he means is that Austria and Germany share a similar culture, including the German language. But this does not constitute, even in Bauer's own theory, a joint nation of Austria and Germany.

Max Adler on Bauer's Concept of the Nation

Max Adler was Austro-Marxism's most important philosopher. He engaged with Bauer's theory of the nation. Adler (1932, 125) argues that the nation is not a natural or biological, but a social phenomenon. To say that the nation is a biological, racial community is racist, whereas defining it as a linguistic community cannot, according to Adler, explain why individuals speaking the same language form different nation-states (126). Adler characterises Bauer's concept of the nation the following way: "Historical fate has bound together groups of humans in common work and common experiences, whereby they have obtained a common physical and psychological character and finally also a common cultural heritage"[8] (126). Adler argues that Bauer's assumptions are too generalising. The notion of the national character is a very imprecise generalisation (127). "So for example someone from Berlin and someone from Munich do not have a common national character. And a naïve East Prussian for example considers the Schuhplattler folk dances performed in Schliersee [Bavaria] as foreign customs"[9] (127). Adler stresses that Bauer is right in defining the nation historically in order to oppose its biological definition. Although Adler sees Bauer's nation concept as too unitary, he does not drop it as ideological, but rather introduces a distinction between a nation-in-itself bound together by historical fate and a nation-for-itself that develops a national consciousness as its ideology (129). He argues that thus far, it has always been the dominant class that has defined national consciousness (129).

Adler defines the nation as "a community of will that has emerged from the historical community of fate for the maintenance of a community of interest or culture that has been defined linguistically or as state"[10] (128). The nation-in-itself is, for Adler, defined by "common historical experience that has resulted in a common physical and spiritual manner and a common community of interests"[11] (130).

Adler sees Bauer's nation-concept as too objectivist and reifying. But he does not drop it, but adds to the reified notion of the nation a subjective one (the nation-for-itself) and argues that in a class society, the dominant class defines national consciousness. This assumption also disregards that workers, to a significant degree, have throughout modern history been nationalist. A significant degree of workers supported Hitler and today support right-wing extremists (Fuchs 2018a). Adler tries to combine a reified and a critical concept of the nation into one overall nation concept instead of extending critique of the nation to the objective dimension.

4.3 The Political Impacts of Austro-Marxism and Otto Bauer's Theory

The two largest failures of Austro-Marxism were its lack of political determination against fascist and imperialist forces and its German nationalism. Whereas some of its rhetoric sounded radical, the politics of the Austrian Social Democrats were largely pragmatic and reformist. At the outbreak of the First World War, the Austro-Marxists did not oppose the war, but supported the Austro-Hungarian Empire's war against Serbia.

The 1919 Peace Treaty of Saint-Germain-en-Laye

After the First World War, the First Austrian Republic was formed. The Social Democrat Karl Renner became the first chancellor and negotiated a peace treaty with the Allied Forces. Given their German nationalist worldview, the Austrian Social Democrats did not accept the establishment of an Austrian nation-state, but argued for Austria's unification with Germany in the negotiations.

Bauer characterised the Peace Treaty of Saint-Germain-en-Laye from 1919 as "a horrible document"[12] (Bauer 1923, 151).

> The Peace Treaty robbed our republic of territories inhabited by more than three million Germans. A third of the Austro-German people fell under foreign rule. [...] The day the Treaty of Saint Germain had to be ratified was the day of the end of proletarian hegemony in German-Austria.[13]
>
> (Bauer 1923, 159)

Also here, Bauer's assessment and idiom is not different from Hitler, who spoke of "the disgraceful treaties [*Schandverträge*] of Versailles and St. Germain" (Hitler 1988, 561) and saw the peace treaties of the First World War as "a scandal and a disgrace" and "an act of highway robbery against our people" (420). Both Bauer and Hitler use the metaphor of the robbery in order to oppose the peace treaties and both employ a nationalist logic for arguing in favour of the *Anschluss*.

As a consequence of the German nationalist ideology of leading Social Democrats, the 1926 Linz Programme of the Social Democratic Workers' Party of Austria (SDAP) demanded the unification of Austria and Germany: "Social Democracy sees the unification of German-Austria and the German Reich as necessary completion of the national resolutions made in 1918. It strives for the Anschluss to the German Republic by peaceful means"[14] (SDAP 1926, 401).

Austrian Social Democracy and the Anschluss

Bauer (1923) describes how during the course of the First World War, Austrian Social Democracy developed the position of demanding Austria's unification with Germany:

> Since 1899, we have demanded the transformation of Austria into a federal state of free nations. But it became evident during the War that the Czechs, the Poles, and the Southern Slavs would no longer be content

with this solution of their national problem if the revolution breaks out and that they would fight for full national autonomy in the revolution. [...] It was already clear in 1917 that the transformation of the monarchy into a federal state of autonomous nations would become a counter-revolutionary slogan. [...] Our considerations led to the following conclusion: if the revolution comes, then we must not defend the existence of Austria hand in hand with the counter-revolutionary powers – the dynasty, the Austro-German bourgeoisie, and the Magyar gentry – against the revolutionary nations. We must accept the Slavic nations' unlimited right to self-determination. And we have to draw the conclusion that if we accept the Slavic nations' right to self-determination, then we must demand the same right to self-determination for the Austro-German people. If the Slavic nations realise their unity and freedom in the form of new nation-states, then we must try to realise the unity and freedom of the German people by the unification (*Anschluss*) of German-Austria and Germany. If the Slavic nations' national revolution blows up the empire, then we must utilise the moment of the revolutionary crisis for the purpose of the social revolution, then we must overthrow the empire also on our soil, erect the democratic republic, and start the struggle for socialism on the democratic republic's soil.[15]

(61–62)

Bauer's argumentation is based on the assumption that cultural nations exist, that German culture is fundamentally different from Slavic cultures and therefore should be organised in different nation-states, that German-speaking Austrians and Germans form one people that should live together in one state, and that Austria and Germany should therefore be unified. Bauer advances a particular form of German nationalism. Already in *The Question of Nationalities and Social Democracy*, which was first published in 1907, he spoke of the existence of Aryans (Bauer 1924/2000, 302, 305) and "Aryan blood" (308). Austro-Marxism had an inadequate analysis of anti-Semitism and there were aspects of anti-Semitism within Austro-Marxism (Peham 2008). It also favoured aspects of eugenics (Trallori 2008).

Bauer and Hitler

Bauer certainly did not like Hitler and the Nazis' belief in the racial superiority of Germans. He rather saw the unification of Austria and Germany as a strategy for the success of the proletarian revolution. It is, however, not clear why a revolution should be more successful in a larger than in a smaller country. Bauer held a nationalist concept of society, like Hitler demanded the *Anschluss* of Austria to Germany, and spoke of the defence of the nation's soil and the existence of Aryans. He disregards in his writings and politics that for Marx and Engels, social revolution and socialism have to have an international character:

> The Communists are further reproached with desiring to abolish countries and nationality. [...] National differences and antagonisms between peoples are daily more and more vanishing, owing to the development of the bourgeoisie, to freedom of commerce, to the world market, to uniformity in the mode of production and in the conditions of life corresponding thereto. The supremacy of the proletariat will cause them to vanish still faster. United action, of the leading civilised countries at least, is one of the first conditions for the emancipation of the proletariat. In proportion as the exploitation of one individual by another is put an end to, the exploitation of one nation by another will also be put an end to. In proportion as the antagonism between classes within the nation vanishes, the hostility of one nation to another will come to an end.
>
> (Marx and Engels 1848, 502–503)

Josef Strasser's Critique of Bauer and Austro-Marxism

Josef Strasser (1982), a communist critic of Austro-Marxism, argues that nationalist ideology can best be challenged by *"intransigent internationalism"*[16] (67). Bauer (1923) saw Austria as unliveable and as too small to be able to survive:

> German-Austria is not a structure that has organically grown. It is nothing but the old empire's remainders after the other nations seceded. It has remained as a loose bundle of diverging countries whose common political solidarity and economic means of existence have been destroyed by the breakup of the old empire and the old economic territory. In the old empire, the Austro-Germans were the politically ruling and economically dominant people. [...] Therefore the dissolution of the old empire had to result in a severe shock to the Austro-German industry and had to severely complicate the nourishment of the Austro-German industrial people. During the time of the revolution, nobody believed that these remainders of the old monarchy that had been torn out of their economic body by a violent operation could autonomously lead a tolerable life.[17]
>
> (113–114)

Schutzbund and Heimwehr

In the 1920s and 1930s, a political-ideological struggle between socialists and conservatives dominated in Austrian politics. Both had armed forces, namely the Social Democrats' Schutzbund and the clerical-fascist Heimwehr. On 30 January 1927, Heimwehr members, in a conflict with Schutzbund members in Schattendorf, a small town in Burgenland, shot Matthias Csmarits and the 6-year-old Josef Grössing.

When a court acquitted Josef Tscharmann, Hieronymous Tscharmann, and Johann Pinter of not having murdered Csmarits and Grössing, the Austro-Marxists did not call for a general strike. On 15 July, workers organised a spontaneous uprising in Vienna and set the Palace of Justice (*Justizpalast*), which they saw as a symbol of class injustice, on fire. The police responded by shooting into the masses, which killed 89 protesters and injured more than 1,000.

Bauer and other leaders of the Social Democrats even condemned the spontaneous uprising of Viennese workers, who saw the Schattendorf-verdict as class injustice. They watched as workers were killed and did not consider arming the Schutzbund to defend the protesting workers who were being shot at (Fischer 1969, 161–186). Bauer explained:

> We had experienced the spontaneous demonstration on the day when the Schattendorf-offences became known to the public. So it was evident that there would be a big upheaval and the following thought was obvious: a big upheaval can arise, so let us not wait until a spontaneous demonstration emerges, but let us ourselves organise a demonstration with all possible safety measures so that public order is not disrupted. [...] we [...] at that time considered it wiser not to do that, but rather to undertake efforts to calm down our comrades in the workshops and that is also what happened.[18]
>
> (cited in Hoke and Reiter 1993, 591)

One can see here that Bauer put order and stability over class struggle and favoured politics that appeased and pacified the working class. There had been political killings of workers before that had resulted in no or just minor punishment. In the First Austrian Republic, "killing workers [...] [was] a peccadillo" (Fischer 1969, 163).

The Dangers of Political Pragmatism

Unitary thinking that overlooks differences was not just a feature of Bauer's concept of the nation, but also shaped his political pragmatism that avoided class struggles, uprisings, general strikes, and armed struggles. It is therefore also no surprise that when Dollfuß' clerical-fascists eliminated the Austrian Parliament in March 1933, the Austro-Marxists first thought their party could continue to legally exist and everything would be back to normal within a couple of weeks. Consequently, the Austro-Marxists did not call for and did not organise armed resistance. Dollfuß erected a clerical-fascist regime and outlawed communist and socialist organisations, as well as the trade union movement.

The clerical-fascists dissolved the Schutzbund in early April 1933. Again, the Social Democratic Party's leaders simply accepted this fact and did not call for or organise armed resistance. The party's mouthpiece, the *Arbeiterzeitung*, simply cited from a party bulletin: "The government has dissolved the Schutzbund. [...] The reactionaries want to hit the working class. They can dissolve organisations, but not the spirit that animates this organisation. The spirit of struggle is alive!"[19] (cited in Hoke and Reiter 1993, 522). The Austro-Marxists not just advanced idealist, Kantian philosophy in Marxian clothes. In decisive political situations, such as the moment of the abolishment of democracy, they advanced political idealism instead of materialist anti-fascist resistance.

Richard Bernaschek was the Social Democratic Party's leader in Upper Austria and also a leader in the Schutzbund. On 12 February 1934, Schutzbund members under Bernaschek's leadership started armed resistance against the Austro-fascist regime in Linz. The armed struggle expanded to other parts of Upper Austria and to Vienna. It was defeated on 15 February. This was the only significant armed socialist resistance against Austro-fascism. Bernaschek (1934) assessed the failures of Austrian Social Democracy: "Austrian Social Democracy was worn down. Worn down by its own indecisiveness and its opponents' resoluteness. [...] The mass of the workers [...] could not understand that they were prepared for revolution and at the same time appeased."[20] These failures had a longer history. When, at the end of the First World War, strikes broke out in Austria, the Social Democrats "did everything in their power to slow down and stop"[21] the strike movement (Baier 2009, 20). After the events of February 1934, many left socialists, including intellectuals such as Ernst Fischer and many members of the Schutzbund, because of their disappointment with Social Democracy, joined the illegal Communist Party of Austria, whose number of members as a consequence increased from 4,000 to 16,000 (Baier 2009, 40). Fischer, who was a member of the Social Democratic Party and a journalist of the party's newspaper *Arbeiter-Zeitung*, writes in his memoirs that there was "a contradiction between words and deeds immanent in Austro-Marxism"[22] (Fischer 1969, 183).

Austro-Marxism and Nazi-Fascism

In 1928, Renner and Bauer signed the Confession of Leading Men and Women of German-Austria to the Idea of the *Anschluss*[23] (Steingress 2008). Shortly before the 1938 referendum on Austria's *Anschluss* to Germany (10 April 1938), Karl Renner (1938) gave an interview, in which he said:

> I would have to deny my whole past as theoretical pioneer of the nations' right to self-determination and as German-Austrian statesman, if I did not welcome the reunification of the German nation wholeheartedly. [...] As Social Democrat I advocate the right to self-determination of the nation. As the first Chancellor of the Republic of German-Austria and as former President of the Republic's Peace Delegation in St. Germain, I will vote in favour of the *Anschluss*.[24]

Karl Renner (1952, 317) still wrote in publications released after the Second World War that Germany without Austria and the Sudeten territories was a "mutilated nation".[25] Otto Bauer also continued to hold a German nationalist position after Hitler had come to power (Baier 2008). In 1936, Bauer (1936) characterised Austria as an "entity not capable of developing"[26] (338), doomed (338), and an "impotent, miserable state"[27] (340). More than 100 years later, Austria is yet smaller than after the First World War, but has managed to successfully survive economically and politically since 1945. It is an ideological myth motivated by German nationalism that the small state of Austria is not able to survive. Out of such complaints speaks the political inferiority complex of nationalists who could not accept that the Austrian Empire came to an end.

Also, Hitler (1988) characterised Austria as not "durable" (nicht lebensfähig) and despised the Austro-Hungarian regime not because of the monarchy, but because of its "babel of tongues" and because he saw a "long and slow Slavization of the Austrian Germans" under way (46). As a consequence, he was in favour of and worked towards what he saw as the "liberating of my German-Austrian people [...] [so that it] would [...] become possible for them to be reunited to the Motherland" (46). The Austrian Social Democrats during the time of the Austro-Hungarian Empire demanded a multi-linguistic state. So, Bauer certainly saw Slavs not as an inferior people, but he nonetheless was a German nationalist, who in the last instance preferred a unified German state to a multi-linguistic state.

Bauer (1938a) without a doubt was an anti-fascist and Marxist who saw democratic socialism as the antidote to fascism. He analysed fascism and Nazi-fascism as a system that is "filled with [...] nationalism" (169), "annihilates all individual liberty, abolishes free elections, destroys the proletarian organizations. [...] Class rule restrained by democratic institutions is replaced by 'totalitarian' dictatorship, that is, by unrestricted class rule" (179). Fascism's "aggressive nationalist foreign policies [...] threaten to end in war" (182). Bauer (1936) saw that fascism tries to make "national consciousness and national sentiments stronger than class consciousness and class struggle"[28] (329).

Ernst Fischer, who knew Bauer in person, shifted sides from Social Democracy to the Communist Party of Austria (KPÖ) after the events of 1934. While in exile during the Nazi period, he was the KPÖ's representative in the Communist International (Komintern). He argues against the view that Otto Bauer betrayed the working class. At the time of Austro-fascism, Fischer saw it, like Bauer, as important that Austria's revolutionary socialists and communists cooperate and therefore help initiate a joint platform (Fischer 1969, 315). Fischer (1969) writes that not the social democrats, but the Austro-fascists, led by Ignaz Seipel and Engelbert Dollfuß, and the Nazis posed the real political threat in Austria in the 1920s and 1930s:

> Social democratic politics prevented the proletarian revolution, saved the bourgeoisie and has bred fatal revolutionary ideas in the working class. Nevertheless, it would be wrong to describe all leaders of social democracy as traitors [...] Austrian social democracy has to be blamed for a major defeat of the working class, but it has at the same time kept alive the idea, or, if you please to say so, the feeling of socialism among the masses. [...] Otto Bauer is not a traitor. It is true that he has failed in a decisive situation, but he has not betrayed us.[29]
>
> (332, 353)

In the light of fascism, Bauer (1936) called for a new revolutionary socialist strategy that would establish an integral socialism that united socialist and communist positions as well as reformist and revolutionary politics. But he nonetheless shared nationalism and essentialism with fascist ideology. Of course, it makes a difference that his nationalist essentialism was not biological, but cultural in character. But his nationalist ideology and politics also made him misjudge the *Anschluss* of Austria to Germany. He argued that Austria had no future, welcomed the *Anschluss*, and argued for a pan-German revolution against Hitler (Bauer 1938b, 1938c). Given the party that represented working-class interests had for a long time favoured the

Anschluss, was it not likely that this class voted for the actual *Anschluss* when Hitler and the Nazis advanced this agenda? And maybe parts of the working class even assumed there is some joint agenda of socialist and the Nazis because they both favoured German nationalism. Even worse, some former members of the Social Democratic Party may have felt encouraged to join the Nazi Party. Bauer did not see that the assumption of the unity and superiority of Germans was an inherent and central feature of Nazi-ideology.

Austro-Marxism's Willingness to Servitude and Submission

A certain willingness to servitude and submission that lacked determinateness and the willingness to call for the organisation of resistance in decisive moments when democracy was under threat seems to have been an inherent feature of Austro-Marxism. This attitude stands in a psychological relationship to German nationalism. Nationalism is an expression of the worldview that individuals are part of and should submit to mythical collectives. Erich Fromm (1942/2001) characterises authoritarian and nationalist personalities as sadomasochistic. Their ideology is based on the "lust for power" (183), "sadistic craving for power" (191), the "projection of social inferiority to national inferiority" (186), sadistic hatred against constructed enemies (194), "the wish to have power over helpless beings" (200), and the masochistic proclamation that "the individual is nothing and does not count" (200). By submitting and sacrificing themselves to the power of the leader and the national community, nationalists see themselves as dying psychologically as weak individuals and as being reborn as *Volk*. Authoritarianism's sadistic side is "the craving for power over men"; its masochistic side is "the longing for submission to an overwhelmingly strong outside power" (204). According to Fromm's theory, the Austro-Marxists' politically sycophantic and servile political behaviour that was not the cause of, but favoured the rise of, clerical-fascism and Nazi-fascism in Austria, stands in relation to their German nationalist ideology.

The Austrian communist Josef Strasser (1982) criticised Austro-Marxism's defencelessness:

> Here and there the Heimwehr killed a worker. After each of these murders, the *Arbeiter-Zeitung* declared that if something like that happened again, then … What would happen 'then' became evident on July 15, 1927. When on that day the workers of Vienna, who were exacerbated about the acquittal

of some fascist murders of workers, set the Palace of Justice on fire, the Social Democrats thought nothing less was appropriate than to offer to the Conservatives to form a coalition government. [...] And now, after Dollfuss, encouraged and alarmed by the events in Germany, set about to provide advantages to the Austrian bourgeoisie that a fascist regime can pose, Social Democracy remains idle. [...] Austro-Marxists face fascism just as clueless as the reformist theoreticians and practitioners face war.[30]

(98)

At the time of Otto Bauer, the following joke was told among radical socialist and communists: If the fascists kill Otto Bauer, the Social Democratic Party's leadership and the *Arbeiter-Zeitung* will release a statement saying, "The fascist reactionaries have killed our leader Otto Bauer. We warn them: If they murder Otto Bauer a second time, then we will organise armed resistance." This piece of black humour contains a bitter truth: Austrian Social Democracy's German nationalism, passiveness, and political pragmatism and idealism supported first the rise of clerical-fascism and then the rise of Nazi-fascism in Austria.

4.4 Rosa Luxemburg's Critical Theory of Nationalism

Rosa Luxemburg's Radical Internationalism

Rosa Luxemburg's (1976, 101–287) *The National Question and Autonomy* was first published in Polish as a series of articles in 1908 and 1909. Luxemburg was a representative of "radical internationalism" (Forman 1998, 12). "Luxemburg's argument was that democracy had to be based not in nations, but in popular institutions that recognized political rights" (Forman 1998, 87). She was critical of Lenin's notion of the nation because in her view, he had betrayed democracy and capitulated to nationalism (Forman 1998, 86).

At the end of the eighteenth century, the Polish–Lithuanian Commonwealth was undergoing partition and ceased to exist. The Commonwealth's territories became part of Austria, Prussia, and Russia. At the end of the nineteenth century, the Polish Socialist Party advanced Polish nationalism as a strategy for creating a Polish nation-state that was independent from Russia. Rosa Luxemburg's Social Democracy of the Kingdom of Poland and Lithuania was critical of these nationalist politics and argued for internationalist politics. This political situation was the background of Luxemburg's *The National Question and Autonomy*.

The Right to National Self-Determination and Nationalism as Ideologies

Otto Bauer argued for the nations' rights to self-determination. He saw anti-imperialist politics, working-class politics, and the struggle for new nations as inherently intertwined: "In the struggle against a violent, genocidal imperialism that increases its exploitation, reduces its political power, and does harm to its class morale, the working class announces its demand for the liberty and self-determination of all nations" (Bauer 1924/2000, 392). Luxemburg (1976) sees the demand for national self-determination as a nationalist ideology that distracts from class issues and the need for class struggle. She argues that not nations, but only the working class, has a "*right* to self-determination" (108). She sees nationalism as "a metaphysical cliché" (110).

One of the reasons why Luxemburg rejects the demand of the right of nations to self-determination is that she thinks the underlying concept of the nation "ignores completely the fundamental theory of modern socialism – the theory of social class" (135). Those talking about the nation often use it as "a homogeneous social and political entity" that is a "misty veil" concealing "a definite historical content" (135). "In a class society, 'the nation' as a homogeneous socio-political entity does not exist" (135). Rather, in a class society, there are historically developing dominating and dominated classes with certain compositions as well as rulers and the ruled. Whereas Bauer stresses that the nation culturally, psychologically, and spiritually constructs society's unity, Luxemburg argues that such an assumption is a myth and ideology that overlooks class society's divisions.

As a consequence, Luxemburg says that "Social Democracy is called upon to realize not the right of nations to self-determination but only the right of the working class, which is exploited and oppressed, of the proletariat, to self-determination" (140). Whereas for Bauer socialism means "national separation", for Luxemburg it means the emergence of an "international culture in which distinct nationalities will disappear" (263). For Luxemburg, the true workers-in-and-for-themselves do not know a national fatherland: "The workers' fatherland, to the defense of which all else must be subordinated, is the socialist International" (Luxemburg 1970, 477). "I feel at home in the entire world, wherever there are clouds and birds and human tears" (Luxemburg 2013, 376).

For Luxemburg (1976), the nation exists as the modern nation-state and as nationalist ideology that helps organising exploitation and imperialism. Nation-states "are today the very same tools and forms of class rule of the bourgeoisie as the earlier,

A Marxist Theory of Nationalism

non-national states, and like them they are bent on conquest" (172). The nation-state is "a tool of domination (or control) and conquest" (175).

Other than Bauer, Luxemburg stresses the ideological character of the nation and nationalism and that nationalism plays a role in the bourgeoisie's attempt to distract attention from class conflicts by trying to construct a national ideological unity of capital and labour that is opposed to an outside enemy. Luxemburg, in contrast to Bauer, grounds her analysis of the nation in Marx's theory of ideology. When Luxemburg speaks of nationalism as a misty veil, then she means that nationalism is a political fetishism that tries to distract attention from how social problems are grounded in class and capitalism.

Rosa Luxemburg and the First World War

The First World War showed that nationalism has an inherent militarist potential and that the idea of national unity beyond class-boundaries can easily result in workers of different nations hating and killing each other. Rosa Luxemburg (1918) characterised the First World War as the "world's explosion of nationalism" (370).[31] Nationalism is ideological diversion from class-structures and class conflict. It is an ideology that acts as a form of political psychology, constructs a national cross-class unity, and directs aggression, hatred, and dissatisfaction against other imaginary nations. In imperialist conquest, the coloniser or imperialist presents the conquered groups inhabiting the colony as backward, inferior, or as being in need of help that advances modernisation, democratisation, development, etc. The ideological argument justifying conquest and oppression is frequently that a common national culture that helps all groups to develop can be established and that this common culture overcomes alleged tribal "primitivism" and "backwardness". Cultural claims justify the establishment of the control over resources, power, people, labour-power, and markets.

Luxemburg (1913/2003) stresses that militarism, nationalism, and war are interconnected features of capitalism:

> Militarism fulfils a quite definite function in the history of capital, accompanying as it does every historical phase of accumulation. It plays a decisive part in the first stages of European capitalism, in the period of the so-called "primitive accumulation", as a means of conquering the New World and the spice-producing countries of India. Later, it is employed to subject the modern colonies, to destroy the social organisations of primitive societies so that their means of production may be appropriated, forcibly to

introduce commodity trade in countries where the social structure had been unfavourable to it, and to turn the natives into a proletariat by compelling them to work for wages in the colonies. It is responsible for the creation and expansion of spheres of interest for European capital in non-European regions, for extorting railway concessions in backward countries, and for enforcing the claims of European capital as international lender. Finally, militarism is a weapon in the competitive struggle between capitalist countries for areas of non-capitalist civilisation. In addition, militarism has yet another important function. From the purely economic point of view, it is a pre-eminent means for the realisation of surplus value; it is in itself a province of accumulation.

(434)

Luxemburg argues that in the First World War, the ideology of the national father-land forced "the masses to slaughter each other",[32] which would not correspond to "human culture"[33] (Luxemburg 1914a, 847).

We rather think that all nations independent of ethnicity, language and beliefs can live in complete peace and friendship with one another and can vie in the fulfilment of their cultural tasks. Naturally we do not surrender to the illusion that this ideal can be realised as long as capitalism exists. [...] As long as capitalism prevails, wars are inevitable.[34]

(Luxemburg 1914b, 444)

There will be no more war, as soon as the masses declare: We do not want any genocide![35]

(Luxemburg 1914b, 445)

Lenin's Critique of Luxemburg

Lenin (1914) published a critique of Luxemburg's analysis of the nation. He draws a distinction between an "oppressor nation" and an "oppressed nation" (412). Lenin says that nationalist mass movements should be supported to the extent they are progressive (437). The problem of this position is that there is no clear boundary between what Lenin terms progressive nationalism and bourgeois, reactionary, chauvinist nationalism. Nationalism tends to grow especially in the context of capitalist crises. In such situations, radical events tend to occur that force radical decisions that can have substantial consequences. For example, in 1938, there was a plebiscite on whether Austria should become part of Nazi-Germany. The Nazis initiated this plebiscite because they saw Austrians as part of the self-proclaimed "Aryan" nation Germany. Social Democrats such as Renner and Bauer favoured the *Anschluss* because they thought class struggle could better be organised in a larger country. But the consequence of both types of nationalism was the same: Austria and Austrians became part of the Nazi-regime's annihilation machinery and an imperialist World War. In the British Brexit referendum, leftist nationalists opposing the EU stood on the same side as right-wing extremists and conservatives who used xenophobic rhetoric for arguing against immigration. Progressive nationalism turns out to often share elements of reactionary nationalism, which renders the distinction between both superfluous.

Jürgen Habermas on Nationalism

Jürgen Habermas (1998) takes a position that is comparable to Luxemburg. He argues that the nation is invented and imaginary (130) and that national identity has again and again been mobilised in the fight against constructed "enemies of the fatherland" (131). Nationalism "is not a necessary or permanent precondition of a democratic process" (132). The constitution of the nation does not precede the formation of states; rather, by the founding of a state, "the participants constitute themselves as a nation of citizens" (140). Nationalism typically expresses itself as the demand of national self-determination (141). Ernest Gellner (2006) argues in this context that nationalism is a particular modern endeavour and political principle that wants "to make culture and polity congruent" (42), holds that "the political and the national unit should be congruent" (1), and aims at the "fusion of will, culture and polity" (54). The problem is that the

> formation of nation-states under the banner of ethnonationalism has almost always been accompanied by bloody purification rituals, and it has generally exposed new minorities to new waves of repression. In late 19th and 20th century Europe it left in its wake a horrific legacy of emigration and expulsion, of forced resettlement, disenfranchisement, and physical extermination, up to and including genocide. Often enough the persecuted themselves mutated into persecutors once they succeeded in emancipating themselves.
>
> (Habermas 1998, 142)

> In general, discrimination can be eliminated not through national independence but only through a process of inclusion that is sufficiently sensitive to the cultural background of individual and group-specific differences.
>
> (145)

Habermas argues that society needs the protection of minorities as well as a common culture. He argues for a cultural politics of unity in diversity.

Writing in 1998, Habermas was confident that "the catastrophes of two world wars have taught Europeans that they must abandon the mind-sets on which nationalistic, exclusionary mechanisms feed. Why should a sense of belonging together culturally and politically not grow out of these experiences" (Habermas 1998, 152). A European public sphere would not emerge from the construction of a "European people" (153), but from a shared political culture, a common civil society, a European party system, European citizen initiatives, European NGOs, European interest groups, etc. (152). The dilemma of the European Union is that it has in the past decades predominantly been an economic union that fostered neoliberal capitalism, not a strong social and political union. Through increasing fears of social decline and inequalities, neoliberal capitalism backfired in the EU and created new nationalisms that resulted in a political and legitimacy crisis of the EU. The EU was not prepared and did not have the political mechanisms to deal with the refugee crisis, which added to opportunities for nationalists to advance anti-refugee ideology and nationalist sentiments. In the Greek debt crisis, the EU advanced a combination of neoliberal austerity and economic nationalism spurred by Germany with false and ideological arguments such as the one that "hard-working Germans" fund "lazy Greeks". In the UK, Thatcher and Thatcherite Eurosceptics portrayed the EU as too "socialist" and as undermining the British nation and British democracy. With increasing inequalities in the UK, nationalist anti-immigration rhetoric gathered momentum and was a major factor influencing Brexit. Brexit in turn advanced the crisis of the EU and right-wing nationalist movements within the EU.

A Neoliberal European Union Instead of the United States of Europe

Rosa Luxemburg warned in 1911 that a capitalist United States of Europe would mean an "imperialist abortion" and "a colonial race war" (Luxemburg 1970, 369). One hundred years later, it has become evident that the European Union was realised as a neoliberal capitalist project of a new imperialism that advanced accumulation by dispossession (Harvey 2003). Many international institutions today "express the prevailing political, economic, and social inequalities at every level" (Forman 1998, 188). "The efforts of today's Left must be directed toward making these international institutions accountable to the citizens of the world" (Forman 1998, 188). The creation of the Socialist United States of Europe could have prevented the EU's crisis and the threat of war and murder that the rise of new nationalism as the negative dialectic of the EU's neoliberal capitalism entails. But of course, the creation of one Socialist United States does not suffice in a global political economy. The struggle for socialism has to be embedded into the creation of one, two, many Socialist United States that aim at overcoming nationalism and capitalism and work towards global socialism.

4.5 Conclusion

Comparing the Approaches of Otto Bauer and Rosa Luxemburg

As a summary of this chapter's results, Table 4.1 presents a summary of the differences between Bauer's and Luxemburg's concepts of the nation.

Whereas Bauer advances a cultural, spiritual, psychological notion of the nation, Luxemburg's notion is materialist and a form of ideology critique: she sees the nation as a question of concrete individuals living in modern capitalist society and their social relations. For Luxemburg, the nation takes on the form of the nation-state and nationalist ideology. Whereas Bauer was a German nationalist who argued for the *Anschluss* of Austria to Germany and saw socialism as a form of people-nationalism, Luxemburg sees nationalism in contrast to Bauer and Lenin as a form of political fetishism that does not have a progressive dimension.

New Nationalisms on Social Media

More than 100 years after Bauer and Luxemburg wrote about the nation, we today experience the rise of new nationalisms that could very well lead up to a new global war or nuclear annihilation of life on Earth. Let us consider two examples of how nationalism is expressed on social media: Twitter posts by Alice Weidel (Alternative for Germany) and Donald Trump:

> Merkel's refugee policies destroy the welfare state. The #AfD will make sure that has an end![37]
>
> (Twitter, @Alice_Weidel, 3 September 2017)

> Refugees from Syria are now pouring into our great country. Who knows who they are — some could be ISIS. Is our president insane?
>
> (Twitter, @RealDonaldTrump, 17 November 2015)

Chapter Four | Theories of the Nation and Nationalism **71**

TABLE 4.1 A comparison of Otto Bauer's and Rosa Luxemburg's concepts of the nation and nationalism

Dimension	Otto Bauer	Rosa Luxemburg
Political context	Multi-linguistic Austro-Hungarian Empire	Russian Poland
Nation	Culture: nation as community of fate and culture	The nation as nationalist ideology and imperialist nation-states; building and maintaining communications is "one of the most urgent economic needs of bourgeois society" (Luxemburg 1976, 217) as well as "the object of international conventions" (190) because capitalism requires global communications
Society	Unification of modern society by culture, spirit, psychology, and fate	Differentiation of modern society by class structures and domination
Language, communication	Language communities and communication are epiphenomena of national communities of fate	The modern nation-state organises the reproduction of a national language[36] and the "uniform arrangement of roads and communications" (Luxemburg 1976, 189) that is necessary for the transportation of commodities, information, workers, commands, ideologies, etc.
Political strategy	Right to and struggles for national self-determination	International solidarity, opposition to the national right to self-determination, only the working class has such a right
Socialism	In socialism, nation and nationalism will be defined not just by the ruling class' culture, but the people's culture and life	Socialism does not need the nation and nationalist ideology; after an international revolution, together with capitalism and imperialism, the nation and nationalism disappear
Political impacts	German nationalism, demand for the unification of Austria and Germany, opposition to the Peace Treaties of the First World War	Opposition to the First World War

Conclusion

In December 2017, Trump's tweet had more than 26,000 likes, Weidel's tweet more than 750. Both tweets communicate a combination of nationalism and the friend/enemy scheme. Refugees are presented as a social threat in the one tweet and as a terrorist threat in the other. Weidel symbolises the German nation by using the German flag, Trump the US nation by calling it a "great country". The symbol of the flag and linguistic intensification are used for communicating nationalism. The nation is opposed to refugees in both cases. The outsider group is characterised negatively as dangerous, which is a typical xenophobic ideological strategy (Reisigl and Wodak 2001, 55).

Bauer's theory does not pose any tools for a theoretical analysis of such forms of nationalism. For Bauer, the nation is a cultural phenomenon. Today, nationalism is expressed via popular cultural communication tools such as Twitter, Facebook, and YouTube. But given that Bauer naturalises the cultural dimension of the nation and does not provide an ideology critique of the nation and nationalism, his approach seems to be unfit for helping us to understand contemporary nationalism and its mediation. Luxemburg's approach in contrast allows a theoretical interpretation: Weidel and Trump communicate nationalism that constructs refugees as scapegoat in order to distract attention from the circumstance that not refugees, but neoliberalism, destroys the welfare state and that refugees are not automatically terrorists and criminals. The tweets construct a "misty veil" that conceals "a definite historical content" (Luxemburg 1976, 135). Weidel leaves out any discussion of German neoliberalism and Trump does not discuss the complex historical-political cause of ISIS. Both veil the complexity of refugees' situation and the true causes of the dismantling of the welfare state and terrorism. Such nationalist veiling strategies have in recent years been ideologically and politically relatively successful in both Germany and the USA, where individuals and groups afraid of social decline have in the past years to a significant degree voted for and supported nationalists.

One, Two, Many Socialist United States

Rosa Luxemburg builds on Marx's theory of ideology and fetishism. Her approach allows us to understand that twenty-first-century nationalism is an ideology and political fetishism. She saw internationalism as the only correct answer. The alternative to neoliberal capitalism is not the strengthening of any form of right-wing or allegedly left-wing nationalism, but the political strategy and goal of advancing a socialist world society as well as the creation of one, two, many Socialist United States.[38]

Notes

1 https://de.wikipedia.org/wiki/%C3%96sterreich-Ungarn#Sprachen_und_Religionen
2 Translation from German: „Otto Bauers Begriff ist idealistisch, denn er erklärt das ideologische Merkmal der nationalen Charaktergemeinschaft als das ausschlaggebende Merkmal der Nation, ohne es in den notwendigen Zusammenhang mit den anderen Merkmalen, mit der Gemeinschaft des Territoriums und des Wirtschaftslebens zu bringen, aus denen es erwächst."

Chapter Four | Theories of the Nation and Nationalism **73**

3 Translation from German: „Bei ihm ergibt sich daraus die kuriose, moderne Nazitheorien vorwegnehmende Idee, dass die Germanen schon im Zeitalter des Sippschaftskommunismus und in der feudalen Gesellschaft des Mittelalters eine Nation bildeten!"

4 "A nation is a historically constituted, stable community of people, formed on, the basis of a common language, territory, economic life, and psychological make-up manifested in a common culture."

5 Translation from German: „österreichischen nationalen Kultur".

6 Translation from German: „Eine Schicksalsgemeinschaft ist jedes gesellschaftliche Gebilde; jede Gesellschaft hat ihre gemeinsamen Schicksale und Traditionen; die Gens, die Gemeinde, der Staat, die Zunft, die Partei, selbst die Aktiengesellschaft. Und viele dieser Gebilde bedeuten auch eine Kulturgemeinschaft, bauen sich auf der gemeinsamen Kultur ihrer Mitglieder auf, denen sie wieder eine gemeinsame Kultur vermitteln. [...] Andererseits aber bildet die Gemeinsamkeit der Schicksale und der Kultur einer Menschengruppe nichts, was eine Nation streng von der anderen sonderte. Den deutschen und französischen Schweizer verbindet trotz der Verschiedenheit ihrer Nationalität eine weit engere Schicksals- und Kulturgemeinschaft, als den deutschen Schweizer und den Wiener oder den Holsteiner. Und wo sich innerhalb einer Nation große Klassenunterschiede herausbilden, erwachsen in ihr auch Kulturunterschiede, die weit tiefer gehen, als viele Kulturunterschiede zwischen Nationen, indes die Gleichheit der Klasse oft auch eine Kulturgemeinschaft zwischen den Angehörigen der gleichen Klasse verschiedener Nationen herstellt. Der deutsche und der dänische Bauer in Schleswig stehen jedenfalls in engerer Kulturgemeinschaft, als der deutsche Bauer und der deutsche Journalist und Künstler in Berlin W., während diese in engerer Kulturgemeinschaft mit den Journalisten und Künstlern von Paris stehen."

7 Translation from German: „Ganz anders sind unsere Aussichten, wenn Deutschösterreich zu einem Gliedstaat der großen Deutschen Republik wird. Die große Deutsche Republik wird kein lockerer Staatenbund sein, sondern ein fest gefügter Bundesstaat mit starker einheitlicher Regierung und gemeinsamen gesetzgebenden Parlament; [...] Und dass diese Staatsgewalt vom Wollen zum Sozialismus beherrscht sein wird, dafür bürgen uns die Zahl, die geistige Reife und die revolutionäre Entschlossenheit der deutschen Arbeiter. Der Anschluß an Deutschland bahnt uns also den Weg zum Sozialismus. Es ist die erste Voraussetzung zur Verwirklichung des Sozialismus. Darum muß der Kampf um den Sozialismus hierzulande zunächst geführt werden als ein Kampf um den Anschluß an Deutschland."

8 Translation from German: „Durch gemeinsames geschichtliches Schicksal sind Gruppen von Menschen zu gemeinsamer Arbeit und gemeinsamen Erleben zusammengeschmiedet worden, die dadurch einen gemeinsamen physischen und psychischen Charakter und schließlich auch einen gemeinsamen Kulturbesitz erworben haben."

74 A Marxist Theory of Nationalism

9 Translation from German: „So ist z.B. der gemeinsame Nationalcharakter zwischen einem Berliner und einem Münchner [...] [nicht] vorhanden. Und ein naiver Ostpreuße sieht z. B. die Schuhplatter-Tänze der Schlierseer wie die Gebräuche eines fremden wilden Volkes an."

10 Translation from German: „die aus historischer Schicksalsgemeinschaft entstandene Willensgemeinschaft zur Erhaltung einer in der Regel sprachlich oder staatlich bestimmten Interessen- und Kulturgemeinschaft."

11 Translation from German: „Verbundenheit durch gleiches geschichtliches Erleben, gleiches daraus enstandenes Wesen in körperlicher und geistiger Art und gleiche Interessensgemeinschaft."

12 Translation from German: „ein furchtbares Dokument".

13 Translation from German: „Der Friedensvertrag raubte unserer Republik Gebiete, die mehr als drei Millionen Deutsche bewohnen; ein Drittel des deutschösterreichischen Volkes fiel unter Fremdherrschaft. [...] Der Tag, an dem der Vertrag von St.-Germain ratifiziert werden mußte, war der Tag des Endes der proletarischen Vorherrschaft in Deutschösterreich."

14 Translation from German: „Die Sozialdemokratie betrachtet den *Anschluß Deutschösterreichs an das Deutsche Reich* als notwendigen Abschluß der nationalen Resolutionen von 1918. Sie erstrebt mit friedlichen Mitteln den Anschluß an die Deutsche Republik."

15 Translation from German: „Wir forderten seit 1899 die Umbildung Österreichs zu einem Bundesstaat freier Nationen. Im Verlaufe des Krieges war es klar geworden, daß sich Tschechen, Polen, Südslawen mit dieser Lösung ihres nationalen Problems nicht mehr begnügen werden, wenn die Revolution ausbricht; daß sie in der Revolution um ihre volle nationale Unabhängigkeit kämpfen werden. [...] 1917 aber war es schon klar: Kommt die Revolution, dann wird die Umbildung der Monarchie zu einem Bundesstaat autonomer Nationen zur Parole der Konterrevolution werden. [...] Unsere Erwägungen führten zu dem Schluß: Kommt die Revolution, so dürfen wir nicht Arm in Arm mit den konterrevolutionären Mächten, mit der Dynastie, mit der deutschösterreichischen Bourgeoisie, mit der magyarischen Gentry die Existenz Österreichs gegen die revolutionären Nationen verteidigen. Wir müssen das uneingeschränkte Selbstbestimmungsrecht der slawischen Nationen anerkennen. Und müssen aus dieser Anerkennung unseren Schluß ziehen: Erkennen wir das Selbstbestimmungsrecht der slawischen Nationen an, so müssen wir dasselbe Selbstbestimmungsrecht für das deutschösterreichische Volk fordern. Verwirklichen die slawischen Nationen ihre Einheit und Freiheit in neuen Nationalstaaten, so müssen wir die Einheit und Freiheit des deutschen Volkes zu verwirklichen versuchen durch den Anschluß Deutschösterreichs an Deutschland. Sprengt die nationale Revolution der slawischen Nationen das Reich, so müssen wir die revolutionäre Krise ausnützen für die Sache der sozialen Revolution; müssen wir auch auf unserem Boden die Dynastie stürzen, die demokratische Republik aufrichten, auf dem Boden der demokratischen Republik den Kampf um den Sozialismus beginnen."

16 Translation from German: „*intransigenter Internationalismus*".

Chapter Four | Theories of the Nation and Nationalism **75**

17 Translation from German: „Deutschösterreich ist kein organisch gewachsenes Gebilde. Es ist nichts als der Rest, der von dem alten Reich übriggeblieben ist, als die anderen Nationen von ihm abfielen. Es blieb zurück als ein loses Bündel auseinander strebender Länder, deren politisches Zusammengehörigkeitsgefühl und deren ökonomische Existenzgrundlagen durch den Zerfall des alten Reiches und des alten Wirtschaftsgebietes zerstört worden waren. Die Deutschösterreicher waren im alten Reich das politisch herrschende und das wirtschaftlich führende Volk gewesen. [...] Die Auflösung des alten Reiches mußte daher die deutschösterreichische Industrie schwer erschüttern und die Ernährung des deutschösterreichischen Industrievolkes empfindlich erschweren. Daß dieser Rest der alten Monarchie, durch eine gewaltsame Operation aus ihrem Wirtschaftskörper herausgerissen, selbständig ein erträgliches Leben zu führen imstande sein werde, hat in der Zeit der Revolution niemand geglaubt."

18 Translation from German: „Wir hatten die spontane Demonstration an dem Tage erlebt, wo die Schattendorfer Taten in Wien bekanntgeworden waren. Es war also klar, daß eine ungeheure Aufregung kommen werde, und es war naheliegend, den Gedanken zu haben: Da kann eine ungeheure Aufregung entstehen, warten wir nicht, ob eine spontane Demonstration entstehen wird, veranstalten wir lieber selber eine Demonstration unter allen möglichen Sicherungen, daß die Ordnung nicht gestört wird. [...] wir haben [...] es damals für klüger gehalten, es nicht zu tun, sondern uns zu bemühen, unsere Genossen in den Betrieben zu beruhigen, wie es auch geschehen ist."

19 Translation from German: „Die Regierung hat den Schutzbund aufgelöst. [...] Die Reaktion will die Arbeiterklasse treffen. Sie kann Organisationen auflösen – nicht den Geist, der diese Organisation beseelt. Der Kampfgeist lebt!"

20 Translation from German: „Die österreichische Sozialdemokratie ist zermürbt worden. Zermürbt durch die eigene Unentschlossenheit und durch die Entschlossenheit des Gegners. [...] Die Arbeitermassen [...] konnten es nicht verstehen, dass man [...] sie auf die Revolution vorbereitete und gleichzeitig beschwichtigte."

21 Translation from German: „alles in ihrer Macht stehende zu unternehmen, um sie zu bremsen und abzubrechen".

22 Translation from German: „[...] Widerspruch von Wort und Tat, der dem Austromarxismus innewohnte".

23 Translation from German: „Bekenntnis führender Männer und Frauen Deutschösterreichs zum Anschlussgedanken".

24 Translation from German: „Ich müßte meine ganze Vergangenheit als theoretischer Vorkämpfer des Selbstbestimmungsrechtes der Nationen wie als deutsch-österreichischer Staatsmann verleugnen, wenn ich die große geschichtliche Tat des Wiederzusammenschlusses der deutschen Nation nicht freudigen Herzens begrüße. [...] Als Sozialdemokrat und somit als Verfechter des Selbstbestimmungsrechtes der Nationen, als erster Kanzler der Republik

76 A Marxist Theory of Nationalism

Deutschösterreich und als gewesener Präsident ihrer Friedensdelegation zu St.-Germain werde ich mit Ja stimmen."

25 Translation from German: „verstümmelte Nation".

26 Translation from German: „kein entwicklungsfähiges Gebilde".

27 Translation from German: „ohnmächtige, armselige Staat".

28 Translation from German: „Nationalbewußtsein und Nationalgefühl stärker als Klassenbewußtsein und Klassengegnerschaft".

29 Translation from German: „Die sozialdemokratische Politik hat die proletarische Revolution verhindert, hat die Bourgeoisie gerettet und in der Arbeiterschaft verderbliche reformistische Illusionen großgezüchtet. Trotzdem wäre es falsch, sämtliche Führer der Sozialdemokratie als Verräter zu bezeichnen [...] Die österreichische Sozialdemokratie hat eine schwere Niederlage der Arbeiterklasse verschuldet, aber sie hat gleichzeitig in den Massen den Gedanken, oder wenn Sie wollen, das Gefühl des Sozialismus wachgehalten. [...] Otto Bauer ist kein Verräter. Er hat in entscheidender Situation versagt, das ist wahr, aber verraten hat er uns nicht."

30 Translation from German: „Bald da, bald dort ermordeten sie [die Heimwehren] einen Arbeiter. Nach jedem solchen Mord erklärte die *Arbeiter-Zeitung:* wenn noch einmal so etwas vorkommt, dann ... Was ‚dann' geschehen sollte, zeigte sich am 15. Juli 1927. Als an diesem Tage die Wiener Arbeiter, erbittert über die Freisprechung einiger faschistischer Arbeitermörder, den Justizpalast in Brand steckten, glaubten die Sozialdemokraten nichts besseres tun zu können, als den Christlichsozialen die Bildung einer Koalition vorzuschlagen. [...] Sie tut auch jetzt nichts, nachdem Dollfuß, durch die Vorgänge in Deutschland ebenso ermuntert wie erschreckt, daran gegangen ist, der österreichischen Bourgeoisie die Vorteile zu verschaffen, die ihr ein faschistisches Regiment zu bieten hat [...] Der Austromarxismus steht dem Faschismus genauso ratlos gegenüber, wie die Theoretiker und Praktiker des Reformismus dem Krieg gegenüberstehen."

31 Translation from German: „Weltexplosion des Nationalismus".

32 Translation from German: „daß man die Massen gegenseitig zur Abschlachtung zwingt".

33 Translation from German: „Menschenkultur".

34 Translation from German: „Wir glauben vielmehr, daß alle Völker ohne Unterschied der Rasse, der Sprache und des Glaubens in völligem Frieden und in Freundschaft miteinander leben und in der Erfüllung ihrer Kulturaufgaben wetteifern. Wir geben uns natürlich nicht der Täuschung hin, dieses Ideal könne verwirklicht werden, solange der Kapitalismus noch besteht [...] solange der Kapitalismus herrscht, sind Kriege unvermeidlich."

35 Translation from German: „Es wird kein Krieg mehr stattfinden, sobald die Massen erklären: Wir wollen keinen Völkermord!"

36 "However, capitalism does not create that intellectual spirit in the air or in the theoretical void of abstraction, but in a definite territory, a definite social environment, a definite language, within the framework of certain traditions, in a word, within definite national

forms. Consequently, by that very culture it sets apart a certain territory and a certain population as a cultural national entity in which it creates a special, closer cohesion and connection of intellectual interests" (Luxemburg 1976, 253).

37 Translation from German: „Merkels Flüchtlingspolitik zerstört den Sozialstaat. Die #AfD wird dafür sorgen, dass das ein Ende hat!"

38 So for example, the only feasible answer to the crisis of Europe is not the attempt to strengthen the nation state and destroy the EU, but to create the Socialist United States of Europe.

Chapter Five
Contemporary Marxist Theories of Nationalism

5.1 Anti-Colonial Nationalism and Internationalism

5.2 Eric J. Hobsbawm's Approach: Characteristics of Nationalism

5.3 Theorising the Communication of the Nation

5.4 Conclusion

Building on the engagement with classical theories of nationalism in previous chapters, this chapter discusses contemporary Marxist approaches to the study of nationalism. It engages with the Marxian concepts and approaches of Étienne Balibar, Partha Chatterjee, Vivek Chibber, Erich Fromm, Eric J. Hobsbawm, Klaus Holzkamp, Ute Holzkamp-Osterkamp, C.L.R. James, Wilhelm Reich, David Roediger, Marisol Sandoval, and Raymond Williams.

Critical theories of nationalism have to deal with questions of whether nationalism can have progressive political features and how it relates to internationalism and anti-colonialism (Section 5.1). They also have to identify general features of nationalism for identifying strategies of critique (Section 5.2). Section 5.2 engages in more detail with Eric J. Hobsbawm's approach on the study of nationalism. This chapter gives specific attention to the way the nation and nationalism are communicated in capitalism. It argues for a communicative, critical, Marxian theory of nationalism. Section 5.3 focuses on some foundations of a communicative critical theory of nationalism.

5.1 Anti-Colonial Nationalism and Internationalism

Raymond Williams on Nationalism and Wales as British Colony

In Europe, movements for regional independence have defined specific regions such as the Basque Country, Catalonia, Scotland, Wales, Northern Ireland, Flanders, Wallonia, Veneto, Lombardy, Corsica, Brittany, Sardinia, and South Tyrol as colonies that should struggle for national autonomy or for national unification with another country. Raymond Williams has in this context given particular attention to the relationship of Wales and England. In the

English language, the word *nationalist* was coined in the eighteenth century and the term *nationalism* in the nineteenth century (Williams 1983a, 213).

For Williams (1983b, 177–199), the nation, race, and nationalism are "divisive ideologies" (196). Nations are frequently formed by conquest, repression, economic domination (181), or war (182). Williams points out an inherent connection of nationalism and capitalism. The paradox of nationalist ideology is that whereas the nationalisation of industries that can benefit the broad population

> can be perceived as "unpatriotic" – "unBritish", "unAmerican" – [...] a transnational strategy, pursued even to a point where a national economy loses heavily within unrestricted competition, is by its structural retention of the most artificial national images perceived as the "patriotic" course.
>
> (192–193)

The ground for hope against nationalism, racism, and xenophobia would neither be some form of left-wing nationalism nor a liberal pluralism that points out that immigrants are also British, but rather the practice of "working and living together, with some real place and common interest to identify with" (196).

It is not just a misjudgement, but also highly inappropriate, that Stuart Hall (1996) argues that many of Williams' works on culture show a "narrow, exclusive nationalism" and are "open to the critique of ethnocentrism" (394) and that Paul Gilroy (1987) accuses Williams of "apparent endorsement of the presuppositions of the new racism" (50). Williams "appears to be constitutively blind to the politics of race and gender, and the dynamics of imperialism" (Higgins 1999, 170). One can certainly say that Williams faces some issues in respect to the question of a left strategy against racism and xenophobia: although there may be common social and political interests of immigrants and national citizens, the problem is that the phenomena of xenophobia without immigrants, racism in a homogenous community, anti-Semitism without Jews, nationalism without foreigners, etc. exist. The problem has to do with the projection of fears into an unknown Other. Common life and work in a community are therefore not always a readily available and possible solution.

The collection of Williams' (2003b) writings on Wales shows that he assumes that an important way of how communal socialism can be imagined and formed is through social struggles, including anti-colonial struggles that do not foreground language or history, but opposition to the ruling class. He argues that Wales has for a long time been an English colony. The 1926 General Strike and the Welsh miners' strike in 1984/85 are, for Williams, important examples and experiences that matter not just for the Welsh working class, but for social struggles in general. Williams (1968) was the primary author of *The May Day Manifesto 1968*. The *Manifesto* argues that a post-colonial new imperialism has emerged that is based on the dependency of developing countries on developed countries, which results in underdevelopment and transnational corporations' exploitation of labour in different parts of the world (Williams 1968, Chapter 19). It also criticises that in the UK and the world, people of colour are suffering from social deprivation (167–168). Given that this important manifesto-like writing contains such a focus, it is absurd to argue that Williams' approach ignores or supports racism and imperialism.

Partha Chatterjee's Critique of Anti-Colonial Nationalism

Partha Chatterjee stresses that anti-colonial nationalism was both imported from the West and created by indigenous elites. There are therefore both Western and indigenous influences on the development of nationalism in India and other former colonies. Chatterjee (1993) argues that Benedict Anderson resists the Western contemporary tendency to see nationalism as being located in the Global South, and having turned there from liberation into corruption, war, and genocide, but sees nationalism purely as a phenomenon of European modernity. He writes that both Anderson and Gellner see Third World nationalism as "profoundly 'modular'" (Chatterjee 1986, 21) and asks: "If nationalisms in the rest of the world have to choose their imagined community from certain 'modular' forms already made available to them by Europe and the Americas, what do they have left to imagine?" (Chatterjee 1993, 5). Based on the example of India, he argues that anti-colonial nationalism combines Western "material" elements (modern economy, statecraft, science, technology, civil society) with non-Western spiritual elements (cultural identity, language, aesthetic forms, family, religion, schooling). The rising political elite would combine and transform both domains for crafting a nationalist project. Anti-colonial nationalism cannot simply imitate "the alien culture, for then the nation would lose its distinctive identity. The search therefore […] [is] for a regeneration of the national culture adapted to the requirements of progress, but retaining at the same time its distinctiveness" (Chatterjee 1986, 2). Anti-colonial nationalism tries to combine "the superior material qualities of Western cultures with the spiritual greatness of the East", which is an ideal that "necessarily implies an elitist programme" (Chatterjee 1986, 51).

Vivek Chibber's Critique of Chatterjee's Approach

Ideas and ideology are not immaterial, but are, just like the economy and politics, socially produced. Materialism in society means that humans co-produce the social world (Fuchs 2017a; Williams 1977). So, Chatterjee dualistically separates the material world from the supposedly immaterial world. Vivek Chibber (2013, Chapter 10) elaborates a critique of Chatterjee that builds on the insight that dualism is a false logic. He argues that there have been material needs for anti-colonial nationalism to establish modernisation projects in post-colonial societies. These forces include global capitalism's threat of military conflict, competition on the world market, and the subaltern classes' demand to improve their living conditions for being willing to participate in nationalist projects. Chibber argues that these material pressures have required post-colonial societies to embrace "industrialization, scientific research, modern administrative techniques, and similar practices" (262). The reason why anti-colonial nationalists "took to modernization was not that they had passively accepted the Enlightenment worldview, but because it was a rational response to their circumstances" (269). Chatterjee, according to Chibber, treats Reason – "rational argument, objectivity, evidence" – as "Western and hence as colonial", and thereby "remains trapped within colonial discourse" as well as "Orientalist" ideology (250). Chibber stresses that it is Orientalist to argue that only the West, and not the Global South, is capable of Reason (262).

The key question that arises from both Chatterjee's and Chibber's account is how to understand reason, modernity, and the Enlightenment. If we thereby (a) mean capitalist modernisation that entails industrialisation, rationalisation, automation, informatisation, bureaucratisation, productivity growth, and scientific progress for the sake of capital accumulation, then it is clear that Chatterjee points towards an important circumstance, namely that under colonialism, capitalist reason used the colonies as source of resources and as markets, whereas the logic of anti-colonial capitalist modernisation backfired and did not abolish class rule, but just created new forms of exploitation, a new national bourgeoisie whose rule is embedded into an international division of labour, where it interacts with the international bourgeoisie so that the post-colonial subalterns are confronted with both national and international capitalist rule. There is a specific negative dialectic of capitalist enlightenment of former colonies that Chatterjee criticises.

If we, however, by modernisation, reason, and the Enlightenment in general understand (b) attempts to establish progressive economic, political, and cultural development, then this also entails the possibility of socialist reason and Enlightenment and a dialectical, alternative modernity, in which technology serves humans and is not a means of surplus-value production. In such a definition, socialist and capitalist modernity are both projects aiming at progress, but they offer two different rationalities of progress – socialism and capitalism. Socialist modernity entails the development of industry, the information and technology sector, and science for the sake of socialist development, which includes collective ownership (worker self-management of certain economic realms, state control of others), the redistribution of wealth, the limitation of the working day to the necessary minimum, and the importance of non-profit organisations in the economy, politics, and culture.

Class struggles between movements, parties, and tendencies that want to advance capitalism on the one side and socialism on the other side shape modernity. There are capitalist and socialist potentials and elements within modern societies and there is a constant struggle about the relationship of both. Modernity contains two contradictory modernities. Nationalism is a project underpinning the class structuration of modernity; it is part and parcel of capitalist modernity.

If modernisation is understood in such a broad sense, then the argument that modernity is colonial and Eurocentric and should be overcome implies establishing an anti-modern or premodern society that is based on hard labour and eschews modern technologies. But Chatterjee opposes Gandhi's anti-industrialism, which is precisely anti-modern in the general understanding of the term because it opposes industrialisation and the use of modern technology.

Chibber (2013, 281–282) is aware that Chatterjee (1986) says that what he opposes is capitalist reason, not reason as such. But Chibber (2013) thinks this argument comes at the very end and therefore too late in Chatterjee's (1986) book. Chibber (2017a) asks:

> [H]ow do postcolonial theorists plan to get out of the current crises – not only economic and politics, but also environmental – if they're saying that science, objectivity, evidence, and concerns with development are to be ditched? Chatterjee has no way out of this.
>
> (24–25)

Let us have a look at some of the passages about Reason in Chatterjee's works:

> Nowhere in the world has nationalism qua nationalism challenged the legitimacy of the marriage between Reason and capital. Nationalist thought [...] does not possess the ideological means to make this challenge. [...] Marx [...] pleaded that Reason be rescued from the clutches of capital. [...] The critique of nationalist discourse must find for itself the ideological

84 A Marxist Theory of Nationalism

> means to connect the popular strength of those struggles with consciousness of a new universality, to subvert the ideological sway of the nation and to challenge the presumed sovereignty of a science which puts itself at the service of capital, to replace, in other words, the old problematic and thematic with new ones.
>
> (Chatterjee 1986, 170)

Also, in another passage, there are indications that Chatterjee argues for an alternative form of universality and Enlightenment: "For Enlightenment itself, to assert its sovereignty as the universal ideal, needs its Other; if it could ever actualize itself in the real world as the truly universal, it would in fact destroy itself" (Chatterjee 1986, 17). Chatterjee (1986) speaks of the

> bourgeois-rationalist conception of knowledge, established in the post-Enlightenment period of European intellectual history, as the moral and epistemic foundation for a supposedly universal framework of thought which perpetuates, in a real and not merely a metaphorical sense, a colonial domination.
>
> (11)

But if there is "bourgeois-rationalist knowledge", then there must also be "socialist-rational knowledge" that contradicts the logic of class and capital. So, there are indications that Chatterjee already early in his book is conceptually open for an alternative form of reason and rationality. But one can certainly criticise that he does not define this alternative form in more detail.

Chatterjee's Response and Chibber's Rejoinder

In a debate with Chibber, Chatterjee (2017, 42–43) argues that Chibber's assumption that there are universal basic needs such as physical well-being is an expression of the contractarian school of liberal political thought. One needs to add that physical well-being is just an example essential human need that Chibber (2013, 197–202) discusses, and that there are also other essential human needs, such as mental well-being and communication (Fuchs 2016b).

One could interpose in support of Chibber that Chatterjee forgets that Marx also assumes that there are basic human needs, but what varies are the concrete historical and social forms of needs and the way production can satisfy these needs depending on the qualities of the mode of production (such as the level of productivity, the use of technology, class relations, natural conditions, etc.). When Marx speaks of the human as species-being, he stresses "the need to maintain physical existence" (Marx 1844b, 276). Only in a communist society, humans produce "in freedom" from "physical need" (Marx 1844b, 276). So, Marx here indicates that depending on the societal context, there are differences in how well human needs can be satisfied. And Marx ascertains that there are different social and natural conditions of need satisfaction within global capitalism so that "the same quantity of labour satisfies a different mass of requirements in different countries, and consequently under otherwise analogous circumstances, the quantity of necessary labour-time is different" (Marx 1867, 650). As a consequence, less productive countries, regions, and corporations have disadvantages on the world market, which is one of the factors advancing uneven development. The universal similarity of class relations is that alienated labour as "*forced labour*" is "not the satisfaction of a need; it is merely a *means* to satisfy needs external to it" (Marx 1844b, 274).

Humans in the West and in the Global South all have to satisfy basic needs that are not static, but develop together with production. The existence of such needs is a human universal. In global capitalism, the existence of class relations is a capitalist universal that takes on different forms in different contexts, in which it results in the exploitation of human labour. Need satisfaction operates under different conditions in various parts of the world that are related through the human universality of need satisfaction and the capitalist universals of exploitation and alienation. Given that capitalism and domination deny and alienate need satisfaction, it is also a universal human condition that there is a potential for resistance to class relations and domination. Human needs are at the same time universal and diverse, general and contextualised, anthropological and historical. Chibber (2017b), in his response to Chatterjee, argues that many anthropologists stress what "Subaltern Studies scholars typically deny – that social actors are motivated by a healthy regard for their well-being, and that this motivational structure appears to be operative across cultures" (66).

Chatterjee (2017), in his response to Chibber, stresses that there are "historical specificities of the political, economic, and cultural institutions and practices" (46). He argues that Subaltern Studies "does not rule out the rise of new universalist principles, but these [...] must be forged anew" and that "the working classes of Europe and North America and their ideologues can no longer act as the designated avant-garde in the struggles of subaltern classes in other parts of the world" (47). It here becomes clear that whereas Chibber stresses the need for global solidarity and cooperation of the subaltern classes, Chatterjee also believes in the feasibility of a universalist political project, but puts more stress on the need for its internal diversity. There is certainly a danger that such a position ends up in too much diversity without unity, which is what Chibber warns against.

For an Alternative, Socialist Modernity

In the last instance, both Chatterjee and Chibber seem to oppose capitalist modernity and argue for an alternative, socialist modernity. We need to add and stress that socialist modernity does not need nationalist ideology, but rather can only work as a project of the working class and other subalterns against capital, which entails the insight that all working people are brothers and sisters who should be united in the struggle for a just world.

Chatterjee shows that anti-colonial nationalism shares with other forms of nationalism the attempt to ideologically and politically unify different classes by constructing a collective identity. In the case of anti-colonial nationalism, the nation is defined against the colonial or imperialist force. But just like in other nationalisms, the problem is that such a construct leaves out the existence of power and class differentials. As a consequence, newly established post-colonial nation-states based on such nationalist projects tend to erect a new ruling class that sustains relations of exploitation. Just like the foreign ruling class imposed imperial rule on the colony's subordinated classes, the new ruling class imposes a new rule. Whereas in the imperial rule of a colony, hegemony — large-scale non-resistance of everyday people in the colony — tends to be achieved by the threat of direct violence against everyday people and ideological consent by a local elite, anti-colonial nationalism achieves consent from below by the ideology of political and/or cultural unity of different classes opposed to the colonisers/imperialists.

Gayatri Spivak on Nationalism

Gayatri Spivak (2009) argues that the nation does not exist before nationalism and that reproductive heteronormativity is the key aspect of nationalism. At the same time, she says that nations as "collectivities bound by birth, that allowed in strangers gingerly, have been in existence long before nationalism came around" (79). "[M]etonymized as nothing but the birth-canal, woman is the most primitive instrument of nationalism" (80). She sees a connection between "[l]anguage, mother, daughter, nation, marriage" (87). Reproductive heteronormativity is "the broadest and oldest global institution" (Spivak 2005, 481). Spivak (2009) argues for de-transcendentalising the nation by a critical regionalism and the comparative study of literature as alternatives to nationalism.

Spivak and Julia Kristeva

Spivak (1981) argues that the Bulgarian-French philosopher Julia Kristeva's (1977) book *About Chinese Women* attempts to speak for Chinese women and therefore ends up advancing an Orientalist account that is self-centred on Western women and only asks "[W]ho am I?" (Spivak 1981, 179), instead of "[W]ho is the other woman? How am I naming her? How does she name me? Is this part of the problematic I discuss?" (179). Spivak concludes that Kristeva's account is symptomatic for an "inbuilt colonialism in First World feminism toward the Third" (184). The "First World feminist must learn to stop feeling privileged *as a woman*" (157). Western feminists would have to stop speaking for subaltern women, but "learn to learn from them, to speak to them" (156). Spivak's point, which she also stresses in the essay *Can the Subaltern Speak?* (Spivak 1988), is that in trying to speak for and give voice to the subaltern, Western intellectuals silence them.

By arguing that Western and subaltern experiences and lifeworlds are radically different and incomparable, Spivak fetishises difference and overlooks that people exploited by capital are not just differently exploited, but share the fact of being exploited and the potential for resistance. What matters for her and similar approaches in the end is not your political position, but which nation you were born into. This kind of reasoning ends up in a reverse Orientalism and reverse nationalism that reifies the subaltern in the Global South as resistant and anyone in Western nations as reactionary and guilty of racism by birth. The danger of postmodern identity politics is that it uncritically celebrates, fetishises, and essentialises subaltern cultures as authentic and necessarily resistant. Cultural hybridisation, global communication, and global entertainment have not, as some postmodernists claim, brought about the end of the nation-state and nationalism.

The Debate between Spivak and Chibber

Vivek Chibber (2013) criticises Subaltern Studies for the assumption that postcolonial societies are fundamentally different from Western societies and therefore cannot "be assimilated into the same general framework" (17). He argues that Subaltern Studies "resurrects the worst instances of Orientalist mythology" (288) and "*relentlessly promotes Eurocentrism*" (291) by assuming that "*Eastern agents operate*

88 A Marxist Theory of Nationalism

with an entirely different political psychology than do Western agents" (288), assigning "*science, rationality, objectivity, and similar attributes to the West, instead of regarding them as common to both cultures*" (290), the "*celebration of the local, the particular*" that "*ends up justifying an exoticization of the East*" (289). Chibber argues that Marxism is not a Eurocentric theory, but a cross-cultural framework analysing dynamics "common to East as well as West" (285). He speaks of capitalism's two universalisms that have emerged in the West and the Global South:

> the universal logic of capital [...] and social agents' universal interest in their well-being, which impels them to resist capital's expansionary drive. These forces impinge on both East and West, even if they do so with different intensities and in different registers.

(291)

So, we can say that there is a unity in diversity of capitalisms. There are general structures of capitalism that Marx described, including the commodity form, labour-power, money, capital, value, exchange-value, surplus-value, exploitation, profit, etc. that take on particular forms in different contexts. The question that arises is how to explain the relation of nationalism in the West and the Global South, nationalism's unity in diversity. For doing so, we need to identify general characteristics of nationalism.

Anti-Colonial Nationalism's Faults

National liberation movements make a political mistake when they do not fight for liberation from the rule of the international and national bourgeoisie, but for a new nation in the name of the unity of all national classes, including the bourgeoisie and other classes. This form of nationalism overlooks that in imperialism, not one nation exploits another nation, but an international capitalist class supported by state and military power and often backed by a national capitalist class exploits the dominated classes in the colonised region (and often in the capitalist centres as well). The subordinated classes in the colonised and the ruling country have a joint class enemy, namely international capital. If the exploited class in one region or country supports the exploitation of workers or a group of workers (e.g. migrant workers, black workers, etc.) in the same or another country, then an alliance is temporarily not possible and the struggle must certainly then also be directed against the ideologies that keep workers from seeing their own interests and make them support the bourgeoisie's interest and love the exploitation of others and/or their own.

A nationalist cross-class alliance fighting against the imperialist force risks new class and political divisions in the newly established nation. This criticism does not imply that cultural domination, i.e. the oppression of a group's language, rights, and customs, should be accepted or is unimportant. But one can doubt that fighting for the establishment of new nations based on nationalist ideology is the right answer. It makes a difference to struggle for cultural, political, and economic rights and relative autonomy or to struggle in the name of nationalism. The problem is that nationalism is not, as Horace Davis (1978) claims, "morally neutral" (31).[1] It constructs a friend/enemy distinction along the lines of who belongs to the nation and who doesn't, which creates a militaristic potential and thereby a potential for annihilation and genocide in the name of the nation. In order to be progressive, liberation struggles need to be struggles for socialism and against class society and for a society that guarantees welfare and political participation for all as well as the protection of minorities' interests.

Nigeria and Rwanda

On the territory of today's Nigeria, Europeans established slave trade in the sixteenth century. In the nineteenth century, Britain gained economic, political, and cultural control of the region. The British Empire obtained control of Lagos in 1861 and expanded its territorial control of the region via the Oil Rivers Protectorate and the Royal Niger Company. In 1901, Nigeria formally became part of the British Empire as a protectorate. At the time of the First World War, the Northern and Southern Nigeria Protectorate were united as one administrative unit in 1914. Nigeria gained independence from the British Empire in 1960. The post-colonial phase featured a civil war (1967–1970) that had to do with different ideas about the Nigerian nation, the relationship to Cameroon, and independence of certain parts, followed by military regimes (1970–1999) and a fragile democracy (since 1999). Conflicts in Nigeria feature questions of control of oil-rich regions, religion (Islam, Christianity), and foreign influence.

Today's Rwanda became a German colony in 1884. In 1916, it became, together with Burundi, the Belgian colony Ruanda-Urundi. The German and Belgian colonisers advanced the idea of a separation between the two groups of the Hutu and the Tutsi. They favoured rule in collaboration with members of the Tutsi group. The Belgian rulers in 1935 introduced identity cards that defined each individual as either Hutu or Tutsi. Colonisation advanced ethnic tensions and violence between the Hutu and the Tutsi. Hutu members organised the 1959 Rwandan Revolution that resulted in Rwanda's independence from Belgium in 1962. Ethnic conflict between the Hutu and the Tutsi continued to exist, culminating in the Rwandan Civil War (1990–1994) that featured a genocide with an estimated 1,000,000 victims, who were predominantly Tutsis. After the civil war, the Congolese wars followed in the years between 1996 and 2003, resulting in several million casualties.

Nigeria and Rwanda are two good examples of how colonial forces artificially created nations in order to rule and exploit the humans living there. Imperial power not only resulted in exploitation and domination, but also during and after the imperial rule reinforced tensions between groups in the region. Regional violence in the post-colonial phase focused on the question of controlling the nation-state or creating new nations. Imperialism created new nations and advanced ethnic tensions and ethnic conflicts within these nations so that nationalism acted as a destructive ideology on behalf of the colonisers and the colonised.

C.L.R. James on Anti-Imperialism and Socialism

Marxist-humanist thinker C.L.R. James (2012) asks "why in African state after African state, with almost the rapidity with which independence was gained, military dictatorship after military dictatorship has succeeded to power" (116). One aspect is that political independence does not eliminate economic dependence on global capitalism and the world market. In addition, new leaders often followed old patterns so that "the newly independent African state was little more than the old imperialist state only now administered and controlled by black nationalists" (James 2012, 117). The new government was often formed by "lawyers and middle-class intellectuals" whose "skins were black", but who "had essentially the same attitude to the great masses of the African people that a liberal colonial official would have. Self-government for them meant the substitution of themselves and members of their case for the colonial officials" (James 1971, 112). Once

> you are changing over from an underdeveloped colonial country, and aim at being a modern country, straight away you have this enormous concentration of power in the hands of the state. [...] The only way it does not take place and doesn't overwhelm you is if the people who are taking charge of the government are aware that this is the danger and take steps to moderate it and keep it in order.

> (James 2009, 138)

James (1973) warns that capitalism can easily corrupt revolutionaries because it is not easily abolished:

Every single African who opposed and wanted to establish political independence somehow talked about the capitalist system which was the source of capitalistic exploitation in the colonies. But when he comes into power, what about this capitalist system well, he can't touch it. So he does something which is very strange. He paints it up as much as he can in red and he calls it African Socialism.

C.L.R. James' Socialist Humanism and Socialist Internationalism

James argues for socialist humanism and socialist internationalism based on political equality, social justice, and human dignity as the guiding forces of social struggles and the establishment of new orders (James 2012, 132). He says that Marxism must struggle for internationalism:

> Mankind must leave behind the outmoded bourgeois class and all the obstacles which the national state now places in the way of an international socialist order. THAT IS MARXISM. It says: no longer the national political state but an international social order.
>
> (James 2013a, 92)

As a consequence, he argues for the creation of the Socialist United States of Europe and the Socialist United States of Africa (James 1943, 2013a).

Nationalism is not inherent in human, social, and societal being. The word appeared in the English language in the eighteenth century and became common in the nineteenth century (Williams 1983a, 213–214). The rise of nationalism was profoundly associated with the establishment of modern nation-states and capitalism. The existence of the nation as national economy, the nation-state, and cultural institutions governed by the nation-state (schools, universities, churches, museums, arts, media, science, hospitals, families, sports, etc.) are a fact of modernity. A national economy, the nation-state, and national cultural institutions are organised as bounded spaces that have an inside and an outside and borders that are defined by membership rules. So, the nation certainly has a very real existence. But nationalism is not the same as the nation. Membership can be fluid and more or less rigid.

That nationalism is an "ism" indicates that it is an ideology and political movement. It is an ideological practice and movement that argues that society, the state, the economy, and culture are the exclusive realm of a certain group and that others need to be excluded from it. Nationalism is not morally neutral because no ideology is morally neutral. It is a form of repressive moralism. Nationalism makes demands for control and ownership based on the pride in collective identity as a nation that has been invented and illusionary shared characteristics that are defined biologically, economically, politically, or culturally. Nationalism defines pride in imagined shared characteristics of a large group as ideological justification for political-economic control of a territory and bounded spaces. Nationalism is moral, ideological, and political devotion to the idea of the nation. It includes the willingness to die and kill for the defence of the nation and its human and non-human symbols. Socialist politics in modern society must take place at the level of the nation-state just like it must take place at the local and global level. But politics at the nation-state level is different from politics in the name of nationalism that fights for a society determined by a unity defined by blood or culture and that excludes others living in the same territory from membership of the nation. References to a unity based on blood, traditions, and culture that exclude others always have a certain potential for annihilation and mass murder.

5.2 Eric J. Hobsbawm's Approach: Characteristics of Nationalism

In order to arrive at general characteristics of nationalism, we will have a closer look at Eric J. Hobsbawm's theory and history of nations and nationalism. Hobsbawm developed this approach out of a critique of Tom Nairn's concept of nationalism.

Tom Nairn's Theory of Nationalism

Tom Nairn (1977/2015) sees nationalism as the consequence of capitalism's uneven imperialist development. In respect to the debate between Rosa Luxemburg and Lenin, Nairn opposes Luxemburg's position that there is no right to national self-determination but rather only a right of exploited classes to self-determination: "There had been no room for the ambiguous and yet central phenomenon of nationalism in her heroic world-view. Nothing existed between socialism and barbarism" (65). Nairn supports Lenin's position and applies it to the UK. He argues that the neo-nationalisms of Scotland, Wales, and Northern Ireland are a result of uneven development and "could contribute to socialist revolution", the break-up of Britain and "the principal factor making for a political revolution of some sort" (69).

Nairn distinguishes between progressive and reactionary nationalism and considers the latter as "abusive versions" of nationalism that "tend towards the encouragement of social and psychological atavism, the exploitation of senseless fears and prejudices, and so towards violence" (298). At the same time, he acknowledges that nationalism is ideology and false consciousness (286) and necessarily populist (291). But given this characterisation of nationalism as containing irrational elements, Nairn's theory and his embrace of anti-imperialist nationalism cannot rule out that the latter develops into a new form of capitalism, imperialism, racism, genocide, anti-Semitism, mass extermination, or fascism. Given the necessarily irrational elements of nationalism, there is always a fascist potential.

German, Italian, and Japanese fascism are for Nairn merely reactions to "a relatively recent experience of 'backwardness'" (297). He reduces Nazi-fascism and therefore also the catastrophe of Auschwitz to a necessary consequence of "the general framework of modern developmental history" (300). Auschwitz is then for Nairn a necessary collateral damage of capitalist history that is tolerable in the light of the emergence of "the great counter-force of anti-imperialist struggle" beyond "the wreckage" (309). Nairn simplifies history and reduces Nazi-fascism to Germany's defeat in the First World War and the Treaty of Versailles. He does not take into account that Hitler and Nazi-fascism may not have happened if the German Revolution of 1918/1919 had been successful or the social democrats and communists had not fought each other and had united in the struggle against Nazi-fascism and for turning the Weimar Republic into a socialist republic. Nazi-fascism and Auschwitz were not a necessary, but an avoidable catastrophe that has its immanent potential in capitalism and nationalism.

Nairn advances a metaphysical concept of history, in which nationalism in the last instance, despite catastrophic setbacks, has progressive tendencies that will prevail with necessity. It is nationalism, and not class struggle, that is a progressive force for him. He argues that all nationalism "is spotted without exception" (299), but seems to think that fascism has to be accepted as a necessary evil, an inevitable stage, and collateral damage on the way to socialism:

> It is through nationalism that societies try to propel themselves forward to certain kinds of goal (industrialization, prosperity, equality with other peoples, etc.) *by a certain sort of regression* – by looking inwards, drawing more deeply upon their indigenous resources, resurrecting past folk heroes and myths about themselves and so on.

(298–299)

Nairn's assessment of Hitler and the Nazis lacks complexity. Nazi-fascism was a mass movement that promised salvation to big and small capital, as well as workers, peasants, and soldiers, by "making Germany great again" and portraying democracy, the Jews, finance, and socialists as causes of social problems. Its nationalism tried to unify German capital and German labour by constructing them as an Aryan race that was under threat by "non-Aryans" and communism. Nazi-fascism's rise was favoured by several factors, including the presence of anti-Semitism, authoritarianism, and hierarchic bureaucracy; the strong limitation of free speech and strong censorship of the press during the nineteenth century; the lack of a democratic revolution and the failure of the democratic revolution in 1848/49 and of the socialist revolution in 1918/19; and the repression against socialists in the form of the Anti-Socialist Laws under Bismarck. Last but not least, Nazi-fascism and other fascisms were also attempts to defeat the internationalist socialist, communist, and trade union movements in the light of events such as the Russian Revolution.

Eric J. Hobsbawm (1995) argues that fascism found fruitful soil especially in countries where "democracy and liberalism were not dominant, or among classes which did not identify with them, that is to say, chiefly in countries which had not undergone a French revolution or its equivalent" (121). After 1917, right-wing forces mobilised in a militant manner because they saw socialism as a realistic threat in the context of the October Revolution. The Nazis' power and influence was based on the combination of the global capitalist crisis that started in 1929, the defeat of the left in the November Revolution, and its resulting weakness and internal hostilities, including infighting between communists and socialists. The Great Slump transformed fascism

> into a world movement, and, more to the point, a world danger. [...] But as the tide of fascism rose with the Great Slump, it became increasingly clear that in the Age of Catastrophe not only peace, social stability and the economy, but also the political institutions and intellectual values of 19th century liberal bourgeois society, were in retreat or collapse.
>
> (Hobsbawm 1995, 108)

Eric J. Hobsbawm's Critique of Nairn's Theory of Nationalism

Eric J. Hobsbawm (1977) questions Nairn's position. He takes a Luxemburgist position and therefore argues that Marxists cannot be nationalists since nationalism by definition subordinates all other interests to those of its specific "nation". [...] any Marxists who are not, at least in theory, prepared to see the "interests" of their own country or people subordinated to wider interests, had best reconsider their ideological loyalties.

(9)

Marxists "see nations in the modern sense as historical phenomena rather than *a priori* eternal data of human society" (10). Hobsbawm argues for a realist socialist position that sees nation-states sceptically and as facts and puts the socialist interest first. The Leninist policy of Marxists who support the right to national self-determination has historically resulted in Marxist movements becoming "subordinate to, or been absorbed by, or pushed aside by non-Marxist or anti-Marxist nationalism. To this extent, the Luxemburgist case is not entirely unrealistic" (11). Hobsbawm argues against Nairn's support of Scottish and Welsh independence that both would probably reinforce English nationalism and xenophobia (17) and that it is naïve to assume that advancing Marxist nationalism will suddenly transform the Scottish National Party or Plaid Cymru into revolutionary socialist parties (11). Hobsbawm warns against Nairn's assumption that Welsh and Scottish separatism and socialism after separation are inevitable historical developments. History would depend on many factors and therefore be unpredictable. Marxists will "continue to be not merely enemies of 'great-nation chauvinism', but also of 'little-nation chauvinism'" (22). Anderson (2006) speaks of "Nairn's good nationalist tendency to treat his 'Scotland' as an unproblematic, primordial given" (89).

Nairn's Response to Hobsbawm

Nairn argues that Hobsbawm (1992b, 131) mistakes Nazi-Germany for "the apogee of nationalism" (Nairn 1997, 51), whereas in his view it was an imperialist system. Nairn argues that in Hobsbawm's account of nationalism, "anything good about national movements turns out actually to derive from some other source or inspiration (quite often internationalism); everything bad is disdainfully highlighted as typical, suspect or ominous" (51).

Nairn (1977/2015) admits that nationalism has a dark side, but thinks this side must be accepted as necessary to achieve progress in history. So, it should not be a surprise that other historians analyse and highlight these immanent aspects of nationalism. Hobsbawm was 16 years old when Hitler came to power in 1933 and he and his Jewish family had to flee from Berlin to the UK. He experienced the

96 A Marxist Theory of Nationalism

horrors of nationalism. Being a communist Jew, it is likely that he may not have survived if he had not been able to flee. It is no wonder that Hobsbawm has a different, more realist, and less romantic perspective on nationalism than Nairn.

Eric J. Hobsbawm's History of Nationalism

Hobsbawm (1992b) argues that nations are not "as old as history" (3), but emerged from the eighteenth century onwards as modern nation-states:

> Like most serious students, I do not regard the "nation" as a primary nor as an unchanging social entity. It belongs exclusively to a particular, and historically recent, period. It is a social entity only insofar as it relates to a certain kind of modern territorial state, the "nation-state", and it is pointless to discuss nation and nationality except insofar as both relate to it.
>
> (9–10)

Based on Gellner, Hobsbawm defines nationalism as the principle of unifying the political and the national unit (9). Nationalism "comes before nations. Nations do not make states and nationalisms but the other way round" (10). Hobsbawm argues that nations and nationalism have to be studied not just "from above", but also "from below" (10), the nation as seen "by ordinary persons" (11). I suggest that the way of doing this is to study how the nation and nationalism are being communicated from above and from below. As a foundation for such studies, a critical theory of communication is needed.

Table 5.1 shows the number of empires and nation-states with more than 1 million inhabitants in particular years. It becomes evident that nation-building has taken place especially since the nineteenth century, which shows that the nation-state is indeed a predominantly modern phenomenon having to do with imperialism, wars, and rapid changes of modernity, capitalism, and class structure. Hobsbawm (1992b, Chapter 1) argues that the Age of Revolution (1789–1848), including the French Revolution, was quite hostile to the nationalist principle of establishing nation-states based on "ethnicity, common language, religion, territory and common historical memories" (20). During that time, one thought of nations primarily as national economies. Nationalism and the quest for the modern nation-state emerged, according to Hobsbawm, from 1875 onwards with the rise of imperialism (or what Hobsbawm terms the Age of Empire).

Hobsbawm argues that common language, religion, and political history are not sufficient criteria for nationalism and nation-states to emerge. These factors could, however, be mobilised by nationalist movements as proto-nationalist symbols. For making capitalism work, institutions such as the governing elite, citizenship, print language, the modern military, state bureaucracy, the census, the police, the school system, etc. are needed. State institutions require a border that defines whom they serve and whom not. The emergence of the modern state "helped to foster the emergence of nationalism" (Hobsbawm 1992b, 100). "The widespread progress of electoral democracy and the consequent emergence of mass politics therefore dominated the invention of official traditions in the period 1870–1914" (Hobsbawm 1983b, 267–268). In the formation of the nation-state and nationalism, the invention of (a) primary education; (b) public ceremonies; and (c) public monuments played an important role (Hobsbawm 1983b, 271–272).

According to Hobsbawm (1992b), nationalism proliferated from the 1880s onwards and stressed differences of language, culture, and "race". "The basis of 'nationalism' of all kinds was the same: the readiness of people to identify themselves emotionally with 'their' 'nation' and to be politically mobilized as Czechs, Germans, Italians or whatever, a readiness which could be politically exploited" (Hobsbawm 1989, 143). Nations and nationalism were "invented in the later 19th century" (Hobsbawm 1989, 146). Hobsbawm (1992b) argues that racism and anti-Semitism grew along with the influence of race theories and social Darwinism. Race and nation were increasingly used as synonyms (108).

TABLE 5.1 Number of empires and nation-states with more than 1 million inhabitants

Year	Number
1700	24
1800	26
1900	87
1939	56
1989	130

Sources: https://en.wikipedia.org/wiki/List_of_countries_by_population_in_1700, https://en.wikipedia.org/wiki/List_of_countries_by_population_in_1800, https://en.wikipedia.org/wiki/List_of_countries_by_population_in_1900, https://en.wikipedia.org/wiki/List_of_countries_by_population_in_1939, https://en.wikipedia.org/wiki/List_of_countries_by_population_in_1989 (accessed 30 December 2017)

The foreigner came to symbolize the disruption of old ways and the capital-ist system which disrupted them. Thus the virulent political anti-Semitism which we have observed spreading across the western world from the 1880s [...] took aim rather against the bankers, entrepreneurs and others who were identified with the ravages of capitalism among the "little men".

(Hobsbawm 1989, 158)

Rapid economic change and changes of the class structure expressed themselves increasingly in ideological, cultural, and linguistic conflicts. The Long/Great Depres-sion (1873–1896) accelerated changes of the class structure and fears of social decline (Hobsbawm 1992b, 109). Individuals, groups, and classes feeling economic-ally under threat increasingly turned to nationalism, racism, anti-Semitism, chauvin-ism, and patriotism as reactive ideologies:

Until the Great Depression something very like global free trade, while per-haps benefiting Britain rather more than others, had been in the interest of all. Yet from the 1870s on such claims ceased to ring true, and as a global conflict came, once more, to be considered as a serious, if not an impend-ing possibility, the sort of nationalism which saw other nations frankly as menace or victims gained ground.

(Hobsbawm 1989, 159)

Imperialist rivalries for the control of markets and international sources of resources and labour spurred nationalist ideology (Hobsbawm 1992b, 91).

Whatever the nature of the nationalism which came to the fore in the fifty years before 1914, all versions of it appeared to have something in common: a rejection of the new proletarian socialist movements, not only because they were proletarian but also because they were, consciously and militantly *internationalist*, or at the very least non-nationalist. [...] And the canonical view among historians is indeed that in this period mass nation-alism triumphed against rival ideologies, notably class-based socialism, as demonstrated by the outbreak of war in 1914.

(123)

The rise of the radical right was directed against socialism and needed scapegoats (such as Jews and foreigners) for its mobilisation. Socialist and nationalist move-ments competed for the same groups of people (124).

Nationalisms, competing capitalisms, and the conflict between socialism and what now took on the form of various fascisms continued to exist in new formations after the First World War. After 1918, the cinema, the radio, and the press acquired an increasing role in the communication of nationalism (141). Sports became an expression of national conflict and events of national self-assertion (143). Fascists used nationalism for mobilising against Bolshevism and socialism (143). The Great Depression increased not just social misery, but also despair (144).

After 1945, anti-colonial nationalism, decolonisation, and liberation struggles gained momentum. Marxism-Leninism and Maoism had a major influence on such movements. Hobsbawm criticises that there was not much thought put into the question of how the "nations" that fought for freedom were defined. They often copied the European principle of national self-determination (Hobsbawm 1992b, 152–153). So, national liberation movements in the Global South were for Hobsbawm often "modelled on the nationalism of the west" (169). When society is failed by capitalism, then the nation and nationalism appear as all-to-easy fixes that cannot substitute the need for socialism as an alternative to capitalism. Hobsbawm argues that anti-capitalist and anti-imperialist movements have to be internationalist and not fall prey to the nationalist fetishism of "ethnicity, language, culture, historical past, and the rest" (179). Ethnicity is an ideology that "links the members of 'we' because it emphasizes their differences from 'them'. What they actually have in common beyond being 'them' is not so clear. [...] ethnicity is one way of filling the empty containers of nationalism" (Hobsbawm 1992a, 4).

We can see certain parallels here between Eric J. Hobsbawm's arguments, Partha Chatterjee's call for dissociating reason and modernity from capital and nationalism, and Vivek Chibber's insight that a new socialist universalism that transcends capitalism's particularistic universalism is needed.

Hobsbawm (1992b) observes that in Germany, "the traditional 19th century concept of 'the nation'" as the unity of state and nation "survived most strongly in the working class" (190). Given the rise of Trump and working-class support for the far-right in many countries, we today unfortunately have to extend this insight to other countries as well (see Fuchs 2018a) so that it is not so certain that we can hope that the "owl of Minerva which", according to Hegel, "brings wisdom [...] is now circling round nations and nationalism" (Hobsbawm 1992b, 192). We can only actively hope that the owl as political principle will ascertain itself over the tendency that history repeats itself, first as tragedy and then as farce.

Nationalism's Psychology

Why do individuals follow nationalist and xenophobic ideologies? Crises, ideological strategies, and authoritarian demagogy are important influencing factors, but only lead to nationalist consciousness on the part of some and certainly not all individuals. There are also psychological factors at play that need to be considered: "In the public debate on the societal basis for racism, political consequences, societal conditions, etc., one common deficit is frequently pointed out: a failure to include subjective, psychological, and emotional aspects" (Holzkamp 2013, 172).

Erich Fromm (1936, 1942/2001) and Wilhelm Reich (1972) show in their analyses how authoritarian education and authoritarian family structures create a fascist and nationalist predisposition. They show that authoritarianism operates at the level of society, ideology, and the individual.

Wilhelm Reich's Political Psychology of Fascism and Nationalism

Reich (1972) characterises fascist ideology as appeal to *"personal honor, family honor, racial honor, national honor"* (55–56), and argues that fascism operates in the individual, ideology, and society, including structures of

> *capitalism, or rather patriarchy; the institution of compulsive marriage; sexual suppression; personal struggle against one's own sexuality; personal compensatory feeling of honor; etc.* The highest position in the series is assumed by the ideology of "national honor," which is identical with the irrational core of nationalism.
>
> (56)

Fascist ideology is a way of "embedding this economic process [of capitalism] in the *psychic structure of the people who make up the society*" (18). There is no automatic link between economic position and political consciousness. Reich shows how Hitler operated upon "the *emotions* of the individuals in the masses" and avoided "*relevant arguments* as much as possible" (34). Authoritarian fathers, bosses, and political leaders play an important role in the formation of individuals' authoritarian character structure. Authoritarianism culminates in the identification with a political Führer (62–63).

> *The Little Man does not know that he is little, and he is afraid of knowing it.* He covers up his smallness and narrowness with illusions of strength and

greatness, of *others'* strength and greatness. He is proud of his great generals but not proud of himself. He admires the thought which he did *not* have and not the thought he *did* have. He believes in things all the more thoroughly the less he comprehends them, and does not believe in the correctness of those ideas which he comprehends most easily.

(Reich 1975, 13)

Wilhelm Reich here indicates that there is a psychological dimension to authoritarian personalities' admiration of leaders and destruction. Authoritarians are sadomasochistic personalities who do not love themselves, love the powerful, and hate the weak. This also results in the irrational belief in unproven claims that appeal to ideologies such as nationalism, racism, xenophobia, fascism, and anti-Semitism that correspond to the authoritarian personality. Today, there are discussions about post-truth knowledge, knowledge determined not by facts, but by emotional and ideological belief. Reich argues that such knowledge is not just based on ideology and the political-economic context, but also the authoritarian psyche.

Erich Fromm's Critical Theory of the Authoritarian Character

Erich Fromm (1942/2001) characterises the fascist as a sadomasochistic personality, someone who loves to hate and to be violent and to submit to and experience authority: "He admires authority and tends to submit to it, but at the same time he wants to be an authority himself and to have others submit to him" (141). Fromm argues that parents' authoritarian behaviour towards the child suppresses spontaneity, freedom, and independence. A fascist personality is not the automatic result, but authoritarian family structures create a fascist predisposition (Fromm 1936, 86) that makes individuals prone to affirm the authoritarian behaviour of teachers, managers, bosses, and political leaders. The "amount of destructiveness to be found in individuals is proportionate to the amount to which expansiveness of life is curtailed" (Fromm 1942/2001, 157). Fromm analyses how authoritarianism operates not just in the family, but also in fascist ideology and capitalist structures. In Nazi-ideology, "[r]acial and political minorities within Germany and eventually other nations which are described as weak or decaying are the objects of sadism upon which the masses are fed" (194).

Fascist ideology conveys that "the individual is nothing and does not count. The individual should accept this personal insignificance, dissolve himself in a higher power, and then feel proud in participating in the strength and glory of this higher power" (200).

102 A Marxist Theory of Nationalism

Authoritarianism also operates in capitalism's structures, a world "in which everybody and everything has become instrumentalized", where the individual "has become a part of the machine that his hands have built" (219). Authoritarianism is built into capitalism in the form of abstraction, quantification, the division of labour, class, and exploitation (Fromm 1956, Chapter 5). Capitalism is based on alienating structures. Alienation is "a mode of experience in which the person experiences himself as an alien" (117).

Fromm, Reich, and other authors close to the Frankfurt School see a fascist potential in capitalism. They therefore argue for changing society's structures, institutions, and forms of socialisation. This entails the strengthening of supportive instead of repressive authority (Fromm 1936, 111, 135), the advancement of humanistic communitarian socialism (Fromm 1956, 354) that is based on "active and intelligent co-operation" and the expansion of democracy and its "principle of government of the people, by the people, for the people [...] from the formal political to the economic sphere" (Fromm 1942/2001, 235). The implication is that the struggle for socialist humanism is the best way of undermining fascist and authoritarian potentials (see Fromm 1966).

Holzkamp's Political Psychology

Racist and nationalist structures are possibilities to act for the subject (what Klaus Holzkamp calls constellations of meaning), to which they respond positively if they see advantages for their individual life-interests by being racist, nationalist, etc. Racist, nationalist, and fascist structures invite subjects to act in racist, nationalist, and fascist ways. Some subjects may accept this invitation. Life-interests are antagonistic and interpretable in different ways. For some, repressing and discriminating others appears as their own interest; for others, overcoming structures that favour such discrimination appears as their own interest.

Racism, fascism, nationalism, anti-Semitism, and xenophobia operate by

> repressing one's factual dependency on capital and state through the unconscious construction of a regional omnipotence at the expense of others, "strangers" whose persecution "supersedes" conflicts with the ruling classes, whereby this displacement also involves the repression of one's self-harming participation in stabilizing powers one is dependent upon; this repression, in turn has to be kept "unconscious" by mythicizing one's own "powerfulness" and demonizing "others".

(Holzkamp 2013, 202)

Holzkamp and Holzkamp-Osterkamp argue that racists and nationalists are not victims, but together with institutions co-responsible for domination. Childhood would just be the starting point of one's own history, not the end point and not the ultimate cause of individual behaviour:

> Fascist ideology exists in the promise that the individual can rapidly and without risk overcome the helplessness and subjection of its existence; [...] Fascism gave content, meaning, a general orientation and distinction to existence that until then had been meaningless, empty, isolated and insecure. It created a seeming superiority and real power over all those who played no part. It conveyed the feeling of being needed.[2]

> (Holzkamp-Osterkamp 1981, 157, 158)

The approaches of Reich, Fromm, Holzkamp, and Holzkamp-Osterkamp are interdisciplinary Marxist approaches that combine political economy, political psychology, and ideology critique for explaining how subject and object, the individual, and society interact. They explain nationalism as the dynamic interaction of institutions, parties, movements, leaders, ideologies, the family, and the individual's experiences, character structure, and psyche. They combine political economy, ideology critique, and political psychology for explaining how authoritarianism works in society and the individual.

David R. Roediger: Wages of Whiteness

Comparable to Holzkamp and Holzkamp-Osterkamp, David R. Roediger (2007), in his book *Wages of Whiteness*, says that when white workers are racist and nationalist, then this is a form of strategic action that aims at actual material advantages of the individual. Basing his argument on W.E.B. Du Bois, Roediger writes that "the pleasures of whiteness could function as a 'wage' for white workers. That is, status and privileges conferred by race could be used to make up for alienating and exploitative class relationships" (Roediger 2007, 13). Roediger does not really take into account that not all white people are part of the working class because there are also white capitalists. He also does not give so much attention to white anti-racism, non-white racism/nationalism, and the "relationship between the struggle against male supremacism and white supremacism" (Allen 2001).

But Roediger's wages of whiteness approach is nonetheless an important contribution that helps us to think about how nationalism, racism, anti-Semitism, and xenophobia are related to the structure of capitalism. We can generalise his concept: whiteness, masculinity, nationality, racial/ethnic superiority, etc. are, in a Bourdieuian understanding, forms of cultural capital that help workers to distinguish themselves from Others. They help to accumulate reputation, status, and social distinction – cultural capital.

Nationalism and Psychological, Ideological, Economic, Political, and Cultural Surplus

The motivation for individuals and groups advancing nationalist, fascist, patriarchal, sexist, racist, etc. ideologies are often feelings of anxiety and alienation that they want to compensate in order to feel better and channel their aggressions. The pleasure derived from nationalism, degrading others, bad-mouthing them, communicating stereotypes, discrimination, oppression, and exploitation can be seen as a psychological "wage". A psychological "wage" is not money, although it might lead to monetary benefits, but a psychological surplus that allows compensation for frustration, aggression, and anxiety. A lack of pleasure and satisfaction is overcome by a psychological "wage"/surplus obtained from repressing others and obtaining a feeling of superiority by downgrading, bad-mouthing, and scapegoating the perceived enemy. Roediger (2007) says that when he uses, based on W.E.B Du Bois, the term "psychological wage" (12), there are parallels to the works of scholars in critical psychoanalysis such as Wilhelm Reich and Erich Fromm (Roediger 2017, 67–69).

The pleasure derived from degrading others, bad-mouthing them, and communicating stereotypes, discrimination, oppression, and exploitation can be seen as a psychological "wage". If the practice and communication of discrimination leads to reputation and status gains, then we can talk of a cultural "wage"/surplus obtained from nationalism, racism, xenophobia, etc. Political advantages derived from discrimination, oppression, and exploitation are a political "wage"/surplus. Political and ideological capital can be transformed into economic resources when, for example, better economic positions, higher wages, salaries, and income can be obtained by the public, semi-public, or organisational communication and support of racism, nationalism, xenophobia, anti-Semitism, etc. In the capitalist economy, authority, culture, and ideology can result in a monetary surplus-wage. And within the political and cultural system, exploitation and oppression can result in certain individuals' and groups' social advantages at the expense of others, or what could, in a metaphorical sense, be termed an ideological wage (a surplus of pleasure, enjoyment, and status), a political wage (a surplus of political influence), and a cultural wage (a surplus of reputation). One aspect that Bourdieu's and Marx's analyses share is the stress on how the logic of accumulation shapes capitalist society and brings about inequalities. Roediger extends this analysis by arguing that: (a) ideology, culture, and authority result in surplus-wages in the economy; and (b) ideology and politics in modern society are systems of accumulation, in which political and cultural surpluses are accumulated.

W.E.B. Du Bois

The surplus that ideology can produce involves not just surplus pleasure and surplus enjoyment in the suffering of others (the psychological wage), but it can also be economic, political, and cultural in character (the economic, political, and cultural wage). W.E.B. Du Bois (1935) argued in this context:

> It must be remembered that the white group of laborers, while they received a low wage, were compensated in part by a sort of public and psychological wage. They were given public deference and tides of courtesy because they were white. They were admitted freely with all classes of white people to public functions, public parks, and the best schools. The police were drawn from their ranks, and the courts, dependent upon their votes, treated them with such leniency as to encourage lawlessness. Their vote selected public officials, and while this had small effect upon the economic situation, it had great effect upon their personal treatment and the deference shown them. White schoolhouses were the best in the community, and conspicuously placed, and they cost anywhere from twice to ten times as much per capita as the colored schools. The newspapers specialized on news that flattered the poor whites and almost utterly ignored the Negro except in crime and ridicule.
>
> (700–701)

Representatives of critical theory and critical psychology, such as Neumann, Fromm, Reich, Adorno, Holzkamp, and Holzkamp-Osterkamp, agree that the friend/enemy logic is a crucial feature of fascism, nationalism, racism, xenophobia, and anti-Semitism. Subjects thereby create feelings of superiority that allow them to overcome their feelings of inferiority, anxiety, alienation, dissatisfaction, etc. They release anger and aggression. David R. Roediger's approach helps us to put these mechanisms into the language of Marxian political economy so that a combination of political psychology and Marx's political

106 A Marxist Theory of Nationalism

economy can be created. Capitalism creates psychological defects, a loss that ideological strategies allow to overcome in the form of psychological surplus, a surplus pleasure and enjoyment in discrimination, scapegoating, and the communication of hatred against the perceived enemy. Capitalism as the society built on the accumulation of surplus is not just a society, in which money-capital is accumulated, but also one in which power structures necessitate the accumulation of power and ideology results in the accumulation of ideological, cultural, and psychological surplus/"wages".

Eric J. Hobsbawm on Nationalism as Invented Tradition

Eric J. Hobsbawm (1983a) argues that traditions are often invented for serving political and social purposes:

> "Invented tradition" is taken to mean a set of practices, normally governed by overtly or tacitly accepted rules and of a ritual or symbolic nature, which seek to inculcate certain values and norms of behaviour by repetition, which automatically implies continuity with the past.
>
> (1)

All kinds of modern organisations have invented traditions in order to create and reproduce identity among their members and communicate power to broader society. Hobsbawm (1983b) discusses International Workers' Day as an example of an invented socialist tradition that was introduced in the late nineteenth century to symbolise and communicate the internationalism and power of the politically organised working class. Invented traditions are partly entirely new and partly build on older practices. The national tradition is a particular kind of invented tradition that aims at advancing the cohesion of the nation-state and nationalism. For doing so, nationalism not only needs to be produced as ideology, but also reproduced through acts of communication. Nationalism is a social practice that produces and communicates divisive ideology that glorifies invented national traditions and practices, creates collective identity, and defines itself against aliens and enemies.

Hobsbawm (1983b) argues that the creation of modern nation-states was accompanied by the mass production and mass invention of traditions. He says that national traditions are often invented from above, but aim at reaching a broad following in the population by speaking to a felt "need among particular bodies of people" (Hobsbawm 1983b, 307). "'Invented traditions' have significant social and political functions, and would neither come into existence nor establish themselves if they could not acquire them" (Hobsbawm 1983b, 307). It is clear that nationalist traditions are invented from above and require hegemony from below. But it is not self-evident that attempts to impose nationalism on the population via national symbols, events, and practices always succeed. The question is how and to which extent the encoded nationalist meaning is decoded in the same or different manner by the audience.

General Features of Nationalism

We can learn from critical theories of nationalism, especially the ones advanced by Eric J. Hobsbawm and Rosa Luxemburg (1976), that there are some general features of nationalism that take on different forms in various contexts:

- *Political movement and ideology, nation-state and national consciousness*: Nationalism is an ideology and political movement that sustains or aims at building a nation-state that unites defined nation-state members (citizens forming a people). Nationalism has two interconnected dimensions, a territorial-political one (the nation-state) and an ideological one (national consciousness). It is both a political relation and collective consciousness. Its territorial aspect contains an actual or claimed bounded natural environment that is the space for the organisation of the nation-state. Nations do not exist prior to nationalism and nation-states.

- *Nature and culture*: Nationalism claims that there is a foundational unity of the nation that is grounded in nature (blood, kinship, soil, "race") and/or culture/society (common language, traditions, myths, history, wars, heroes ["great men of history"], symbols, memories, moral practices and moral values, habits, tastes, everyday life and ways of life, art, literature, structure of feeling, emotions, worldviews, ideas, wars, philosophy, religion, education, cuisine, sports, law, experiences, identity, means of communication, etc.). Nationalism fabricates and invents fictive ethnicity (Balibar and Wallerstein 1991, 49, 96–100).

- *Domination and hegemony*: Nationalism is imposed and constructed from above by political elites and intellectuals, but it is also lived and hegemonically produced and reproduced from below by everyday people in their everyday practices and beliefs. Nationalism as ideology does not necessarily and not automatically work. There is a continuum of reactions to nationalism, ranging from active participation, on the one end, to opposition and resistance, on the other end.

- *Ideology and class*: Nationalism as ideology legitimates and distracts from the division of society into classes and relations of domination by constructing, inventing, and fabricating a national unity of the people that is said to be stronger than class divisions. Nationalism is a false appearance of unity that is a feature of modern class societies. It is a political fetishism that mystifies the nation as a natural and thing-like entity existing above and transcending actual relations of power and exploitation. Nationalism is not just a phenomenon of the ruling class. Groups and classes threatened by or afraid of social decline are prone to nationalism and to leading, supporting, and joining nationalist movements. Crises and rapid changes of the class structure in light of crises and capitalist transformation increases the chance of the emergence of nationalist movements.
- *Enemies of the nation*: Nationalism always has an outside. Its collective unity is defined against proclaimed outsiders of and enemies to the nation. The other of the nation and nationalism can be inner enemies and outsiders and/or outer enemies and competitors. Nationalism is ideological violence that tries to naturalise class relations and exploitation and tries to "convince" workers and other subalterns that their exploitation and domination is without alternative and natural, and that social problems have other roots than the class structure. Nationalism is one of the ideologies that tries to construct a feeling of unity between the subaltern classes and the capitalist class in order to distract attention from class differences, the class structure, and power inequalities associated with class societies. Nationalist language is war by other means, intellectual warfare that often aims at denigrating the foreign by the nation's positive self-presentation or negative othering.
- *Modernity*: Nationalism is a feature of the modernisation of capitalist and class societies. Modern class society *requires* nationalism as ideology in order to justify the exploitation of workers, the domination of consumers, and the geographic expansion of capitalist production and markets. Nationalism justifies the nation-state that with the help of a monopoly of the means of violence and the law secures the control of a national labour-market, the rule of the political elite, the ideological dominance of capitalism, and the biological and social reproduction of labour-power and citizens, as well as economic and military expansion in order to enable capital export and capital's access to international markets for labour-power, resources, and commodity sales. Nationalism and the nation-state enable the control of a national territory that is a power

container for the accumulation of money-capital (economic power), political decision power (political power), and ideological influence (cultural power).

- *Crisis*: Economic and political crises open up periods of uncertainty, in which the future is open and rapid political change can occur. Right-wing authoritarianism and associated nationalism are likely to grow in situations of capitalist crisis, especially if the left is weak, disjointed, and disorganised.

- *Forms of nationalism*: Nationalism as ideology takes on four forms: biological nationalism, economic nationalism, political nationalism, and cultural nationalism (see Table 5.2).

- *Imperialist and anti-colonial nationalism*: The difference between imperialist and anti-colonial nationalism is that the first considers the enemy as immigrants and other minorities in developed capitalist countries or as other competing nations or political groups, whereas the second sees the imperial force as the enemy. Imperialist nationalism not only justifies a national society's class structure, but also its imperialist, colonial, or neo-colonial expansion and wars that tend to be justified by the ideology of the "national interest" and "national security" which claim that the nation needs to be defended against foreign enemies and by the ideology of "national superiority" which claims that the superior nation must "civilise" and thereby "help" the world's primitive, underdeveloped, and backward regions. The danger of all nationalism is that as a class project, it sustains and ideologically legitimates the power and dominance of a ruling class by eliding class structures. When the rule of one nationalism substitutes another one, it may just mean the shift from one ruling class to another, not the end of class society.

- *Racism and nationalism*: There is a dialectic of racism and nationalism. Racism is an integral super-nationalism that calls for the preservation of the nation's biological and/or cultural origin, character, and purity. Racism is an ideological construction of the out-group as an alien biological (classical racism) or cultural (new racism) group that is not part of the illusionary national collective.

- *Ideological strategies*: Nationalism requires ideological strategies that communicate and practise the feeling of superiority of the nation and its members over the outsiders and enemies. These ideological strategies feature positive self-presentation of the nation and negative other-presentation. Nationalism ideologically promises a better life to members of the nation if the alien group is subdued.

110 A Marxist Theory of Nationalism

TABLE 5.2 Types of nationalism's ideological discourse structures

Type	Definition	Examples of nationalist we-identity	Examples of nationalist other-presentation
Biological nationalism	Nationalism that relates to biology, nature, blood and soil. It proclaims the superiority of and pride in an invented national "race" and the inferiority of other "races".	"Our people are by nature hard-working, decent, peaceful, rational, winners, inventive, creative, superior, etc."	"They look different from us", "They are by nature aggressive, dirty, criminal/ lazy, noisy, smelly, ill-adapted, violent, etc."
Economic nationalism	Nationalism that relates to society's economic system and resources. It proclaims the superiority of and pride in aspects of the national economic system (labour, capital, commodity types and industries, productivity, technologies, entrepreneur-ship, etc.) and the inferiority of competing economies.	"Our economy is particularly competitive", "Our workers are decent and hard-working individuals proud of their skills and industrious-ness", "Our companies and entrepreneurs are particu-larly inventive and creative", "German jobs for German people!", "Buy British"	"They take away our jobs/ benefits/houses/educational or healthcare opportunities, etc.", "They degrade our social system/wages/educa-tion system/pension system/welfare system/ healthcare system/housing system, etc."
Political nationalism	Nationalism that relates to society's political system and power structures. It pro-claims the superiority of and pride in aspects of the national political system and the inferiority of other political systems.	"We are proud of our polit-ical values of freedom and our long political history of freedom and human rights", "We are proud of our heroes and army who have fought for the defence of our nation", "We are proud of our government/head of state/political system/mon-arch", "We have to fight for and maintain our independ-ence and sovereignty from foreign political influences", "I love my country and my flag – I'd die for them"	"They come from an authoritarian country that shapes their political world-view and behaviours", "They do not know/respect Western political values", "They are used to a political system dominated by crime", "They are criminals/ do not follow our laws"
Cultural nationalism	Nationalism that relates to society's cultural system. It proclaims the pride in and superiority of national cul-ture and the inferiority of foreign cultures.	"We can be proud of our traditions, arts, artists, lan-guage, intellectuals, scien-tists, achievements in sports, celebrities, philoso-phy, education system, cuis-ine, etc.", "We have won the World Cup", "We can be proud that our team won and because of its superior-ity defeated the others"	"They have different values and morals", "In their cul-ture it is usual to …", "They speak a different lan-guage/have different habits/ways of behaviour/ mentality/symbols/tradi-tions, etc.", "They destroy our language/culture/tradi-tions/character, etc.", "They come from a culture of

(Continued)

TABLE 5.2 (Cont.)

Type	Definition	Examples of nationalist we-identity	Examples of nationalist other-presentation
			aggression/laziness/criminality, etc.", "They have a different lifestyle", "They do not want to adapt", "They treat women badly", "They have too many children", "They wear strange clothes", "They have bad food tastes/habits", "Their food stinks", "Their religion does not belong here and threatens our culture – it is inherently disrespectful, violent, terrorist, etc."

- *Communicating nationalism*: Nationalism is an ideology that is communicated through events, symbols, practices, and the media system in everyday life and in extraordinary situations (such as national holidays, commemorations, parades, and wars).

- *Inclusive and exclusive nationalism*: The hatred of the enemy and outsiders implies the exploitative or exclusive/exterminatory character of nationalism. One can distinguish between inclusive nationalism that ideologically degrades outsiders in order to justify their exploitation and exclusive nationalism that ideologically scapegoats and debases outsiders in order to justify and organise their exclusion and/or extermination.

- *Militarism and war*: Nation-states are often the historical results of wars and political conflict. Nationalism implies the need for militarism, a police state, and law and order policies. Nationalism has a tendency for war and annihilation.

- *Psychological aspects of nationalism*: Nationalism and (new) racism appeal to authoritarian character structures that have been acquired through socialisation. They are possibilities to act for the subject in order to feel empowered and create meaning in a meaningless, empty, isolated, and insecure world. Individuals may respond positively to nationalism and racism if they see advantages for their individual life-interests. Nationalism is a complex interaction of political economy, ideology, and the human psyche.

- *Surplus-generating nationalism*: The pleasure derived from nationalism, degrading others, bad-mouthing them, communicating stereotypes, discrimination, oppression, and exploitation can be seen as a psychological "wage" and surplus. This is a surplus of pleasure, enjoyment, and status. Psychological surplus allows compensation for frustration, aggression, and anxiety. Nationalism and other ideologies can also create higher economic wages (higher monetary income/surplus wage), a political wage (a surplus of political influence), and a cultural wage (a surplus of reputation).
- *Socialist humanism as the alternative*: Nationalism can only be effectively challenged by socialist humanism, the combination of humanism that stresses human unity in diversity, i.e. what humans have in common despite of and through their differences, and socialism that empowers the human self-management of society.
- *Struggles against capitalism are struggles against the nation and nationalism*: The subaltern have no need for nations and nationalism. They can only become free through solidarity and struggles against capital and capitalism on the local, nation-state, regional, international, and global levels.
- *Nationalism and anti-imperialist struggles*: In anti-imperialist struggles, there is the danger that anti-imperialist forces advance a nationalist position and as a consequence merely replace the foreign ruling class with a new national ruling class.

5.3 Theorising the Communication of the Nation

A Critical Theory of Nationalism Needs to Be Underpinned by a Critical Communication Theory of Nationalism

Hobsbawm (1992b) argues that the national question "is situated at the point of intersection of politics, technology and social transformation" (10). A proper critical understanding of nationalism needs to be based on a combination of political economy, history, ideology critique, political psychology, and communication theory. With the rise of new technologies that stand in the context of societal transformations of politics, economy, ideology, and class structures, the way nationalism is communicated takes on new forms. A critical communication theory of nationalism is not a stand-alone theory of nationalism, as claimed by Karl Deutsch (1966), but needs to interact with and underpin the analysis of other dimensions. Marxian theory is an interdisciplinary theory approach that allows bringing together and combining various fields in the analysis of society, including the role of nationalism in society. A Marxian theory of communication is a foundational aspect of a critical theory of nationalism.

Nationalism needs to be produced and then communicated. The communication of nationalism is based on a dialectic of content/ideology and social form. Nationalism is communicated as textual content that has particular semiotic, linguistic, textual, and discursive structures of ideology. Nationalist texts are communicated in specific social forms. At the level of content, nationalism takes on particular semiotic and linguistic discourse structures. Table 5.2 gives an overview of different types of nationalist discourse as well as typical examples. We can distinguish between biological, economic, political, and cultural nationalism. Nationalist ideology creates a boundary between "us" and "them" by self- and other-presentation strategies. The dimensions shown in Table 5.2 are ideal-types. Concrete nationalist texts can be combinations of various dimensions and elements of nationalist ideology.

Communicating Nationalism: Types and Structures of Nationalist Ideology

Raymond Williams' and Marisol Sandoval's Typologies of the Media

The media make "national symbols part of the life of every individual, and thus [...] break down the divisions between the private and the local spheres in which most citizens normally lived, and the public and national one" (Hobsbawm 1992b, 142). So, media as social forms of communication play an important role in the communication of nationalist content and ideology. Raymond Williams (1980/2005, 53–63, 1981, Chapter 4) argues that the means of communication take on particular social forms. He distinguishes between communication that is based on immediate human physical resources (verbal communication, non-verbal communication) and communications (= communication systems) that are based on non-human materials that are socially produced by human labour (amplificatory communications, durative storage communications, alternative communications; for a discussion of Williams' theory of communication(s), see Fuchs 2017a).

114 A Marxist Theory of Nationalism

Marisol Sandoval (2014, 42–50) presents a typology of forms of media and communication that overcomes the theoretical ungroundedness and arbitrariness of most media typologies. She draws on the political economy distinction between the production, distribution, and consumption of goods. In the case of the media, these goods are information and symbols. She adds the prosumption of information, i.e. contexts where consumers become producers of information, as a further dimension. Comparable to Williams, Sandoval draws distinctions based on whether each of these dimensions is organised only with the help of the human mind and body or as a combination of external technologies and the human mind and body. This results in a distinction of five ways of how media content can be produced, distributed and consumed (see Figure 5.1):

> In the first case no media technology is involved for production, distribution, or consumption. [...] In the second case media technology is used for encoding content, but distribution and consumption is possible without media technology, as is the case with all print media. In the third case media technology is

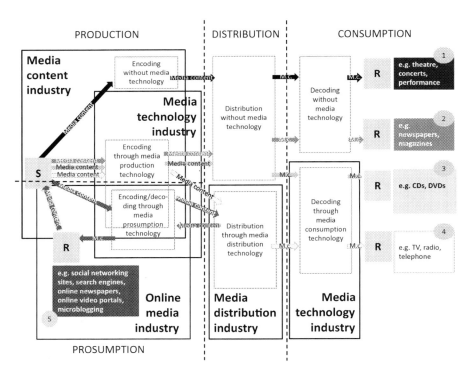

FIGURE 5.1 Five types of communications/mediated communication
Source: Sandoval (2014, 47)

needed for both encoding and decoding of media content; distribution, however, takes place without the involvement of media technology. [...] In the fourth case all stages of the media production, distribution and consumption processes are based on media technology. [...] With computers and the Internet a fifth way of circulating media content has emerged, which allows the use of the same media technologies for both production and consumption of media content. These technologies can therefore be called media prosumption technologies. Based on these technologies a more interactive way of producing media content has emerged in which all users have the technological means to not only consume but also produce media content.

(48)

Social Forms of Communicating Nationalism

We can apply Sandoval's systematic typology of media/communications types to the realm of nationalist communication in order to distinguish different social forms of nationalist communication (see Table 5.3).

There are five basic types of nationalist communication forms that correspond to Sandoval's five types. In addition, I distinguish between entities, social relations/practices, and events that play a role in nationalist communication. Entities are specific systems that enter the communication process. These are humans, social systems, and non-human entities. Such entities enter into human beings' social relations, in which they socially produce and reproduce society. Events are social practices and relations that are routinised, take place at specific times in particular spaces, and are typically periodically repeated. Nationalist communication always involves entities and social practices. It is also a form of ideological communication that quite frequently is practised in the context of particular national events. In nationalism, entities, events, and social practices become symbols of nationalism that are embedded into the communication of nationalism. Michael Billig (1995) argues that nationalism is embedded into everyday life as banal nationalism, symbols, and "ideological habits" (6) that enable the reproduction of nations. Nationalism is not an exception and extraordinary, but built into the banality of everyday life. "Daily, the nation is indicated, or 'flagged', in the lives of its citizenry" (6). Such everyday symbols and habits act as continuous "reminders of nationhood" (93). Most "of the occasions when people become conscious of citizenship as such remain associated with symbols

116 A Marxist Theory of Nationalism

TABLE 5.3 Social forms of nationalism (media types, entities, social relations/practices, events)

	Entities (examples)	Social relations and social practices (examples)	Events (examples)
Primary media (human body and mind, no media technology for production, distribution, reception): theatre, concert, performance, interpersonal communication	National heroes, soldiers, national mottos, head of state, president, prime minister, ministers, government, parliament, ministries, public authorities, national performing artists, national celebrities, entertainers and athletes, national museums, national sports teams, national anthem, national flag, formal national language/print language, typical national dishes, folk dance, folk music	Teaching, learning and speaking the formal national language (print language), participation in national events, basic military service, conscription, fighting as a soldier in a war, the work of parliament, parliamentary committees, ministries, and other public institutions, participation in elections, attending and organising sports events, attending and organising artistic performances, attending and organising national museums/exhibitions, singing the national anthem, speeches on the occasion of national events, government campaigns, flag rituals, cooking and eating typical national dishes, folk dancing, listening to or performing folk music	National events (ceremonies, commemorations, and festivals), national day, wars, bank holidays, parliamentary sessions, elections and election campaigns, state opening of parliament, sports events, national theatre and other art performances, national food festivals, national prize ceremonies, folk dance festivals and events, folk music events and festivals
Secondary media (media technology for production): newspapers, magazines, books, technologically produced arts and culture	National flags, national emblems and symbols, military and other national uniforms, national monuments, national artworks, public buildings, coins, banknotes, national money, stamps, national seals, national badges and medals, passport, maps, government publications, national literature and philosophy, national press, national history books, national language textbooks and	Writing for the national press (journalists), reading the national press, reading of national literature and government literature, waving the national flag, wearing national uniforms, emblems, symbols, badges, medals, etc., using one's passport at border controls, working in or using national buildings, building or looking at national monuments, use of coins/banknotes/	Press reports on national events, national sporting events, parliamentary sessions, national political events, national artistic or other cultural events, national economy, national fine arts exhibitions, public reading events

(Continued)

Chapter Five | Contemporary Marxist Theories **117**

TABLE 5.3 (Cont.)

	Entities (examples)	Social relations and social practices (examples)	Events (examples)
	dictionaries, national encyclopaedias, national visual and fine artworks, national museums, libraries and archives	national money for commodity purchases, organising or attending exhibitions of national fine arts, reading national literature and philosophy	
Tertiary media (media technology for production and consumption, not distribution): CDs, DVDs, tapes, records, Blu-ray discs, hard disks	Recordings of national politics, national economic developments, and national culture distributed on disks	Production and consumption of national politics, national economic developments, and national culture distributed on disks	Events where recorded national politics, national culture, or national economic developments are shown (e.g. cinematographic presentation of the newest movie of an acclaimed national filmmaker, national film festivals, etc.)
Quaternary media (media technology for production, distribution, and consumption): TV, radio, film, telephone, Internet	National radio and television (state broadcaster, public service broadcaster), national film, national telephone and Internet infrastructure, web pages operated by national institutions and nationalists	Producing and consuming broadcasts on national radio and television, use of national telephone and Internet infrastructure, production, distribution, and consumption of national institutions and nationalists' web content	Broadcast of national events, national sporting events broadcasts, broadcasts of parliamentary sessions, broadcast news about national events, broadcast of national artistic or other cultural events, web content created by national institutions on the occasion of national events
Quinary media (digital media prosumption technologies, user-generated content): Internet, social media	Nationalist and nation-related user-generated websites, blog posts, wikis, pages and groups on social networking sites, threads on discussion boards and mailing lists, videos distributed on video platforms, microblog posts, images spread via image sites, memes, etc.	Online production, distribution, and consumption of user-generated nationalism and nation-related user-generated content	User-generated nationalist content on the occasion of national/nationalist events

118 A Marxist Theory of Nationalism

and semi-ritual practices (for instance, elections), most of which are historically novel and largely invented: flags, images, ceremonies and music" (Hobsbawm 1983a, 12).

An Example: The Royal Christmas Message

Let us consider an example of how the nation is communicated at different levels set out in Table 5.3. The Royal Christmas Message has been broadcast in the UK annually since 1932. It started as a radio broadcast in 1932, moved to television in 1957, and is today broadcast via the Internet, television, and radio.

> The evolution of the British royal family into a domestic as well as a public icon of national identification, would have been impossible but for the modern mass media, and its most deliberate ritual expression was actually devised specifically for radio – later adapted to television: the royal Christmas broadcast, instituted in 1932.

> (Hobsbawm 1992b, 142)

In 2017, 7.6 million viewers watched the Queen's Christmas Message broadcast on BBC One, ITV, and Sky News (BBC 2017). In 2002, the total number of viewers was 9.3 million.[3] In 1987, 28 million watched (BBC 2002; Plunkett 2011). The number of TV channels has constantly increased, which may have been one factor influencing the dropping numbers. But the fact that since 1997, not just the BBC, but also ITV, has broadcast the Royal Christmas Message, and in 2011 Sky News also joined the simultaneous broadcast, has not stopped the trend of a decreasing number of viewers.

The Royal Christmas Message involves the Queen as main actor and other actors such as speech-writers, technicians, producers, a public relations team, etc. The production of the message takes place at the level of secondary media: human actors produce a text that the Queen performs as an event on Christmas Day by reading the speech. For reaching the public, the media event is simultaneously organised as a secondary media event that moves to the level of a quaternary media event that is broadcast via television and radio and on the Internet. A DVD presenting all Christmas Messages the Queen has given since 1952 would be a tertiary media technology. In the age of social media, the Royal Christmas Message has also reached the level of social media: the Queen's online team operates official social media accounts. In August 2019, the Twitter profile @RoyalFamily had more than 4 million followers.

Figure 5.2 shows the British Royal Family's official Twitter profile promoting the Queen's 2017 Christmas Message. Within four days, it had reached more than 660,000 views, 23,500 likes, more than 8,000 retweets, and around 1,110 comments. The tweet also contains a video of the speech, so the message's recorded video also moves to and circulates on social media and is thereby not limited to traditional broadcasters (BBC, ITV, Sky).

The example shows that at the level of quinary media, we both find official accounts as well as users communicating about media events and other events in everyday life. One user, for example, replied: "May God bless our Sovereign and keep her safe. The only monarch I have ever known; she has been a solid thread throughout my life, a mother figure to the Nation, a sensible head advising sometimes questionable politicians." Another user commented: "nothing about the e.u. only the commonwealth. that's what I like to hear." The Queen's Message communicates that the Queen is a symbol of the British nation, cares about Britain and Britain's citizens, and thinks of them on a day that is special to many and a public holiday. It is a way of how the British nation is produced and communicated to a broad public. And given quinary media technologies' capacities for prosumption, citizens take the mediated event of the Queen's Message as an occasion for imagining the nation and communicating what they think about Britain and the monarchy, sometimes in quite nationalist ways. In her 2017 speech, the 70th anniversary of the first televised annual Royal Christmas Message, the Queen said:

> My own family often gather round to watch television, as they are at this moment. And that is how I imagine you now. Six decades on, the presenter has evolved somewhat, as has the technology she described. Back then, who could have imagined that people would one day be watching this on laptops and mobile phones, as some of you are today?

One should add that mediated national events are an occasion for citizens to imagine and communicate the nation. Raymond Williams (1974/2003) argues that radio and television are technologies of mobile privatisation that give opportunities to individuals and groups to satisfy their desire for mobility in the privatised context of the home and the family, where they receive "news from 'outside', from otherwise inaccessible sources" (21). Broadcasting is an individualised but *"unified* social intake" (21) of broadcast reality.

National media events are particular forms of mobile privatisation, where not just the Queen or other national actors imagine citizens, but citizens imagine and construct the nation. National and nationalist media events are constructions of the nation from above

FIGURE 5.2 @RoyalFamiliy's tweet about the Queen's Christmas Message 2017
Source: Twitter, @RoyalFamily, posted on 25 December 2017

and from below. In the age of social media, it has become possible that citizens share and communicate their images, constructs, visions, and illusions about the nation and participate not just in the individual and mobile privatised construction of the nation, but to a wider degree also in the social construction, invention, ideological production, reinvention, and ideological reproduction of the nation.

5.4 Conclusion

This chapter elaborated some foundations of a critical, Marxist theory of communication.

Against approaches that welcome nationalism as anti-imperialist struggles, this book advances an internationalist perspective grounded in the works of Karl Marx and Rosa Luxemburg. It stresses that nationalist anti-imperialism has in history often resulted in the mere substitution of one ruling class by another. Internationalism requires the insight that exploitation has a structure of unity in diversity; it operates based on diverse capitalisms that are united by the two universalisms of exploitation and potential resistance.

Nationalism is an ideology and political movement that sustains or aims at building a nation-state that unites defined nation-state members (citizens forming a people). Modern class society *requires* nationalism as ideology in order to justify the exploitation of workers, the domination of consumers, and the geographic expansion of capitalist production and markets. Nationalism as ideology legitimates and distracts from the division of society into classes and relations of domination by constructing, inventing, and fabricating a national unity of the people that is said to be stronger than class divisions. Right-wing authoritarianism and associated nationalism are likely to grow in situations of capitalist crisis, especially if the left is weak, disjointed, and disorganised. For understanding nationalism, we need to combine political economy, history, ideology critique, and political psychology.

Nationalism is not the consequence of modern technology, as Benedict Anderson implies, but information technologies play an important role in communicating the nation and nationalism. A theory of nationalism requires a theory of communication. Some foundations of theorising how the nation and nationalism are communicated were pointed out in this chapter.

The communication of nationalism is based on a dialectic of content/ideology and social form. At the level of content, nationalism takes on a particular semiotic and linguistic discourse structure. At the level of the structure of ideology, we can distinguish between biological, economic, political, and cultural nationalism. Nationalism is communicated through different social forms. Five media types were introduced that operate on the levels of symbolic entities, social relations and practices, and events.

We live in a time where new nationalisms proliferate all over the world as a reaction to economic, political, and ideological crises of capitalism. Given that we live in a digital age, these nationalisms are also communicated via the Internet, social media, and mobile phones. A critical theory of nationalism and a critical communication theory of nationalism are tools for better understanding what is going on in the world and what may be done against it before it is too late.

The five chapters in Part I of this book have established some foundations of a Marxian theory of nationalism. Part II will put these foundations to empirical work. It presents two case studies that analyse how nationalism has been communicated on social media. Germany and Austria, the two countries that together constituted Nazi-Germany, form the political, historical, and contemporary background of these case studies.

Notes

1 For Davis, nationalism is an empty instrument that can be filled with content, the struggle for something. He says that nationalism is any "resistance to alien domination" (Davis 1978, 4).
2 Translation from German: „Die faschistische Ideologie besteht also in dem Versprechen, kurzfristig und risikolos die Ohnmacht und Ausgeliefertheit der individuellen Existenz zu überwinden; [...] Der Faschismus gab der bis dahin bedeutungslosen, inhaltsleeren, isolierten, verunsicherten Existenz Inhalt, Bedeutung und eine allgemeine Ausrichtung und Auszeichnung, eine scheinbare Überlegenheit und reale Macht gegenüber allen Nicht-Dazugehörigen. Er vermittelte das Gefühl, gebraucht zu werden."
3 http://ukchristmastv.weebly.com/ratings.html (accessed 29 December 2017).

Part II

Nationalism on Social Media

Chapter Six
German Nationalism on Social Media in the 2017 Elections to the Bundestag

6.1 Background

6.2 Methodology

6.3 Analysis

6.4 Conclusion

6.1 Background

The 2017 German Federal Elections

The German federal elections to the Bundestag in 2017 took place in the midst of a crisis of the European Union, the refugee crisis, and the expansion and intensification of nationalism and right-wing extremism throughout the world. Germany in 2015 took a leading role when the troika of the European Commission, the European Central Bank, and the International Monetary Fund implemented harsh austerity measures in Greece. Germany also took a leading role in Europe in respect to the refugee crisis: the number of asylum applications in the EU increased from 626,960 in 2014 to 1,322,825 in 2015. In 2016, the number was 1,260,910. In 2016, 59.1 per cent of all EU asylum applications were made in Germany, followed by 9.8 per cent in Italy and 6.7 per cent in France. In 2017, Germany issued 56.0 per cent of the positive asylum permits to refugees in the EU and in France 18.7 per cent. Hungary issued 0.35 per cent, Poland 0.58 per cent, the Czech Republic 0.18 per cent, and Slovakia 0.01 per cent of the permits. This means that the four countries of the political alliance of the Visegrád Group accounted for 1.2% (Eurostat 2019).

If one assumes that in a refugee crisis, the refugees receiving asylum should be evenly distributed across the EU based on some criteria, then one can construct, based on population statistics, various composite indicators. One example indicator is shown in Table 6.1.

The reasonable share of the EU's asylum permits granted by one country is, in this example indicator, calculated as the average of its shares of the GDP and the total population of the EU minus the level to which unemployment exceeds the average of the GDP and population shares. Germany, France, Sweden, and Greece are the EU

TABLE 6.1 Composite indicator for a country's reasonable share of asylum permits in the EU

Variable	Germany	France	Visegrád Group	UK
EU's GDP share (GDP)	21.2%	15%	5.4%	16.1%
EU's population share (POP)	16.1%	13.1%	12.5%	12.8%
EU's unemployment share (UNE)	8.5%	14.2%	8.5%	7.6%
Reasonable share of asylum permits = AVERAGE (GDP, POP) + [AVERAGE (GDP, POP) − UNE]	28.8%	13.9%	9.4%	21.3%
Actual share of asylum permits	56.0%	18.7%	1.12%	6.2%

Source: Eurostat (2019)

countries that have provided significantly larger shares of asylum permits than they can reasonably be expected to issue, whereas most other EU countries, including the Visegrád Group and the UK, have much lower shares. The EU's problem is that it is primarily an economic union governed by neoliberalism that does not have agreed mechanisms for dealing with social crises. The Visegrád countries have nationalist governments that see refugees as a threat and therefore refuse to give asylum to refugees. In autumn 2015, the EU came up with a relocation scheme for distributing 120,000 asylum seekers from Greece, Hungary, and Italy to the other EU countries. The distribution key consisted of a weighted indicator taking into account 40 per cent of a country's population size, 40 per cent of the GDP, 10 per cent of the average number of past asylum applications, and 10 per cent of the unemployment rate (European Commission 2015). In 2017, the relocation scheme practically collapsed because countries such as the Visegrád Group and Austria had refused to host asylum seekers.

The EU's Crisis and Rising Nationalism

Neoliberalism has divided the EU in many respects and has advanced nationalist ideology that blames refugees and migrants for capitalism's social problems. Germany has refused nationalist responses to the refugee crisis but has at the same time advanced neoliberal austerity logic against Greece. There seems to be a lack of understanding that neoliberalism polarises society and fosters social crises, which increases the risk for a rise of nationalism, xenophobia, right-wing extremism, and in the end war and the collapse of the EU. The German elections of 2017 took place in the context of the EU's crisis and rising nationalism.

This chapter asks: How has German nationalism been expressed during the 2017 German Bundestag elections on social media? For giving an answer, a critical social media discourse analysis of political communication data collected on Twitter, Facebook, and YouTube in the days and weeks before the election was conducted. The chapter proceeds by introducing the study's methodology in Section 6.2, presenting results in Section 6.3, and drawing conclusions in Section 6.4.

The Alternative for Germany (AfD)

Alexander Häusler (2018) bases his analysis of the AfD on Ruth Wodak's (2015) concept of right-wing populism and Stuart Hall's (1988) notion of authoritarian populism. He characterises the AfD's ideology and politics as *völkisch*-authoritarian populism. Features of this concept are nationalism that distracts from the class conflict (*völkisch*), a hierarchic, anti-democratic understanding of politics (authoritarian), and the combination of anti-intellectualism and the politics of scapegoating and fear (populism). The problem is that the meanings given to the concept of populism vary widely. Its use tends to create more confusion than theoretical revelation. Populism is, in general, associated with making something popular to "the people". But the concept of the people can refer to all humans, all citizens, the members of a nation-state, or the members of a culturally or biologically defined nation. Populism has been associated with employing popular culture and the media for reaching out to the people. It has also been associated with the attempt to manipulate the public by scapegoating, steering fears and simplifying political reality, and the use of media strategies such as tabloidisation, scandalisation, entertainment, and banalisation. It has been associated with racist far-right politics that scapegoat immigrants, people of colour, and refugees. In order to avoid the confusion associated with the notion of right-wing populism, I prefer to use the term right-wing authoritarianism, which characterises an ideological and political practice that combines top-down leadership, nationalism, the friend/enemy scheme, militarism, and patriarchy (Fuchs 2018a). The AfD can better be characterised as a right-wing authoritarian than a right-wing populist party.

Table 6.2 gives an overview of the 2017 Bundestag election's results.

Angela Merkel's Christian Democratic Union (CDU) and its sister party CSU together lost 8.5 per cent of the voting share, which is for both parties the worst result since 1949. The right-wing extremist Alternative für Deutschland (AfD, Alternative for Germany) became, with 12.6 per cent of the voting share, the third-largest party in the

TABLE 6.2 Results of the 2017 Bundestag elections

Party	Worldview	Voting share 2017	Change in comparison to the 2013 elections	Number of MPs, change to previous Bundestag
CDU	Conservatism	26.8%	−7.4%	200 (−55)
SPD	Social democracy	20.5%	−5.2%	153 (−40)
AfD	Right-wing extremism	12.6%	+7.9%	69 (+5)
FDP	Liberalism	10.7%	+6.0%	67 (+4)
Die Linke	Socialism	9.2%	+0.6%	46 (−10)
Greens	Green politics	8.9%	+0.5%	80 (+10)
CSU	Conservatism	6.2%	−1.2%	94 (-)
Voter turnout	76.2%			

Source: www.bundeswahlleiter.de

Bundestag. The Social Democrats lost a significant share of voters, the liberal FDP re-entered parliament, and the Greens and the Left Party (Die Linke) made minor gains. It is the first time in the history of post-Nazi-Germany and the Bundestag, which was founded in 1949, that a right-wing extremist party has entered it. According to post-election research, the typical AfD voter is male, between 30 and 59 years old, a blue-collar worker or unemployed, and does not have a school leaving examination and university education (Forschungsgruppe Wahlen 2017a, 2017b)

Forty-four per cent said that refugees and foreigners were the most important election topic, followed by pensions (24 per cent) and social justice (16 per cent) (Forschungsgruppe Wahlen 2017b). Sixty-eight per cent of the AfD voters say that the party is not right-wing extremist, whereas 74 per cent of those not voting for it say it has such a character (Forschungsgruppe Wahlen 2017b). Thirty-five per cent of AfD voters had not voted in 2013, 24 per cent had voted for the AfD, and 21 per cent for CDU/CSU (Forschungsgruppe Wahlen 2017b). Class, age, gender, and education are factors that influence the likelihood that a German citizen votes for the AfD.

A study shows that a large share of AfD voters show xenophobia, nationalism, and fear of social degradation (Hans Böckler Stiftung 2017). Eighty-three per cent of the respondents who vote for the AfD say that immigration makes you feel a foreigner in your own country (compared to 44 per cent of all respondents). Eighty-eight per cent of the AfD respondents argue that the state should stop migration (compared to 54 per cent of all respondents). Sixty-four per cent of the AfD-supporting respondents say that Germany should focus on its national interests, even if this means having to harm other EU countries. AfD voters' largest fears are bad financial security in old age (63 per cent), becoming victims of crime and violence (62 per cent), the future of their kids (60 per cent), and their financial situation (53 per cent). Seventy-two per cent of AfD-voting respondents say that politicians do less for them than for other groups.

6.2 Methodology

The success of the AfD stands in the context of rising nationalisms, the socio-economic crisis of capitalism, and the political crisis of the European Union. Nationalism

> divides the world into "us" and "them", "friends" and "foes", positing a homogeneous and fixed identity on either side and stressing the characteristics that differentiate "us" from "them". [...] The nationalist discourse always looks back in time, seeking to demonstrate the "linear time of the nation", its undisputed diachronic presence. [...] The nationalist discourse is also haunted by a fixation on territory, the quest for a "home", actual or imagined. This involves the reconstruction of social space as national territory.
>
> (Özkirimli 2010, 208–209)

Nationalism is a "misty veil" that "conceals in every case a definite historical content" (Luxemburg 1976, 135). The theoretical foundations of this book have shown that nationalism is an ideology that tries to veil class antagonisms and to distract public attention from class structures. Nationalism is a political fetishism that naturalises the nation in the form of a "we"-identity (a national people) that is distinguished from enemies (outsiders, other nations, immigrants, refugees, etc.) that are presented as intruders, aliens, subhuman, uncivilised, parasites, etc. in order to deflect attention from class contradictions and power inequalities.

Empirical Ideology Critique

Given that nationalism is a particular form of ideology, empirical ideology critique is a suited method for studying how nationalism is expressed in the public sphere. Empirical ideology critique analyses the structure (*text*) of ideological communication in the *context* of society's power structures in order to draw conclusions for political *prospects*. The methodology of the presented case study proceeded in four steps:

1) Data collection, including research ethics.
2) Identification of discursive macro-topics.
3) Analysis of the structure of ideology and discourse for each macro topic; analysis and theorisation of how online discourses and ideology are related to the broader societal context, i.e. the relations of the online-semiotic elements to the broader societal context.
4) Prospective critique.

As a *first step*, data were collected from social media platforms. Online research poses special challenges in respect to research ethics because the boundaries between private and public communication are blurred in online spaces. Social media research ethics guidelines suggest assuming that no informed consent for data collection is needed if users in a certain online setting can reasonably expect to be observed by strangers (Fuchs 2017b, 60; Townsend and Wallace 2016). For this study, data were only collected from Twitter accounts run by politicians and parties, Twitter users posting under election-relevant hashtags, and YouTube channels and Facebook groups run by parties and politicians. These profiles fulfilled a public communication role. It is reasonable to assume that users going there are aware that the information posted is intended for achieving public visibility. Therefore, no informed consent is needed for gathering and analysing data from such profiles. In the presentation of results in Section 6.3, the names of users who are public figures (such as politicians and parties) have not been anonymised. The names of other users are not mentioned.

Data were collected in the days and weeks before the German election from three data sources: Twitter, YouTube, and Facebook. Table 6.3 provides an overview of the collected data. Two streams of data were collected from Twitter with the help of the online data collection tool DiscoverText. The first one collected tweets posted by the main contending parties and politicians that mentioned keywords such as nation, *Volk* (the people), Germany, migration, foreigners, Europe, Brexit, Greece, and Islam or Muslim. Appendix 6.A gives an overview of the relevant Twitter profiles. The collection started one month before the election (on 23 August 2017, 22:00 BST) and ended three days after it (on 27 August 2017, 15:34 BST). The result was a dataset consisting of 2,086 elements. The second Twitter dataset used the same keywords in combination with hashtags at two key points of time during the election campaign, when major media events took place: (a) the only TV debate between Chancellor Angela Merkel (CDU) and SPD frontrunner Martin Schulz that ARD broadcast on 2 September; and (b) the TV debate between the frontrunners of the other five main contending parties: Joachim Herrmann (CSU), Christian Lindner (FDP), Cem

Chapter Six | German Nationalism on Social Media **131**

TABLE 6.3 Overview of collected social media data

Data source	Search keywords	Number of data elements
Twitter	(Nation OR Volk OR contains:Deutsch OR contains:Einwand OR contains: migr OR contains:immig OR contains:flüchtl OR contains:auslä EU OR contains:Europ OR contains:Brexit OR contains:Griech OR #TrauDichDeutschland OR contains:Islam OR contains:muslim OR contains:moslem) AND (from:RegSprecher OR from:CDU OR from:CSU OR from:MartinSchulz OR from:SPDde OR from:AfD_Bund OR from:AfDKompakt OR from:FraukePetry OR from:Alice_Weidel OR from:DieLinke OR from:SWagenknecht OR from:DietmarBartsch OR from:Die_Gruenen OR from:Cem_Oezdemir OR from:GoeringEckart OR from:fdp OR from:C_Lindner OR from:FrankFranz OR from:NPDde)	2,086
Twitter	Event 1 (ARD debate Merkel/Schulz): (Nation OR Volk OR contains:Deutsch OR contains:Einwand OR contains: migr OR contains:immig OR contains:flüchtl OR contains:auslä EU OR contains:Europ OR contains:Brexit OR contains:Griech OR #TrauDichDeutschland OR contains:Islam OR contains:muslim OR contains:moslem) AND (#tvduell OR #bundestagswahl OR #btw17) Event 2 (ARD debate Herrmann/Lindner/Özdemir/Wagenknecht/Weidel): (Nation OR Volk OR contains:Deutsch OR contains:Einwand OR contains: migr OR contains:immig OR contains:flüchtl OR contains:auslä OR contains:Europ OR contains:Brexit OR contains:Griech OR #TrauDichDeutschland OR contains:Islam OR contains:muslim OR contains:moslem) AND (#fuenfkampf OR #Fünfkampf OR #5kampf OR #derfuenfkampf OR #DerFünfKampf OR #der5kampf)	26,468 + 5,006 = 31,474
Facebook	FB1: Posting about the EU from Angela Merkel's (CDU) Facebook page FB2: Posting about immigration from the CSU's Facebook page FB3: Posting opposing the AfD from Martin Schulz's (SPD) Facebook page FB4: Posting about the integration of migrants from Cem Özdemir's (Green Party) Facebook page FB5: Posting about the immigration of refugees' family members to Germany on Alice Weidel's (AfD) Facebook page FB6: Posting about immigration on the FDP's Facebook page	2,689 403 451 584 908 1,387 Total comments: 6,422
YouTube	YT1: CDU campaign video focusing on good life in Germany YT2: YouTube campaign video about social injustice in Germany, refugees, and the AfD (Die Linke)	91,488 views, 765 comments 66,459 views, 267 comments Total comments: 1,032

Özdemir (Bündnis 90/Die Grünen), Sahra Wagenknecht (Die Linke), and Alice Weidel (AfD). ARD broadcast this debate on 4 September. Keywords focusing on Germany, migration, foreigners, Europe, Brexit, Greece, and Islam or Muslim were combined with event-specific hashtags. The result was a dataset consisting of 31,474 tweets. One collected Twitter dataset focuses on politicians and parties' tweets, the other one on citizens' tweets.

An analysis of the Merkel/Schulz debate shows that 31.1 per cent of the discussion time was devoted to migration and deportation, 10.8 per cent to Turkey, 9.2 per cent to terror and inner security, and 9.2 per cent to Islam (Segger et al. 2018). So, more than 60 per cent of the airtime was used for very similar topics that often are associated with scapegoating refugees, immigrants, and Muslims. Issues such as education, healthcare, or digital media were not at all discussed.

For collecting data from Facebook and YouTube, relevant channels of the main contending politicians and parties were identified (see the lists in Appendix 6.A). The Facebook-based data collection app Netvizz was used for collecting comments to specific postings made on relevant Facebook pages. Netvizz/YouTube Data Tools was used for collecting comments from YouTube channels. There was a focus on postings about refugees and the European Union that attracted a relatively large number of reactions and comments in comparison to other postings. Only postings made in August or September 2017 were considered because these were the two main election campaign months. The collection of comments from Facebook and YouTube was conducted on 25 September 2017, one day after the Bundestag election. A total of 6,422 comments were collected from seven relevant Facebook postings. A total of 1,032 comments were collected from two YouTube videos.

As a *second methodological step*, macro discourse topics were identified as a preparation for the data analysis. A discourse topic is a semantic macro-proposition that relates to a key aspect of a particular topic (van Dijk 1987, 48–50). Three macro discourse topics were defined by the research question this chapter poses, which coincided with four major themes in the election campaign – the German nation, the European Union, refugees and migrants in Germany, and Islam. The German nation and the EU are two themes that have to do with citizens' identity in Europe. These two macro discourse topics are important because the crisis of the EU and rising nationalism were two key contexts of the 2017 Bundestag elections. The German nation and the EU are two contradictory poles of German citizens' political identity. On one end of the spectrum are those who perceive themselves primarily as German and oppose the EU, whereas on the other end of the spectrum are those who perceive themselves as European cosmopolitans. The relationship between Germany and the EU has to do with questions of nationalism, internationalism, and how the boundaries of political identity are drawn. The refugee crisis was another major context of the 2017 Bundestag elections and therefore constituted a macro discourse topic of the analysis. Refugees are on the one end of the political spectrum welcomed, and on the other end seen as enemies that should be kept out and deported. A fourth important topic in the German elections was Islam and the question of what role it plays and should play in German society. Refugees, migrants, and Islam pose questions for political identity and about who should be seen as friend or enemy. Nationalism is closely connected to the friend/enemy scheme (Fuchs 2018a).

Table 6.4 shows the most frequently mentioned words in the Facebook dataset. The keyword *Obergrenze* (upper limit) refers to the suggestion that there should be a maximum number of refugees accepted per year. The CSU in particular advanced this idea. The table indicates that the discourse topics of Europe, Germany, and refugees seem to have been of particular importance in the 2017 German election. The issue of refugees is closely related with the discourse topic of Islam because many refugees arriving in Europe flee from countries whose faith structure is predominantly Islamic.

As the *third methodological step*, the application of methodological tools from critical discourse analysis, was used in order to analyse the structure of the four discourse topics (Reisigl and Wodak 2001; Wodak and Meyer 2016). In this analysis, for each macro discourse topic, interesting cases were identified and analysed with the help of critical theories of nationalism as well as in the context of the broader societal context. This analysis is presented in Section 6.3. Drawing political conclusions about the communication of nationalism in Germany was the *fourth step* (see Section 6.4).

TABLE 6.4 Most frequently mentioned words in the Twitter dataset

Keyword	Frequency
Merkel	736
Deutschland (Germany)	548
Europa (Europe)	236
Deutsche (Germans)	153
Flüchtlinge (refugees)	132
Obergrenze (upper limit)	120
Schulz	112

Source: Generated with NVivo

6.3 Analysis

Twitter Posting Frequencies

Table 6.5 shows who posted most frequently in the Twitter dataset that features politicians and parties' tweets.

Most Frequently Mentioned Twitter Users

Taken together, the AfD accounts (two party accounts and the accounts by AfD politicians Alice Weidel and Frauke Petry), with 32.6 per cent of all tweets, accounted for a relative majority, followed by SPD accounts (18.5 per cent). CDU/CSU profiles made up 15.4 per cent of the tweets, Green Party profiles 12.0 per cent, FDP profiles 9.7 per cent, and profiles of Die Linke 9.1 per cent. It is evident that on Twitter, the AfD dominates the discourse on migration, refugees, Islam, and the EU. Table 6.6

TABLE 6.5 The political Twitter accounts posting most frequently about Germany, the nation, refugees, migrants, the EU, and Islam

Twitter user	Tweets	Relative share
@SPDde	370	17.7
@AfD_Bund	239	11.5
@CDU	213	10.2
@Alice_Weidel	182	8.7
@AfDKompakt	164	7.9
@FDP	158	7.6
@DieLinke	146	7.0
@Die_Gruenen	139	6.7
@Cem_Oezdemir	110	5.3
@CSU	97	4.7
@FraukePetry	93	4.5
@NPDde	46	2.2
@C_Lindner	43	2.1
@DietmarBartsch	26	1.2
@SWagenknecht	19	0.9
@MartinSchulz	16	0.8
@FrankFranz	14	0.7
@RegSprecher	11	0.5

shows that among the analysed tweets by politicians and political parties, AfD accounts were, with 262 mentions, the most frequently referenced ones.

Filter Bubbles

Tables 6.7 and 6.8 indicate that Twitter communication about the nation, refugees, migrants, the EU, and Islam form filter bubbles (Pariser 2011): both Alice Weidel (AfD) and Martin Schulz (SPD) are predominantly referenced by their own parties' profiles.

The AfD's Dominance on Social Media

In the Twitter dataset collected during election TV debates, the AfD profiles also dominated (see Table 6.9). They achieved a total of 3,562 direct references to their usernames. There were 830 references to Martin Schulz's profile, the third most referenced account. Although the main television debate was between Merkel and Schulz and the vast majority of tweets were collected during that time period, the AfD managed to be the most frequently mentioned user. Table 6.10 shows that AfD supporters dominated Twitter postings about the nation, migrants, refugees, the EU, and Islam during the TV debates.

Two hundred and nineteen of the user anonymous1's 220 tweets in the television debate dataset are retweets (especially of the AfD accounts @Alice_Weidel, @FraukePetry, @AfD_Bund, and @AfD), either pure retweets or retweets into which

TABLE 6.6 The ten most frequently mentioned users in politicians' tweets about Germany, the nation, refugees, migrants, the EU and Islam in the Twitter-politician dataset

Rank	User	Frequency
1	@MartinSchulz	176
2	@AfD	105
3	@Alice_Weidel	97
4	@Cem_Oezdemir	97
5	@C_Lindner	93
6	@AfD_Bund	60
7	@Die_Gruenen	49
8	@KatjaKipping	38
9	@SPDde	37
10	@GoeringEckardt	37

136 Nationalism on Social Media

TABLE 6.7 Users mentioning Alice Weidel in the Twitter-politician dataset

Username	Frequency
@AfD_Bund	43
@AfDKompakt	23
@Alice_Weidel	28
@Die_Gruenen	1
@DieLinke	1
@FraukePetry	1

TABLE 6.8 Users mentioning Martin Schulz in the Twitter-politician dataset

Username	Frequency
@SPDde	173
@CSU	1
@DieLinke	1
@FraukePetry	1

TABLE 6.9 Users mentioned most frequently in the Twitter-television debate dataset

Rank	Username	Mentions
1	@FraukePetry	1,490
2	@Alice_Weidel	1,115
3	@MartinSchulz	830
4	@oler (Oler Reißman, journalist at Spiegel Online)	828
5	@Die_Gruenen	706
6	@Cem_Oezdemir	617
7	@AfD	587
8	@CDU	547
9	@AfD_Bund	370
10	@FDP	354

hashtags (such as #AfDwaehlen [#voteAfD] or #TrauDichDeutschland) or small comments were inserted. Seventy-nine of anonymous2's 82 tweets, 54 of 60 tweets by anonymous5, and 46 of 53 tweets by anonymous6 were retweets. Seventy-two of 73

Chapter Six | German Nationalism on Social Media **137**

TABLE 6.10 The users with the largest number of postings made in the Twitter-television debate dataset

Rank	Username		Number of tweets
1	anonymous1	AfD supporter	220
2	anonymous2	AfD supporter	82
3	@TrauDichDe	AfD Niedersachsen	73
4	anonymous3	AfD supporter	65
5	anonymous4	AfD supporter	62
6	anonymous5	AfD supporter	60
7	anonymous6	AfD supporter	53
8	anonymous7	SPD supporter	50
9	anonymous8	AfD supporter	49
10	@AfD_Tweets	AfD support account	44

tweets by the AfD Niedersachsen were retweets. All of the postings in the dataset made by anonymous3, anonymous4, anonymous8, and @AfD_Tweets were retweets.

Bots and Fake News

In bot analysis, Twitter accounts posting more than 50 times a day have been classified as being automated/bots (Kollanyi et al. 2016). Other criteria have been the number of retweets, the time distribution of tweets, linguistic cues, and sentiment features (Davis et al. 2016). The self-description of @AfD_Tweets indicates that it is likely to be a bot. The other pro-AfD users present themselves as regular users. But given the high share of retweets, it is likely that at least some of them are semi-automated or automated retweet accounts. The strong visibility of the AfD during German election TV debates could very well be related to the activities of social media bots.

Digital Forensic Lab (2017) during a two-week period in August 2017 analysed all 41,000 tweets mentioning the official AfD Twitter profile @AfD_Bund. Also, in this dataset, @anonymous1 was the most active user, mentioning @AfD_Bund 225 times: "As of August 22, over 90 % of its most recent tweets were retweets, marking it as a likely cyborg account" (Digital Forensic Lab 2017). DFL's analysis also documented other amplification strategies, for example one that first disguised itself by posting info about cooking recipes and lifestyle for gathering followers and during the election campaign turned into an AfD-supporting account:

It was mentioned almost twice as often as the AfD main feed, and by more than twice as many accounts. [...] Its support base is far more international, boosted by hyperactive (and possibly automated) users on the German, French, Dutch and American far right, as well as probable bots which significantly amplify Kremlin propaganda. It thus appears to be a relative rarity: an initially German account which has attracted a following among the international far right. It is regularly retweeted by far-right accounts in a number of other countries, including the U.S.; it sometimes retweets far-right accounts from those countries.

(Digital Forensic Lab 2017)

Sängerlaub et al. (2018) analysed fake news in the context of the German 2017 federal elections. They identified ten fake news stories related to the Bundestag elections and conducted a telephone survey about them ($N = 1,037$). The maximum number of online engagements (shares, likes, comments) these fake news stories achieved was 500,000. AfD Facebook profiles, especially the ones of the federal party and the two AfD co-chairpersons Jörg Meuthen and Frauke Petry, played a major role in the online circulation of seven of these ten fake news stories. Five of the seven fake news stories that AfD accounts helped circulate had to do with refugees: "The way the phenomenon presents itself empirically in Germany is that especially the right, right-wing populists and right-wing extremists spread fake news"[1] (Sängerlaub et al. 2018, 73). "All of our fake news-cases have clearly been disseminated by right-wing populists and right-wing extremists, including the AfD as well as media such as Junge Freiheit or right-wing blogs such as Philosophia Perennis"[2] (Sängerlaub et al. 2018, 84–85). The phone survey showed that 28 per cent of all respondents believed that the presented fake news stories were true. In the case of AfD voters, the share was on average 42.3 per cent and therefore significantly higher than among the general population. So, there is evidence that right-wing organisations and individuals are to a significant degree involved in the dissemination of fake news and that supporters of right-wing groups tend to believe to a higher degree than the average citizen in fake news. One underlying reason might be that right-wing ideology tends to be close to conspiracy thinking. Another one is that given that fake news tends to a significant degree to be produced and disseminated by right-wing demagogues and is to a large degree right-wing in character, those who support this ideology tend to find them credible because they stem from sources (individuals, organisations, media) they trust.

Neudert (2019) collected 984,713 tweets related to the Bundestag election of 2017 in the days from 1 September until 10 September. Ninety-two automated accounts were identified that created 73,012 tweets (7.4 per cent of the total). Automated tweets were most frequently found in tweets related to the AfD (15.0 per cent of all AfD-related tweets): "The overwhelming majority of bot-generated posts supported views on the political right and extreme right of the spectrum. Hateful comments on immigration, xenophobic conspiracy theories, and racist slurs were common themes, as well as support for the right-wing AfD" (Neudert 2019, 165). Some 32.2 per cent of a random sample of non-professional political news and info (N = 3,277) shared on Twitter presented false news as factual:

> The right-wing, anti-Islam blog Philosphia Perennis (156 shares) leads in shares, followed by the conservative, right-extremist Junge Freiheit (91). Mirroring the findings from the enquiry on social bots, the majority of the misinformation pages identified were politically right, and xenophobic, nation-alist, pro-Pegida, pro-AfD, and Islamophobic content was common.
>
> (172–173)

The AfD's Social Media Strategy

Right-wing extremists often have the public image of being opposed to technology, bad at using the newest communication tools, and not innovative and creative in using IT. The analysed dataset showed that in contrast to all other parties, the AfD again and again asked users to contribute by recording and posting their own videos supporting the AfD, commenting on AfD postings, using the hashtag #Trau-DichDeutschland (#DareYouGermany), and spreading the AfD's YouTube videos. For example, the main AfD account @AfD_Bund (now transformed into @AfD) posted two user-videos accompanied by the request "Record your own video now!"[3] (Twitter-politician dataset, #1480, @AfD_Bund). It also asked users to spread links to the AfD's YouTube videos: "Did you like our TV spot? Then please spread the YouTube-version – Thank you! #TrauDichDeutschland: #AfD [embedded YouTube Video]"[4] (Twitter-politician dataset, #1980, @AfD_Bund). Alice Weidel, for example, posted the following request: "Dear supporters, participate and write your com-ments under #Wahl2017! #TrauDichDeutschland #AfD #Btw17"[5] (Twitter-politician dataset, #1843, @Alice_Weidel). "How did you like our first TV-campaign spot? I am very interested in your opinion"[6] (Twitter-politician dataset, #2025, @Alice_-Weidel). Part of the AfD's high visibility on social media may have been that it actively fostered an online culture of spreading, sharing, and commenting on right-wing extremist ideology.

The German Nation

Communicating the German Nation on Social Media

The election campaign of Angela Merkel's CDU focused on the image of good life in Germany under Merkel's rule:

> A Germany, in which we have a good life and like to life. That is what Angela #Merkel and the #CDU work for. #fedidwgugl
> [CDU campaign video, shows a foetus at the start, text spoken by Angela Merkel:] In what kind of Germany will you live? Will it be the Germany that we care about? A country of education, where everyone can make something out of their life. A Germany of opportunities, where more people than ever before find work. A country that does not rest on its laurels, but rather finds new solutions for the future. It's in our hands! We can take this decision for Germany. For a country that already today ensures that there is also good work tomorrow, that does not leave people alone in old age and illness. For a country, in which we fight together against hatred and envy. A country that resolutely defends its European values. We can choose a political programme that respects and supports families. For an economy that creates prosperity for all. For a homeland, where everyone can feel free and secure. Your Germany should be a country, in which we all live well. For this Germany, I would like to continue to commit myself with all my strength. And I ask for your support of this task!
> [Written text:] On September 24, with both votes for the CDU.[7]
>
> (Twitter-politician dataset, @CDU, ID 1680, http://twitter.com/CDU/statuses/908417730830852098)

In terms of predication, the CDU campaign video tries to construct a sense of solidarity and unity of all persons living in Germany by using inclusive language and the third-person plural ("we", "everyone", "for all"). The symbol of the foetus is used as a metaphor signifying future prosperity of Germany and of those groups and individuals living in it. The CDU also based its election programme on the image of good life in Germany. "Germany is a loveable and livable country, where one can reside, work and live well. [...] Today, we live in the most beautiful and best Germany we ever had"[8] (CDU 2017, 4, 5). The CDU's election discourse was based on a feel-good programme that promised long-term stability, peace, and prosperity through a social market economy. The problem of this approach is that not everyone feels like having benefited from Merkel's three governments in the years from 2005 to 2017. The CDU's programme did not speak to those who were afraid of or experienced social decline. For example, the inequality of income distribution measured by the ratio of total income received by the 20 per cent with the highest and lowest incomes increased from 3.5 in 2005 to 4.1 in 2016. The share of people living at risk of poverty after social transfers increased from 12.2 per cent in 2005 to 16.5 per cent in 2016. The in-work at-risk-of-poverty rate increased from 4.8 per cent in 2005 to 9.5 per cent in 2016.[9]

The SPD answered with a video to the CDU campaign video that it spread on Twitter and YouTube. It presented itself as the party that would create a socially just Germany:

> Replying to @CDU: In what kind of Germany do we want to live? Our answer to your spot is a bit different. #TimeForMartin
>
> [Video showing a foetus. Text spoken by Martin Schulz:] In what kind of country do you want to live? Hopefully in a country that invests more money into schools and education than into tanks and drones. Hopefully in a country, in which you can lead a good life based on your old-age pension and do not have to work until you are seventy. In a country, where all receive fair wages and women earn as much as men do. Hopefully in a country, where things are tackled and not waited out. In a just country. Fortunately, you live in a country, where your parents can put the cross on the right place.
>
> [SPD-logo and text "Time for more justice"]
>
> (Twitter-politician dataset, @SPDde, ID 1256, https://twitter.com/spdde/statuses/900651836537024514)

The SPD in its video also uses the foetus as symbol of prosperity and positive development. Whereas the CDU more stresses economic development, the SPD focuses on social justice and social development by foregrounding schools, education, pension levels, wages, and the retirement age. The SPD's political strategy was to portray Merkel and the CDU as not doing enough for fostering social justice in Germany and Europe. Accordingly, the title of the SPD's election programme was "Time for More Social Justice" (SPD 2017).

AfD supporters responded to Merkel and the CDU on social media. Here are some typical examples:

> For a Germany, where you can become everything: unemployed, destitute, without a homeland!
>
> (YouTube dataset, ID 44)

142 Nationalism on Social Media

> Merkel in any case fights for a future Germany, where no more Germans live, but only Germans with migration background.

> (YouTube dataset, ID 98)

> Since 2015, Europe has been overrun by terror and she talks about peace and a country, where we live well and like to live. The security of the nation is not on the agenda, or what?

> (Facebook dataset, ID 1960)

The Friend/Enemy Scheme

The logic used in these postings uses the friend/enemy scheme that constructs a friend and an enemy group and stresses negative things about the enemy group (see Fuchs 2018a, Chapters 3 and 4; Reisigl and Wodak 2001, 45–46; van Dijk 2011). Migrants and foreigners are portrayed as a social, cultural, and security threat. They are portrayed as destroying the homeland (*Heimat*), as being untrue Germans, and as being terrorists. The postings operated based on ethnonyms and nationyms (Reisigl and Wodak 2001, 50) that stress a purist concept of the German nation by claiming that it is important that people living in Germany were born in Germany. In nationalism, individuals are "represented in the past or in the future *as if* they formed a natural community" (Balibar and Wallerstein 1991, 96).

The first tweet puts the nationalist stress on preserving the German nation on equal grounds with solving social problems. The second example comment advances the assumption that there are two types of citizens in Germany: Germans and "Germans with migration background". The first are presented as a group of superior human beings. The argumentative structure of the third posting combines the topos of large numbers ("Europe has been overrun") with the topos of danger ("the security of the nation", "Europe has been overrun by terror"; Reisigl and Wodak 2001, 79, 77). It is based on the assumption that masses of foreigners pose a terror threat.

The three example postings reproduce the nationalist and nativist ideology that the AfD advanced in its election campaign. So, for example, the AfD's election programme said:

> The AfD's goal is the self-preservation and not the self-destruction of our nation-state and our people. The future of Germany and Europe must be secured in the long term. We want to leave a country to our descendants that

can still be recognised as our Germany. [...] The AfD avows itself to the German lead culture [...] It [the German lead culture] besides the German language also encompasses our customs, traditions, spiritual and cultural history.[10]

(AfD 2017, 28, 47)

The programme advances a cultural and exclusionary form of racism that aims at excluding elements that are perceived as non-German.

The AfD uses an ideological rhetoric that assumes there is a culturally pure German nation that is under threat by foreigners who aim at culturally and militarily destroying the imagined unitary German nation. The AfD's arguments that are also used by AfD supporters in the analysed datasets are mistaken because they overlook that nation-states are never pure, but "are without exception ethnically hybrid – the product of conquests, absorptions of one peoples by another" (Hall 1993, 356). Nationalism is a political form of fetishism, a "misty veil", as Rosa Luxemburg (1976, 135) says, which blames society's problems on foreign elements, in this case what is presented as being non-German, and thereby distracts from how social problems are grounded in class, capitalism, and domination. Part of the AfD's success is that it speaks to the emotions of Germans, who fear change, loss, and decline. One reaction to fear is the search for possibilities to emotionally channel anger, hatred, and anxiety. The AfD's political propaganda offers opportunities for channelling negative emotions into the hatred against foreigners who are presented as threatening the German nation.

Theodor W. Adorno warns that the friend/enemy scheme was part of Nazi-Germany's ideology and that Germany must be careful not to repeat its own history:

> The fabrication of national collectivities, however – common practice in the abominable jargon of war which speaks of the Russian, the American, and certainly also of the German – is the mark of a reified consciousness hardly capable of experience [*Erfahrung*]. Such fabrication remains within precisely those stereotypes which it is the task of thinking to dissolve. [...] The fabrication of stereotypes, on the other hand, promotes collective narcissism. Those qualities with which one identifies oneself – the essence of one's own group – imperceptibly become the Good; the foreign group, the others, Bad. The same thing then happens, in reverse, with the image the others have of the German. Yet after the most heinous deeds [*Unheil*] were perpetrated under National Socialism in the name of an ideology which privileged the collective subject at the expense of any and all individuality, there is in

144 Nationalism on Social Media

Germany a double reason to guard against relapsing into the production of ideola-
trous, self-glorifying stereotypes

(Adorno 1985, 121)

The European Union

Scapegoating Greece and the European South

The AfD presents Germany as subsidising the European Union's Southern member states:

[Alexander Gauland:]	Mrs. Merkel does not have a cash cow, but a plan. That's also why she keeps her plans for Europe secret. I bet with you that after the election there will be a debt haircut for Greece – at the expense of German citizens.
[Alice Weidel:]	Not with the AfD! The Germans need a party that at last represents its interests! German interests! Not right-wing – but for rights. And more than 15 %. (AfD campaign video on YouTube, www.youtube.com/watch?v=RRoHZ-QKwhk, 92,850 views [26 October 2017])

The AfD argues that under Merkel, Germans have to pay for bailing out Greece from debt. Opposing this argument, critical economists stress that the Greek debt crisis has to do with centre–periphery relations in Europe, in which Southern economies depend on capital from core countries so that debt is artificially created for fostering capitalist interests (Lapavitsas 2012; Laskos and Tsakalotos 2013). Another counter-argument concerns the question of who is the creditor and who the debtor.

"When am I getting my money back?" (Varoufakis 2015, 6), a German junior minister asked then-Greek finance minister Yanis Varoufakis at the latter's first meeting with the German Finance Minister Wolfgang Schäuble. This question also characterises the logic of the AfD. Nazi-Germany in 1941 forced an interest-free loan on Greece. LSE economics professor Albrecht Ritschl says that Germany's unpaid Nazi debt to Greece is today worth over €2 trillion (Nevradakis 2014), which is much more than Greece's outstanding debt to the troika. The question about Greece's debt therefore heeds to be reversed. One needs to ask: When will Germany pay back its debt to Greece? When will Greece get its money back from Germany?

The EU, Immigration, and Refugees

In the analysed datasets, the discussion of Europe was dominated by immigration and the refugee crisis. Some examples:

> Europe is a peace project ?! We in Germany and Europe experience an invasion by foreign peoples and foreign culture
>
> > (Facebook dataset, ID 1887)
>
> Why Merkel is to blame ??? Her invitation has set off this unbelievable refugee invasion, by which thousands of Islamist terrorists have come to Europe in an uncontrolled manner !!! Those who do not see this, are completely blind !
>
> > (Facebook dataset, ID 1127)
>
> We need a Fortress Europe and it will only exist under the AfD
>
> > (Facebook dataset, ID 1023)
>
> Fortress Europe! CLOSE OFF the borders!
>
> > (YouTube dataset, ID 409)
>
> We need a wall around Europe!
>
> > (YouTube dataset, ID 472)

Interdiscursivity is a feature of the first and the second example. Interdiscursivity means the co-occurrence and combination of discourse types or discourse topics (Fairclough 2015, 38). In the first example, three of our four discourse topics are combined: Germany, Europe, and foreigners. Germany and Europe are identified as political communities the speaker identifies with, whereas "foreign peoples and foreign culture" are characterised as threatening these communities ("invasion"). In the second example, the three discourse topics of refugees/foreigners, Islam, and Europe are combined.

These postings use militarionyms (Reisigl and Wodak 2001, 51) for characterising the relationships of Europe and refugees. Migrants and refugees are characterised as "invading" Europe. Invasion is a frequently used military metaphor in racist discourse (Reisigl and Wodak 2001, 59–60). But the demand to close the EU's borders is also formulated in military jargon by calling for building a "wall around Europe" and the "fortress Europe". The friend/enemy logic is not just polarising black-and-white thinking that dualistically opposes groups. It, in the last instance, leads to military action and calls for military action, i.e. the willingness to kill the constructed enemies. Speaking of an invasion and having to build fortresses implies military actions. Those using such language are likely to think that the EU should let refugees crossing the sea to Europe drown, that battleships should attack and sink such ships, or that refugees should be deported or killed. In authoritarian politics, as conceived by the Nazi-political theorist Carl Schmitt (1932/1996), the "foe is in the last resort anyone who must be exterminated physically" (Neumann 1944/2009, 45).

Opposition to Nationalism on Social Media

One strategy of opposing such logic that could be identified in the dataset was the appeal to learn from German history where right-wing extremism could lead to:

> German RIGHT-WING EXTREMISTS have caused a massive bloodbath in Europe. Only complete idiots are still right-wing today!

> (YouTube dataset, ID 831)

Refugees and Migration

Immigrants and Refugees as Constructed Social Burden

One argument that was found frequently in the analysed datasets was that immigrants and refugees are a burden for the German state and its social security system:

> #AliceWeidelLive on the #TVDebate: Merkel's refugee politics destroy the welfare state: The #AfD will make sure that this comes to an end! Open borders and a sustainable welfare state do not go together.

> (Twitter-politician dataset, @Alice_Weidel, ID 1368, https://twitter.com/Ali ce_Weidel/statuses/904414469090148355, 341 retweets, 768 likes [25 October 2017])

> #TVDebate Of course we have to work until we are 70. Someone must fill the social fund for the refugees. #voteAfD #AdD

> (Twitter-television debate dataset, ID 149)

> We Germans need our money that we work for, for our families, the sick and our old people, who have worked their whole life for their pensions. That is how it looks like and not differently. The AfD has good approaches and that's how everything can change. In our Germany.
>
> (Facebook dataset, ID 4409)

These examples combine the topos of burdening and the topos of finances (Reisigl and Wodak 2001, 78), so it is claimed that refugees cost lots of money and threaten and destroy the welfare state, the pension system, family allowance, and healthcare.

Such claims can best be tested by looking at actual budget and statistical data (Table 6.11).

At the height of the refugee crisis in 2015, 974,551 asylum seekers received state support in Germany. In the same year, 326,872 individuals from Syria, 94,902 from Afghanistan, and 73,122 from Iraq were seeking refuge in Germany.[11] In 2016, 728,239 received asylum seekers' benefits in Germany. The largest groups of recipients were refugees from Afghanistan (18.8 per cent), Syria (16.4 per cent), Iraq (11.5 per cent), and Montenegro/Serbia/Kosovo (5.6 per cent) (Statistisches Bundesamt 2015). Of the 1,261,335 asylum applications made in the EU-28 countries in 2016, 16.9 per cent were made by Syrian citizens, 14.8 per cent by Afghan citizens, and 10.3 per cent by Iraqi citizens (Eurostat 2019). The wars in Afghanistan (since 2001) and Iraq (2003–2011) destabilised the entire region and contributed to creating conditions that enabled the rise of ISIS. The UK, Poland, and the Netherlands were involved in the Iraq War, and Germany, the UK, Italy, Bulgaria, Poland, Romania, Spain, and the Czech Republic in the Afghanistan War. ISIS was founded in 1999 and became active as a terrorist group in Iraq after the NATO intervention in 2003. The wars and the failed states created after Western interventions fostered conditions for the growth of Islamic terrorism (Alexander 2015; Anderson 2014). These conditions and the role EU countries played in the destabilisation of the Western Asian region are often forgotten in discussions of the refugee crisis. It is not a coincidence that the largest share of refugees coming to the EU flee from Syria, Afghanistan, and Iraq.

EU countries such as Hungary, Poland, the Czech Republic, Slovakia, and Romania have refused to take in refugees. The UK, Ireland, and Denmark are exempt because they have opted out of participating in EU asylum policies. Lacking coordination and EU solidarity, Germany was taking a leadership position and has taken in the absolute majority of refugees who have fled from their countries to the EU since 2015. Have social services in Germany suffered under this condition, as claimed by the AfD and its supporters?

TABLE 6.11   Selected spending items of the German federal budget

	2017	2016	2015	2014	2013
Total budget	€329.1 bn	€317.4 bn	€311.7 bn	€295.9 bn	€308.2 bn
Pensions	€98.3 bn (29.9%)	€93.1 bn (29.3%)	€90.2 bn (28.9%)	€88.3 bn (29.8%)	€85.2 bn (27.6%)
Military	€37.0 bn (11.2%)	€35.1 bn (11.1%)	€34.0 bn (10.9%)	€33.1 bn (11.2%)	€32.8 bn (10.6%)
Health insurance	€16.0 bn (4.9%)	€15.4 bn (4.9%)	€12.9 bn (4.1%)	€11.9 bn (4.0%)	€12.8 bn (4.2%)
Universities	€5.7 bn (1.7%)	€5.4 bn (1.7%)	€5.0 bn (1.6%)	€5.0 bn (1.7%)	€4.9 bn (1.6%)
Family assistance	€7.7 bn (2.3%)	€7.5 bn (2.4%)	€7.7 bn (2.5%)	€7.1 bn (2.4%)	€6.0 bn (1.9%)
Net benefits for asylum seekers	N/A	€9,234,622,000 (2.9%)	€5,230,723,000 (1.7%)	€2,364,284,000 (0.8%)	€1,491,289,000 (0.5%)

Sources: Bundesministerium für Finanzen (www.bundeshaushalt-info.de) and Statistisches Bundesamt (www.destatis.de)

While the share of net benefits for asylum seekers in the German budget has increased from 0.5 per cent in 2013 to 2.9 per cent in 2016, there have been no cuts to major social services: the budget share of family assistance increased from 1.9 per cent in 2013 to 2.3 per cent in 2017, the share of universities from 1.6 per cent to 1.7 per cent, the share of health insurance payments from 4.2 per cent to 4.9 per cent, and pension payments from 27.6 per cent to 29.9 per cent. The German budget for military affairs has in 2016 been four times as large as the one for asylum benefits. This circumstance is significant because military interventions played a role in creating chaotic conditions in the Middle East that benefited the rise of ISIS. Given that the German budget shares for social services such as healthcare, pensions, family assistance, and education have been rising and not shrinking, the claim of the AfD and its supporters that refugees are destroying the German welfare state is untrue. Data expose these claims as ideologies that aim at scapegoating and creating prejudices and negative sentiments against refugees and migrants in order to blame them for social problems and portray them as dangerous and a financial burden that harms society. The implication is that those voicing anti-refugee sentiments question the human right to asylum and wish that asylum seekers are deported to countries where they could be killed, that the boat people perish by drowning, or that refugees are exterminated.

Überfremdung/Over-Foreignerisation

Consider the following excerpt from an AfD campaign video that is organised as a dialogue between the two frontrunners Alice Weidel and Alexander Gauland:

[AliceWeidel:]	I have dared to do lots of things in my life. I gave up my job – in order to make politics for the AfD! They of all people. Concerned citizens, patriots and young wild ones – really not easy to find a common denominator! Why are you so worried about Germany?
[Alexander Gauland:]	I was in the CDU for 40 years. When they illegally opened the borders, it was clear to me that something was going wrong! If we now do not dare to say "This is our country – we say what is happening here!", then Germany will be erased from the map. Isn't that true, Ms. Weidel?
[Weidel:]	I rather prefer to say that all of this does not pay off. No country in the world can pay alimonies for hundred thousands of immigrants a year. [The slogan "Millions are already here!"

	appears in the video] Either Mrs. Merkel has a cash cow or she embezzles German taxes. One of both.
	[...] Dare you, Germany! AfD
[Gauland:]	Citizens with (cou)rage (Mutbürger) are needed now. Take back your country on the 24th of September!
[Other voice:]	Be brave, Germany! AfD
	(AfD campaign video on YouTube, www.youtube.com/watch? v=RRoHZ-QKwhk, 92,850 views [26 October 2017])

Gauland uses German nationalism for arguing that refugees are "erasing" Germany "from the map". The German *Volk* is presented as ethnically pure and under threat. In a speech to supporters on the election evening, Gauland said: "We will hunt them. We will hunt Mrs. Merkel or whomever. And we will take back our country and our people (*Volk*)."[12] To speak of "hunting" politicians is a militaristic diction that suggests combat and war. It also here becomes evident that Gauland sees refugees as anti-German elements that should not be allowed into the country and that one should get rid of. Weidel uses the ideological topoi of burdening and finances that we already discussed. The AfD in its campaign and also in this video used the term *Mutbürger* (citizens with courage). *Mut* (courage) rhymes on *Wut* (rage). *Mutbürger* is related to the term *Wutbürger* (enraged citizen). By speaking of *Mutbürger*, the AfD wants to communicate that those who are enraged about refugees should as response show the courage to vote for the AfD. Given the connotation of *Mut* with *Wut*, we have translated *Mutbürger* as "citizens with (cou)rage".

The discourse of over-foreignerisation (*Überfremdung* in German) could also be found in postings by the CSU and regular users:

So that Germany remains Germany! #Integration #ElectionArena
[Video, written text]: So that Germany remain Germany! (German) lead-culture Instead of multi-culturalism! Our country is and stays shaped by Christianity! Integration means demands and support! The Bavarian house rules: Learn German! Respect law and order! Earn your own living! Burka – No, thanks!

(Twitter-politician dataset, @CSU, ID 1586)

Germany needs an upper limit for refugees – We will enforce it! #Fünfkampf #5Kampf

(Twitter-politician dataset, @CSU, ID 1618)

Megalomaniac and self-destructive mass immigration advanced by the CDU. The Germans do not want Islamic terror, parallel societies and over-foreignerisation (*Überfremdung*). For the future of our kids, vote AfD!!!

(YouTube dataset, ID 22)

This is no longer to be surpassed in audacity. The world turns away in horror. Merkel destroys Germany and Europe with her multicultural racial fanaticism. The EU splinters itself. Our wives and children are sacrificed.

(YouTube dataset, ID 169)

The CSU is the Bavarian sister party of Merkel's CDU. Since the end of the Second World War, the CSU has held the position of the Minister-President of Bavaria in all but four years. In its 2017 election campaign, the CSU demanded an upper limit of 200,000 refugees in Germany per year. In the cited tweet as well as its election programme, the party opposes the German *Leitkultur* (lead-culture) to other cultures. It defines this lead-culture the following way: "Lead-culture entails the system of values shaped by Christianity that applies here with us, our morals and traditions as well as the basic rules of our living together"[13] (CSU 2017, 13).

Speaking of "over-foreignerisation", "multicultural racial fanaticism", or opposing German culture to multiculturalism, as the CSU does, is a version of nationalism and the friend/enemy logic that opposes an imagined unitary German culture to all other cultures. National unity is defined against an alien and intruding outside that should be kept at a distance or excluded. German lead-culture is defined in terms of language, morals, and religion.

TABLE 6.12 The development of the share of the members of specific religions in the total German population

	1956	2011	2015
Roman Catholic	45.9%	31.2%	28.9%
Protestant	50.1%	30.8%	27.1%
Islam	-	-	5.4%–5.7%
No religious conviction	-	33.0%	36.0%
Other (incl. no religion)	4.0%	-	-

Sources: Eicken and Schmitz-Veltin (2010), Forschungsgruppe Weltanschauungen in Deutschlandin (2019), Statistische Ämter des Bundes und der Länder (2014), Stichs (2016)

How has religious conviction changed in Germany (see Table 6.12)? In 2011, 31.2 per cent of German citizens said they were Roman Catholic and 30.8% said they were Protestant (Statistische Ämter des Bundes und der Länder 2014, 41). More than 26.3 million Germans (33.0 per cent) said they do not belong to or believe in any religion. According to estimations, the share of Muslims in the German population is between 5.4 per cent and 5.7 per cent (Stichs 2016). In 2015, the share of individuals without religious affiliation had increased to 36.0 per cent, whereas the share of Roman Catholics had decreased to 28.9 per cent and the share of Protestants to 27.1 per cent.[14]

In 1956, 50.1 per cent of Germans were Protestant and 45.9 per cent Roman Catholic (Eicken and Schmitz-Veltin 2010). This means that the major cultural change of Germany in the past 60 years was that the country became much more secular. The main cultural trend is not the increase of the share of Muslims that, with a total of around 5 per cent, is relatively modest, but rather the fact that those who today say that they do not belong to and do not believe in a religion form the largest population group. Germany has, independent of refugees, turned into a more heterogeneous culture that is not primarily defined by Christianity, but by secularism.

Demographic development is another reason why fears about immigration are unjustified. The Green Party stressed this circumstance in a campaign video:

> Germany needs immigration in the long term. That is why we propound an innovative and up-to-date immigration law. [...] We want to enable immigration for demographic purposes. Because in our ageing society, today's immigrants will help us tomorrow to keep up our social security systems in the long term.
>
> (Excerpt of spoken text in campaign video by Green Party, YouTube, www .youtube.com/watch?v=MGZc7lbW3DM, 1,166 views [26 October 2017])

In 2013, 15 per cent of the German population were aged 65 to 79 and 5 per cent were aged 80 or older (see Table 6.13). According to estimations, given current demographic

TABLE 6.13 Age groups in Germany

	2013	2060
65–79	15%	20%
>80	5%	13%
Total	20%	33%

Source: Statistisches Bundesamt (2015)

developments, in 2060 the German population will shrink from 80.8 million in 2013 to 67.7 million, the share of the 65–79 age group will have increased to 20 per cent, and the share of the group aged 80 older to 13 per cent (Statistisches Bundesamt 2015). As a consequence, the number of pensioners will increase under the given conditions. Pensions already today account for 30 per cent of the German budget and this share has increased rapidly. There are just four choices: either the pension system will in the future become unfundable; or pension contributions are increased, which weakens wages and thereby can have negative effects on the level of consumption, and thereby the total economy; or the pension age is drastically increased so that citizens work until they are dead or work until they are very old; or more immigrants and refugees are taken into the country and are allowed to work. In 2016, 83 per cent of first-time asylum seekers in the EU-28 countries were less than 35 years old, and 51 per cent were aged between 18 and 34 (Eurostat 2019). Refugees and immigrants do not threaten Western pension systems, but are an opportunity for guaranteeing these systems' sustainability if they are allowed to work.

Islam

Islam and Germany

We have seen in the previous section that some users and the CSU oppose German culture and Christianity to multiculturalism. The AfD radicalises this friend/enemy dualism by characterising Islam as not belonging to or being part of Germany. So, for example, Frauke Petry, who was then the AfD's federal spokesperson, tweeted:

> Islam does not belong to Germany! And the Greens obviously not into the Bundestag! #AfD #TrauDichDeutschland ow.ly/eXNz30fgYK7
> [Link to a Facebook posting by Petry, written text:]
>
> [...]
>
> ++ The Greens are unelectable ++
>
> Despite all horror messages all over the world and also in Germany, evidently the Greens hold on to the idea that Islam is part of Germany. Who does not remember when Göring-Eckardt said in 2015: "We suddenly get humans as a gift." Well, thank you very much for such presents! And now she even tops this and ridicules the victims of radical Islamism: "It would be very odd if we only had to deal with ourselves."

> The AfD says: Islam is not part of Germany. It is time for changes. Time to remove the Greens from the Bundestag. Time for the #AfD!
>
> (Twitter-politician dataset, #1811, @FraukePetry, https://twitter.com/FraukePetry/statuses/910186992993996800, 378 retweets, 1,127 likes [25 October 2017])

Intertextuality means a "combination of parts of other texts" in and with a specific text (Fairclough 2015, 37). A text is a semiotic unit of spoken, written, audiovisual, or digital elements that are the result of social practices and social production, enter the human meaning-making process, and are part of the human communication process: "Texts relate to other texts, represented by the media, through quotes or indirect references, thus already adding particular meanings or decontextualizing and recontextualizing meanings. Media thus produce and reproduce social meanings" (Wodak and Busch 2004, 106). Because of the World Wide Web and therefore also web-based social media's hypertextual, connected nature, intertextuality is prevalent online. Online texts are "multi-semiotic" texts (Fairclough 2015, 8). Frauke Petry's Twitter posting shows that right-wing authoritarianism online makes use of the interlinked structure of social media so that there are intertextual cross-references between texts published on Twitter, Facebook, YouTube, Instagram, Flickr, and other platforms. Twitter (4,026 references), YouTube (197) and Facebook (92) were particularly popular sources of interlinked social media texts in the dataset. The only traditional news medium receiving more links than YouTube was the website of the German newspaper *Die Welt* (welt.de, 285 links). Other news media mentioned as links, but much less popular than social media links, included, for example, Deutschlandfunk (99), ARD (daserste.de, 72), *Süddeutsche Zeitung* (64), *Der Spiegel* (50), and *Die Zeit* (49). There were 112 links to the news aggregation site pressportal.de. This result indicates that references to other social media texts are a very important source of intertextuality on social media.

The AfD and Islam

In its 2017 election programme, the AfD (2017) makes clear that it sees Germany as a religiously, culturally, morally, and linguistically unitary country and that it considers Islam as intrusive and alien:

> Islam does not belong to Germany. The AfD sees the expansion of Islam and the presence of 5 million Muslims, whose number is constantly growing, as a large danger to our state, our society, and our moral order. [...] The clash of cultures between the Occident and Islam as doctrine and carrier of cultural traditions and legal norms that are not capable of being integrated can only be averted by a bundle of defensive and

restrictive measures that prevent the further destruction of our European values based on which enlightened citizens live together. The AfD will not allow that Germany because of falsely understood tolerance loses its cultural face.[15]

(AfD 2017, 34, 47)

The AfD advances a cultural/new racism that operates with the topos of large numbers and constructs a clash of cultures between Germany and Europe on the one side and Islam and the Middle East on the other side. It characterises the first as enlightened, free, and Christian, and the latter as uncivilised and barbaric. This nativist discourse also uses the topos of culture that naturalises culture by arguing that "because the culture of a specific group of people is as it is, specific problems arise in specific situations" (Reisigl and Wodak 2001, 80). The AfD's ideology is characterised by new racism:

[New racism] is a racism whose dominant theme is not biological heredity but the insurmountability of cultural differences, a racism which, at first sight, does not postulate the superiority of certain groups or peoples in relation to others but "only" the harmfulness of abolishing frontiers, the incompatibility of life-styles and traditions.

(Balibar and Wallerstein 1991, 21)

The AfD's argumentation overlooks that this very logic of radical dualism has in Germany resulted in Auschwitz as the culmination of the dialectic of the Enlightenment (Horkheimer and Adorno 2002). To claim that Germany has been a historical project of Enlightenment and moral progress downplays Nazi-Germany's horrors.

By mentioning the claim that "Islam is not part of Germany" together with the "victims of radical Islamism", Petry, on the one hand, uses a victimonym (Reisigl and Wodak 2001, 52) that presents the Germans and Europeans as victims of Islam that is presented as being inherently hostile, violent, and terrorist. Many social media postings in the analysed datasets used the same logic:

No other country in the world lets hundreds of thousands of people into the country without any controls and registration! But the worst is that these are people from cultures that considers us Europeans as infidels and that should according to religious scriptures like the Koran be fought. This is exactly what we experience in numerous terror attacks and it is far from over.

(Facebook dataset, #1130)

Do you want to live in a country whose security ranking has dropped 40 positions behind Rwanda and Oman? That houses 5 million Muslims and builds mosques while churches are demolished? That is not capable of deporting highly dangerous Islamists? Where parents are afraid to send their child to the kindergarten, where hardly anyone speaks German? Where the Romani and the Sinti inhabit whole streets, throw garbage out of the window or into the garden. In an EU, where the Greeks can no longer afford cancer medication, but rejected asylum seekers are in Germany insured at the expense of the state? If so, then Angela Merkel is your first choice.

(YouTube dataset, ID 131)

A country, where you must take care that there is not one who shouts Allahu Akbar in order to drive a lorry into human beings. For a Germany where Islamic terrorists have a good life and like to life! Thank you, Merkel.

(YouTube dataset, ID 627)

ISIS

In such postings, Islam, Muslims, non-Europeans, and other cultures are associated with the topos of large numbers, "numerous terror attacks", "dangerous Islamists", "Islamic terrorists", and driving "a lorry into human beings". Since 2015, a number of terrorist attacks conducted by supporters of ISIS in the name of Allah have been conducted in Germany. ISIS's ideology is based on a minority interpretation of Sunni Islam that wants to advance the Ummah and create a caliphate, calls for a war against non-Muslims and Shia Muslims, is anti-socialist and anti-Marxist, and is strongly patriarchal. It is culturally conservative and opposes homosexuality as well as extramarital and premarital sex. ISIS wants to create a religiously politicised economy and society, in which non-Muslims can be enslaved, women who are polytheistic or worship representations of god can be turned into sex-slaves, and non-Muslims can be turned into feudal serfs who have to pay rent to the Ummah. Transforming enemies into slaves is also considered as a practice of warfare. ISIS's use of technology, such as social media, the Internet, the politics of mediated spectacle and glossy magazines such as *Dabiq*, or the role of fighters who are citizens of, grew up in, and were educated in Western countries, also shows that it is not a pre- or anti-modern movement, but rather appropriates modernity and modern media for its own religious and political purposes: "Instead of seeing in ISIS a case of extreme resistance to modernization, one should rather conceive of it as a case of perverted modernization and locate it into the series of conservative modernizations" (Žižek 2014).

ISIS and its ideology certainly pose threats to humanism. But a minority ideology is not characteristic of Islam as such. The AfD and its supporters present Islam as such as militaristic and terrorist by, on the one hand, using militarionyms (Reisigl and Wodak 2001, 51) that associate Islam in general with violence and terror and by, on the other hand, using generalising synecdoches. "Synecdoches (from the Greek: 'to take up with something else') are substitutions within one and the same field of reference: a term is replaced by another term" (Reisigl and Wodak 2001, 57). The generalising synecdoche is a linguistic construct, in which a whole is presented as standing for a part. In the discourse of AfD supporters, Islam is presented as a whole that is characterised in general by features of a small part, namely supporters of ISIS. In the mentioned examples, synecdoches such as "people from cultures that consider us Europeans as infidels [...] that should [...] be fought [...] in terror attacks" or "one who shouts Allahu Akbar in order to drive a lorry into human beings" can be found.

The Logical Fallacy of Inductive Generalisation

It is a logical fallacy to generalise from single examples to the whole. Inductive generalisations are logical inferences that are often incorrect. They do not abstract from single individuals, observations, events, or experiences, but take them to be the nature and essence of the whole. This reductionist logic fails because it reduces the complexity of the world to individual instances of the world. Inductive generalisation and generalising as well as particularising synecdoches are characteristic for the logic of stereotypical ideologies such as racism, nationalism, and fascism.

Donald Trump also used the logic of inductive generalisation to argue for banning citizens from Iran, Iraq, Libya, Somalia, Sudan, Syria, and Yemen from entering the United States

TABLE 6.14   ISIS supporters' terror attacks in Germany

Date	Location	Terrorist(s)	Country of origin	Lived in Germany since ...
17 September 2015	Berlin	Rafik Mohamed Yousef	Iraq	1996
26 February 2016	Hannover	Safia S.	Morocco	her birth
16 April 2016	Essen	Yusuf T., Mohammed O.	Germany	their birth
18 July 2016	Würzburg	Riaz Khan Ahmadzai (also known as Muhammad Riyad)	Afghanistan	2015
24 July 2016	Ansbach	Mohammed Daleel	Syria	2014
19 December 2016	Berlin	Anis Amris	Tunisia	2015
28 July 2017	Hamburg	Ahmad A.	Palestine	2015

and to suspend Syrian refugees from coming to the USA. In the "100-Day Plan to Make America Great Again", Trump announced a plan to "suspend immigration from terror-prone regions where vetting cannot safely occur" (Trump 2016). "Everybody is arguing whether or not it is a BAN. Call it what you want, it is about keeping bad people (with bad intentions) out of country!" (Twitter, @RealDonaldTrump, 1 February 2017). The basic argument is that all citizens from certain predominantly Muslim countries are potential terrorists. Trump uses generalising logic for ideologically justifying the "Muslim ban".

The AfD's inductive generalisation that ISIS's ideology and terrorism are characteristic for all of Islam disregards that it is a very small share of Muslims in Germany who commit terrorist attacks. Table 6.14 provides an overview of terrorist attacks committed by ISIS supporters in Germany.

About 4.7 million Muslims live in Germany (Stichs 2016). Eight of them committed terrorist attacks since 2015, which is a share of 0.00017 per cent of the total German Muslim population. Between January 2015 and September 2017 when the German elections took place, 1,390,500 applications for asylum were made in Germany (Bundeszentrale für politische Bildung 2017). Four out of eight terrorists came into Germany at the time of the refugee crisis; the other four had either been born in Germany or had lived there for a very long time. This circumstance shows that closing off the borders and letting no refugees in is no solution because a significant share of terrorists are citizens of the country where they commit attacks. Four out of 1.4 million refugees, which is 0.0003 per cent, committed terror attacks in Germany. It is a logical fallacy to assume that all Muslims in Germany are terrorists because 0.00017 per cent of Muslims and 0.0003 per cent of asylum seekers committed terrorist attacks. In a response to one of the above-cited social media postings, a user stressed the absurdity of this logic:

> The sentence "A country, where you must take care that there is not one who shouts Allahu Akbar in order to drive a lorry into human beings" is absurd because it suggests that something like that happens frequently (and that one must be afraid of it), although just 12 people were killed in comparable events. Compared to other causes of death in Germany this is extremely rare.

> (YouTube dataset, ID 633)

The problem, however, is that racist prejudices and stereotypes have an emotional and ideological character that cannot easily be challenged by facts and numbers. In the age of social media, right-wing authoritarian ideology that scapegoats and intensifies stereotypes circulates and spreads online.

6.4 Conclusion

Global, neoliberal capitalism has in recent years experienced an economic, political, and ideological crisis that has resulted in the strengthening of nationalist and right-wing authoritarian movements, parties, and leaders. In the EU, the political crisis has been worsened by the EU Commission's predominant focus on neoliberal market policies that rendered Europe unprepared for the refugee crisis. The institutional lack of social solidarity in the EU has benefited the rise of nationalist and xenophobic sentiments against refugees. Neoliberalism's logic of global accumulation by dispossession (Harvey 2003) has backfired and turned into the rise of authoritarian capitalism (Fuchs 2018a).

Right-Wing Authoritarianism

In Germany, right-wing authoritarianism was strengthened by the AfD becoming the third-largest party in the 2017 Bundestag elections. The typical AfD voter is male, unemployed or a blue-collar worker, and has a low level of education. The declassed classes or those having fears of being declassed form the mass base of right-wing authoritarian movements. The AfD appeals to these classes' fears and emotions by a highly polarising ideology. Figure 6.1 presents a model of right-wing politics.

The AfD and Right-Wing Authoritarianism

Authoritarian leadership, nationalism, the friend/enemy logic, and militarism interact in right-wing authoritarian ideology (Fuchs 2018a). The AfD managed to achieve visibility on social media, which has allowed it to circulate right-wing authoritarian ideology online.

In terms of leadership, the AfD has chosen the combination of a man (Alexander Gauland) and a woman (Alice Weidel). Weidel is a woman who lives in a relationship with another woman and is articulate and media-savvy. Gauland was an active CDU member for 40 years before he helped create the AfD. He is the more traditional rightwing authoritarian leader, who uses highly polarising statements with simplified messages, whereas Weidel tries to convey the same ideological message in a calmer, more nuanced, more intellectual, and less provocative manner.

FIGURE 6.1 Right-wing politics

In the contemporary information society, political communication and media presence play an important role in elections. The presented analysis provides indications that the AfD and its supporters dominated the online discourse on refugees, migration, the EU, and Islam by appealing to users' fears of social decline, crime, terror, and cultural change, using social media bots and fostering an online culture of spreading, sharing, commenting, and user-generated content. The AfD's main social media accounts, such as the Twitter profiles @AfD_Bund (now @AfD), @Alice_Weidel, and @FraukePetry, acted as online leaders who choreographed the participation and engagement of AfD supporters in online nationalism and online right-wing authoritarianism. The AfD used social media as a medium where dissatisfied and anxious citizens can channel their frustrations, fears, and disappointments into nationalism and (new) racism. Other parties and politicians largely missed the opportunity to foster online campaigns in which activists could have challenged the AfD's ideology. There is also empirical evidence that the AfD and other far-right groups are particularly active in spreading fake news and that their supporters, to a much higher degree than the average voter, believe in the truth of fake news.

The discourse topics of Germany, the EU, refugees, and Islam were closely linked in the analysed datasets. The typical logic of argumentation is that the German nation and a European Occident are unitary communities that are under attack and face the threat of being destroyed by refugees and Muslims. We have seen that the main cultural change in Germany is not the increase of the share of Muslims, but the weakening of Christianity by the strengthening of secularism. Germany, like other Western countries, has for a long time been culturally heterogeneous.

Capitalist Donors and Supporters

In capitalist society, spreading ideas, worldviews, propaganda, and ideology in the public sphere is work-intensive and expensive. It is a time-intensive activity operating in a high-speed, superficial capitalist attention economy with short attention time, in which attention is short-lived and a key resource, time is money, and money purchases attention time. Producing attention in the capitalist public requires public relations labour and money invested into PR and advertising.

In late 2018, the German newspaper *Süddeutsche Zeitung* published an article which argued that Alice Weidel had received illegal donations from a company in Switzerland (Pittelkow and Riedel 2018). The newspaper wrote that in 2017, the AfD district chapter Bodensee, where Weidel lives, received donations amounting to a total of around €130,000 from the Swiss pharmaceutical company PWS PharmaWholeSale International AG (Pittelkow and Riedel 2018). According to German law, donations to parties from non-EU countries are illegal (Party Law [*Parteiengesetz*], §25).[16] Donations by EU citizens form an exception. The newspaper wrote that the donor indicated "campaign donation Alice Weidel SocialMedia" ("WAHLKAMPFSPENDE ALICE WEIDEL SOCIALMEDIA") as purpose of the financial flows (Grill et al. 2018). It is not known if and how the donations were used. According to news sources, the AfD transferred the donations back nine months after having received them (Grill et al. 2018), which was long after the

Bundestag election, in which the AfD made major gains, had taken place. The images of a bank statement published by German public service broadcasters ARD, WDR, and NDR indicate that the donor intended that at least some of the money should have been used for social media propaganda, which shows that capitalists supporting nationalists consider social media an important way of influencing the public and see money as a means for purchasing attention given to ideology. On 21 November 2018, Alice Weidel said in a speech in the German Bundestag: "Yes, it is right that we made mistakes in dealing with campaign donations."[17]

Die Zeit reported that the shipping company owner Folkard Edler donated significant amounts to the AfD and gave a loan to the party under very favourable conditions (Kartheuser and Middelhoff 2017). The newspaper also wrote that former officials of the Federation of German Industries (BDI: Bundesverband der Deutschen Industrie) had supported the AfD (Kartheuser and Middelhoff 2017). News media reported that the Swiss PR agency Goal AG helped to organise ads, election posters, papers, billboards, images, and websites of the AfD (Bensmann and von Daniels 2017; Frontal21 2017a, 2017b). *Der Spiegel* and *WOZ* reported that it is likely German billionaire August von Finck Jr., who in 2018 was the world's 167th richest person,[18] indirectly supported the AfD (Jikjareva et al. 2018; Spiegel 2018). AfD politicians Alice Weidel, Peter Boehringer, and Beatrix von Storch are members of the Hayek Gesellschaft (Hayek Society) that spreads the economist Friedrich Hayek's neoliberal ideology (Riedel and Pittelkow 2017), which shows an ideological affiliation of key AfD politicians with neoliberalism. The far-right has historically always supported capitalism and has depended on capitalist support.

The Logic of Nationalism and Racism

All forms of racism and nationalism define a national community in opposition to an outside. The friend/enemy logic is closely interlinked with nationalism. Table 6.15 provides a systematic overview of nationalism and racism's friend/enemy logic.

In the analysed dataset, the AfD and AfD supporters especially used cultural and socio-economic forms of racism. The duality of cultural and socio-economic racism, for example, is evident in the AfD campaign video, in which Gauland says that refugees are erasing Germany from the map, whereas Weidel claims that Germany cannot pay "alimonies for hundred thousands of immigrants a year". In the socio-economic form of the friend/enemy scheme, refugees were presented as a financial burden for Germany. In reality, Germany's welfare budget for pensions, education,

TABLE 6.15 A typology of racism's friend/enemy logic along societal dimensions

Type of ascertained difference in nationalism and racism	Examples
Natural	"They look different", "They are by nature aggressive/dirty/criminal/lazy/noisy/smelly/ill-adapted/violent, etc.", etc.
Socio-economic	"They take away our jobs/benefits/houses/educational or healthcare opportunities, etc.", "They degrade our social system/wages/education system/pension system/welfare system/healthcare system, etc.", etc.
Political	"They come from an authoritarian country", "They do not know/respect Western political values", "They are used to a political system dominated by crime", "They are criminals/do not follow our laws", etc.
Cultural	"They have different values and morals", "In their culture, it is usual to ...", "They speak a different language/have different habits/ways of behaviour/mentality/symbols/traditions, etc.", "They destroy our language/culture/traditions/character, etc.", "They come from a culture of aggression/laziness/criminality, etc.", "They have a different lifestyle", "They do not want to adapt", "They treat women badly", "They have too many children", "They wear strange clothes", "They have bad food tastes/habits", etc.

Source: Based on van Dijk (1987, 59)

healthcare, etc. has not been reduced in recent years. Given its demographic development, Germany needs immigrant workers in order to be able to fund its pension system in the future. The cultural version of the friend/enemy scheme characterises Germany and Europe as humane, civil, democratic, and enlightened, and Islam and refugees as holding an inhumane, uncivil, backward, and barbaric religious ideology, culture, and lifestyle that fosters terror and threatens the existence of German culture. This new cultural racism uses generalising synecdoches and the logic of inductive generalisation in order to construct the stereotype that all refugees and all Muslims are violent and terrorists. Single examples of religiously motivated terrorists are generalised, and it is claimed that violence and terror form an inherent and natural essence of the refugees' culture and religion.

The friend/enemy logic tends to be combined with calls for the defence of the friend community against the constructed enemies. Militarism is the practical political-ideological expression and the friend/enemy scheme's logic. In the final instance, militarism sees war as the appropriate response to conflict. In the analysed datasets, militarist discourse was present in calls for building a wall around Europe, constructing a fortress Europe, or hunting people.

The communication of right-wing authoritarianism online was a significant element in the AfD's 2017 election campaign. Social media accounts were used for communicating right-wing authoritarianism online and for leading and choreographing the engagement of supporters in communicating nationalism, friend/enemy logic, and militarism online. Whereas social media as means for communicating right-wing authoritarianism are relatively new, the ideology itself is as old as capitalism. Right-wing authoritarianism tries to distract from the complex causes of society's problems and how they are grounded in structures of class and domination by constructing scapegoats, nationalism, and blaming certain groups for social problems and the alleged threats to the nation. Karl Marx, in 1870, discussed the role of ideology in distracting attention from class struggle and benefiting the ruling class. Marx dealt with the question of nationalism's creation of false consciousness among the working class in one country so that it hates immigrant workers and workers in the colonies. He specifically addressed that question in respect to Ireland, which he saw as a British colony:

> Ireland is the BULWARK of the *English landed aristocracy.* The exploitation of this country is not simply one of the main sources of their material wealth; it is their greatest *moral* power. [...] And most important of all! All industrial and commercial centres in England now have a working class *divided* into two *hostile* camps, English PROLETARIANS and Irish PROLETARIANS. The ordinary English worker hates the Irish worker as a competitor who forces down the STANDARD OF LIFE. In relation to the Irish worker, he feels himself to be a member of the *ruling nation* and, therefore, makes himself a tool of his aristocrats and capitalists *against Ireland,* thus strengthening their domination *over himself.* He harbours religious, social and national prejudices against him. [...] This antagonism is kept artificially alive and intensified by the press, the pulpit, the comic papers, in short by all the means at the disposal of the ruling class. *This antagonism* is the *secret of the English working class's impotence,* despite its organisation. It is the secret of the maintenance of power by the capitalist class. And the latter is fully aware of this.
>
> (Marx 1870, 473, 474, 475)

Opposition to the AfD on Social Media

In the analysed datasets, there were different reactions of the AfD's opponents to right-wing authoritarianism. The *first reaction* was the call for ignoring or closing right-wing extremist comments and threads:

Maybe one should turn off the comment section on YouTube. Only insults and insinuations of the worst kind can be found there.

(YouTube dataset, ID 640)

The *second reaction* was that users stressed facts as counter-evidence to right-wing authoritarian ideology:

Facts instead of horror scenarios. #TVDuell #Refugees
[Image showing a family, the Earth, and migration flows, written text:] 65 million people worldwide are currently seeking refuge. Developing countries take in 90% of them.

(Twitter-politician dataset, @Die_Gruenen, ID 1735)

The *third reaction* was that users and politicians characterised ideological claims as racism and Nazi-ideology:

#Gauland talks like a Nazi. The #AfD is a disgrace for Germany.
[Excerpt from a speech by Martin Schulz, in which he says:] We are a country, where there will never ever again be room for Nazi-ideology. But we have guys of this type. Guys, who hold the opinion that nobody wants to be the neighbour of Jérôme Boateng.[19] This organisation of agitators is not an alternative for Germany, but a disgrace for the Federal Republic.

(Twitter-politician dataset, @SPDde, ID 1386, http://twitter.com/spdde/sta tuses/902424311625113600, 140 retweets, 399 likes [25 October 2017])

[Anonymous] what do you have against refugees? They are only human beings. Oh, I forgot that you are a racist XD

(YouTube dataset, ID 540)

The *fourth reaction* was the attempt to deconstruct ideology by arguing that the topic that really matters is social (in)justice:

The tax refugees are the most expensive refugees. @DietmarBartsch #btw17 #linke
(Twitter-politician dataset, @DieLinke, ID 1654)

Let us take back the country!. Socially. Just. Peace. For all.

[Dietmar Bartsch]: Comrades, Die Linke will never put up with politics that washes dead children up to the beaches.

[Bernd Riexinger:] For those who have a bit of reason it must be the most important goal to keep the AfP out of the Landtage [regional parliaments] and the Bundestag.

[Dietmar Bartsch:] Comrades, the fact remains: The tax refugees are the most expensive refugees.

(Excerpt of spoken text in campaign video by Die Linke, YouTube, www .youtube.com/watch?v=wddS9dCXXGc)

Such communicative strategies can to a certain degree appeal to those who already oppose right-wing authoritarianism. But they have a limited capacity to convince AfD supporters because right-wing authoritarianism does not operate with facts and rational arguments. It operates with emotions and appeals to fears and hopes. Counter-strategies therefore need to take political psychology into account.

Appendix 6.A

Social Media Data Collection

Tables 6.16–6.18 show the relevant political profiles on Twitter and the relevant Facebook pages and YouTube channels that were used for data collection.

TABLE 6.16 Twitter profiles used in the analysis

Party	Worldview	Twitter profile
CDU	Conservativism	@RegSprecher @CDU
CSU	Conservativism	@CSU
SPD	Social democracy	@MartinSchulz @SPDde
AfD	Right-wing extremism	@AfD_Bund @AfDKompakt @FraukePetry @Alice_Weidel
Die Linke	Socialism	@DieLinke @SWagenknecht @DietmarBartsch
Die Grünen	Green politics	@Die_Gruenen @Cem_Oezdemir @GoeringEckart
FDP	Liberalism	@FDP @C_Lindner
NPD	Right-wing extremism	@FrankFranz @NPDde

168 Nationalism on Social Media

TABLE 6.17 Facebook pages used in the analysis

Party	Worldview	Facebook page
CDU	Conservativism	www.facebook.com/AngelaMerkel www.facebook.com/CDU www.facebook.com/Bundesregierung/
CSU	Conservativism	www.facebook.com/HorstSeehofer www.facebook.com/joachim.herrmann.csu https://de-de.facebook.com/CSU/
SPD	Social democracy	https://de-de.facebook.com/martinschulz/ https://de-de.facebook.com/SPD/
AfD	Right-wing extremism	www.facebook.com/alternativefuerde www.facebook.com/afdkompakt/ www.facebook.com/Dr.Frauke.Petry www.facebook.com/aliceweidel/
Die Linke	Socialism	https://de-de.facebook.com/linkspartei/ www.facebook.com/sahra.wagenknecht/ www.facebook.com/DietmarBartschMdB
Die Grünen	Green politics	www.facebook.com/B90DieGruenen www.facebook.com/Cem https://de-de.facebook.com/GoeringEckardt/
FDP	Liberalism	www.facebook.com/FDP https://de-de.facebook.com/lindner.christian/

TABLE 6.18 YouTube channels used in the analysis

Party	Worldview	YouTube channel
CDU	Conservativism	www.youtube.com/user/bundesregierung www.youtube.com/user/cdutv www.youtube.com/user/cducsu/
CSU	Conservativism	www.youtube.com/user/csumedia
SPD	Social democracy	www.youtube.com/channel/UCZxdUyoP3mJY496WCjVKgBQ www.youtube.com/user/SPDvision
AfD	Right-wing extremism	www.youtube.com/channel/UCq2rogaxLtQFrYG3X3KYNww
Die Linke	Socialism	www.youtube.com/user/dielinke
Die Grünen	Green politics	www.youtube.com/user/GRUENE
FDP	Liberalism	www.youtube.com/user/FDP

Appendix 6.B

German Originals of the Analysed Social Media Postings

Ein Deutschland, in dem wir gut und gerne leben. Dafür arbeiten Angela #Merkel und die #CDU. #fedidwgugl

[CDU campaign video, shows a foetus at the start, text spoken by Angela Merkel:] In welchem Deutschland wirst Du einmal leben? Wird es das Deutschland sein, das uns am Herzen liegt? Ein Land der Bildung, in dem jeder etwas aus einem Leben machen kann? Ein Deutschland der Chancen, in dem mehr Menschen Arbeit haben als je zuvor? Ein Land, das sich nicht aus seinen Erfolgen ausruht, sondern immer neue Lösungen für die Zukunft findet? Es liegt in unserer Hand! Wir können uns für dieses Deutschland entscheiden. Für ein Land, das schon heute dafür sorgt, dass es auch morgen gute Arbeit gibt, das Menschen im Alter und bei Krankheit nicht alleine lässt. Für ein Land, in dem wir gemeinsam gegen Hass und Neid eintreten. Ein Land, das seine europäischen Werte entschlossen verteidigt. WIr können uns für eine Politik entscheiden, die Familien respektiert und unterstützt. Für eine Wirtschaft, die für alle Wohlstand schafft. Für eine Heimat, in der sich jeder Einzelne frei und sicher fühlen kann. Dein Deutschland soll ein Land sein, in dem wir alle gut und gerne leben. Für dieses Deutschland möchte ich auch in Zukunft mit ganzer Kraft einsetzen. Dafür bitte ich um Ihre Unterstützung!

[Written text:] Am 24. September mit beiden Stimmen CDU.

(Twitter-politician dataset, @CDU, ID 1680, http://twitter.com/CDU/statuses/ 908417730830852098)

In welchem Deutschland wir leben wollen? Unsere Antwort auf Euren Spot fällt etwas anders aus. #ZeitFürMartin

[Video showing a foetus. Text spoken by Martin Schulz:] In welchem Land möchtest Du mal leben? Hoffentlich in einem Land, das mehr Geld in Schulen und Bildung investiert als in Panzer und Drohnen. Hoffentlich in einem Land, in dem du von deiner Rente gut leben kannst und nicht bis Siebzig arbeiten mußt. In einem Land, in dem alle gerechte Löhne bekommen und Frauen so viel verdienen wie Männer. Hoffentlich in einem Land, in dem Dinge angepackt

statt ausgesessen werden. In einem Land, in dem es gerecht zugeht. Zum Glück lebst du in einem Land, in dem deine Eltern das Kreuz an der richtigen Stelle machen können
[SPD-Logo and text „Zeit für mehr Gerechtigkeit"]

(Twitter-politician dataset, @SPDde, ID 1256, https://twitter.com/spdde/statuses/ 900651836537024514)

Für ein Deutschland, in dem man alles werden kann: arbeitslos, mittellos, heimatlos!

(YouTube dataset, ID 44)

Auf jeden fall kämpft merkel dafür, daß im zukünftigen deutschland keine deutschen mehr leben, sondern nur noch deutsche mit migrationshintergrund.

(YouTube dataset, ID 98)

Seit 2015 wird Europa vom Terror überrannt und sie redet von Frieden und einem Land, in dem wir gern und gut leben. Sicherheit des Volkes steht nicht auf der Agenda, was ?

(Facebook dataset, ID 1960)

[Alexander Gauland:] Frau Merkel hat keinen Goldesel, doch einen Plan. Deshalb hält sie auch ihre Europapläne geheim. Ich wette mit Ihnen, dass es nach der Wahl einen Schuldenschnitt Griechenlands gibt – zu Lasten der deutschen Bürger.
[Alice Weidel:] Nicht mit der AfD! Die Deutschen brauchen eine Partei, die endlich wieder ihre Interessen vertritt! Deutsche Interessen! Nicht rechts – sondern rechtens. Und größer als 15 Prozent.

(AfD campaign video on YouTube, www.youtube.com/watch?v=RRoHZ-QKwhk, 92,850 views [26 October 2017])

Europa ist ein Friedensprojekt ?! Wir in Deutschland und in Europa erleben eine Invasion fremde Völker und fremde Kultur

(Facebook dataset, ID 1887)

Was Merkel dafür kann ??? Sie hat durch ihre Einladung erst diese unglaubliche Flüchtlingsinvasion in Gang gesetzt, wodurch zig tausende islamistische

Terroristen unkontrolliert nach Europa gekommen sind !!! Wer das nicht sieht ist völlig blind ! (Facebook dataset, ID 1127)
Festung Europa! Macht die Grenzen DICHT!

(YouTube dataset, ID 409)

Wir Brauchen eine Festung Europa und die wird es nur mit der AfD geben

(Facebook dataset, ID 1023)

Wir brauchen eine Mauer um ganz Europa!

(YouTube dataset, ID 472)

Deutsche RECHTSRADIKALE haben in Europa ein gewaltiges Blutbad angerichtet. Nur Vollidioten sind heute noch rechts!

(YouTube dataset, ID 831)

#AliceWeidelLive zum #TVDuell: Merkels Flüchtlingspolitik zerstört den Sozialstaat ⬤: Die #AfD wird dafür sorgen, dass das ein Ende hat!
[Video showing Alice Weidel, saying:] Merkels Flüchtlingspolitik zerstört den Sozialstaat der Bundesrepublik Deutschand. Wir als #AfD werden dafür sorgen, dass das ein Ende hat! Denn offene Grenzen und ein nachhaltiger Sozialstaat funktioniert nicht.

(Twitter-politician dataset, @Alice_Weidel, ID 1368, https://twitter.com/Alice_ Weidel/statuses/904414469090148355, 341 retweets, 768 likes [25 October 2017])

#TVDuell Natürlich müssen wir bis 70 arbeiten. Irgendjemand muss die Sozialkassen für die Flüchtlinge ja füllen. #AfDwaehlen #AfD

(TV-debate Twitter dataset, ID 149)

Wir Deutsche selber brauchen unser Geld dafür wir auch arbeiten gehen für unsere Familien und Kranke und unsere Alten Leute die ihr Leben lang gearbeitet haben für ihre Rente. So sied es aus und nicht anders die Afd hat gute Ansetze und so kann sich alles Ändern. In unserem Deutschland.

(Facebook dataset, ID 4409)

[Alice Weidel:] Ich hab mich einiges in meinem Leben getraut. Meinen Job an den Nagel gehängt – um Politik zu machen für die AfD! Ausgerechnet für die. Besorgte Bürger, Patrioten und junge Wilde – wirklich nicht leicht hier einen Nenner zu finden! Warum machst du dir überhaupt so viele Gedanken um Deutschland?

[Alexander Gauland:] Ich war 40 Jahre in der CDU. Die illegale Öffnung der Grenzen, da war mir klar: Hier läuft etwas schief! Wenn wir uns jetzt nicht trauen zu sagen: „Das ist unser Land – wir bestimmen hier!", dann wird Deutschland von der Landkarte verschwinden. Nicht wahr, Frau Weidel?

[Weidel:] Ich sage lieber, das rechnet sich nicht. Kein Land der Welt kann jährlich hunderttausende Zuwanderer alimentieren. [Slogan „Millionen sind schon hier!" erscheint im Video] Entweder hat Frau Merkel einen Goldesel oder sie veruntreut deutsches Steuergeld. Eins von beidem.

[…]

[Gauland:] Die Mutbürger sind jetzt gefragt. Holen Sie sich am 24. September Ihr Land wieder zurück!

[Other voice:] Trau dich Deutschland! AfD

(AfD campaign video on YouTube, www.youtube.com/watch?v=RRoHZ-QKwhk, 92,850 views [26 October 2017])

Damit Deutschland Deutschland bleibt! #Integration #Wahlarena

[Video, written text:] Damit Deutschland Deutschland bleibt! Leitkultur statt Multikulti! Unser Land ist und bleibt christlich geprägt! Fordern & Fördern bei der Integration! Bayerische Hausordnung: Deutsch lernen! Recht & Gesetz achten! Lebensunterhalt verdienen! Burka – Nein Danke!,

(Twitter-politician dataset, @CSU, ID 1586)

Deutschland braucht eine Obergrenze für Flüchtlinge – Wir werden das durchsetzen! #Fünfkampf #5Kampf

(Twitter-politician dataset, @CSU, ID 1618)

größenwahnsinnige und selbstzerstörerische Masseneinwanderung der CDU. Die Deutschen wollen keinen Islamistischen Terror, keine Parallelgesellschaften und keine Überfremdung. Für die Zukunft unserer Kinder AfD wählen!!!

(YouTube dataset, ID 22)

Das ist an dreistigkeit nicht mehr zu übertreffen. Die Welt wendet sich mit entsetzen ab. Merkel zerstört Deutschland und Europa mit ihrem multi kulti Rassenwahn. Die EU zersplittert sich. Unsere Frauen und Kinder werden geopfert.

(YouTube dataset, ID 169)

Deutschland ist langfristig auf Einwanderung angewiesen. Deshalb legen wir ein innovatives und zeitgemäßes Einwanderungsgesetz vor. [...] Wir wollen demografische Zuwanderung ermöglichen. In unserer alternden Gesellschaft werden uns die Einwanderer von heute nämlich morgen dabei helfen, unsere sozialen Sicherungssysteme langfristig zu behalten.

(Excerpt of spoken text in campaign video by Green Party, YouTube, www .youtube.com/watch?v=MGZc7lbW3DM, 1,166 views [26 October 2017])

Islam gehört nicht zu Deutschland!▇▇und Grüne offenbar nicht in den▇▇
  Bundestag! #AfD #TrauDichDeutschland ow.ly/eXNz30fgYK7
  [Link to a Facebook posting by Petry, written text:]
  ++ Grüne unwählbar ++
  Trotz aller Horrorbotschaften weltweit und auch in Deutschland halten die Grünen offenbar daran fest, dass der Islam zu Deutschland gehöre. Wer erinnert sich nicht an den Ausspruch von Göring-Eckardt aus 2015: „Wir kriegen jetzt plötzlich Menschen geschenkt." Na, vielen Dank für solche Geschenke!
  Nun setze Sie noch einen drauf und verhöhnt die Opfer des radikalen Islamismus: "Es wäre sehr langweilig, wenn wir nur mit uns zu tun hätten"
  Die AfD erklärt: Der Islam gehört nicht zu Deutschland. Es ist Zeit für Veränderungen. Zeit, die Grünen aus dem Bundestag zu entfernen. Zeit für die #AfD!

(Twitter-politician dataset, #1811, @FraukePetry, https://twitter.com/FraukePetry/ statuses/910186992993996800, 378 retweets, 1,127 likes [25 October 2017])

Kein anderes Land der Welt lässt hunderttausende Leute völlig unkontrolliert und ohne Registrierung in sein Land! Das Schlimme ist noch, dass es Leute aus Kulturkreisen sind, für die wir Europäer Ungläubige sind, die es laut religiöser Schriften wie dem Koran zu bekämpfen gilt. Genau das erleben wir in zahlreichen Terroranschlägen und es ist noch lange nicht vorbei.

(Facebook dataset, #1130)

Wollen Sie in einem Land leben, das im Sicherheitsranking 40 Plätze hinter Ruanda und Oman gefallen ist? Welches 5 Millionen Muslime beherbergt und Moscheen errichtet, wÃhrend Kirchen abgerissen werden? Welches nicht in der Lage ist, brandgefährliche Islamisten abzuschieben? In welchem Eltern Angst haben ihr Kind in einen Kindergarten zu stecken, in dem kaum jemand deutsch kann? In welchem ganze Straßenzüge von Roma und Sinti bewohnt werden, die Müll aus dem Fenster oder in den Garten werfen. In einer EU, in dem sich Griechen keine Krebsmedikamente mehr leisten können, abgelehnte Asylanten aber auf Staatskosten in D versichert sind? Dann, ja dann, ist Angela Merkel ihre 1.Wahl.

(YouTube dataset, ID 131)

Ein Land in dem man sich umgucken muss das nicht einer Allahu Akbar ruft um kurz danach mit einerm LKW in Menschen reinzurasen. Für ein Deutschland in dem Islamische Terroristen gut und gerne leben! Danke Merkel

(YouTube dataset, ID 627)

Der Satz "Ein Land in dem man sich umgucken muss das nicht einer Allahu Akbar ruft um kurz danach mit einerm LKW in Menschen reinzurasen." ist absurd, da er suggeriert, so etwas würde häufig passieren (und man müsse Angst davor haben), tatsächlich jedoch nur 12 Menschen bei vergleichbaren Vorfällen umgekommen sind. Verglichen mit anderen Todesursachen in Deutschland ist das extremst selten.

(YouTube dataset, ID 633)

Vielleicht sollte man einfach auf Youtube den Kommentarbereich ausschalten. Nur Beleidigungen und Unterstellungen schlimmster Sorte sind hier zu finden.

(YouTube dataset, ID 640)

Fakten statt Horrorszenarien. #TVDuell #Flüchtlinge
[Image showing a family, the Earth, and migration flows, written text:] 65 Millionen Menschen sind derzeit weltweit auf der Flucht. 90% von ihnen werden von Entwicklungsländern aufgenommen.

(Twitter-politician dataset, @Die_Gruenen, ID 1735)

"#Gauland redet wie ein Nazi. Die #AfdD ist eine Schande für Deutschland.

[Excerpt from a speech by Martin Schulz, in which he says:] Wir sind ein Land, in dem die Nazi-Ideologie nie wieder einen Platz haben wird. Aber Typen dieser Art, die haben wir auch. Typen, die der Meinung sind, keiner wolle Jérôme Boateng zum Nachbarn haben. Diese Organisation der Hetzer ist keine Alternative für Deutschland, sondern sie ist eine Schande für die Bundesrepublik.

(Twitter-politician dataset, @SPDde, ID 1386, http://twitter.com/spdde/statuses/902424311625113600, 140 retweets, 399 likes [25 October 2017])

[Anonymous] was hast du gegen Flüchtlinge? Sind doch nur Menschen. Ach stimmt ja, du bist ein Rassist XD

(YouTube dataset, ID 540)

Die Steuerflüchtlinge sind die teuersten Flüchtlinge. @DietmarBartsch #btw17 #linke

(Twitter-politician dataset, @DieLinke, ID 1654)

Holen wir uns das Land zurück! Sozial. Gerecht. Fieden. Für alle.

[Dietmar Bartsch:] Die Linke wird sich nie mit einer Politik abfinden, die tote Kinder an Strände spült, liebe Genossinen und Genossen.

[Bernd Riexinger:] Wer etwas Verstand besitzt, für den muss es das wichtigste Ziel sein, die AfD aus den Landtagen und den Bundestagen herauszuhalten.

[Dietmar Bartsch:] Es bleibt dabei, die teuersten Flüchtlinge sind die Steuerflüchtlinge, liebe Genosinnen und Genossen.

(Excerpt of spoken text in campaign video by Die Linke, YouTube, www.youtube.com/watch?v=wddS9dCXXGc)

Notes

1 Translation from German: „Fake News, so wie sich das Phänomen in Deutschland empirisch darstellt, werden vor allem von den Rechten, Rechtspopulist:innen und Rechtsextremen verbreitet."

2 Translation from German: „Eindeutig werden alle unsere Fake-News-Cases durch Rechtspopulist:innen und Rechtsextremist:innen verbreitet, wir zählen hierunter sowohl die AfD, als auch Medien, wie die Junge Freiheit, oder rechte Blogs wie Philosophia Perennis."

3 Translation from German: „Nimm jetzt Dein eigenes Video auf!"
4 Translation from German: „Unser TV-Spot hat Ihnen gefallen? Dann verbreiten Sie bitte die YouTube-Version – Danke! #TrauDichDeutschland: #AfD [embedded YouTube Video]."
5 Translation from German: „Liebe Unterstützer, macht mit und schreibt Eure Kommentare unter #Wahl2017! #TrauDichDeutschland #AfD #Btw17".
6 Translation from German: „Wie hat Ihnen unser 1. TV-Wahlspot gefallen? Ihre Meinung würde mich sehr interessieren!"
7 The original German postings of all cited and analysed social media content can be found in Appendix 6.B. They were translated into English by the author.
8 Translation from German: „Deutschland ist ein liebens- und lebenswertes Land, in dem man gut wohnen, arbeiten und leben kann. [...] Heute leben wir im schönsten und besten Deutschland, das wir je hatten."
9 Source of all data: Eurostat (2019).
10 Translation from German: *Ziel der AfD ist Selbsterhaltung, nicht Selbstzerstörung unseres Staates und Volkes.* Die Zukunft Deutschlands und Europas muss langfristig gesichert werden. Wir wollen unseren Nachkommen ein Land hinterlassen, das noch als unser Deutschland erkennbar ist. [...] Die AfD bekennt sich zur deutschen Leitkultur. [...] Sie umfasst neben der deutschen Sprache auch unsere Bräuche und Traditionen, Geistes- und Kulturgeschichte."
11 Source: Statistisches Bundesamt (2015).
12 Translation from German: „Wir werden sie jagen. Wir werden Frau Merkel oder wen auch immer jagen. Und wir werden uns unser Land und unser Volk zurückholen", www.youtube.com/watch?v=48Z4H2pRw4w
13 Translation from German: „Leitkultur umfasst die bei uns geltende Werteordnung christlicher Prägung, unsere Sitten und Traditionen sowie die Grundregeln unseres Zusammenlebens. Leitkultur ist das Gegenteil von Multikulti und Beliebigkeit."
14 https://fowid.de/meldung/religionszugehoerigkeiten-deutschland-2015
15 Translation from German: „Der Islam gehört nicht zu Deutschland. In der Ausbreitung des Islam und der Präsenz von über 5 Millionen Muslimen, deren Zahl ständig wächst, sieht die AfD eine große Gefahr für unseren Staat, unsere Gesellschaft und unsere Werteordnung. [...] Der in Europa bereits stattfindende Kulturkampf zwischen Abendland und dem Islam als Heilslehre und Träger von nicht integrierbaren kulturellen Traditionen und Rechtsgeboten kann nur abgewendet werden durch ein Bündel von defensiven und restriktiven Maßnahmen, die eine weitere Zerstörung der europäischen Werte des Zusammenlebens aufgeklärter Bürger verhindern. Die AfD wird nicht zulassen, dass Deutschland aus falsch verstandener Toleranz sein kulturelles Gesicht verliert."
16 www.gesetze-im-internet.de/partg/__25.html, accessed 24 December 2018.
17 "Ja, es ist richtig, dass bei uns Fehler im Umgang mit Wahlkampfspenden gemacht wurden", Deutscher Bundestag, 21 November 2018. Stenografischer Bericht, 64. Sitzung,

Plenarprotokoll 19/64, http://dip21.bundestag.de/dip21/btp/19/19064.pdf, accessed 24 December 2018.

18 www.forbes.com/profile/august-von-finck/?list=billionaires#26de781c7327, accessed 24 December 2018.

19 Jérôme Boateng is a football player at FC Bayern München. He was part of the German national team that won the FIFA World Cup in 2014. Boateng was born and grew up in Berlin. His mother is German, his father from Ghana. In 2016, Gauland said about Boateng: "People are fond of him as footballer. But they do not want to have one like Boateng as their neighbour" (Translation from German: „Die Leute finden ihn als Fußballspieler gut. Aber sie wollen einen Boateng nicht als Nachbarn haben"; Wehner and Lohse 2016).

Chapter Seven
Online Nationalism and Social Media Authoritarianism in the Context of the ÖVP/FPÖ Government in Austria

7.1 Introduction

7.2 The Austrian Political Context

7.3 Methodology

7.4 Analysis of Debate Excerpts

7.5 Social Media Analysis

7.6 Conclusion

7.1 Introduction

After the coalition government of the Social Democratic Party of Austria (SPÖ) and the conservative Austrian People's Party (ÖVP) collapsed, snap parliamentary elections took place in October 2017. The results are shown in Table 7.1.

The People's Party under Sebastian Kurz's leadership made strong gains and became the largest party, putting the Social Democrats under Chancellor Christian Kern into second position. The far-right Freedom Party (FPÖ) under the leadership of Heinz-Christian Strache increased its voting share by 5.5% and achieved 26.0% of the votes. The liberal NEOS party made slight gains. Before the election, the Green Party split, which resulted in the formation of a new party ("Peter Pilz List") led by former Green MP Peter Pilz. It crossed the 4% threshold and made it into parliament.[1] The Greens suffered a major loss and fell out of parliament.

On 18 December, ÖVP and FPÖ formed a new government that formulated a right-wing working programme for its five-year period of governance. Aged 31, Sebastian Kurz took on the role of Chancellor and became the world's youngest serving state leader. Heinz-Christian Strache became Vice-Chancellor. ÖVP and FPÖ had already formed a coalition government in 2000 under ÖVP Chancellor Wolfgang Schüssel. The EU in February 2000 reduced its diplomatic relations with Austria as protest against the inclusion of the far-right FPÖ in the Austrian government.

180 Nationalism on Social Media

TABLE 7.1 Results of the 2017 Austrian federal elections

Party	Percentage of votes	Change of % compared to the 2013 elections	Number of MPs	Change of MPs
Austrian People's Party (ÖVP)	31.5%	+7.5%	62	+15
Social Democratic Party of Austria (SPÖ)	26.9%	±0.0%	52	±0
Freedom Party of Austria (FPÖ)	26.0%	+5.5%	51	+11
NEOS	5.3%	+0.3%	10	+1
Peter Pilz List	4.4%	+4.4%	8	+8
The Greens	3.8%	−8.6%	0	−24
Voter turnout: 80.0%				

Source: https://wahl17.bmi.gv.at/

The 2017 Austrian election debates were dominated by the European refugee crisis and the question of if and how many refugees and migrants should be allowed to come to Austria. The FPÖ repeatedly argued that Kurz copied its programme and demands in respect to asylum seekers and Islamism.

Table 7.2 shows that in 2017, the typical ÖVP voter was self-employed or a white-collar worker and the typical FPÖ voter a younger, male blue-collar worker. The typical SPÖ voter was a pensioner. An important change was that in 2013, the relative majority of white-collar workers and pensioners voted for the SPÖ, whereas in 2017 many white-collar workers shifted to the ÖVP. The latter's voting share increased from 19 per cent to 31 per cent among white-collar workers. It is therefore interesting to observe that workers in Austria in 2017 did not predominantly vote for the Social Democrats, but for the two right-wing parties. Whereas in 2017 the Social Democratic Party of Austria had been the dominant party among pensioners and white-collar workers, in 2017 it was no longer dominant among any faction of the working class, but only among pensioners.

In 2017, 53 per cent of those voters, who thought that Austria is a rather unjust country, voted for the FPÖ, 24 per cent for the ÖVP, and only 4 per cent for the SPÖ. This shows that in Austria, the Social Democrats are not perceived as the party of social justice among those who have fears of social decline. Forty-two per cent of ÖVP voters said they primarily voted for that party because of the frontrunner, and 15 per cent because of the party's political standpoints. Five per cent of FPÖ voters primarily cast their ballot for that party because of the frontrunner,

TABLE 7.2 Voting behaviour of various groups in the 2017 and 2013 Austrian federal elections (per cent of total voters)

	ÖVP	FPÖ	SPÖ	NEOS	Greens	Pilz List
Blue-collar workers, 2017/2013	15/18	59/33	19/24	4/3	1/5	2/-
White-collar workers, 2017/2013	31/19	26/25	26/26	7/6	4/15	5/-
Self-employed, 2017/2013	41/35	23/18	14/5	10/13	4/12	6/-
Pensioners, 2017/2013	33/31	16/17	39/34	2/2	2/6	5/-
Men, 2017/2013	33/19	29/28	25/22	5/5	2/10	4/-
Women, 2017/2013	30/29	22/16	29/29	5/5	6/13	5/-
Age group 16–29, 2017/2013	28/21	30/22	17/20	9/6	7/21	5/-
Age group 30–59, 2017/2013	31/22	28/24	27/25	5/6	4/11	5/-
Age group 60+, 2017/2013	36/30	19/18	34/33	3/3	2/5	4/-
University-educated voters, 2017/2013	32/29	7/4	31/9	9/12	10/30	9/-
Voters who only completed compulsory education, 2017/2013	25/23	33/15	33/34	2/5	3/8	2/-

Source: SORA (2013, 2017)

and 34 per cent because of its standpoints. Twenty per cent of SPÖ voters primarily supported the Social Democrats because of frontrunner Christian Kern, and 22 per cent because of their political programme (SORA 2017). These data provide indications that many voters supported the ÖVP because of the relative youthfulness of its party leader.

According to respondents in a post-election survey, asylum and integration was the most discussed election topic, followed by social benefits and security (SORA 2017). The three main themes (asylum/integration, social benefits, security) are interlinked because social security and terrorism were often discussed in the context of refugees, migration, and Islam. The public service broadcaster ORF and the private channels Puls 4, ATV, and Ö24-TV broadcast dozens of television debates featuring different combinations of frontrunners. Given the prominence of TV in political communication, it is evident that refugees and migration must have played a major role in the broadcast debates. So, the media certainly played an important role in providing a forum for Strache and Kurz's radical anti-refugee positions.

The new ÖVP/FPÖ government formulated a 180-page programme for its five-year period of government. Key points of policy plans include the following ones (ÖVP/FPÖ 2017):

- Popular petitions signed by more than 100,000 voters shall be discussed by parliament and the responsible minister and committees. The initiator shall be allowed to speak in parliament on the petition topic. A popular petition signed by more than 900,000 voters shall result in a plebiscite.
- Law and order policies; upgrade of the security apparatus; extension of surveillance capacities.
- Confiscation of asylum seekers' cash and mobile phones and access to their social media profiles; expedited deportation of illegal migrants and rejected asylum seekers; cuts of social welfare benefits for refugees; shift from monetary to in-kind social welfare benefits for refugees.
- Strict upper limit of social welfare benefits per family; access to social welfare benefits only for those who have paid into the contribution system for at least five years during the past six years.
- Abolition of emergency benefit (*Notstandshilfe*), a social welfare benefit for the long-term unemployed. It is planned to replace this type of benefit by access to a needs-based minimum benefit (*Bedarfsorientierte Mindestsicherung*). The state can seize the wealth of recipients of the second type of benefit (such as savings or an owner-occupied dwelling), but not of those who receive the first type. In 2016, there were 167,075 recipients of emergency benefits (Statistik Austria 2019) whose wealth could be seized under the planned rules.
- Award of Austrian citizenship to South Tyroleans in addition to their Italian citizenship.
- Compulsory German tests before children start attending school; children with insufficient German skills shall attend separate school classes; stronger control of Islamic organisations, kindergartens, schools, and mosques.
- Introduction of university tuition fees; maintenance and deepening of the Austrian dual secondary school system; marking at all levels of schooling; advancement of entrepreneurial thought as part of education.
- Increase of the minimum pension for those with 40 contribution years; reduction of income tax for families with children.
- Reform of the structure of public social insurance agencies.
- Reduction of ancillary wage cost and the corporation tax level; flexibilisation of maximum daily and weekly working time; reduction of the public expenditure quote to 40 per cent of the GNP.

Overall, the ÖVP/FPÖ programme focuses on the restriction of the rights of refugees and immigrants, law and order politics, control, commitment to performance and entrepreneurship, stricter rules for the long-term unemployed, and the strengthening of capital's interests. Such measures construct refugees, immigrants, and the unemployed as problem groups who can easily be mobilised as scapegoats. The ÖVP/FPÖ agenda clearly is a right-wing government programme. Reducing taxes and public expenditures will very likely result in cuts to social services. Often one can then hear the argument that the state "has lived beyond its means", although tax gifts have been made to corporations and the wealthy. The ÖVP/FPÖ government may well privatise and commodify parts of public services in order to reduce state expenditures. If this happens, then one can expect that it will argue that the concerned services (e.g. healthcare, education, public housing, public transportation) can no longer be funded because allegedly so many immigrants and long-term unemployed are overburdening them. Such arguments would then aim at distracting attention from the political project of supporting the interests of capital and the wealthy. ÖVP Finance Minister Hartwig Löger announced shortly after the government had commenced its work: "We will now have to make restrictive savings for the next budgets. We have an excessive debt level"[2] (Pink and Rief 2017).

This chapter asks: How was nationalism expressed in the 2017 Austrian federal elections? Empirical ideology critique was used as method for the analysis of relevant texts gathered from television and social media.

Section 7.2 explains the political context and Section 7.3 the case study's methodology. Sections 7.4 and 7.5 present results. Section 7.6 draws conclusions.

7.2 The Austrian Political Context

The FPÖ

The FPÖ was founded in 1955. It was the successor party of the Association of the Independents (Verband der Unabhängigen, VdU) that was created in 1949. Many former Nazis were VdU supporters. The FPÖ had German nationalist and liberal wings. In 1983, the FPÖ, under its liberal leader Norbert Steger, formed a coalition government with the SPÖ. In 1986, Jörg Haider replaced Steger as FPÖ leader. SPÖ Chancellor Franz Vranitzky ended the coalition government because he saw Haider becoming the party leader as the

FPÖ's political shift to the far-right. Since 1986, the FPÖ has continuously focused on foreigners as the main theme in its election campaigns. When Sebastian Kurz became ÖVP leader in 2017, observers argued that this meant a shift of the party from the centre-right to the right, and that Kurz in the election campaign adopted parts of Strache's positions and arguments. Figure 7.1 shows the FPÖ's results in federal elections.

Haider was a controversial politician, which, for example, became evident in 1991 when he said about the employment policies in Nazi-Germany: "In the Third Reich, they carried out an orderly employment policy, which is not even accomplished by your government in Vienna."[3] Haider simply ignored that these policies served the purpose of imperialist warfare and armament: "This respectable occupation of people, which is described here in such positive terms, served, as we all know, to prepare for a war of extermination" (Wodak 2002, 40). Brigitte Bailer-Galanda and Wolfgang Neugebauer (1997) hold the view that the "FPÖ represents a successful new adaptation of old right-wing extremism" (102).

Under Haider, the FPÖ vastly increased its share of the votes from election to election, and in 1999 reached 26.91 per cent. In its campaigns, it used slogans such as "Stop der Überfremdung!" (*Stop the overforeignisation!*). In 1993, Haider and the FPÖ, under the title "Österreich zuerst!" (*Austria first!*), initiated an anti-immigration popular petition that was supported by 416,531 voters (7.35 per cent of the electorate). The

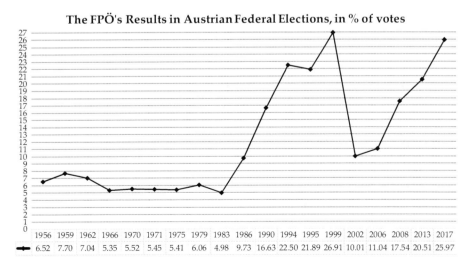

FIGURE 7.1 The FPÖ's results in Austrian federal elections

petition, for example, demanded fully ceasing immigration to Austria and wanted to amend the Austrian Constitution by a passage saying that "Austria is not an immigration country". After the 1999 elections, the ÖVP and FPÖ formed a government that was isolated in the European Union. In 2005, the FPÖ split into two parties: Haider founded the Alliance for the Future of Austria (Bündnis Zukunft Österreich, BZÖ) and Strache became the new leader of the FPÖ. The split weakened both parties in the following elections. Jörg Haider died in a car accident in 2008. Strache became the new uncontested leader of the parliamentary far-right that he rebuilt, so that in 2013 the FPÖ again reached more than 20 per cent of the votes in the federal elections.

In elections, the FPÖ under Strache campaigned with slogans such as „Daham statt Islam. WIR für EUCH" ("Homeland instead of Islam: WE are for YOU"), „Wien darf nicht Istanbul werden" ("Vienna must not turn into Istanbul"), „Mehr Mut für unser ‚Wiener Blut': Zu viel Fremdes tut niemandem gut" ("More courage for our 'Viennese Blood': Too much foreignness is not good for anyone"), „Die Islamisierung gehört gestoppt" ("Islamisation must be stopped"). Strache also used slogans such as „Willst Du eine soziale Sonderleistung haben, musst Du nur ein Kopftuch tragen" ("If you want to have extra-welfare aid, just put a veil on your head") or „Willst du eine Wohnung haben, brauchst du nur ein Kopftuch tragen" ("If you want to have a flat, just put a veil on your head") (Kleine Zeitung 2015; Lagler 2008). Michał Krzyżanowski (2013) writes that the FPÖ has ideologically transformed itself from radical opposition to immigration while Haider was its leader (1986–2005) to Islamophobia.

Austria is one of EU countries that was least hit by the new economic crisis that started in 2008. While Austria's unemployment rate has since 2008 stayed around 5 per cent, it increased in Greece from 7.8 per cent in 2008 to 23.6 per cent in 2016 and from 11.3 per cent to 19.6 per cent in Spain (Eurostat 2019). The example of Austria shows that support for the far-right has not necessarily directly to do with citizens' socio-economic decline, but with fears of potential social decline in the context of crises, social change, and globalisation that are projected into foreigners and minorities. Heribert Schiedel (2007, 49–50, 59) writes that capitalist crises pose a potential for the increase of fears of social degradation. Therefore, it would in such situations be a key question if meaningful alternatives existed to far-right ideology. The far-right offers surrogate objects for the projection of fears.

FPÖ politician Norbert Hofer became Minister for Infrastructure in the ÖVP/FPÖ government. In 2016, he achieved 46.2 per cent of the votes in the Austrian presidential elections (see Fuchs 2016a). He co-authored the 2011 party programme of the FPÖ. This programme defines Austria as a nation that is culturally German:

> We are committed to our homeland of Austria as part of the German-speaking linguistic and cultural community, to the groups of people native to our country and to a Europe of free peoples and fatherlands. [...] The language, history and culture of Austria are German. The vast majority of Austrians are part of the German peoples' linguistic and cultural community. [...] Austria is not a country of immigration.
>
> (FPÖ 2011, 2, 5)

It becomes evident in this passage that the FPÖ defines the nation as a linguistic, cultural, and historical community and sees Austria as belonging to the German cultural nation. It opposes multiculturalism and thinks that "nations" should be kept separate. Austria was part of Nazi-Germany from 1938 until 1945, but has outside of this period had its own distinct history. At the time of the Habsburg Empire, there were many multicultural influences that have shaped Austrian culture until today.

The FPÖ and the Burschenschaften

Burschenschaften are right-wing fraternities. Table 7.3 shows that 20 of the FPÖ's 51 parliamentarians who were elected in 2017 are members of organisations that belong to the milieu of the Burschenschaften. In addition, Norbert Hofer, the FPÖ's candidate in the 2016 Austrian presidential election and Minister for Infrastructure in the ÖVP/FPÖ government, is a member of the Burschenschaft Marko-Germania zu Pinkafeld. Vice-Chancellor Strache is a member of the Burschenschaft Vandalia Wien.

Bernhard Weidinger (2015) analysed the role of the Burschenschaften in Austria since 1945. He argues that Burschenschaft members "rather possess best prospects in Strache's FPÖ as long as they are ready to take a certain distance from the folkish doctrine in their external appearance"[4] (555). Hans-Henning Scharsach (2017) argues the Burschenschaften have quietly conquered power in Austria. He characterises their milieu as the "folkish-German national spearhead of the FPÖ"[5] (9) and writes that this milieu features individuals who "downplay the Nazis' crimes", "promote right-wing extremist and racist activities of young people", and "carry out neo-Nazi indoctrination"[6] (18).

Chapter Seven | Social Media-Authoritarianism **187**

TABLE 7.3 FPÖ parliamentarians and ministers who are members of organisations that belong to the milieu of the Burschenschaften

Member of Parliament	Organisation
Hannes Amesbauer	Oberösterreicher Germanen Wien
Reinhard Eugen Bösch	Teutonia Wien
Hermann Brückl	Scardonia Schärding, Markomannia Eisenstadt
Martin Graf	Olympia Wien
Johann Gudenus	Vandalia Wien und Aldania Wien
Christian Hafenecker	Nibelungia Wien
Roman Haider	Donauhort Aschaach
Christian Höbart	Tauriska Baden
Hans-Jörg Jenewein	Nibelungia Wien
Gerhard Kaniak	Albia Wien
Axel Kassegger	Germania Graz, Thessalia Prag in Bayreuth
Anneliese Kitzmüller	Iduna Linz
Wendelin Mölzer	Vandalia Graz
Werner Neubauer	Gothia Meran, Markomannia Graz
Walter Rosenkranz	Libertas Wien
Carmen Schimanek	Sigrid Wien
Philip Schrangl	Oberösterreicher Germanen Wien
Harald Stefan	Olympia Wien
Heinz-Christian Strache	Vandalia Wien
Wolfgang Zanger	Vandalia Wien

Minister:

Norbert Hofer, Minister for Transport, Innovation, and Technology	Marko-Germania Pinkerfeld

Sources: FIPU (2016), Kurier (2017), Scharsach (2017, 14–15)

Germania zu Wiener Neustadt is a high school Burschenschaft based in Wiener Neustadt, Austria's eleventh largest city and the second largest city in the federal state of Lower Austria. Udo Landbauer was the FPÖ's frontrunner in the 2018 elections to Lower Austria's regional parliament (Landtag), where the FPÖ achieved 14.76 per cent of the votes. Landbauer was a member of Germania zu Wiener Neustadt since the year 2000 and its deputy chairman. Shortly before the regional elections, a songbook appeared in public that the fraternity had published in 1997 for its members. The book contained the lyrics of a version of the Burschenschaft drinking song „Es lagen die alten Germanen", to which new anti-Semitic, racist, and neo-Nazi verses were added:

> Then the Jew Ben Gurion stepped into their middle: "Step on the gas, old Teutones, we'll accomplish the seventh million". [...] Then a slit-eyed Chinese stepped into their middle: "We are also Indo-Germanic and want to join the Waffen-SS".[7]
>
> (Horaczek 2018)

The song verse calls for the continuation of the Shoah. Facing public pressure, Landbauer stepped down as a member of Lower Austria's regional parliament and made his FPÖ membership dormant. The songbook affair gives an impression of the mindset that can be found in the milieu of the Burschenschaften.

Sebastian Kurz and the ÖVP

The journalists Nina Horaczek and Barbara Tóth (2017) argue in their book on Sebastian Kurz that the Austrian Chancellor is strongly focused on his image and on marketing himself in the traditional media and on social media such as Facebook, Twitter, Instagram, and YouTube. They characterise Kurz as a "more polite Strache" (32) who "adopted FPÖ-positions and presented them less aggressively, even politely" (118) and advances neoliberal policies of performance, individual responsibility, and entrepreneurship that lack a sense for solidarity. Isolde Charim (2017) argues that Kurz's combination of youthfulness and the stress on image, appearance, and change is the "embodiment of the neoliberal ideal". Ruth Wodak (2017) characterises Kurz's policies the following way:

> At the end of September 2015, the ÖVP changed to the tracks of the FPÖ. [...] There is a major difference in perception if I call humans, who flee from death, war and torture, refugees or if I call them illegal migrants or economic migrants, which denies them the legal status of refugees. Repeated often enough and propagated by the media, this image solidifies collectively. [...] Kurz's ÖVP has given up certain traditional characteristics of the ÖVP and has taken on characteristics of right-wing populist parties such as the emphasis on border protection, the stop of "illegal migration", the tightening of asylum conditions, as well as the law and order orientation and the party's strong hierarchisation.[8]

Table 7.4 gives an overview of the largest donors of Kurz and the ÖVP's 2017 election campaign. The largest donor was Stefan Pierer, CEO of the motorcycle and sports car manufacturer KTM. Individuals and companies representing the following industries in particular have supported Kurz: the transport, mobility, fuel, and automotive industries; the real estate industry; the hotel and leisure industry; the finance industry; and the manufacturing industry. The data show that big capital supports Sebastian Kurz's election campaign. It may therefore not come as a surprise that the reduction of the corporation tax, the flexiblisation of working hours, and the deregulation of the economy are part of the ÖVP/FPÖ government programme.

Why has the far-right become so strong in Austria? There are several influencing factors that form a complex whole.

Austria's Incomplete Denazification

The first dimension has to do with incomplete denazification. Austria's Second Republic, which was created after the Second World War, is based on the myth that Austria was Hitler's first victim, which resulted in its incomplete denazification. Far-right ideology could thereby continue to exist.

The myth of Austria as Hitler's first victim can also be found in the Austrian State Treaty that established Austria's sovereignty as an independent state. It says that "on March 13, 1938, Hitlerite Germany annexed Austria by force and incorporated its territory in the German Reich" (United Nations 1955, 225). But in the April 1938 referendum, 99.73 per cent of the voters opted for Austria becoming part of the German Reich. There was a voter turnout of 99.71 per cent. The Austrian population overwhelmingly welcomed the country's *Anschluss* to Germany. Austria was not Hitler's victim. It played a very active role in the Nazi-regime.

Today there is a widespread political tendency that Austrians tend to see themselves as victims of alleged "foreign forces" and do not want to see that Austrian right-wing extremism has to do with anti-democratic tendencies in the country itself.

In 1986, Kurt Waldheim, a member of the Nazi Sturmabteilung (SA) during the Second World War, became Austria's President. During his presidency, the USA declared him a *persona non grata* so that he was not allowed to enter the country. Waldheim's diplomatic contacts and travels as Austrian President remained limited. Conservative politicians at that time often portrayed Waldheim as a victim of

TABLE 7.4 Main donors of the ÖVP's 2017 election campaign

Donor	Industry	Amount (€)
Stefan Pierer	Motorcycles and automotive	436,563
Rudolf Gürtler	Lawyer, hotel and food industries	50k
M. Kaindl KG	Manufacturing industry	50k
Martin Böhm	Transport and mobility technologies	40k
Dr Markus Braun	Finance industry	40k
MAM Babyartikel GesmbH	Clothing industry	40k
Happy-Foto GmbH	Photo industry	35k
Markus Braun	Finance industry	30k
GMIM Immobilienmanagement	Real estate sector	30k
Senger-Weiss GmbH	Transport industry	30k
IGO Industries GmbH	Building equipment	30k
Richard Ramsauer	Consultancy	25k
BM 454 GRA GmbH	Equipment rental and leasing	20k
Benedikt Abensperg	Agriculture	20k
Vitalis Food VertriebsgmbH	Food industry	20k
Supernova Baumärkte Holding GmbH	Real estate sector	20k
Dorit Muzicant	Real estate sector	20k
Georg Muzicant	Real estate sector	20k
Teresa Pagitz	Hotel industry, real estate sector	14k
Allinvest Unternehmensbeteiligung	Real estate sector	11k
Kurt Mann	Food industry	10k
Wilhelm Klepsch	Plastics processing industry	10k
Münzer Bioindustrie GmbH	Biofuel industry	10k
Harald Hild	Real estate sector	10k
MRP Investmentmanagement	Real estate sector	10k
Gottfried Wurpes	Leisure industry	10k
SMILE GmbH	Manufacturing industry	10k
Nikolaus Goriany	Real estate sector	10k
Bettina Glatz-Kremsner	Gambling industry	10k
Martin Kurschel	Real estate sector	10k

Sources: www.sebastian-kurz.at/spendenuebersicht, https://kontrast.at/das-sind-die-kurz-spender/

a foreign conspiracy against Austria. One of the slogans in his 1986 campaign read „Wir Österreicher wählen wen *wir* wollen! Jetzt erst recht Waldheim" ("We Austrians vote for whom *we* want! Now more than ever Waldheim").

Austrian Nationalism: Mia San Mia, Vernaderer, and Nestbeschmutzer

A second dimension is Austrian nationalism. Austria's status as a small country in Europe that was a former superpower and now often stands in the shadow of Germany has resulted in a schizophrenic national identity. Identity-building of in-groups often makes use of the negative definition of out-groups.

In Austria, this political schizophrenia tends to be expressed by nationalists in the form of an "us versus them" ideology that lacks the capacity of self-criticism and in situations of political crisis blames Europe, immigrants, the USA, Jews, socialists, liberals, everything foreign („das Ausland"), etc. Linguistically, this repressive nationalist inwardness and isolationism is known as the „Mia san Mia" ("we are we") ideology that opposes Austrian patriots to imagined foreign enemies and what this ideology terms „Vaterlandsvernaderer" ("denouncers of the fatherland", "traitors") or „Nestbeschmutzer" ("denigrators", "defilers of their own country").

Austrian Neoliberalism

Third, Austrian Neoliberalism plays a role. In the 1970s, Austria was under Bruno Kreisky's (SPÖ) chancellorship one of the world's leading welfare democracies. The rise of neoliberalism has also shifted social democracy in Austria towards the right. Right-wing populists have used citizens' fears of social decline and projected them into racist ideology. Many citizens who traditionally identified with the Social Democrats felt that this party no longer represents the interests of ordinary people and therefore looked for alternatives. The FPÖ has presented itself as such an alternative, as a party that listens to the fears of ordinary people. It tries to project the population's fears of social decline into the construction of immigrants as scapegoats.

Kronen Zeitung

Right-wing media form the fourth dimension. Austria has a highly concentrated press system. The right-wing *Kronen Zeitung* is the most widely read newspaper. In

2005, it had around 3 million readers, which means a reach of almost 45 per cent. In 2015, its reach was 30.1 per cent.[9] The *Kronen Zeitung* has for a long time supported the FPÖ and has practised anti-immigrant rhetoric.

An example of *Kronen Zeitung*'s coverage: in the days before the 2017 elections, *Krone* ran stories with headlines such as:

- "People smuggler lived underground" („Schlepper lebte als 'U-Boot'", 15 October 2017);
- "Upper Austria: 26-year-old rioted in asylum accommodation" („OÖ: 26-Jähriger randaliert in Asylunterkunft", 13 October 2017);
- "Totally sloshed: Moroccan smashed everything to bits in asylum seekers' hostel" („Im Vollrausch: Marokkaner schlug in Heim alles kurz und klein", 15 October 2017); and
- "Viennese 'Islamic State bride' (39) flown home from Kabul!" („Wiener ‚IS-Braut' (39) aus Kabul heimgeflogen!", 13 October 2017).

Such headlines create the impression that Austrians are surrounded and under constant threat by violent and criminal asylum seekers, people smugglers, and Islamic terrorists.

Al-Youssef (2018) conducted a data analysis of all content that FPÖ leader Heinz-Christian Strache posted on his Facebook profile from 24 December 2017 until 24 April 2018. During that period, Strache made 232 postings that contained links. A relative majority of 111 (47.8 per cent) posts linked to articles published in *Kronen Zeitung*'s online version. Postings on the Facebook page of *Kronen Zeitung* reach on average 240 reactions ("like", "wow", "haha", "sad", "angry") and 53 comments, and are on average shared 45 times (Al-Youssef 2018). If Strache links to a *Kronen Zeitung* article, the average response is multiple times larger: 1,965 reactions, 199 comments, and 354 shares. "Angry" accounted for 60.1 per cent of all analysed reactions on Strache's page. Strache often links to *Krone* articles about refugees and migrants that have to do with crime and other problems and portray migrants and refugees negatively. Often he adds populist comments and demands. That the share of angry reactions to his postings is so large is an indication that most readers of Strache's page are supporters who buy into the scapegoating of migrants and refugees and support xenophobic policies.

Strache's social media presence and *Kronen Zeitung*'s articles are mutually beneficial: (1) *Kronen Zeitung* provides material for Strache that allows him to create, mobilise, and reinforce anti-refugee sentiments. *Krone*'s articles are Strache's everyday political "capital" that enter into his political propaganda as ideological information. They form a basic building block that he uses for inductively generalising from single examples to the groups of refugees and migrants as a whole, who are often presented as criminals and benefit scroungers. (2) *Kronen Zeitung* benefits from Strache's social media links: many more users read *Krone* articles when Strache shares and comments on them. As a result, *Krone* reaches wider attention and higher reputation in the public, which translates not only into higher reputational and symbolic capital, but also into more profit reached via the increase of the amount of advertising clicks, subscriptions, and paper copies sold.

The Containment of Class Struggle

The institutional containment of class struggle is the fifth dimension. Austria's political system is based on the consensus culture of consociationalism: in industrial policy, there is a social partnership (*Sozialpartnerschaft*) between the organised representatives of capital and labour that negotiates compromises on wages and working conditions. As a result, Austria has hardly seen strikes since 1945. Class struggles have remained contained. Long-term containment of class struggles can explode into the wrong direction and be turned against scapegoats such as migrants and refugees. The Austrian class system has undergone changes so that a new middle class has emerged and the blue-collar working class has decreased in numbers, which has strengthened blue-collar labour's fears of social decline.

The Weakness of the Left

The weakness of the Austrian political left is the sixth dimension. The political left has in Austria been traditionally very weak, which has to do with the containment of class struggle and the fact that during the time of the Cold War, Stalinism was widely spread in the Austrian left, but unappealing to ordinary citizens. Given a weak left, it is easier for the far-right to strive.

Low Level of General Education and Hauptschule

The low level of general education in Austria is the seventh dimension. According to a study of the Austrian federal election of 2013, where the FPÖ achieved 20.5 per cent of the vote, it was the strongest party among men (28 per cent), blue-collar workers (33 per cent), those aged 16–29 (22 per cent), and those whose highest educational attainment is a polytechnic school (35 per cent; a one-year practical education that prepares pupils at the age of 14 for starting an apprenticeship; SORA 2013). The typical FPÖ voter is a young, male blue-collar worker with a low level of education. In 2014, the EU-wide average share of those who were aged 25 or above and held at least a bachelor's degree was 22.3 per cent. Austria had, with 12.25 per cent, the lowest share of all 22 EU countries for which data are available.[10]

In Austria, there has been a long-standing political debate about the abolishment of the *Hauptschule* (secondary modern school). Secondary school is a dual system in Austria: pupils aged 10–13 have to decide if they either attend grammar school (the so-called *Gymnasium*) or secondary modern school (*Hauptschule*, now called *Neue Mittelschule* [new secondary school]). Often this choice is one that has to do with the children's family and class background. There is a tendency that especially children from lower-income families attend secondary modern school and that those attending the *Gymnasium* are much more likely to later attend university. Austrian Social Democrats and Greens tend to criticise that the dual secondary school system fosters an educational gap, whereas the Austrian Conservatives paint fears of the end and decline of education if a combined secondary school system for all children aged 10–14 were introduced. Austria's dual secondary school system is one of the reasons why the level of higher education is very low in the population. A reform has resulted in the stepwise transition of secondary modern schools into new middle schools (*Neue Mittelschule*) that use new forms of teaching and learning. But the basic distinction between the *Gymnasium* and a less demanding type of secondary school has not been abolished. There is a relationship between parents' class and educational status and the educational achievements of their children (Volkshilfe 2015). Austria's dual secondary education system not only creates educational gaps and is a system divided by social class, but can also contribute to the prevalence of political support for far-right movements.

Education is one of the factors that influences political worldviews. In the 2016 presidential election, such divisions of the social structure of voters became evident (SORA 2016). In the second round, 60 per cent of male voters cast their ballot for FPÖ candidate Hofer, but only 40 per cent of women voters. Eighty-six per cent of blue-collar working-class voters supported Hofer, whereas 60 per cent of white-collar working-class voters opted for the Green candidate Alexander van der Bellen. Fifty-five per cent of voters who only completed compulsory education cast their vote for Hofer. The same can be said about 67 per cent of those voters who completed apprenticeships and about 58 per cent of those whose highest educational attainment is the completion of a vocational school (Berufsbildende mittlere Schule, BMS). In contrast, 73 per cent of voters who had passed school leaving examinations and 81 per cent of university-educated voters opted for van der Bellen. Class and education are key influencing factors on voting behaviour in Austria.

Proporz: The Austrian Patronage System

The Austrian patronage system forms the eighth dimension. In the Austrian political system, the Conservative Party ÖVP traditionally represented capital and farmers, and the Social Democratic Party SPÖ represented labour. A particular system of clientelism, called the *Proporzsytem* (patronage system), developed, in which the ÖVP and the SPÖ divided power. Getting and keeping the job one wants to hold has often been a question of party membership and having the right kind of political connections. There is even a term in everyday language that characterises the specific Austrian system of patronage: *Parteibuchwirtschaft* (party book economy).

It is therefore no accident that in Austria, the population's relative level of party membership is the highest in Europe: a study showed that whereas the average share of political party members in the total electorate was 4.7 per cent in the European Union, this ratio was 17.27 per cent in Austria in the year 2008 (Van Biezen et al. 2012). In 1980, the share was around 28.5 per cent in Austria. The existence of Austrian clientelism has political reasons: both the Social Democrats and the Conservatives have seen it as a way of avoiding a repetition of the military conflict and civil war between conservative and socialist forces in the 1920s and early 1930s and as a means for containing the power of the far-right. The FPÖ has presented itself over the decades as the one force that can end the *Proporz* system's dual concentration of power in the hands of the Conservatives and the Social Democrats.

The interaction of these eight factors has, over the decades, again and again resulted in electoral successes of the far-right. Economic and political crises in Europe and the world do not determine the strength of far-right movements, but have in political history often been important contexts of its popularity and support.

7.3 Methodology

Empirical ideology critique analyses the structure (*text*) of ideological communication in the *context* of society's power structures in order to draw conclusions for political *prospects*. The research was conducted by adopting a methodology consisting of four steps:

1) Data collection, including research ethics.
2) Identification of discursive macro-topics.
3) Analysis of the structure of ideology and discourse for each macro-topic; analysis and theorisation of how online discourses and ideology are related to the broader societal context, i.e. the relations of the online-semiotic elements to political economy.
4) Prospective critique.

Data collection was the *first step*. Nationalist ideology operates from above and below. It is therefore important to study how politicians communicate ideology "from above" and how citizens respond to it "from below". The analysis therefore focused on material from the main television debate as well as on online comments.

Table 7.5 gives an overview of the audience rates of the main television debates that involved Kurz and/or Strache. The so-called "round of elephants" (*Elefantenrunde*) is a television debate of all frontrunners of parties represented in parliament. Whereas the round of elephants shown by the public service broadcaster (Austrian Broadcasting Corporation, ORF) only featured the frontrunners of the five elected parliamentary parties, the ones on private channels also included Peter Pilz, the frontrunner of the Pilz List, a new party that had split off from the Green Party. ORF argued that it only features representatives of elected parties. The round of elephants shown by Austria's public service broadcaster ORF was the debate that achieved the highest rating. In general, election debates on ORF were watched by more viewers than on private channels such as Puls 4 or ATV.

Given that the ORF round of elephants was the most watched election debate, we can assume that it had significant influence. For the purpose of the analysis in this chapter, we therefore focus on excerpts from this debate, where Kurz and Strache talk about Austria, refugees, migrants, and Islam.

Given that social media enable user-generated content, social media critical discourse analysis is a good way of analysing ideology from below. The analysis focused on all

TABLE 7.5 Audience rates of main television debates in the 2017 Austrian federal elections that involved Sebastian Kurz and/or Heinz-Christian Strache

Debate	TV channel	Date	Audience rate
Round of elephants (*Elefantenrunde*): Christian Kern (SPÖ), Sebastian Kurz (ÖVP), Ulrike Lunacek (Greens), Heinz-Christian Strache (FPÖ), Matthias Strolz (NEOS)	ORF	12 October 2017	1,210,00
Kurz/Kern	ORF	10 October 2017	970,000
Strache/Kurz	ORF	10 October 2017	904,000
Kern/Strache	ORF	9 October 2017	887,000
Strache/Irmgrad Griss (NEOS)	ORF	27 September 2017	697,000
Kurz/Lunacek	ORF	28 September 2017	636,000
Kurz/Kern	Puls 4	8 October 2017	623,000
Strache/Kurz	Puls 4	8 October 2017	587,000
Round of elephants: Kern, Kurz, Lunacek, Peter Pilz (Pilz List), Strache, Strolz	Puls 4	24 September 2017	560,000
Round of elephants: Kern, Kurz, Lunacek, Pilz List, Strache, Srolz	ATV	1 October 2017	526,000

Source: Der Standard (2017)

comments posted to three Facebook postings and two online newspaper articles that dealt with the topics of immigrants, refugees, and Islam and were published in the days after the ÖVP/FPÖ government assumed office (for an overview, see Table 7.6). We selected one relevant Facebook posting each by Sebastian Kurz (Chancellor, ÖVP), Heinz-Christian Strache (Vice-Chancellor, FPÖ), and Herbert Kickl (Minister of the Interior, FPÖ). In addition, we collected comments from two online articles in *Kronen Zeitung*, Austria's main tabloid, which often runs stories having to do with migrants and refugees. Data collection resulted in a dataset of 2,367 comments.

Kurz and Strache are the two Austrian politicians with the highest number of followers on Facebook: on 4 January 2018, Kurz's page had around 720,000 followers and 717,000 likes, and Strache's page around 746,000 followers and 772,000 likes. Kickl's PR team created a Facebook profile on 19 December 2017, one day after the ÖVP/FPÖ government's inauguration. Given that he attracted a lot of media attention, the page quickly achieved 10,000 followers. *Kronen Zeitung* is Austria's most read newspaper. In 2017, it had an average of 2.2 million daily readers (30.1 per cent of all readers) and 2.8 million (37.2 per cent of all readers) at weekends.[11] *Kronen Zeitung* is a tabloid that very frequently publishes stories about crimes committed by foreigners. Its coverage was clearly

198 Nationalism on Social Media

TABLE 7.6 Facebook postings and online newspaper articles selected for analysis

Posting	Source	Date of posting	Number of comments
Posting about criminal foreigners	H.-C. Strache's Facebook page, www.facebook.com/HCStrache/	2 January 2018	717
Posting about criminal refugees	Herbert Kickl's Facebook page, www.facebook.com/herbertkickl/	30 December 2017	90
Posting about illegal migration and refugee policies in Europe	Sebastian Kurz's Facebook page, www.facebook.com/sebastiankurz.at/	24 December 2017	831
Article titled „Türkis-blaue Pläne: Neu: Asylwerber müssen Handy und Bargeld abgeben" ("New ÖVP/FPÖ Plans: Asylum Seekers Must Hand in Their Mobile Phones and Cash")	*Kronen Zeitung* Online, www.krone.at/604492	19 December 2017	428 (4 January 2018)
Interview with Herbert Kickl: „Das große Interview: Wird Österreich jetzt sicherer, Herr Kickl?" ("The Great Interview: Will Austria Now Become More Secure, Mr Kickl?")	*Kronen Zeitung* Online, www.krone.at/1603409	31 December 2017	301 (4 January 2018)
			Total: 2,367

favourable to Jörg Haider during his political rise. During the 2017 election campaigns, it gave significant positive attention to both Kurz and Strache.

Figures 7.2, 7.3 and 7.4 show the three selected Facebook postings and provide translations of the main posting texts.

I watched an online video of the selected ORF debate and identified passages where Strache and Kurz talked about migrants, refugees, or Islam. These excerpts were transcribed. The Facebook app Netvizz was used for collecting all comments posted under the three chosen Facebook postings, which resulted in three Excel files that were merged into one file. The text of the comments to two articles in *Kronen Zeitung* were collected manually because there was no automated data collection possibility. All comments were copied into an Excel sheet. The resulting file was merged with the Facebook file, which resulted in one analysis file with a total of 2,367 comments.

FIGURE 7.2 Facebook posting by Heinz-Christian Strache
Translation: No misconceived tolerance for foreign criminals! [*Image text*: Consequent deportation of foreign violent criminals! FPÖ – The party for a social homeland]

Social media research ethics guidelines suggest informed consent for data collection is not needed if users in a certain online setting can reasonably expect to be observed by strangers (Fuchs 2017b, 60; Townsend and Wallace 2016). For this study, data were only collected from public sources, including Facebook profiles of politicians, online newspaper articles, and television debates. If you post a political opinion on the public Facebook profile of a politician or to an online newspaper article, then you certainly take into account that others will have public access to it and you have to expect that such texts may be analysed and quoted by others. One can therefore assume that in these cases, no informed consent needs to be obtained. Usernames have in the analysis been anonymised.

As a *second methodological step*, discourse topics were identified as a preparation for the data analysis. A discourse topic is a macro-topic (Reisigl 2018) and a semantic macro-structure (van Dijk 2018). The discourse topics were chosen according to the structure of nationalist ideology identified in the book at hand: nationalism defines a "we"-identity that is posited against outsiders and enemy groups. We can distinguish between biological, socio-economic,

FIGURE 7.3 Facebook posting by Herbert Kickl

Translation: To Chechens just like to all others, who abuse the right to asylum in Austria, it applies that we will exhaust all legal means in order to end the stay of criminals [Link to an article posted on the news platform Ö24 titled "Chechens: Will Deportation Come Now?" (www.oe24.at/oesterreich/chronik/wien/Tschetschenen-Kommt-jetzt-Abschiebung/315071148) that reports on the injury of three police officers at the arrest of Chechens]

political, and cultural nationalism. (New) racism is an inherent characteristic of nationalism. Table 7.7 presents an overview of nationalist macro discourse topics and identifies typical examples of nationalist attitudes. In addition to different forms of nationalism, other elements of authoritarianism were also used as macro discourse topics: top-down leadership, the friend/enemy scheme, and law and order-politics (see Fuchs 2018a).

As a *third methodological step*, methodological tools from critical discourse analysis were used in order to analyse the structure of the nationalist discourse topics (Reisigl and Wodak 2001; Wodak and Meyer 2016). In this analysis, for each macro discourse topic, typical cases were identified and analysed with the help of critical theories of nationalism as well as in the context of the broader societal context.

FIGURE 7.4 Facebook posting by Sebastian Kurz

Translation: We need a united, strong Europe in order to preserve affluence in Germany & Austria. First, we must correct refugee- & migration-policies' aberrations & especially stop illegal migration to Europe [Image of an interview with Kurz conducted by Germany's largest newspaper, the tabloid *Bild* (The article holds the title "Chancellor Kurz Exclusively in Sunday Bild!", online version: www.bild.de/bild-plus/politik/ausland/angela-merkel/soll-kanzlerin-bleiben-54290876)]

Drawing political conclusions about the communication of nationalism in Austria was the *fourth step*.

7.4 Analysis of Debate Excerpts

Let us first have a look at the ORF election debate excerpt that is the source of analysis. Appendix 7.A shows the German original that was translated into English.

HEINZ-CHRISTIAN STRACHE (FPÖ): The reality is that we want that those who have not paid into the system receive benefits in kind instead of cash benefits because then the

TABLE 7.7 Nationalist discourse topics used in the analysis

Type of nationalism	We-presentation (ideal-type)	Other-presentation (ideal-type)
Biological nationalism	"We are a superior race."	"They are an inferior race that shows negative characteristics and behaviour."
Socio-economic nationalism	"We are a hard-working and industrious nation."	"They are lazy and social parasites who live from our money. They take away our jobs and houses and are a burden to our healthcare system, our education system, our social services, etc."
Political nationalism	"We are a democratic nation that values freedom."	"They are undemocratic and are in favour of dictatorship. They pose a terrorist and criminal threat and a threat to our nation's security."
Cultural nationalism	"Our nation's culture, language, and religion have a long history and traditions that need to be preserved."	"Their culture, language, and religion is different from ours and threatens the survival of our culture, language, and religion. If they want to live here, then they have to adopt our culture, speak our language, and accept our religion. Their culture is uncivilised."

knock-on effect of economic refugees can certainly be clearly reduced. […] This is something that nobody in Austria, who is full-time employed and earns a bit more than the minimum benefit, understands. All of this is not fair.

And if you have worked for 40 or 45 years and then you receive a minimum pension of €940, then that's not fair. That's something nobody understands. And then there are women, who are so often referred to in Sunday-speeches and who are left alone in poverty with just €250 or €350 when they are old. These are unfair systems. The system needs to be made fair and changed so that minimum pensioners who have worked 40 or 45 years then really receive €1,200 and mothers' child-rearing time is taken into account in the calculation of their pension so that they receive at least the minimum pension. That would mean that one shows respect and decency towards the people.

[…]

SEBASTIAN KURZ (ÖVP): In Vienna, there is the situation that in the meantime every other recipient of needs-based minimum benefit is a foreign national. A family with three children receives in Vienna €2,500 of minimum benefits and other social benefits such as child support. That is a sum that somebody who works does not earn that easily. You have to earn pretty well in order to get that. And in this

Chapter Seven | Social Media-Authoritarianism **203**

respect we need a change. We spend billions on refugee support, in the meantime 1 billion on minimum benefits alone, and we transfer 300 million of family aid to foreign countries. If we do not counteract, then it will become ever harder to finance our social system.

STRACHE: And we have aberrations that are due, as I mentioned, to the lack of border control in 2015. And there have been developments that have taken place not just since then, but that also took place earlier on. And there one has to be honest and has to say correctly that in the year 1973 we had 73,000 fellow Muslim citizens in Austria, and a very, very undifferentiated policy of mass immigration has over the past decades resulted in today already more than 700,000. And also schools in Vienna experience in the realm of primary education that we already have more Muslim than Catholic children.

And then there are structures of associations and Islamic kindergartens and mosques that have been concretely observed by the authorities for the protection of the constitution not just since a year, but over more than 15 years. And it is suggested that there are radical Islamist aberrations.

Very dangerous developments take place that also concern recruitment. This has led to the point that now one fortunately could a couple of days ago discover an IS-guy in a refugee home in Salzburg who was in touch with the Paris assassins. This means that there is a need for action.

KURZ: Anyone who sets off to illegally enter Europe by human trafficking should not have a chance to file an asylum request, but has to be returned. And at the same time we have to extend development cooperation and help on the ground because this way we can help substantially more people and in a substantially more sustainable manner with the same amount of money.

STRACHE: We must start here in order to avoid conditions like in Vienna. And that is necessary. Due to the aberration that has already been caused, our children here in Vienna have become a minority in their own city. And you please have to recognise that circumstance. And then there is the political question if you want to further promote this development or not. Not with us.

Nationalist ideology works with positive presentations of the nation and negative presentations of foreigners. Let us therefore look at how Strache and Kurz predicate Austrians and non-Austrians.

Foreigners and refugees are referred to as "foreign countries" that receive "300 million of family aid" from Austria (Kurz) or a "foreign national" who is a "recipient of needs-based minimum benefit" (Kurz). These predications combine the xenonym (see Reisigl and Wodak 2001, 48) of being foreign with negationyms (52) that make a negative statement about a certain group in the form of problematisations (50). Foreigners are presented as passive objects who are not active subjects, but receivers and recipients of money. They are thereby declared to be a social problem. Other negationyms that construct foreigners as a social problem and as passive include the use of the formulations "those who have not paid into the system" (Strache) and that a "family with three children receives in Vienna €2,500 of minimum benefits and other social benefits such as child support" (Kurz).

In contrast, Austrians are referred to as those who are "full-time employed and earn a bit more than the minimum benefit" (Strache), those who "worked for 40 or 45 years" (Strache), those who "receive a minimum pension of €940" (Strache), "minimum pensioners who have worked 40 or 45 years" (Strache), or "somebody who works" (Kurz). In the speech that opened the ÖVP's 2017 election campaign, Kurz (2017a) made a similar argument, saying that a poor retired peasant woman who has worked her whole life finds it unfair that refugees receive minimum benefits:

> I have for example met a peasant woman in Salzburg, who told me that with her small pension, she can hardly make ends meet although she has worked her whole life long hard and even physically hard. And she quite rightly does not understand why a refugee receives the full minimum benefit from the start.[12]

Professionyms present humans in terms of their work (Reisigl and Wodak 2001, 50), and victimonyms in terms of being a victim. The mentioned predications combine professionyms and victimonyms. They present Austrians as hard-working and receiving little for their work. Another predication that was employed uses a combination of a victimonym and an origionym (reference in terms of origin; Reisigl and Wodak 2001, 48) when speaking of "our children here in Vienna" who are a "minority in their own city" (Strache). "Our children" is a reference in terms of family origin that communicates particular vulnerability.

Taken together, the combination of the construction of Austrian victims and foreign recipients of Austrian money and benefits results in a sharp us/them difference that presents foreigners as "social parasites" and Austrians as victims of foreigners.

A consequence is that refugees are not seen as individuals who predominantly flee from war, murder, and terror, but as "parasites" who come to Austria in order to exploit Austrians by living from taxes.

Kurz says directly that he fears that given immigration and refugees, "it will become ever harder to finance our social system". That foreigners get more out of the system than they pay in is not just an idea advanced by politicians, but also believed by a significant share of the population. In the 2014 wave of the European Social Survey, 55.9 per cent of the Austrian respondents said that immigrants took out more from the social system than they put in, 17.3 per cent held the opposite opinion, and 26.7 per cent said that neither of both was true.[13] The reality looks different than the majority thinks: according to data, in 2015, non-Austrian citizens paid €5.3 billion into the social security system and received services and benefits for the total amount of €3.7 billion. Their contributions amounted to 9.5 per cent of the social system's budget, and the benefits that they got out of the system to just 6.1 per cent. As part of these payments and benefits, non-Austrian citizens paid €2.8 billion in pension contributions and received pensions in the amount of €1.1 billion (John 2016).

Strache combines the topos of numbers and the topos of culture (Reisigl and Wodak 2001, 79, 80) in order to present Muslims as a threat. The first uses the logic of large numbers in order to construct a problem, and the second fetishises cultural difference in order to argue that there is a problem. Strache criticises that there are "more than 700,000 Muslims" (Strache) and says there are "more Muslim than Catholic children" in Vienna and that "our children here in Vienna have become a minority in their own city". He uses the possessive determiners "our" and "their" in order to express the claim that Muslim children are aliens and only non-Muslim children of Austrians ("our children") belong to the in-group of Austrians. He implies that Islam is non-Austrian and Christianity Austrian. A split between religions is constructed and one side is identified with the nation and the other side split off the nation. Being Muslim is presented as a cultural problem and the presence of Muslims in Austria as cultural destruction and as a threat to language, religion, and culture. Strache argues that these perceived problems are the results of "a very, very undifferentiated policy of mass immigration". He here uses the strategy of linguistic intensification ("very, very", "mass") in order to try to communicate that there is a threat and an urgent need for political change.

In a speech at the 2017 FPÖ New Year Meeting, Norbert Hofer (2017), who was the party's candidate in the 2017 presidential election and became Minister for Transport, Innovation, and Technology in the ÖVP/FPÖ government, said:

> Our traditions apply. Our culture applies. Our unnegotiable community of values, my dear friends, applies. And he who does not like that may ultimately return to his Islamic country. [...] Not we Austrians have to adapt, but rather those immigrated guests who want to live with us permanently. And they have to accept that Christianity has shaped Austria's culture and its way of life. [...] We need a commitment to our culture, our history, our identity, and our way of life. And I am tired of us Austrians having to constantly worry about whether some people, who have migrated to us, agree or not. The one who does not like it, dear friends, does not have to be here. We have our rules, our culture, our language, here. And we predominantly speak German, not Arabic and not Turkish or other languages.[14]

In this short passage, Hofer uses the possessive pronoun "our" 14 times and the personal pronoun "we" four times. He makes clear that "we" and "our" stands for Austria, German, and Christianity. By "he", "they", "them", and "his", he refers to Muslims, Arabs, and Turks, who in his opinion should go home if they do not assimilate their culture to the dominant one. Hofer constructs an us/them differential and codes this differential as Austrian on the one side and as Islamic, Arabic, and Turkish on the other side.

In its party programme, the FPÖ defines "our homeland of Austria as part of the German-speaking linguistic and cultural community. [...] The language, history and culture of Austria are German" (FPÖ 2011, 2, 5). One of the FPÖ policy guidelines is that "we are committed to protecting our homeland of Austria, our national identity and autonomy as well as our natural livelihood" (FPÖ 2011, 3). Christianity and German language are, for the FPÖ, inherent parts of the Austrian nation. It is therefore no surprise that the party and its representatives see Muslims and those who speak another language than German as un-Austrian and as a threat to the constructed German nationhood of Austria.

In September 2017, Austrian tabloid media reported that there are more Muslim than Catholic pupils in Vienna's schools (Heute 2017; Kronen Zeitung 2017; Österreich 2017). *Kronen Zeitung* ran an article with the title "32,000 in the Schools:

More Muslims Than Catholics in Vienna". Strache may have taken this information from tabloid media. The tabloids only focused on primary schools (*Volksschule*) and new secondary schools (*Neue Mittelschulen*), but left out pupils aged 10–14 who attend secondary academic schools (*Gymnasium, Allgemeinbildende Höhere Schulen* [AHS]). The majority of pupils in new secondary schools are Muslims, which has to do with the fact that Austria's secondary school system is class-structured and there is a tendency that traditional working-class parents tend to send their children to this type of school. According to data, in the school year 2016/17, there were 47,132 Roman Catholic children, 31,984 Muslim children, 29,395 other Christian children, and 22,133 children of no conviction in Vienna's schools (Katholische Kirche Österreich 2017). The claim that there is a majority of Muslim school children seems to be fake news.

Table 7.8 shows the development of religious conviction in Austria. Although the share of Muslims has increased, the major tendency is that Austria has in the past 50 years become a much more secular country. The share of people without religious conviction has increased from 3.8 per cent in 1961 to 16.9 per cent in 2011. Austria's major religious trend is not, as claimed by the FPÖ, a supposed "Islamisation", but rather the trend of secularisation. The cultural change that far-right observers whine about has, to a significant degree, to do with the circumstance that fewer and fewer individuals find the idea of god meaningful and perceive religious faith and communities as not giving adequate answers to contemporary society. Atheism and agnosticism are, just like Christianity and Islam, important parts of Austrian culture and world culture.

In its political handbook, the FPÖ (2013) argues: "Islam is a religion that sees the world as a war zone – until the whole of humanity is Islamic"[15] (53). This is a generalising statement that subsumes all members and versions of Islam into a whole that is

TABLE 7.8 The development of the share of the members of specific religions in the total Austrian population (in per cent)

Religion	1951	1961	1971	1981	1991	2001	2011
Roman Catholic	89.0	89.0	87.4	84.3	78.0	73.6	64.2
Protestantism	6.2	6.2	6.0	5.6	5.0	4.7	4.8
Islam	-	-	0.3	1.0	2.0	4.2	7.9
No religious conviction	3.8	3.8	4.3	6.0	8.6	12.0	16.9

Sources: Österreichischer Integrationsfonds (2017), Statistik Austria (2019)

presented as violent. In its 2017 election programme, the FPÖ (2017) says that "Islam is not part of Austria"[16] (3). The FPÖ has a nativist understanding of culture. It sees Austria as part of the "German linguistic and cultural community"[17] (FPÖ 2013, 3). It considers language, religion, art, tradition, morals, customs, songs, prayers, literature, poesy, music, and thought as forming the nation (FPÖ 2013, 258). By defining Austria's nation as German and excluding Islam from Austria, the FPÖ presents a static and one-dimensional understanding of culture. Austria has been a multicultural social formation since the time of the Austro-Hungarian Empire so that its culture has never been homogeneous. All social groups living in Austria shape a certain part and play a certain role in Austria's culture.

Kurz and Strache also refer to refugees by using criminonyms (Reisigl and Wodak 2001, 52), i.e. linguistic constructs that communicate that there is the threat of crime or terror. Strache speaks of the "IS-guy in a refugee home in Salzburg" who "was in touch with the Paris assassins", and Kurz of those who "set off to illegally enter Europe". Strache, by evoking the terror of the Islamic State in the context of a refugee home, not just uses a criminonym, but also the fallacious logic of inductive generalisation, i.e. a "hasty generalisation" known as *secundum quid*, which argues "on the basis of a quantitative sample that is not representative" (Reisigl and Wodak 2001, 73). By mentioning terrorism and the refugee home together, the generalisations that refugee homes give shelter to terrorists and are breeding grounds for terrorism are constructed. Strache underlines this meaning by saying that "very dangerous developments take place that also concern recruitment". Kurz constructs refugees as "illegals", which does not take into account that there are people fleeing from war, persecution, and terror. The Universal Declaration of Human Rights defines the right for everyone "to seek and to enjoy in other countries asylum from persecution"[18] (§14). The UN Convention Relating to the Status of Refugees specifies persecution of refugees as the "fear of being persecuted for reasons of race, religion, nationality, membership of a particular social group or political opinion".[19] All EU countries have ratified both conventions. Therefore, those arriving in Europe and declaring to seek asylum shall be treated as asylum seekers and not as illegal immigrants.

The overall effect of nationalist ideology, as communicated by Strache and Kurz, is that attention is distracted from real economic power differentials between capital and labour as well as the rich and the poor. A study estimates that in Austria, the richest 1 per cent owns 37.0 per cent of the wealth, whereas the share of the poorest 50 per cent in total wealth is just 2.2 per cent (Eckerstorfer et al. 2013).

Figure 7.5 shows the development of the wage share (at market prices) in Austria and the EU-15 countries in the period from 1960 until 2019. The wage share is the share of total wages in the gross domestic product.

In Austria, the wage share dropped during the period of analysis from a height of 66.1 per cent in 1978 to a level of 54.3 per cent in 2019. In the EU-15 countries, the highest level of 65.5 per cent was reached in 1975. Ever since, there was, just like in Austria, a drop to 55.5 per cent in 2019. The drop of the wage share means an increase of the capital share, the share of capital in the gross domestic product. Many societies have, after the economic crisis of the mid-1970s, introduced neoliberal policies that have privileged capital at the expense of labour. The dropping wage share is an expression of the class conflict at the macro-economic level. Capital has expanded its share of the economy, whereas the share of the collective worker has significantly dropped.

The data show that the increasing gap between capital and labour and the inequality between the rich and the poor is a real social problem. Nationalist ideology that pits

FIGURE 7.5 Development of the wage share in Austria and the EU-15 countries
Source: AMECO (2019)

Austrians (or members of another nation) as a hard-working nation against immigrants and refugees who are presented as a social burden that negatively impacts the living conditions of common people distracts attention from the class conflict. By constructing and presenting refugees and immigrants as a social burden and "scroungers" who live from the wealth of national citizens, right-wing demagogues "nationalise" social problems and circumvent discussions of the huge wealth differentials and deepening inequalities that exist in contemporary capitalist countries. Right-wing politicians such as Strache and Kurz fulfil an ideological role that serves the interest of capital.

Nationalist ideology is not just produced from above, but also finds responses from below. Social media is a realm of communication, where such responses can be observed.

7.5 Social Media Analysis

Heinz-Christian Strache and Sebastian Kurz are the two Austrian politicians with the highest number of followers and likes on their Facebook pages. In the middle of January 2018, Strache's Facebook page had around 780,000 likes and 750,000 followers, and Kurz's Facebook page around 720,000 likes and approximately the same number of followers.

Austrian data journalists captured all comments made on 40 Austrian political Facebook pages from August to October 2017 (Khomenko 2018). The resulting dataset consists of 2.9 million comments posted by 400,000 users. Some 8,900 power users (2 per cent) posted around half of all comments (49 per cent). Some 400 users (0.1 per cent) who posted at least 500 comments accounted for 18.9 per cent of all comments. The results show that political commenting on Facebook tends to be dominated by a group of small, highly active users. The study did not analyse if there were bots among this commenting elite and if the dominant users' comments received significant attention (views, likes, referencing comments).

The Austria Press Agency (2017) analysed 4.2 million user reactions to Facebook postings of the main parties' frontrunners during the 2017 Austrian federal elections. Sixty-four per cent of the followers of Pilz List's frontrunner Peter Pilz were also active on other frontrunners' pages. The activity share was 59 per cent for followers of NEOS frontrunner Matthias Strolz, 58 per cent in the case of Green Party frontrunner Ulrike Lunacek, 37 per cent in the case of SPÖ frontrunner Christian Kern, 29 per cent in the case of Sebastian Kurz (ÖVP), and 22 per cent in the case of Heinz-Christian Strache (FPÖ).

The analysis shows that the pages of Kurz and Strache are, to a much higher degree than the other frontrunner pages, self-contained filter bubbles.

Data journalist Muzayen Al-Youssef (2017) gathered reactions (comments, shares, emoticons – "like", "love", "haha", "wow", "sad", "angry") from the pages of the frontrunners of Austria's major parties from 1 August until 28 September 2017 (see the overview in Table 7.9). Strache received the largest number of reactions, followed by Kurz and Kern. The average number of reactions per posting was largest for Kurz, followed by Strache and Kern. Given that Strache and Kurz are the two Austrian politicians with the largest number of Facebook followers, this result is not surprising. Strache received by far the highest average number of "angry" reactions to his postings, which may have to do with the fact that opponents of the ÖVP and the FPÖ are less organised in filter bubbles and therefore tend to also react to FPÖ and ÖVP postings. It may also indicate that Strache's politics and postings are especially polarising.

The FPÖ also produces, maintains, and uses its own media, such as Unzensuriert.at and FPÖ TV. Unzensuriert.at ("Uncensored") is a news platform that was founded in

TABLE 7.9   Analysis of reactions to Facebook postings of the frontrunners in the 2017 Austrian federal elections

Politician	Number of reactions	Number of postings	Average number of reactions per posting	Average number of "angry" emotions per posting
Heinz-Christian Strache (FPÖ)	677,789	313	2,165	216
Sebastian Kurz (ÖVP)	565,309	200	2,826	43
Christian Kern (SPÖ)	395,429	230	1,719	7
Matthias Strolz (NEOS)	31,489	201	157	2
Peter Pilz (Pilz List)	26,939	52	518	5
Ulrike Lunacek (Green Party)	10,142	141	72	0.3
Barbara Rosenk-ranz (FLÖ)	8,277	135	61	4
Mirko Messner (KPÖ)	418	9	46	0
Isabella Heydarfa-dai (Die Weißen)	178	29	6	0.03

Source: Al-Youssef (2017)

2009 by people around FPÖ politician Martin Graf, who was then the Third President of the Austrian Parliament. FPÖ TV is a YouTube channel that in January 2018 had about 19,000 followers. Alexander Höferl, Fritz Simandl, and Walter Asperl have played important roles at Unzensuriert. On 12 January 2018, Unzensuriert was the 746th most accessed web platform in Austria.[20] In December 2017, Höferl switched from his work for Unzensuriert and as the FPÖ's director of communication to the job of the communication director of FPÖ Minister of the Interior Herbert Kickl. Unzensuriert also spreads links to its articles via social media, especially on Facebook, where it had more than 60,000 followers in January 2018.

In 2017, the German investigative journalist Stefanie Albrecht made an undercover report about Unzensuriert. She applied to work at Unzensuriert and documented how fake news was adopted from the blog Philosophia Perennis for an article without checking for correctness. Höferl told Albrecht: "We do not make this medium because we feel so strongly about independent journalism, but rather because we want to support this political movement in a certain way. [...] We report purely positively about it"[21] (RTL Extra 2017). In 2016, the Austrian Office for the Protection of the Constitution and the Suppression of Terrorism assessed that Unzensuriert "publishes content that is partly extremely xenophobic und has anti-Semitic tendencies. Also conspiracy theory approaches and pro-Russian ideology are represented"[22] (Bundesamt für Verfassungsschutz und Terrorismusbekämpfung 2016).

The journalists Jakob Winter and Ingrid Brodnig (2016) analysed all 124 articles published by Unzensuriert during a two-week period in 2016. Whereas the coverage of refugees, migrants, Muslims, the EU, presidential candidate Alexander van der Bellen, and the left was purely negative, reports about FPÖ presidential candidate Norbert Hofer, the FPÖ, Donald Trump, and Russia were almost entirely positive.

An analysis has documented nationalist reactions to Strache's and Hofer's Facebook postings during the 2016 Austrian presidential elections (Fuchs 2016a). Hans-Henning Scharsach (2017) argues that three types of violent comments can be found among the reactions to Strache's Facebook postings: "insults"[23] (122), "calls for violence"[24] (123), and "fantasies of violence expressed in typical Nazi-diction"[25] (123).

Strache often posts links to online articles from *Kronen Zeitung*, especially those that focus on crimes committed by asylum seekers and immigrants: "It is a business based on reciprocity, in which both sides win: Strache benefits polit-ically. [...] *Krone* profits economically"[26] (Scharsach 2017, 130). And the FPÖ also supports *Krone* by buying ad space: according to a report, over a six-week period during the Austrian 2017 election campaign phase, the FPÖ was, with €953,778, the party that invested the highest amount of money into newspaper ads. The largest share of this sum, namely 33 per cent, was spent on ads in *Kronen Zeitung* (Dossier 2017).

Table 7.10 shows that the postings in the analysed dataset predominantly communicate support for the ÖVP/FPÖ coalition government. A small minority of 14.1 per cent voiced opposition.

Authoritarianism is a character structure, ideology, and mode for the organisation of society that is shaped by the belief in top-down leadership, nationalism, the friend/enemy scheme, and militarism/law and order politics (for a detailed elaboration of this model, see Fuchs 2018a). In the analysed dataset, all four elements could be found to a significant degree in the ideological structure of postings supporting the ÖVP/FPÖ government (see Table 7.11). Top-down leadership is an authoritarian organisation principle of social systems and society that is anti-democratic and believes in centralising power in the hands of single persons or groups. Whereas nationalism is an ideology that organises the inner identity and self-understanding of nationalist groups, the friend/enemy scheme is a corresponding ideological principle that defines the inner identity ("we", "us") against outer enemies ("they", "them"). The law and order principle and militarism are modes of dealing with the identified enemies. They suggest repressing the enemy by direct, structural, or symbolic violence.

Table 7.11 shows that all four principles of authoritarianism could be identified in the analysed dataset. The friend/enemy scheme was the discourse principle used most frequently for justifying support for the ÖVP/FPÖ government: 65.2 per cent of all postings supporting the right-wing Austrian government employed a reference to

TABLE 7.10 Share of specific types of postings in the analysed dataset, $N = 2,367$

Position	Absolute number	Relative share
Support	1,607	67.9%
Opposition	334	14.1%
Unclear	426	18.0%

TABLE 7.11 Dimensions of authoritarianism in the analysed dataset among postings supporting the ÖVP/FPÖ government, $N = 1{,}607$

Position	Absolute number	Relative share
Leadership	387	24.1%
Nationalism	193	12.0%
Friend/enemy scheme	1,047	65.2%
Law and order	615	38.3%

enemies. Law and order discourse was the second most frequently employed discourse principles used for justifying support, followed by references to strong leadership and nationalism. The four discursive elements of authoritarianism cannot always be clearly separated; there are cases where they appear in combined forms.

We will now have a look at examples found in the analysed dataset for each of the four dimensions of authoritarianism. The examples have been translated from German to English.

The Leadership Discourse

Consider the following example postings from the analysed dataset:

A young man who has more intellect than the current rulers who are out of touch with reality. Hope he remains healthy and can implement the signs that he sets.[27] (#968)

Dear Mr Minister of the Interior, please redeem the Austrian people from this plague …[28] (#757)

Thank you, Sebastian Kurz. Finally steps into the right direction are taken in respect to the topic of 'refugee policy'. Please close down the borders and control closely who comes into our country![29] (#1057)

A new government that also translates its election promises into action is something entirely new. That's almost like President Donald Trump. BRAVO, just keep it up.[30] (#1967)

If Mr Kickl as minister clamps down just half as hard as he did as oppositional politician, then he is a big gain for Austria's security.[31] (#2187)

Dear Sebastian, please come to Berlin and rule us as well! Otherwise Merkel will soon turn Germany into an Islamic caliphate.[32] (#877)

Maybe Germany and Austria can form a grand coalition and Mr Kurz then rules both countries!!!!!!!![33] (#1773)

In these passages, Sebastian Kurz is predicated by anthroponyms. An anthroponym is a characterisation that uses human capacities, such as references to the human body or mind. Kurz is presented as a "young man" with "intellect". In a similar vein, other postings characterise Kurz, for example, as "a 31-year-old politician in Europe, who recognises the sorrows and hardships of the people"[34] (#277), a "reasonable, routinised and convincing [...] 31-year-old, young politician"[35] (#1281), or a "young, dynamic man"[36] (#1095).

Such anthroponyms reproduce the tendency that in contemporary politics, the focus on personality, personal life, and looks replaces the engagement with political topics and causes of society's problems. Politics has become a marketplace where politicians try to present and sell themselves as brands and celebrities. In his government declaration to the Austrian Parliament, Kurz stressed that his team consists of "younger ones and the ones who are young at heart"[37] (Kurz 2017b, 4). Neoliberalism has advanced the ideal of everyone being an entrepreneur of the self, who is responsible for him or herself, has to dynamically adapt to changes, and is individually responsible for failure just like for success. In order to find work and stay in work, the neoliberal entrepreneurial subject, who often works as precarious freelancer, has to sell not just his services, but him or herself, in order to attract clients. Being young is, in the context of neoliberalism, a symbol of agility, strength, and hard, productive labour, whereas old age is, in the same context, a symbol of unproductiveness and dependence: "Human capital's constant and ubiquitous aim, whether studying, interning, working, planning retirement, or reinventing itself in a new life, is to entrepreneurialize its endeavors, appreciate its value, and increase its rating or ranking" (Brown 2015, 36). The effect of neoliberal entrepreneurialism is the stepwise destruction of the welfare state. Sebastian Kurz is a manifestation of neoliberal subjectivity. In reality, the age and look of a politician say nothing about the policies he or she stands for. The focus on personality distracts public attention from and destroys the potential dedication of time to a thorough analysis of society's problems.

In authoritarian thought, leaders are often seen as both close to the people and godlike. A clear example is the posting that speaks of Kickl as being able to "redeem the Austrian people from this plague" of refugees. Using the topos of the saviour (Wodak 2015, 10), Kickl is presented as the godlike redeemer and the hatred of refugees as a holy, religious struggle. It almost seems like their hatred of refugees has, for many citizens, the status of a twenty-first-century crusade. God stands for love, whereas the characterisation of refugees and migrants as a disease (the plague) expresses absolute hatred. Authoritarianism preaches love for the leader and the fictive collective of the nation and hatred against constructed enemies. Also, the logic of comparison is used for stressing the leadership qualities of Kurz, Strache, and Kickl. The government is, for example, compared to Trump.

Authoritarian leaders are not only religiously worshiped by their followers. The latter also stress that powerful leaders are required to bring about change by taking harsh measures. In the examples, this becomes evident in the formulations that Kurz should "close down" and "closely control" the borders, that Kickl will "clamp down" on foreigners and is "a big gain for Austria's security", that the government takes "action", and that Kurz immediately brings about "steps in the right direction". Strong leadership is, on the one hand, envisioned as the centralisation of power and, on the other hand, as the use of that power for implementing law and order politics.

There were also postings that called for a reunification of Austria and Germany under Sebastian Kurz's rule. Kurz is, in this context, posited as a strong leader and is positioned against Angela Merkel, who is presented as refugee-friendly chancellor destroying Germany: "Merkel will soon turn Germany into an Islamic caliphate" (see above), Sebastian Kurz "could spare us mummy Merkel"[38] (#922), "The delusion of our mummy must be confronted by competent, fresh leaders"[39] (#1330), "Your mummy nevertheless wants to again fly in around 2 million Muslim asylum seekers on planes (on your costs !) !! The decline is already predetermined. One wants a complete substitution of the people !!"[40] (#838). Users who employ the genderonym "mummy" for characterising Angela Merkel want to express that in their view, she shows love for refugees and thereby hatred for the German nation. Refugees are defined as not belonging to the nation and as un-German. It is a tragedy of history that 73 years after the end of the Second World War and Nazi-Germany's terror, some Germans and Austrians take Kurz's politics as an opportunity for demanding an *Anschluss*, this time not of Austria to Germany, but of Germany to Austria ("Kurz then rules both countries", "come to Berlin and rule us as well").

Chapter Seven | Social Media-Authoritarianism **217**

Nationalism

Let us have a look at some examples of nationalism in the analysed dataset:

At last Austrian politics is being made![41] (#1851)

Bravo, finally politics is being made for the Austrians.[42] (#1876)

Please only look out for Austria and its people! (#2112) [43]

The first difference to the red government of Kern is that politics is first of all made for the Austrians and not for the refugees.[44] (#1830)

First we are tolerant, and then we are foreign in our own country.[45] (#600)

Austria first! Thereby I mean the autochthonous Austrians who are in need and not some Chechen guardians of public morals, criminals committing violence against our police and other migrating criminals.[46] (#190)

In the next 10 years, we want to again feel like Austrians and masters of our own country.[47] (#1727)

Restore a liveable, secure Austria for its citizens! That's only possible through harshness![48] (#2347)

Kickl was the best choice! He is tough, correct and loves Austria![49] (#2297)

The nation is, in these postings, characterised as a political unit ("our own country", "Austrian politics", "Austrian citizens"), an economic unit ("a liveable, secure Austria for its citizens"), and a people ("the Austrians", "Austria and its people"). In some of the examples, the use of the first-person plural pronoun "we" ("We are tolerant", "we are foreign in our own country") and of the possessive personal pronoun "our" ("Our own country", "our police") marks a nationalist in-group identity that is defined against an alien outside against which it closes itself off and that it considers as enemy. The postings show the close relationship of nationalism, (new) racism, and the friend/enemy scheme. The Austrian nation is defined against refugees and migrants, who are seen as intruders and aliens against whom the nation must be defended by political measures. As a consequence, there are calls for toughness, harshness, and law and order politics. The nation is imagined as culturally pure, homogenous, and unitary. There is a call to an imagined lost origin. Migrant and refugees are blamed for this loss. In reality, Austria has never been culturally homogenous, but has since the time of the Austrian Empire been a multicultural society.

Among the 200 most widely used family names in Austria, one finds not just names whose linguistic origin is German (such as Wagner, Gruber, or Winkler), but also Hungarian names such as Horvath and Toth, Czech names such as Novak, and Serbian names such as Jovanović.[50] In the Austrian online phone book, one can find 9,210 entries for Gruber, 6,939 for Wagner, and 4,499 for Winkler, but also 3,280 families named Horvath or Horvat.[51] Families originally speaking Hungarian, Czech, Slovakian, Slovenian, Croatian, Serbian, or Polish have been settling and living in cities such as Vienna for hundreds of years. Austria is not and has never been an originally and purely German country.

Nationalist rhetoric that is quite similar to the rhetoric found in the analysed dataset and that defines Austria as a homeland against migrants can also be found in the ÖVP/FPÖ government programme: "We protect our welfare state from abuse and will stop illegal migration to Austria"[52] (ÖVP/FPÖ 2017, 7). "We want to preserve our homeland Austria as liveable country with all its cultural amenities. This includes to decide on our own who is allowed to live with us as immigrants and to stop illegal migration"[53] (ÖVP/FPÖ 2017, 9). Social protection (the welfare state, good livelihood) and culture are defined as being part of the nation ("our", "we"). Both sequences oppose the nation and its claimed ownership of culture and the welfare state to migrants, implying that they are a threat to welfare, uncivilised and uncultured.

The Friend/Enemy Scheme

The friend/enemy scheme was the most frequently employed ideological discourse principle in the analysed dataset. Table 7.12 provides an analysis of specific enemies mentioned in the dataset.

Migrants and refugees (70.6 per cent of all mentions of enemies) are by far the most common enemy mentioned by those who employed the friend/enemy scheme in the dataset. The political left and Angela Merkel are the second and third most mentioned enemies. Given that the refugee topic dominated the 2017 Austrian parliamentary election campaigns and debates, this result is not a surprise.

Those who advance nationalist, xenophobic, or racist arguments do so by using specific ideological forms of communication (see Table 7.7) — biological, socio-economic, political, and cultural discourse themes. Biological arguments, namely the claim that

TABLE 7.12 The mentioning of specific enemies in the analysed dataset

Position	Absolute number	Relative share
Migrants and refugees	814	70.6%
The political left	97	8.4%
Angela Merkel	90	7.8%
Political opposition	63	5.5%
EU	44	3.8%
Islam and Muslims	33	2.9%
Criminals and terrorists	6	0.5%
The media and journalists	4	0.3%
The unemployed and welfare recipients	2	0.2%
Total number of times specific enemies were mentioned	1153	

refugees and immigrants are an inferior race, could, with some exceptions, hardly be found in the dataset. In contrast, socio-economic, political, and cultural forms of nationalism and new racism prevailed. Let us have a look at some examples:

> It can also not be right that in Vienna council flats are filled with foreigners! And Austrians do not get a flat![54] (#191)

> 50% foreigners is cool! Keep it up … 90% of the school children do not speak our language.[55] (#146)

> And then Europe is soon just as overpopulated, impoverished, violent, ghettoised as well as economically and educationally run down as the countries of origin of the skilled workers seeking asylum. Then patriarchal ways of thinking, the oppression of women, religious fanaticism and ethnic conflict prevail here again; a really nice future for Austrian children.[56] (#944)

> The central problem is not just illegal immigration ! Also official immigration from the Arab region is no longer bearable !! Alien to our culture, – An innate aversion to our lifestyle respectively our culture and religion, – Therefore they have already a long time ago begun to create their own society. They live according to their own laws and rules, – We and our country are only there to guarantee them a convenient and carefree and socially secure existence !! The 'con' of multiculturalism has been unmasked, – at the latest since the rapes, robberies, etc., etc., etc. …! In 2016, asylum seekers committed more than 15,000 crimes !! THAT is the reality !! And every sceptic should once look

over the border, – In Berlin, Arab clans call the shots and have practically eliminated the rule of the state. When will we have the same problems ?? Or is it already happening ??[57] (#1083)

I do not want to go to work for supporting people, who do not learn our language, do not integrate and do not even remotely accept our values and our culture. Furthermore, many of them will never contribute something to the functioning of our welfare state, but will forever 'remain stuck' on minimum benefits. Unfortunately this problem, as described above, concerns many refugees[58] (#1057)

We can find a number of claims in these examples that dominate not just the discourse structure of the dataset, but contemporary discussions about migration and refugees in general:

- Discourse topic of economic enemies: "They are social parasites who live from our money. They take away our jobs and houses and are a burden to our healthcare system, our education system, our social services, etc."
- Discourse topic of political enemies: "They pose a terrorist and criminal threat and a threat to our nation's security. We have to be afraid about what could happen to our children."
- Discourse topic of cultural enemies: "Their culture, language, and religion are different from ours and threaten the survival of our culture, language, and religion. If they want to live here, then they have to adopt our culture, speak our language, and accept our religion. Their culture is uncivilised, and they come from countries where religious fundamentalism is prevalent. They oppose our culture and language and are a threat to the development of our children and the survival of our nation."

The first example focuses on constructing immigrants as a socio-economic problem. The use of the verb "filling" (*befüllen* in German) for characterising immigrants living in council flats communicates that there is a mass of people that constitutes a burden to the housing system. The posting combines the topos of (large) numbers and the topos of burdening (Reisigl and Wodak 2001, 78–79) for arguing that the insinuated large number of immigrants results in problems for Austrians. The second example uses the same logic and claims that there is a very large share of immigrants in the population, resulting in a vast majority (90 per cent) of children not speaking German. Immigrants are presented as constituting a cultural problem.

The third example combines the socio-economic, the political, and the cultural discourse topics. Immigrants are presented as a socio-economic problem (overpopulation, impoverishment, ghettos), a political problem (violence, oppression of women, fanaticism, ethnic conflicts), and a cultural problem (educational decline). The topos of threat, which argues that "if a political action or decision bears specific dangerous, threatening consequences, one should not perform or do it" (Reisigl and Wodak 2001, 77), is used by claiming that refugees and immigrants pose a large threat to society and "Austrian children". Both the second and third examples refer to children, which is a rhetoric strategy that plays with the fear of parents that something could happen to their children.

Also, the fourth example uses the topos of immigrants as threat to culture ("aversion to our lifestyle" and "religion"), political life ("they live according to their own laws", "rapes, robberies", "asylum seekers committed more than 15 000 crimes", "Arab clans" eliminate "the rule of the state"), and the economy (we "guarantee them a convenient and carefree and socially secure existence"). Immigrants and Muslims are presented as criminals, social "parasites", and cultural aliens. The example combines socio-economic, political, and cultural themes, and advances cultural nationalism ("our culture") and political nationalism ("our country").

The fifth example constructs refugees as a socio-economic problem ("I [...] work for supporting [these] people", they "never contribute something to the functioning of our welfare state", they "remain stuck" on "minimum benefits") and as a cultural problem (they "do not learn our language, do not integrate and do not even remotely accept our values and our culture"). By making use of the topos of threat, refugees are presented as a socio-economic burden and cultural threat.

All five examples use the logic of the friend/enemy scheme for constructing an us/them difference between Austrians and foreigners. We-identity is expressed by reference to the ethnonyms "Austrians" and "Austrian children" and the use of collective nouns and possessive pronouns as in "we and our country", "our lifestyle", "our religion", "our language", "our culture", "our welfare state", etc. Refugees and immigrants are purely negatively characterised as "parasites", criminals, and cultural aliens.

It was already shown in Section 7.4 that immigrants contribute more to Austria's welfare system than they take out, and that secularisation is one of the largest cultural changes. Austria is not on the way to becoming a predominantly Muslim country, but is becoming an ever-more secular country. How has the number of asylum seekers coming to Austria developed in recent years? Table 7.13 shows an overview.

The year 2015 saw the peak of asylum seekers in recent years. At that time, the Islamic State had captured significant parts of Syria and Iraq. By 2017, the number was lower than in 2014. The majority of asylum seekers have been coming from Syria, Afghanistan, and Iraq, from where many families and individuals had to flee because of war and the Islamic State's terror. The whole region has been politically destabilised by the wars in Afghanistan (since 2001) and Iraq (2003–2011), in which EU countries such as the United Kingdom, Poland, the Netherlands, Germany, Italy, Bulgaria, Romania, Spain, and the Czech Republic participated. The political turmoil and chaos benefited the rise of the Islamic State. Given the falling levels of asylum seekers after the 2015 peak, to speak directly or metaphorically of masses of refugees is certainly a gross exaggeration that does not correspond to reality.

Table 7.14 shows that in 2015, Germany was the country that received the largest share of asylum application, followed by Hungary, Sweden, Austria, Italy, and France. In 2016, the countries with the largest shares were Germany, Italy, France, Greece, and Austria. Paragraph 18 of the Charter of Fundamental Rights of the European Union defines a right to asylum under the rules of the Geneva Convention (Convention Relating to the Status of Refugees 1951). The implication is that denying refugees the right to flee from persecution, hindering them to do so, or setting a maximum limit to the annual number of asylum application denies them human rights and the right to life. The problem the EU has faced is that it does not have a quota system that regulates the distribution of refugees and asylum seekers in a legally binding manner. As a result, some countries have very low shares of the overall number of asylum seekers.

TABLE 7.13 Asylum seekers in Austria

	2017	2016	2015	2014
Asylum seekers	24,296	42,285	88,340	28,452
Positive asylum decisions	29,588	26,517	19,003	11,535
Negative asylum decisions	27,474	25,487	24,017	14,596
Top four countries of origins of asylum seekers	Syria Afghanistan Pakistan Iraq	Afghanistan Syria Iraq Pakistan	Afghanistan Syria Iraq Iran	Syria Afghanistan Russia Kosovo

Source: BMI, www.bmi.gv.at/301/Statistiken/, accessed 28 January 2017

TABLE 7.14   Asylum applications in the EU

	Asylum applicants 2015	Asylum applicants 2016	Share of EU total 2015, in %	Share of EU total 2016, in %
EU-28	1,322,825	1,260,910	-	-
Belgium	44,660	18,280	3.4	1.4
Bulgaria	20,365	19,420	1.5	1.5
Czech Republic	1,515	1,475	0.1	0.1
Denmark	20,935	6,180	1.6	0.5
Germany	476,510	745,155	36.0	59.1
Estonia	230	175	0.0	0.0
Ireland	3,275	2,245	0.2	0.2
Greece	13,205	51,110	1.0	4.1
Spain	14,780	15,755	1.1	1.2
France	76,165	84,270	5.8	6.7
Croatia	210	2,225	0.0	0.2
Italy	83,540	122,960	6.3	9.8
Cyprus	2,265	2,940	0.2	0.2
Latvia	330	350	0.0	0.0
Lithuania	315	430	0.0	0.0
Luxembourg	2,505	2,160	0.2	0.2
Hungary	177,135	29,430	13.4	2.3
Malta	1,845	1,930	0.1	0.2
Netherlands	44,970	20,945	3.4	1.7
Austria	88,160	42,255	6.7	3.4
Poland	12,190	12,305	0.9	1.0
Portugal	895	1,460	0.1	0.1
Romania	1,260	1,880	0.1	0.1
Slovenia	275	1,310	0.0	0.1
Slovakia	330	145	0.0	0.0
Finland	32,345	5,605	2.4	0.4
Sweden	162,450	28,790	12.3	2.3
United Kingdom	40,160	39,735	3.0	3.2

Source: Eurostat (2019)

It is in this context surprising that Sebastian Kurz sees the attempt to establish EU-wide quotas as a failure and argues that "the member states should decide themselves if and how many people they take in. [...] To force states to admit refugees does not help Europe"[59] (Die Welt 2017). Implicitly, this implies that he thinks that EU member states have the right to say they want to accommodate no refugees and to deny asylum seekers the right to life by sending them collectively back or not letting them in.

Table 7.15 shows that the rate of violent crime in total crime has in Austria in the past ten years had a relatively constant value between 7.5 per cent and 8.0 per cent. The absolute number of violent crimes has in 2015 and 2016 been lower than in 2009, 2011, and 2012. Table 7.16 shows that the murder rate (the number of intentional homicides per hundred thousand inhabitants) has in the years 2009, 2014, and 2015 been the lowest in the EU-28 countries. Overall, one cannot observe a drastic rise of crime and violent crime in Austria in the context of an increased number of refugees. Tabloid media report daily about single acts of violent crimes, often those committed by foreigners. Single examples are used for stoking fear and distracting attention from the circumstance that Austria is one of the securest countries in the world. The result is that the subjective feeling of being threatened by crime increases and citizens become more prone to right-wing propaganda that constructs asylum seekers and immigrants as criminals.

Tables 7.17 and 7.18 show some aspects of Austria's demographic development. Austria has an ageing population. The share of people aged 65 or older will, according to forecasts, increase from 18.5 per cent in 2017 to 28.1 per cent in 2060. Between 1951 and

TABLE 7.15   Reported crimes in Austria

	Annual number of crimes reported to the police	Annual number of violent crimes reported to the police	Share of violent crimes in total crimes reported
2008	570,952	43,090	7.5%
2009	589,961	43,447	7.4%
2010	534,351	40,532	7.6%
2011	539,970	43,353	8.0%
2012	547,764	44,290	8.1%
2013	546,396	42,344	7.7%
2014	527,692	40,184	7.6%
2015	517,869	40,333	7.8%
2016	537,792	43,098	8.0%

Source: Bundeskriminalamt (2016)

2017, the average population age in Austria has increased from 35.7 to 42.5 years. If this trend continues at the same pace, then the average age will be 49.0 years in 2080. That we live longer on average is a positive development that has to do with medical and social progress. At the same time, given that the share of pensioners increases, there is a danger that the pension system will be difficult to fund in the future. If the pension age is further increased, then this would mean that more people may work until they die and not be able to enjoy life as pensioners. In order to secure the pension system, countries such as Austria need immigrants, who tend to be younger and to be part of the workforce. Enabling refugees who have come to Austria in recent years to learn German, to engage in education and skills development, and to become part of the workforce is a positive investment in the future of the Austrian population and its social conditions. Seen from this point of view, migration and refugees may be seen not as a threat, but as an opportunity. In contrast, the ÖVP/FPÖ government programme defines migration explicitly as a security threat:

> Because of the changed geopolitical situation in and around Austria, the government however also requires a security architecture that is adapted to new threats and challenges (transnational terrorism, foreign agitation, migration), in the context of which in the future much higher priority needs to be given to prevention.[60] (ÖVP/FPÖ 2017, 31)

Law and Order Politics

Authoritarianism does not stop at defining the nation in opposition to enemies and as being best organised top-down and by strong leaders. It often argues in addition for repressing the constructed enemies, i.e. for law and order politics, militarism, or militancy.

Calls for law and order politics were widely present in the analysed dataset. The basic logic or argument is that refugees, Muslims, and immigrants pose a threat to Austrian society, its economy, political system, and culture, and that the presence of threats justifies repressive measures.

First, there were general calls for law and order in the dataset that did not further specify specific measures:

> The dogs must feel that they are not wanted here![61] (#48)

> Ultimately those who just want to nest with us are sorted out.[62] (#714)

226 Nationalism on Social Media

TABLE 7.16 Number of intentional homicides per hundred thousand inhabitants

	2008	2009	2010	2011	2012	2013	2014	2015
Belgium	1.90	1.76	1.74	1.95	1.85	1.84	1.86	1.96
Bulgaria	2.29	2.01	1.99	1.74	1.92	1.50	1.60	1.79
Czech Republic	1.09	1.01	1.00	0.79	0.90	0.87	0.80	0.80
Denmark	0.99	0.85	0.89	0.88	0.77	0.73	1.05	0.81
Germany	0.80	0.88	0.85	0.86	0.77	0.77	0.80	0.81
Estonia	6.28	5.24	5.25	4.89	4.75	3.94	3.12	3.19
Ireland	2.00	1.95	1.96	1.44	1.72	1.81	1.74	1.32
Greece	1.24	1.29	1.58	1.65	1.49	1.28	0.96	0.79
Spain	0.89	0.89	0.86	0.82	0.78	0.65	0.69	0.65
France	1.60	1.27	1.23	1.32	1.20	1.18	1.20	1.53
Croatia	1.65	1.14	1.44	1.14	1.19	1.08	0.85	0.88
Italy	1.05	1.00	0.89	0.93	0.89	0.84	0.78	0.77
Cyprus	1.16	2.38	0.85	0.95	2.20	1.27	1.17	1.42
Latvia	4.52	4.99	3.30	3.33	4.74	3.41	3.85	4.08
Lithuania	8.90	7.54	6.33	6.19	6.03	5.79	5.27	5.75
Luxembourg	1.45	1.01	1.59	0.78	0.57	0.19	0.73	0.89
Hungary	1.46	1.39	1.33	1.42	1.14	1.39	1.31	1.00
Malta	1.47	0.97	0.97	0.72	2.39	1.42	1.41	0.93
Netherlands	0.91	0.93	0.87	0.86	0.87	0.74	-	-
Austria	0.70	0.61	0.73	0.96	1.05	0.73	0.47	0.49
Poland	1.21	1.29	1.15	1.18	0.99	0.78	0.74	0.75
Portugal	1.17	1.23	1.17	1.08	1.16	1.37	0.88	0.96
Romania	2.28	1.94	1.88	1.56	1.88	1.68	1.49	1.46
Slovenia	0.55	0.64	0.54	0.83	0.68	0.58	0.82	0.97
Slovakia	1.75	1.56	1.65	1.78	1.39	1.44	1.33	0.89
Finland	2.51	2.25	2.22	2.05	1.63	1.66	1.63	1.61
Sweden	0.89	1.00	0.97	0.86	0.72	0.91	0.90	1.15
England and Wales	1.17	1.08	1.14	0.94	0.97	0.92	0.91	-
Scotland	1.83	1.61	1.91	1.76	1.19	1.15	1.11	-
Northern Ireland	1.36	1.62	1.28	1.27	1.15	1.09	0.93	1.25
EU-28 average	1.90	1.78	1.65	1.56	1.63	1.43	1.39	1.44

Source: Eurostat (2019)

Chapter Seven | Social Media-Authoritarianism

TABLE 7.17 Share of population aged 65/75 or older, in per cent

Year	Share of population aged 65 or older	Share of population aged 75 or older	Average population age
1869	5.2%	1.2%	29.6
1900	5.7%	1.5%	29.3
1934	7.9%	2.2%	33.5
1951	10.6%	3.2%	35.7
1971	14.2%	4.7%	36.1
1991	15.0%	6.7%	38.1
2011	17.8%	8.1%	41.7
2017	18.5%	9.1%	42.5
2025 (forecast)	20.7%		
2030 (forecast)	23.0%		
2040 (forecast)	26.0%		
2050 (forecast)	27.2%		
2060 (forecast)	28.1%		

Source: Statistik Austria (2019)

TABLE 7.18 Share of pensioners in total population, in per cent

Year	Share of pensioners in total population
1971	17.3%
1981	18.2%
1991	19.8%
2001	21.5%
2011	22.1%

Source: Statistik Austria (2019)

A *second demand* found in the dataset was that the borders should be closed and no asylum seekers should be let in:

Asylum needs to be categorically abolished.[63] (#2349)

I still do not understand that they simply come into our country, do not let them in, that all costs mega bucks.[64] (#224)

A *third demand* was the mass deportation of refugees and criminal migrants. The Austrian military owns three C-130 Hercules transport planes. In 2008, Strache demanded that these planes should be used for deportations so that the deportees would not be on regular flights together with other passengers: "And do you know how deportation works today? In civil aviation planes, where passengers go off on holiday, the deportee flies along. Well, what approach to deportation is this? What for do we have military transport planes such as the Hercules? I say: The Hercules needs to be converted into a departure plane. That's where they can then scream and pee themselves. Nobody is disturbed then. And then they are deported".[65] Echoing Strache, similar demands could be found in the analysed dataset:

> Put them into the next Hercules, make it fully occupied, and one needs a great many planes.[66] (#24)

> Immediate changes of the law, please, and fill up the Hercules.[67] (#260)

> The Hercules is just waiting for its use.[68] (#395)

> I wish that 2018 will become the year of deportations![69] (#2307)

Fourth, there was the *demand* to dispossess refugees:

> Seizure of cash, yes of course, they partly have more in their rucksacks than some might think.[70] (#1779)

> Seizure of cash, screening of mobile phone data, that's all completely appropriate. That's how one immediately identifies various criminals and terrorists.[71] (#1786)

> Why not also watches and necklaces, let's go the whole hog.[72] (#1725)

Fifth, there was the *demand* to build internment camps for refugees in the analysed dataset:

> Even if other states do not take back their citizens, one can intern them in order to protect citizens from danger.[73] (#301)

> Maybe one can talk to Putin, Siberia would lend itself.[74] (#254)

FPÖ politicians have demanded using mass quarters or barracks for "concentrating" asylum seekers. In December 2017, FPÖ parliamentarian Johann Gudenus demanded the creation of "mass quarters" (*Massenquartiere*) for refugees (Facebook, www.facebook.com/pg/jgudenus, 18 December 2017). Minister of the Interior Herbert Kickl argued in January 2018 for "holding asylum seekers concentrated in one place"[75] (Facebook, www.facebook.com/herbertkickl/posts/1998249077120059, 11 January 2018). The BBC reported that "Austria's far-right interior minister has caused outrage by using a term associated with Nazi death camps to say asylum seekers should be concentrated in one place" (BBC 2018). The *New York Times* wrote that for "many observers, Kickl's wording evoked Nazi-era concentration camps, where Nazis held and killed millions of Jews, political dissenters, disabled people, Roma and Sinti during World War Two" (New York Times/Reuters 2018).

In January 2018, Heinz-Christian Strache suggested the "state supervision"[76] of asylum seekers, including in military barracks. This would concern those who live in private accommodations supervised by NGOs. He said: "And it is definitely worth considering that it can make sense here and there to use vacant barracks."[77] He furthermore argued that one should think about curfews for asylum seekers:

> Already in the past there was a discussion on whether it should be the case that from a certain evening time onwards all have to be back in the barracks. There needs to be order as long as there is an open asylum procedure. Also you will certainly be aware of the existence of problems in our society.[78] (*ORF Wien Heute*, 4 January 2017)

Such logic generalises that all asylum seekers are a security threat because some are, and that therefore special control is needed.

The constitutional jurist Heinz Mayer argues that such suggestions violate the Constitution: "To lock them in at night is a problem. It is a restriction of freedom. One cannot lock in asylum seekers for no reason just because they are asylum seekers"[79] (*ORF Wien Heute*, 5 January 2017).

Sixth, there were suggestions in the analysed dataset to kill refugees and Muslims:

> In an emergency, drop them from the air …[80] (#26)

> Deportation is of no use as they come back around another corner. My opinion is that we should let them swim back, these animals.[81] (#196)

> The Muslims are in a 'holy war' with us. So proclaim martial law for a week and ask the Austrians to take matters into their own hands![82] (#747)

Everyday right-wing constructions of dangerous refugees and immigrants in tabloid media and politics have radicalised Austrian citizens' fears of change, difference, and decline. They try to cope with this fear by externalising it communicatively: they formulate violent fantasies on social media that range from tough laws to mass murder. By imagining the suffering of others, nationalists derive pleasure and feelings of superiority and omnipotence over their illusionary enemies. They act like online soldiers who constantly fight a war of words against illusionary enemies. According to Klaus Theweleit (1989), authoritarians aim at the symbolic or physical creation of a "bloody miasma, the empty space, the blackout" as "a moment of survival devoid of threat" by which they guarantee their "own survival, [...] self-preservation and self-regeneration" (221).

> The key quality of the blow as an act of physical violence is its capacity to break and crack open, to smash to pieces. It produces the man as "I," not by "switching him in" to some different reality, but by an eruption of muscular activity whose goal is to crush all existing distinction and to raise the man above the undifferentiated miasma. The civilian forms of the physical blow are many. They include verbal annihilation – also most often in revenge for "insults" [...] The movement toward miasma may also be disguised as criticism: the "searing critique," a rude encroachment that renders its objects unrecognizable, ripping them apart till they begin to resemble the critic's image of them as "bloody crap." (274).

7.6 Conclusion

Main Results

The analysis of speeches, interviews, discussions, programmes, and citizens' online and social media comments that stand in the context of Austria's ÖVP/FPÖ governments and its political plans has shown several tendencies:

- *The friend/enemy scheme*: A widespread use of the friend/enemy scheme was identified that presents refugees and immigrants as socio-economic, political, and cultural threats to Austrian society. At the socio-economic level, refugees and immigrants were presented as benefit "scroungers" (*Sozialschmarotzer*) living from Austrians' taxes and as a threat to employment, wages, funding, and the maintenance of the healthcare system, the housing system, and the pension system. At the political level, refugees and immigrants were presented as criminals, rapists, and terrorists who pose threats to Austrian citizens, public life, democracy, children, and women. At the cultural level, migrants and refugees were constructed as posing a threat to German language, Christianity, and established traditions such as Christmas.

- *Nationalism*: Widespread nationalism was identified as the flip side of the new racist friend/enemy scheme. Nationalism today mostly takes on non-biologistic forms that do not argue that there are biologically inferior and superior nations and races. Rather, nationalism today tends to take on cultural, political, and socio-economic forms: migrants and refugees are culturally presented as threats to "our culture", "our language", "our traditions", and "our lifestyle"; politically as threats to "our state", "our country", "our democracy", and "our security"; and economically as threats to "our jobs", "our economy", "our resources/infrastructures", and "our social system". Cultural, political, and socio-economic nationalisms are not strictly separate ideological topics, but often appear in combined forms.

- *Authoritarian leadership*: Followers of the ÖVP and the FPÖ expressed their admiration of these parties' leaders Sebastian Kurz and Heinz-Christian Strache. They especially admire Kurz's youthfulness and see Strache, Kurz, and Kickl as political leaders and godlike political figures who will use their power to "redeem" Austria from refugees, immigrants, and Muslims.

- *Law and order politics*: Many followers of the FPÖ and the ÖVP called in the analysed online comments for law and order politics directed against refugees, immigrants, and Muslims. In order to counter their own fears, they argued for taking tough measures. Six types of favoured law and order politics were identified: general calls for law and order, the closure of all borders to refugees, mass deportation of refugees and criminal migrants, the dispossession of refugees, the creation of internment camps for refugees, and the killing of refugees and Muslims. There was a continuum of law and order politics with increasing levels of violence that start at the tightening of laws and end at the fascist mass extermination of perceived enemies.

Taken together, empirical research shows indications that among supporters of the ÖVP/FPÖ government, there is a significant degree of right-wing authoritarian ideology that combines the friend/enemy scheme, nationalism, the belief in the need for top-down leadership, and law and order politics.

Both parties have managed to convince a significant proportion of the Austrian population that refugees, immigrants, and Muslims constitute a major problem of society, to which right-wing responses are required. In this ideology, social problems derive from cultural, political, and socio-economic conflicts between Austrians on the one side, and refugees, immigrants, and Muslims on the other side. There are no class conflicts in the ideologies of the ÖVP and the FPÖ. But at the same time, the ÖVP in particular has been supported by big capital and both parties advance policies that favour capitalist interests.

The conducted case study shows how authoritarian capitalism uses nationalist ideology, the friend/enemy scheme, the leadership ideology, and law and order politics for distracting attention from the class conflict. The class conflict is ideologically "nationalised", which means that social problems are explained in terms of a conflict between nations. Refugees and immigrants are constructed as scapegoats: "Important fissures and divides within a society, such as class [...] are neglected in focusing on such 'Others'" (Wodak 2015, 4).

Challenging Authoritarianism

Some 14.1 per cent of the analysed online comments opposed the ideology of the followers of the FPÖ and the ÖVP, which shows that there are significant attempts to challenge authoritarian ideology on the online profiles and social media pages of right-wing politicians and groups. The key question that arises in this context is whether rational counterarguments that use logic, statistics, and reason can convince nationalists, racists, xenophobes, authoritarians, and fascists to take on a different opinion.

One critic commented on Kurz's Facebook posting that claimed that one must "correct refugee- & migration-policies' aberrations & especially stop illegal migration" in order to "preserve affluence in Germany & Austria". The critic indicated, like many others who formulated doubts, that given the history of Austria and Germany, it is problematic that an Austrian politician makes claims about both Germany and Austria by evoking negative sentiments directed against refugees and migrants: "It is impudent to mention Germany in the same breath with Austria when it comes to Europe. The majority of Germans do not want a nationalist and xenophobic

Europe"[83] (#1638). Another comment put this critique more directly: "Anyone who wishes that once again an Austrian rules in Berlin has not paid attention to history!"[84] (#826).

The critic's posting resulted in 73 replies, of which 58 were right-wing in character and defended xenophobia. Many of them also attacked the critic:

Shut your trap.[85] (#1605)

We can fairly well dispense with the agitation by a left-wing German, who stands for even more migration.[86] (#1569)

I am sure that your flat has a door with a lock, right? Otherwise, please reveal your address. We would then immediately accommodate two refugee families there on your costs. Of course without identity checks because that would be racist.[87] (#1574).

You and the established parties are the problem, simply shut your trap. Not everyone is as silly as you and considers the flood of illegal immigrants from all over the world as acceptable.[88] (#1616)

A 20 metre high ring of fire around Europe![89] (#1621)

These responses are indicative of the tendency that the attempt to use logical, empirical, or historical arguments to challenge xenophobia and nationalism often result in an intensification of these very ideologies. Given that these ideologies are irrational and operate with emotions, it is hard to challenge them with rational arguments.

One question that arises is if satire and humour can challenge xenophobia, racism, and nationalism. The German satirical magazine *Titanic* printed cartoons that portrayed Sebastian Kurz as "Baby Hitler", which resulted in the creation of the hashtag #BabyHitler. The ÖVP in turn considered taking the magazine to court, which reminded some observers of the Turkish President Recep Erdoğan's attempt to silence the German comedian Jan Böhmermann's artistic critique of Turkey's president by legal means.

Satire and humour are certainly means for creating attention for the critique of nationalism, racism, xenophobia, and authoritarianism and unifying oppositional

234 Nationalism on Social Media

movements by cultural means. But a proper anti-fascist politics requires a new socialism that advances policies that establish alternatives to neoliberalism and show that the real causes of social problems have to do with class and capitalism. In addition, we also required new forms of political debate, such as Club 2.0, that overcome the acceleration, superficiality, and anonymity of discussion and give time and space to the exploration of the causes of society's problems.

#IbizaGate

On 17 May 2019, the German newspaper *Süddeutsche Zeitung*, the German weekly magazine *Der Spiegel*, and the Austrian weekly *Der Falter* published excerpts of a secretly taped video showing Strache and FPÖ parliamentarian Johann Gudenus in discussion with an alleged Russian oligarch in a finca in Ibiza. The video was recorded shortly before the 2017 Austrian general election. The published excerpt shows a discussion about how the oligarch could unofficially donate large sums to the FPÖ's election campaign and in return benefit from reciprocal deals with the Austrian state initiated by the party. Mentioned deals include state building contracts, the privatisation of water, corporate tax cuts, and the privatisation of one of the channels of Austria's public service broadcaster ORF.[90] In the video, Strache also suggests that the oligarch buys Austria's largest newspaper *Kronen Zeitung* and that people who are critical of the FPÖ are fired and the party installs supporters as journalists. Strache says:

> Look, if she [the oligarch] really does take over the newspaper first, if there's really a chance to push us in this newspaper two or three weeks before [the election], then there's an effect that others will not get. If the medium pushes us two, three weeks before the election, if this medium suddenly pushes us [...] Then we do not make 27, then we male 34 [percent] [...] As soon as she takes over the *Kronen Zeitung*, as soon as she does, we have to talk openly. Then we must talk completely openly and sit down together: With us at the *Krone* – Chop! Chop! Chop! – there are three, four people whom we have to push; three, four people that we have to throw out. And we bring in five new ones that we build up. And that's the deal.[91]

The video shows how right-wing politicians favour corruption and illegal financial flows and their disrespect for the freedom of the press. It shows that they are willing to use economic and political means for manipulating democracy. The video was widely shared on Facebook, Twitter, and YouTube. Twitter users used the hashtag

#IbizaGate for spreading the video and commenting on it. FPÖ critics also used the Vengaboys' 1999 hit song "We're Going to Ibiza!" as a protest song at demonstrations and on social media. As a consequence, the song became number 1 on iTunes Austria's download charts. On 18 May, both Strache and Gudenus resigned, the ÖVP/FPÖ coalition government collapsed, and Chancellor Kurz called for a snap election in September.

Information technology played a dual role in Strache's fall. First, the video documented ideas about political corruption. Second, social media helped spread the information. Right-wing authoritarians often keep their real faces and true nature hidden from the public. In public appearances, they often talk about how they represent the interest of everyday people. The secretly recorded video reveals how a politician talks about abusing taxpayers' money for his own political advantage, turning public services into private assets as a return favour for large donations, and manipulating the public sphere. It documents a deeply authoritarian mindset that disrespects democracy. "Ibiza-gate" shows how political power, ideological power, and economic power intersect. The scandal makes evident that the power of the far-right can be challenged by documenting how it advances the political economy of corruption for ideological reasons. Video surveillance and social media were not the cause of Strache's fall, but helped to publish information on how the mindset and potential actions of a politician diverge from the interests of the common people that he pretends to represent in his public appearances. The general lesson that can be learned from Ibiza-gate is that right-wing demagogues' ideology can best be unmasked by showing how they betray the interests of everyday people by favouring the interests of the rich, corporations, and the powerful and their own interests at the expense of the public interest and democracy.

Notes

1 In German, Liste Peter Pilz. The party's name was changed to JETZT – Liste Pilz in December 2018.
2 Translation from German: „Wobei wir jetzt einmal restriktiv Einsparungen für die nächsten Budgets vornehmen werden müssen. Wir haben einen Schuldenstand, der überbordend ist."
3 Translation from German: „Im Dritten Reich haben sie ordentliche Beschäftigungspolitik gemacht. was nicht einmal Ihre Regierung in Wien zusammenbringt" (Protokoll der Sitzung des Kärntner Landtags, 13 June 1991).

4 Translation from German: „Korporierte verfügen in der Strache-FPÖ vielmehr über beste Zukunftsaussichten – solange sie im Auftreten nach außen zu gewissen Abstrichen von der völkischen Lehre bereit sind."

5 Translation from German: „völkisch-deutschnationale Speerspitze der FPÖ".

6 Translation from German: „verharmlosen die Verbrechen der Nazis", „fördern rechtsextreme und rassistische Aktivitäten der Jugend", „betreiben neonazistische Indoktrination".

7 Translation from German: „Da trat in ihre Mitte der Jude Ben Gurion:Gebt Gas, ihr alten Germanen, wir schaffen die siebte Million. […] Da schritt in ihre Mitte ein schlitzäugiger Chines': Auch wir sind Indogermanen und wollen zur Waffen-SS."

8 Translation from German: „Die ÖVP schwenkte Ende September 2015 auf den Kurs der FPÖ um. […] Es macht einen großen Unterschied in der Wahrnehmung, ob ich Menschen, die vor Tod, Krieg und Folter flüchten, als Flüchtlinge bezeichne. Oder ob ich sie als illegale Migranten oder Wirtschaftsmigranten bezeichne und ihnen damit auch den rechtlichen Flüchtlingsstatus abspreche. Wenn das oft genug wiederholt und von den Medien propagiert wird, dann verfestigt sich dieses Bild kollektiv. […] die Kurz'sche ÖVP hat bestimmte traditionelle Merkmale der ÖVP aufgegeben und Charakteristika rechtspopulistischer Parteien angenommen, wie die Betonung des Grenzschutzes, den Stopp der ‚illegalen Migration', die Verschärfung von Asyl. Ebenso die Law-and-Order-Ausrichtung und starke Hierarchisierung innerhalb der Partei."

9 Data source: www.media-analyse.at

10 Data source: http://uis.unesco.org

11 Data source: Media Analyse 2016/2017, www.media-analyse.at/

12 Translation from German: „Ich hab zum Beispiel in Salzburg eine Bäuerin kennengelernt, die mir erzählt hat, dass sie mit ihrer knappen Pension fast nicht über die Runden kommt, obwohl sie ein Leben lang hart und sogar körperlich hart gearbeitet hat. Und sie versteht zu Recht nicht, warum ein Flüchtling die volle Mindestsicherung von Anfang an erhält."

13 Data source: ESS Data, http://nesstar.ess.nsd.uib.no/webview/, accessed 10 January 2018.

14 Translation from German: „Es gilt unsere Tradition. Es gilt unsere Kultur. Es gilt unsere Wertegemeinschaft, liebe Freunde, die nicht verhandelbar ist. Und wem das nicht passt, der möge letztlich in sein islamisches Land zurückgehen. […] Nicht wir Österreicher haben uns anzupassen, sondern jene zugewanderten Gäste, welche auf Dauer bei uns leben wollen. Uns sie müssen akzeptieren, dass Österreichs Kultur und Lebensart die vom Christentum geprägt ist. […] Ein Bekenntnis zu unserer Kultur, zu unserer Geschichte, zu unserer Identität und zu unserer Lebensweise. Und ich hab es daher satt, wenn wir Österreicher uns ständig Sorgen machen müssen, ob das irgendwelchen Leuten, die zu uns zugewandert sind, passt oder nicht. Wem's nicht passt, liebe Freunde, der braucht nicht hier sein. Hier haben wir unsere Regeln, unsere Kultur, unsere Sprache. Und wir sprechen überwiegend Deutsch, nicht Arabisch und nicht Türkisch oder andere Sprachen."

15 Translation from German: „Der Islam ist eine Religion, die die Welt als Kriegsschauplatz ansieht – und zwar solange, bis die gesamte Menschheit islamisch ist."

16 Translation from German: „Der Islam ist kein Teil Österreichs".

17 Translation from German: „deutschen Sprach- und Kulturgemeinschaft".

18 www.un.org/en/universal-declaration-human-rights/

19 www.unhcr.org/uk/3b66c2aa10

20 www.alexa.com/siteinfo/unzensuriert.at, accessed 12 January 2018.

21 Translation from German: „Wir machen ja nicht dieses Medium, weil uns am unabhängigen Journalismus so sehr gelegen ist, sondern weil wir diese politische Bewegungen in gewisser Weise unterstützen wollen. [...] Eine rein positive Berichterstattung zu fahren."

22 Translation from German: „veröffentlichten Inhalte sind zum Teil äußerst fremdenfeindlich und weisen antisemitische Tendenzen auf. Es werden auch verschwörungstheoretische Ansätze und eine pro-russische Ideologie vertreten."

23 Translation from German: „Beschimpfungen".

24 Translation from German: „Gewaltaufrufe".

25 Translation from German: „Gewaltfantasien in typischer NS-Diktion".

26 Translation from German: „Es ist ein Geschäft auf Gegenseitigkeit, bei dem beide Seiten gewinnen: Strache profitiert politisch. [...] Die *Krone* profitiert wirtschaftlich."

27 Translation from German: „Ein junger Mann mit mehr Verstand als die realitätsfremden aktuellen Bestimmer. Hoffentlich bleibt er gesund und kann die Zeichen die er setzt umsetzen."

28 Translation from German: „Bitte Herr Innenminister erlösen sie das Österreichische Volk von dieser Plage ..."

29 Translation from German: „Danke Sebastian Kurz. Endlich werden Schritte in die richtige Richtung zum Thema ‚Flüchtlingspolitik' gesetzt. Bitte macht die Grenzen dicht und kontrolliert genau, wer in unser Land hineinkommt!"

30 Translation from German: „Eine neue Regierung welche ihre Wahlversprechen auch umsetzt, ganz was neues. Das ist ja fast wie bei Präsident Donald Trump. BRAVO, nur weiter so."

31 Translation from German: „Falls Herr Kickl als Minister nur halb so hart durchgreift wie er als Oppositionspolitiker aufgetreten ist, dann ist er ein großer Gewinn für die Sicherheit Österreichs!"

32 Translation from German: „Lieber Sebastian, bitte komm nach Berlin und regiere uns gleich mit! Ansonsten macht Merkel aus Deutschland bald ein islamisches Kalifat."

33 Translation from German: „Vielleicht können Deutschland und Österreich eine GroKo bilden und Herr Kurz regiert dann beide Länder!!!!!!!"

34 Translation from German: „einen 31 jährigen Politiker in Europa der die Sorgen und Nöte der Menschen erkennt".

35 Translation from German: „Schon Irre wie vernünftig, routiniert und überzeugend ein 31 jähriger junger Politiker sein kann."

36 Translation from German: „jungen dynamischen Mann".
37 Translation from German: „Es ist ein breites Team aus Männern und Frauen, aus Jüngeren und jung Gebliebenen, ein Team, das bereit ist, für unser Land zu arbeiten."
38 Translation from German: „Er könnte uns Mutti Merkel ersparen!"
39 Translation from German: „Dem Wahn unserer Mutti müssen fähige unverbrauchte Köpfe entgegentreten."
40 Translation from German: „Trotzdem will eure Mutti nochmals ca. 2 Millionen moslemische Assys per Flugzeug (auf eure Kosten !) einfliegen !! Der Untergang ist schon vorbestimmt. Man will einen kompletten Volksaustausch !!"
41 Translation from German: „Na Endlich wird eine Österreichische Politik gemacht".
42 Translation from German: „Bravo endlich wird Politik für die Österreicher gemacht".
43 Translation from German: „Nur auf Österreich und sein Volk schauen, bitte!"
44 Translation from German: „Der erste Unterschied zur roten Kern-Regierung ist, dass Politik zuerst für die Österreicher gemacht wird und nicht für die Flüchtlinge."
45 Translation from German: „Erst sind wir tolerant dann sind wir fremd im eigenen Land."
46 Translation from German: „Austria first! Damit meine ich die bedürftigen autochthonen Österreicher und nicht irgendwelche tschetschenische Sittenwächter, Gewalttäter gegen unsere Polizei und noch andere zugewanderte Verbrecher."
47 Translation from German: „Wir wollen uns die nächsten 10 Jahre wieder als Österreicher und Herren im eigenen Land fühlen."
48 Translation from German: „Ein lebenswertes, sicheres Österreich für seine Staatsbürger wiederherstellen! Das geht nur mit Härte!"
49 Translation from German: „Kickl war die beste Wahl! Er ist hart, korrekt und liebt Österreich!"
50 Data source: http://namenskarten.lima-city.at/oesterreichs-haeufigste-nachnamen.php?p=0, accessed 26 January 2018.
51 Data source: www.herold.at/telefonbuch/(Personensuche), accessed 26 January 2018.
52 Translation from German: „Wir schützen unseren Sozialstaat vor Missbrauch und werden die illegale Migration nach Österreich stoppen."
53 Translation from German: „Wir wollen unsere Heimat Österreich als lebenswertes Land mit all seinen kulturellen Vorzügen bewahren. Dazu gehört auch, selbst zu entscheiden, wer als Zuwanderer bei uns leben darf, und illegale Migration zu beenden."
54 Translation from German: „Es kann auch nicht sein, daß in Wien die Gemeindewohnungen mit Ausländern befüllt werden! Und Österreicher bekommen keine Wohnung!"
55 Translation from German: „50 % Ausländer geil! weiter so. 90 % der Kinder in der Schule sprechen unsere Sprache nicht."
56 Translation from German: „Dann ist Europa bald ebenso überbevölkert, verarmt, gewalttätig, ghettoisiert sowie wirtschaftlich und bildungsmäßig heruntergewirtschaftet wie die Herkunftsländer der Asyl-Fachkräfte. Dann herrschen hier wieder patriarchale Denkweisen,

Frauenunterdrückung, religiöser Fanatismus und ethische Konflikte, eine wirklich schöne Zukunft für österreichische Kinder."

57 Translation from German: „spätestens nach den Vergewaltigungen, Raubüberfällen,und, und,und..! 2016 wurden von Assys über 15 000 Straftaten verübt !! DAS ist die Realität !! Und jeder Skeptiker soll einmal über die Grenze schauen,-In Berlin haben Arabische Clans das Sagen und praktisch die Staatsmacht ausgeschaltet. Wann haben wir die selben Probleme ?? Oder ist es gar schon soweit ??"

58 Translation from German: „Ich möchte nicht arbeiten gehen, um Menschen mitzutragen, die unsere Sprache nicht lernen, sich nicht integrieren ja noch nicht einmal im Entferntesten unsere Werte, unsere Kultur akzeptieren. Weiters werden viele von ihnen nie etwas zum Funkltionieren unseres Sozialstaates beitragen, sondern ewig in der Mindestsicherung ‚hängen'. Leider sehe ich das Problem bei einer Vielzahl der Flüchtlinge wie oben geschildert"

59 Translation from German: „Die Mitgliedstaaten sollten selbst entscheiden, ob und wie viele Menschen sie aufnehmen. [...] Staaten zur Aufnahme von Flüchtlingen zu zwingen, bringt Europa nicht weiter."

60 Translation from German: „Aufgrund der veränderten geopolitischen Lage in und um Österreich braucht die Regierung aber auch eine auf die neuen Bedrohungen und Herausforderungen (transnationaler Terrorismus, ausländische Agitation, Migration) angepasste Sicherheitsarchitektur, in deren Rahmen der Prävention in Zukunft eine wesentlich höhere Bedeutung zukommen muss."

61 Translation from German: „Die Hunde müssen spüren dass sie hier nicht gewollt sind!"

62 Translation from German: „Endlich werden jene aussortiert die sich bei uns nur einnisten woollen."

63 Translation from German: „Asyl gehört grundsätzlich abgeschafft."

64 Translation from German: „i vasteh nu imma ned das de afoch in unsa Laund kumman, gor ned einalossn, kost ois nur mega Kohle !!!"

65 Translation from German: „Und wissen Sie, wie der Abschub heute funktioniert? In zivilen Luftfahrmaschinen, wo heute Passagiere auf Urlaub fliegen, wird daneben der Abzuschiebende mitgeflogen. Ja, was ist denn das für eine Abschubvorgangsweise? Für was haben wir militärische Transportflugzeuge wie die Hercules? Ich sage: Die Hercules umrüsten zu einer Abflugmaschine. Da können sie dann schreien und sich anurinieren. Da stört's dann niemanden. Da werden sie abgeschoben", www.youtube.com/watch?v=0iym1miowSU, accessed 28 January 2018.

66 Translation from German: „in die nächste Herkules und zwar vollbesetzt und da braucht es noch sehr viel Maschinen."

67 Translation from German: „Bitte sofortige Gesetzesänderung und die Hercules volltanken."

68 Translation from German: „Die Hercules wartet nur auf ihren Einsatz."

69 Translation from German: „Wünsche mir, dass das Jahr 2018 das Jahr der Rückführungen wird!"

240 Nationalism on Social Media

70 Translation from German: „Bargeldabnahme, na selbstverständlich, die haben teilweise mehr im Rucksack als so mancher glaubt."

71 Translation from German: „Abnahme von Bargeld, Handy Daten durchleuten alles völlig richtig. So erkennt man diverse Kriminelle und Terroristen sofort."

72 Translation from German: „Warum nicht auch Uhr und Halsketten, wenn schon, denn schon."

73 Translation from German: „Selbst wenn andere Staaten ihre Mitbürger nicht zurücknehmen,so kann man sie doch Internieren um die Bürger vor Gefahren zu schützen."

74 Translation from German: „Vielleicht kann man mit Putin reden, Sibirien würde sich anbieten."

75 Translation from German: „Asylwerber konzentriert an einem Ort halten."

76 Translation from German: "staatliche Betreuung".

77 Translation from German: "Und dass es da oder dort auch Sinn ergeben kann, vielleicht die eine oder andere leerstehende Kaserne auch zu nutzen, das ist durchaus überlegenswert."

78 Translation from German: "Es ist ja bereits in der Vergangenheit darüber diskutiert worden, ob es nicht so sein soll, dass ab einer gewissen Abendzeit alle wieder in der Kaserne zu sein haben. Es braucht ja auch Ordnung, so lange es ein offenes Asylverfahren gibt. Und dass es Probleme gibt in unserer Gesellschaft, das wird sicherlich auch Ihnen schon durchaus bewusst sein."

79 Translation from German: „Sie in der Nacht einzusperren, ist ein Problem. Das ist eine Freiheitsbeschränkung. Und man kann Asylwerber nicht ohne Grund, nur deshalb einsperren, weil sie Asylwerber sind."

80 Translation from German: „Notfalls Luftabsetzung …"

81 Translation from German: „Abschieben bringt doch nichts denn die kommen doch über ne andere Ecke wieder. Ich bin der Meinung lasst die zurück schwimmen das viehzeug."

82 Translation from German: „Die Moslems befinden sich mit uns im ‚heiligen Krieg'. Also ruft für eine Woche das Kriegsrecht aus und fordert die Österreicher auf, das Problem selber in die Hand zu nehmen!"

83 Translation from German: „Schon dreist Deutschland in einem Atemzug mit österreich zu nennen,wenn es um Europa geht. Die Mehrzahl der Deutschen möchte kein nationalistischen und fremdenfeindliches Europa."

84 Translation from German: „Wer sich wünscht, dass wieder mal ein Österreicher in Berlin regiert, der hat in Geschichte nicht aufgepasst!"

85 Translation from German: „Halt den Schnabel".

86 Translation from German: „wir können sehr gut auf die Hetze eines Linken Deutschen, der für noch mehr Zuwanderung steht verzichten."

87 Translation from German: „Ich bin sicher, dass Ihre Wohnung auch eine Tür mit Schloss hat, oder? Sonst geben Sie doch Ihre Adresse preis. Wir würden dann gleich zwei

Flüchtlingsfamilien auf Ihre Kosten bei Ihnen einquartieren. Natürlich ohne Identitätsprüfung, das wäre ja sonst rassistisch."

88 Translation from German: „du und die etablierten Parteien sind das Problem, halt einfach deinen Schnabel wenn nicht jeder so blöd ist wie du und die Überflutung mit illegalen Immigranten aus aller Herren Länder noch für tragbar hält."

89 Translation from German: „Feuerring um Europa, 20 Meter hoch !"

90 Data source: www.spiegel.de/video/fpoe-chef-heinz-christian-strache-die-videofalle-video -99027174.html, https://orf.at/stories/3122824/, accessed 28 May 2019.

91 Translation from German: „Schau, wenn sie wirklich die Zeitung vorher übernimmt. Wenn's wirklich vorher, um diese Wahl herum, zwei, drei Wochen vorher die Chance gibt, über diese Zeitung uns zu pushen, dann passiert ein Effekt, den die anderen ja nicht kriegen. Wenn das Medium zwei, drei Wochen vor der Wahl, dieses Medium, auf einmal uns pusht [...] Dann machen wir nicht 27, dann machen wir 34. [...] Sobald sie die *Kronen Zeitung* übernimmt, sobald das der Fall ist, müssen wir ganz offen reden, da müssen wir uns zusammenhocken. Da gibt es bei uns in der *Krone*: Zack, zack, zack. Drei, vier Leute, die müssen wir pushen. Drei, vier Leute, die müssen absorviert werden. Und wir holen gleich mal fünf Neue herein, die wir aufbauen. Und das ist der Deal". Video source: www.spiegel.de/video/fpoe-chef-heinz-christian-strache-die-videofalle-video-99027174.html, accessed 28 May 2019.

Appendix 7.A

German original of an excerpt from the main ORF election debate, 12 October 2017

SEBASTIAN KURZ (ÖVP): Ich glaub, das große Thema, das wir haben, ist: Wir haben ein starkes Sozialsystem geschaffen, aber dieses Sozialsystem wird weiter nur existieren können, wenn wir einerseits es sicherstellen, im System sparsamer zu werden, Stichwort 21 Sozialversicherungsträger, die viel Geld brauchen, das in Wahrheit dann bei den Betroffenen, bei den Patienten, fehlt. Und zum Zweiten braucht es aus meiner Sicht dringend auch einen Stopp der Zuwanderung ins Sozialsystem. Warum? Weil sonst vieles einfach nicht finanzierbar sein wird. Und da sollten wir eine Trendwende schaffen, wenn wir unser Sozialsystem von den Spitälern bis hin zu den Pensionen auch langfristig absichern woollen.

[…]

HEINZ-CHRISTIAN STRACHE (FPÖ): Wir wollen in Wahrheit Sachleistungen statt Geldleistungen für jene, die nicht in das System eingezahlt haben, weil dann diese Sogwirkung von Wirtschaftsflüchtlingen sicherlich deutlich zurückgehen wird. […] Denn es versteht ja niemand in Österreich, der heute Vollzeit beschäftigt ist und dann ein bisschen mehr als heute eine Mindestsicherung verdient. Das ist ja alles nicht mehr gerecht.

Und wenn man 40 und 45 Jahre gearbeitet hat und dann durchschnittlich eine Durchschnittspension von 940 Euro erhält. Das ist ja nicht gerecht. Das versteht ja niemand. Bis hin auch zu den Frauen, die immer wieder auch in Sonntagsreden bemüht werden, aber die man dann gerade im Alter oftmals in der Altersarmut alleine lässt mit 250/350 Euro. Und das sind unfaire Systeme. Da gehört das System fair gestaltet und geändert, sodass Mindestpensionisten, die 40/45 Jahre gearbeitet haben, dann wirklich 1,200 Euro bekommen und Mütter ihre Kindererziehungszeit angerechnet kriegen und zumindest eine Mindestsicherung erhalten im Alter. Das wäre Respekt und Anstand gegenüber den Menschen

[…]

KURZ: Wir haben in Wien die Situation, dass mittlerweile jeder zweite Mindestsicherungsempfänger ein ausländischer Staatsbürger ist. Eine Familie mit drei Kindern bekommt in Wien an Mindestsicherung und an anderen Leistungen wie Kinderbeihilfe insgesamt 2,500 Euro netto pro Monat. Das ist eine Summe, die muss jemand, der arbeiten geht, einmal verdienen. Da muss man schon ziemlich gut verdienen. Und insofern braucht es hier eine Veränderung. Wir geben Milliarden aus für die Flüchtlingsversorgung, eine Milliarde mittlerweile für die Mindestsicherung und wir überweisen 300 Millionen an Familienbeihilfe ins Ausland. Also wenn wir hier nicht gegensteuern, dann wird unser Sozialsystem immer schwerer zu finanzieren.

STRACHE: Und wir haben Fehlentwicklungen, wie ich angesprochen habe, durch die fehlende Grenzsicherung 2015, wo ja natürlich hier auch Entwicklungen passiert sind nicht nur seit dieser Zeit, sondern auch davor, da muss man ehrlich sein, wo wir alleine im Jahr 1973, um das auch korrekt zu sagen, 73,000 muslimische Mitbürger in Österreich hatten, und durch eine sehr sehr undifferenzierte Massenzuwanderungspolitik der letzten Jahrzehnte heute über 700,000 bereits haben, und auch Schulen in Wien erleben, wo wir insgesamt in den Volksschulbereichen schon mehr muslimische Kinder als katholische Kinder haben.

Und da gibt's dann Vereinsstrukturen und islamische Kindergärten und auch Moscheen, die unter der konkreten Beobachtung des Verfassungsschutzes stehen, nicht erst seit diesem Jahr, seit über 15 Jahren, und darauf hingewiesen wird, da gibt's radikal-islamistische Fehlentwicklungen.

Da passieren ganz gefährliche Entwicklungen, auch der Rekrutierung bis hin, dass man jetzt auch in einem Flüchtlingsheim vor kurzen Tagen in Salzburg einen IS-Mann auch zum Glück entdecken konnte, der mit den Paris-Attentätern auch in Verbindung stand. Das heißt, wir haben hier Handlungsbedarf.

KURZ: Wer sich illegal auf den Weg macht nach Europa mit dem Schlepper, der soll keine Chance haben, bei uns einen Antrag zu stellen, sondern er muss zurückgestellt werden. Und gleichzeitig müssen wir die Entwicklungszusammenarbeit und die Hilfe vor Ort ausbauen, weil wir so mit demselben Geld wesentlich mehr Menschen und wesentlich nachhaltiger helfen können.

STRACHE: Wir müssen hier ansetzen, dass wir nicht so wie in Wien, und das bitte ist notwendig. Durch die Fehlentwicklung, die schon verursacht wurde, sind unsere Kinder hier in Wien zur Minderheit in der eigenen Stadt geworden. Und das muss man bitte schon erkennen. Und da ist dann die politische Frage, will man das weiter fördern oder nicht. Wir nicht.

KURZ: Ich glaub, das große Thema, das wir haben, ist: Wir haben ein starkes Sozialsystem geschaffen, aber dieses Sozialsystem wird weiter nur existieren können, wenn wir einerseits es sicherstellen, im System sparsamer zu werden, Stichwort 21 Sozialversicherungsträger, die viel Geld brauchen, das in Wahrheit dann bei den Betroffenen, bei den Patienten, fehlt. Und zum Zweiten braucht es aus meiner Sicht dringend auch einen Stopp der Zuwanderung ins Sozialsystem. Warum? Weil sonst vieles einfach nicht finanzierbar sein wird. Und da sollten wir eine Trendwende schaffen, wenn wir unser Sozialsystem von den Spitälern bis hin zu den Pensionen auch langfristig absichern wollen.

Chapter Eight
Conclusion: Towards a Society of the Commons beyond Authoritarianism and Nationalism

8.1 Theorising Nationalism

8.2 The Communication of Nationalism in the Age of Social Media

8.3 Fake News

8.4 Authoritarian Capitalism, Authoritarian Movements, Authoritarian Communication

8.5 From the Antagonism of the Empire and the Multitude Towards a Society of the Commons

---

8.1 Theorising Nationalism

We today experience a surge of new nationalisms. Donald Trump, Brexit, Recep Tayyip Erdoğan, Marine Le Pen, Viktor Orbán, Heinz-Christian Strache, Geert Wilders, the Alternative for Germany (AfD), Narendra Modi, Rodrigo Duterte, and Vladimir Putin are some of the symbols of contemporary nationalisms. Far-right movements and new nationalisms are the "cicatrices and scars of a democracy [...] that until today has still not lived up to its own concept"[1] (Adorno 1967). They are the result of the negative dialectic of neoliberal capitalism and the new imperialism. The commodification of everything, entrepreneurialism, privatisation, deregulation, financialisation, globalisation, deindustrialisation, outsourcing, precarisation, and the new individualism, have backfired, and extended and intensified inequalities and crisis tendencies, which created a futile ground for new nationalisms, right-wing extremism, and new fascism. Eric Hobsbawm (1983a, 1983b, 1992a, 1992b) has, based on Marx and Luxemburg, shown that nationalism is an ideology that is invented for political purposes and invents everyday symbols through which nationalism is communicated. That nationalism is invented means that it is constructed, fabricated, inculcated, illusionary, false, and ideological. In the age of digital capitalism, nationalist ideology and nationalist symbols are constantly invented and reinvented online, on social media, and as user-generated content.

Understanding contemporary nationalism and how it is communicated on social media, the Internet, and other media requires a critical theory of nationalism that can be put to use as a theoretical foundation for empirical studies in order to inform political praxis that is directed against authoritarianism.

Approaches to the study of nationalism include primordialism, perennialism, ethnosymbolism, modernism, and postmodernism. This book has argued that such approaches are often fetishist and/or do not adequately explain the role of nationalism in capitalist society. A Marxian theory of nationalism grounded in the works of Karl Marx, Rosa Luxemburg, Eric J. Hobsbawm, and other critical thinkers has been suggested.

Marx's contribution to the study of nationalism is often overlooked. Too many observers consider him as a purely economic theorist and underestimate the relevance of his thought for the critique of politics. It has been argued that especially Marx's concepts of ideology, fetishism, Bonapartism, internationalism, and his critique of nationalism as ideology can inform the contemporary critique of nationalism. Marx allows us to understand nationalism as an ideology that divides and distracts, is communicated over the media, and reproduces capitalism and the hegemony of the ruling class and dominant elites.

The First World War was an expression of the culmination of the combination of imperialism and nationalism. Marxist theorists living at that time tried to make sense of nationalism's role in political economy. Otto Bauer and Rosa Luxemburg both established profound analyses of nationalism that are grounded in Marx's works. The main difference between the two approaches is that Bauer sees the nation as a community of fate and culture, whereas Luxemburg characterises the nation as both nationalist ideology and imperialist nation-states. Whereas Bauer, just like Lenin, believes in the existence of a national right to self-determination, Luxemburg characterises national liberation struggles as part of nationalist ideology and stresses the importance of international solidarity. Whereas for Bauer the nation and nationalism are democratically defined by the people in a socialist society, Luxemburg stresses that society is not socialist if it advances nationalism. Whereas Bauer was a German nationalist who argued for the *Anschluss* of Austria to Germany and saw socialism as a form of people-nationalism, Luxemburg saw nationalism, in contrast to Bauer and Lenin, as a form of political fetishism that could not have a progressive dimension. For Luxemburg, nationalism is a misty veil, a form of ideological politics that fetishises the nation in order to distract attention from class conflicts and the fundamental causes of capitalism's problems.

For developing a critical theory of nationalism, this book has built on the approaches of Marx and Luxemburg. It has furthermore taken up elements from the approaches of Eric J. Hobsbawm, Étienne Balibar, Partha Chatterjee, Vivek Chibber, Erich Fromm, Klaus Holzkamp, C.L.R. James, Ute Holzkamp-Osterkamp, Wilhelm Reich, David Roediger, Marisol Sandoval, and Raymond Williams.

Nationalism is an ideology and political movement that sustains or aims at building a nation-state that unites defined nation-state members (citizens). Nationalism has two interconnected dimensions, a territorial-political one (the nation-state) and an ideological one (national consciousness). It is both a political relation and collective consciousness. Nationalism claims that there is a foundational unity of the nation that is grounded in nature and/or culture/society. Nationalism as ideology legitimates and distracts from the division of society into classes and relations of domination by constructing, inventing, or fabricating a national unity of the people that is said to be stronger than class divisions. Nationalism is a false appearance of unity that is a feature of modern class societies. Nationalism's collective unity is defined against proclaimed outsiders of and enemies to the nation. There is a dialectic of racism and nationalism. That new nationalisms have emerged in the context of a large capitalist crisis validates the assumption that right-wing authoritarianism and associated nationalisms are likely to grow in situations of capitalist crisis.

8.2 The Communication of Nationalism in the Age of Social Media

Today, nationalism is expressed via popular cultural communication tools such as Twitter, Facebook, and YouTube. Two case studies that put the Marxist theory of nationalism to empirical use were presented in this book. The first case study analysed the communication of nationalism on social media during the 2017 German federal election campaigns. The analysis focused on a dataset consisting of 31,474 tweets collected during television debates, 6,422 comments posted to the Facebook profiles of German politicians, and 1,032 comments posted to YouTube videos generated by political parties. The second case study focused on authoritarianism and nationalism in the context of the right-wing ÖVP/FPÖ government formed in late 2017. The study analysed the main television debate and 2,367 comments posted by users to the profiles of ÖVP Chancellor Sebastian Kurz, FPÖ Vice-Chancellor Heinz-Christian Strache, FPÖ Minister of the Interior Herbert Kickl, and comments posted on online articles of Austria's most widely read newspaper, the tabloid *Kronen Zeitung*.

Nationalism is imposed and constructed from above by political elites and intellectuals, but it is also lived and hegemonically produced/reproduced from below by everyday people in their everyday practices and beliefs. The two presented case studies show how on social media, far-right political influencers (politicians, parties, right-wing media, etc.) communicate nationalism from above, to which users respond by reproducing and spreading nationalist ideology and adding specific elements to it.

Communicating nationalism requires both discursive structures as well as social forms. Four types of nationalist discourse have been identified and analysed: biological nationalism, socio-economic nationalism, political nationalism, and cultural nationalism. Nationalism is an ideology that is communicated through social forms such as events, symbols, practices, and the media system in everyday life and in extraordinary situations (such as national holidays, commemorations, parades, and wars). The mediation of nationalist symbols, nationalist practices/relations, and nationalist events takes place through different types of media. One can distinguish the communication of nationalism via primary media (based on the human body), secondary media that uses media technology for the production of nationalist information, tertiary media that uses media technology for the production and consumption of nationalist information, quaternary media that uses media technology for the production, distribution, and consumption of nationalist information, and quinary media where digital technologies are used in such a way that the production, distribution, and consumption of nationalist ideology can all be organised via converging digital media technologies and platforms that enable prosumption (productive consumption) and user-generated content production.

The two critical discourse analyses of nationalism online show that contemporary nationalism stands in a relation to top-down leadership, the friend/enemy scheme, and militarism/law and order politics. Together, these four interlinked elements form the ideology of right-wing authoritarianism. Far-right social media profiles act as media that choreograph the online nationalism of dissatisfied and anxious citizens who channel their frustrations, fears, and disappointments into online nationalism and (new) online racism. Social media's anonymity, high speed, superficiality, personalisation, individualisation, interactivity, attention economy, structures of reputation accumulation, and its networked and multimedia character support the spreading of far-right ideology online.

The analyses also provide empirical indications for the use of social media bots, fake accounts, and fake attention in social media politics. Fake news has become an important aspect of contemporary right-wing online politics.

8.3 Fake News

The *Collins English Dictionary* named "fake news" as Word of the Year 2017. Collins defines fake news as "false, often sensational, information disseminated under the guise of news reporting".[2] Here are some more definitions of fake news:

- Fake news is news that has "deliberately misleading elements incorporated within its content or context. A core feature of contemporary fake news is that it is widely circulated online" (Bakir and McStay 2018, 154).
- "We define 'fake news' to be fabricated information that mimics news media content in form but not in organizational process or intent. Fake-news outlets, in turn, lack the news media's editorial norms and processes for ensuring the accuracy and credibility of information. Fake news overlaps with other information disorders, such as misinformation (false or misleading information) and disinformation (false information that is purposely spread to deceive people)" (Lazer et al. 2018, 1094).
- "We define 'fake news' to be news articles that are intentionally and verifiably false, and could mislead readers" (Allcott and Gentzkow 2017, 213).
- Fake news is "the deliberate presentation of (typically) false or misleading claims as news, where the claims are misleading *by design*. [...] That is to say, the originator of an instance of fake news either intends a specific claim to be misleading in virtue of its specific content, or deliberately deploys a process of news production and presentation that is designed to result in false or misleading claims. What makes contemporary fake news a novel phenomenon, and gives it its significance, is the extent to which systemic features inherent in the design of the sources and channels through which fake news is disseminated ensure its proliferation. The latter, I wish to suggest, adds a sense of urgency to the recent spate of fake news, as propagated especially on electronic social media" (Gelfert 2018, 85–86, 111).

According to these definitions, fake news is factually false, circulated online predominantly on social media, lacks journalistic professional norms, and tries to systematically and deliberately mislead and misinform.

But "fake news" is not new. It started much earlier than the age of the Internet and social media. For example, in August 1835, the *New York Sun* ran a six-part story that claimed that life on the Moon had been discovered, including "a small kind of rein-deer, the elk, the moose, the horned bear, and the biped beaver" and human bats that were "doubtless innocent and happy creatures". The Great Moon Hoax increased the newspaper's circulation.

Edward S. Herman and Noam Chomsky (1988) argue in their propaganda model that the capitalist and ideological character of the media results in biases and the reflection of partial interests in the news (for a discussion on the topicality of this model, see the contributions in Pedro-Carañana et al. 2018). They argue that there are five factors that act as filters creating news biases: (a) private ownership, profit orientation, and monopolies; (b) advertising; (c) powerful actors as news sources; (d) "flak": the lobbying operations of powerful organisations; and (e) ideology (understood in a Lukácsian sense as attempts to create false representations of reality in order to legitimate class, domination, and capitalism). If, in a class society, political economy and ideology result in certain biases of capitalist media, then all media operated as for-profit businesses show some aspects and degrees of falseness. Public service media and community media are alternative media that try to avoid such biases. Given they also have to operate in a capitalist society, they are also facing issues such as resource precarity or attempts of political actors to influence reporting and decision-making. In digital capitalism, the propaganda model needs to take phenomena such as algorithm-driven news and visibility, targeted and algorithmic online advertising, native online advertising, branded online content, the online attention economy, political bots, online hate speech, filter bubbles, ideologies of and on the Internet, digital labour, digital surveillance, digital warfare, and the tabloidisation and acceleration of online information into account (see Fuchs 2018b).

So, fake news is not new. It is at least as old as the tabloid press, for which it serves as a means for increasing its audience, sales, advertising rates, and profits. Lies, scandalisation, and tabloidisation are profit strategies. Fake news is news that pretends to give a true picture of the world but does not correspond to reality. It is a way of trying to misinform citizens and to manipulate reality by spreading lies. Fake news can better be characterised as false news in the sense of the Marxist term "false consciousness", i.e. ideologies that take on the form of lies and manipulated information in order to disguise the true condition of certain aspects of society. False consciousness is consciousness that "by-passes the essence of the evolution of society and fails to pinpoint it and express it adequately" (Lukács 1971, 50).

Claire Wardle (2017) argues that there are different types of mis- and disinformation: misleading information that frames issues in a biased manner, the impersonation of sources, the fabrication of content, the misleading use of headlines, visuals, and captions in manners not supported by the content, the use of false contextual information, and the manipulation of information, sound, or images. The falseness of false news can relate to the informational content, context, presentation style, and use of text, visuals, sounds, or audiovisuals.

Wardle (2017) also includes news satire and news parody that have "no intention to cause harm" but have "potential to fool" into a typology of mis- and disinformation. Tandoc et al. (2018) include news satire and news parody besides news fabrication, photo manipulation, advertising and public relations (including native advertising), and propaganda into their typology of fake news. They make clear that news satires and news parodies do not have the intention to deceive, but given that these genres aim at making clear to the average audience members that false and overdrawn claims are not presented as news, but are used as artistic means of entertainment and critique whose ultimate aim is to create laughter, news satire and news parody should not be characterised as being "fake"/false news. They are forms of art and not news. Both news and art are forms of culture. Comedy is a form of art that aims to make people laugh, whereas the goal of news is to report novel factual developments about society that matter to a large public.

The use of the term "fake news" is somewhat problematic because Donald Trump and other right-wing demagogues have adopted it in order to try to discredit criticism of their political programmes. Factually true information is thereby often presented as "fake", whereas real fake news that is factually false is presented as true. Lies are presented as truth, truth as lies. For example, Trump tweeted about media that have reported critically about him – the *New York Times*, NBC, ABC, CBS, and CNN – that they spread fake news and were enemies of the American people: "The FAKE NEWS media (failing @nytimes, @NBCNews, @ABC, @CBS, @CNN) is not my enemy, it is the enemy of the American People!"[3]

False news is as old as tabloid media. What is new is the way false news is organised: they have moved from traditional media to the networked online and social media environment, where false news created in troll factories by low-paid false news labour spreads through targeted advertisements, personal networks, false profiles, and bot-generated attention and likes.

It is a mistake to assume that false news has technological causes and exists because of the technological possibilities for creating and spreading digital content that tries to deceive, manipulates reality, and reports invented/fictive stories as facts. Technologies do not determine society and human behaviour, but are rather embedded into society's contradictions and complexities (Fuchs 2017b). There are therefore no technological fixes to the problems associated with false news, political bots, and false social media accounts. Solutions need to focus on changing society by legislation, regulation, and media reforms.

Empirical Research of False News on Social Media

Empirical research has provided indications that the content of false news that humans and bots spread on social media tends to more support right-wing than left-wing and centrist politics (Allcott and Gentzkow 2017; Kollanyi et al. 2016, Silverman 2016; Woolley and Guilbeault 2019). Right-wing voters seem to believe more in the truth of false news stories when confronted with them than other voters (Silverman and Singer-Vine 2016).

A study analysed false news stories collected over 114 days from 70 domains known for spreading such stories (Fourney et al. 2017). It found that social media platforms were the source of 68 per cent of all visits to these stories, which shows that social media is an important medium fostering access to false news. An analysis of 14 million tweets found that super-spreaders of false news were more likely to be bots than humans and that such bots frequently mentioned usernames that had a large amount of followers in order to attract visibility and attention (Shao et al. 2018).

The Cambridge Analytica Scandal

According to reports by the *Guardian*, Cambridge Analytica paid Global Science Research (GSR) for conducting fake online personality tests on Facebook via the Facebook Developer Platform in order to obtain personal Facebook data of almost 90 million users,[4] including likes and friendships (Cadwalladr 2018 ; Cadwalladr and Graham-Harrison 2018; Kang and Frenkel 2018; Rosenberg et al. 2018). The *New York Times* reported that the data breach "allowed the company to exploit the private social media activity of a huge swath of the American electorate, developing techniques that underpinned its work on President Trump's campaign in 2016" (Rosenberg et al. 2018). According to the reports, the data were used for targeting political advertisements in various elections. Steve Bannon, who in 2017 was Donald Trump's White House Chief of Staff and was involved in forming and managing the far-right website Breitbart, is also a former vice-president of Cambridge Analytica.

In the US presidential election of 2016, Trump's digital election campaign was called Project Alamo. Theresa Hong, who worked for the digital arm of Donald Trump's election campaign, said in a BBC interview that Cambridge Analytica "came up with the Alamo data set" that was used for targeting ads on Facebook.[5] In the US Senate Select Committee on Intelligence (2017), Facebook's Vice-President and General Counsel Colin Stretch stated that the Trump and Clinton campaigns purchased targeted ads on Facebook for a total of US$81 million. Trump's digital director Brad Parscale said in an interview that the Trump campaign had targeted ads on Facebook, Google, and Twitter, with 80 per cent of them on Facebook (CBS 2017). According to campaign finance data from the Federal Election Commission, Trump's campaign spent a total of US$361,671,328.40.[6] According to the data, US$6.3 million was spent on data services, of which US$5.9 million went to Cambridge Analytica. Brad Parscale's company Giles-Parscale received a total of US$87.8 million for website development, digital consulting, and online advertising. Some US$85.3 million of this sum was spent on online advertising. In addition, the data indicates that Trump's campaign directly paid US$300,000 to Twitter and US$79,717.60 to Facebook for online advertising. If Parscale's information that around 80 per cent of the online ads were run on Facebook is correct, then Trump's campaign must have spent around US$70 million on Facebook ads. If the estimation of a total of US$85.7 million paid for online ads is correct, then this means that almost a quarter of Trump's campaign budget was spent on online ads.

The Canadian company AggregateIQ (AIQ) worked on building the Ripon tool. Christopher Wylie, who had been employed by Cambridge Analytica and is the whistle-blower whose information sparked off the scandal, characterises Ripon as "the software tool that utilised the algorithms from the Facebook data" (Digital, Culture, Media and Sport Committee 2019, 45). According to Facebook, AIQ ran 1,398 ads with a total ad value of US $2,032,860 for the pro-Brexit campaigns Vote Leave, BeLeave, Veterans for Britain, and DUP Vote to Leave (Facebook Ireland 2018). Some 88.3 per cent of the ads and 79.7 per cent of the ad value was related to Vote Leave, the campaign where politicians such as Boris Johnson and Gisela Stuart were involved (Facebook Ireland 2018). According to AggregateIQ's COO, the total amount these organisations paid to the company was more than £3.6 million, of which around 80 per cent was paid by Vote Leave (Digital, Culture, Media and Sport Committee 2019, 50)

The Cambridge Analytica data breach has caused concerns about social media corporations' business model of targeted advertising and its dangers to democracy. The Cambridge Analytica scandal was possible because the regulation of data processing for corporate purposes is lax and based on the idea of corporate self-regulation, which invites Facebook, Google, and other digital companies to gather massive amounts of user data and use them for achieving profits. Facebook is built on the idea that gathering and storing as much data as possible about users is good for its profits. Personal data as a big data commodity that is used for selling and targeting personalised online advertisements is the underlying business principle of corporate social media, including Facebook, Google, and Twitter.

The Cambridge Analytica scandal seems to have influenced the Trump campaign's capacity to target social media users. On the one hand, it is certainly one-dimensional to assume that social media is the cause of the rise of Trump because there are many factors that play a role in the rise of right-wing authoritarianism, including changes of the class structure, rising inequalities, crises, increasing economic, political, cultural, and social alienation, the weakness of the political left, the spread of ideology and political anxiety, the antagonisms of capitalist globalisation, etc. (Fuchs 2017c, 2018a). On the other hand, it is also short-sighted to argue that social media does not play any role in political changes. In an antagonistic, class-based society, social media has an antagonistic character and is a field of social struggles in which society's antagonisms express themselves. It is no surprise that in digital capitalism, groups, movements, parties, and politicians from the political right, left, and centre try to utilise social media as a means of political communication. That it is especially the far-right that has utilised social media for spreading false news and ideology might have to do with a combination of several factors, such as the general rise of the far-right in the context of capitalism's general crisis, its unscrupulousness in manipulating the public sphere, significant monetary and resource investments into online media campaigns, and the receptiveness of their followers for emotionally laden, ideological stories that are not built on facts, but on the moral and political values of right-wing authoritarianism.

Cambridge Analytica is a story about how the combination of far-right ideology, digital capitalism, and neoliberal politics threatens democracy:

1. *Far-right activists and movements* advance use of dubious and manipulative information and communication strategies in politics. *Far-right ideologues* will do everything necessary and use all means necessary in order to win elections and increase their power.
2. *Capitalist social media platforms* operate based on the logic "the more data and engagement on our platform, the more ads can potentially be

sold". Their for-profit character has led them to opening interfaces to third-party data use that was used for privacy-violating data collection. Targeted ads and ad algorithms are programmed to maximise profits. Targeted ads are not controlled by humans, but by algorithms. Their fetishistic character is blind to the content of ads. It does not matter to these software programmes if ads are about chocolate cake, diapers, or far-right ideology. Social media corporations have no interest in human control because it costs money and means less profits.

3. Proponents of the *neoliberal state* believe that self-regulation of companies is the best form of regulation, which has, especially in the USA, resulted in lax data protection regulation and privacy-invading practices of corporations in general and online companies in particular.

The Internet Research Agency

The US Senate Select Committee on Intelligence investigated Russian interferences into the 2016 US presidential election. It gave special attention to the activities of the Internet Research Agency (IRA), a troll farm based in Saint Petersburg that, according to the Mueller Report, was "funded by Yevgeniy Viktorovich Prigozhin and companies he controlled, including Concord Management and Consulting LLC and Concord Catering" (Mueller 2019, 14).

> By early to mid-2016, IRA operations included supporting the Trump Campaign and disparaging candidate Hillary Clinton. The IRA made various expenditures to carry out those activities, including buying political advertisements on social media in the names of U.S. persons and entities. Some IRA employees, posing as U.S. persons and without revealing their Russian association, communicated electronically with individuals associated with the Trump Campaign and with other political activists to seek to coordinate political activities, including the staging of political rallies.
>
> (Mueller 2019, 14)

Two teams of researchers analysed data posted by the IRA on Twitter, YouTube, Instagram, and Facebook for the period from 2013 until 2018 (Howard et al. 2018; New Knowledge 2018). The social media companies provided these data to the US Senate Select Committee on Intelligence, which enabled the researchers to conduct analyses. According to these reports, the IRA invested US$25 million into targeting

US voters and reached 77 million engagements on Facebook, 187 million on Instagram, and 73 million on Twitter (New Knowledge 2018, 6–7). Facebook estimated that 126 million users were reached on its platform (Isaac and Wakabayashi 2017; New Knowledge 2018, 8). A total of 10.4 million tweets, 1,110 YouTube videos, 116,000 Instagram posts, and 61,500 unique Facebook posts (New Knowledge 2018, 7) originated from the IRA. In 2016, there was a monthly average of 564 IRA Facebook ads, 2,442 Facebook posts, 2,611 Instagram posts, and 57,247 tweets (Howard et al. 2018, 5). On Facebook and Instagram, black voters in particular were targeted by trying to suppress their votes, but left-wing and right-wing voters were also targeted. There was a pro-Trump and an anti-Clinton bias of the content. On Facebook, 3.3 million page followers, 30.4 million shares, 37.6 million likes, and 3.3 million comments were reached (New Knowledge 2018, 21, 32). On Instagram, 3.4 million followers, 183 million likes, and 4.0 million comments were achieved (New Knowledge 2018, 32). Some 3,519 ads were run on Instagram and Facebook (New Knowledge 2018, 34).

The IRA was also active on Twitter:

> Individualized [Twitter] accounts used to influence the U.S. presidential election included @TEN_GOP […]' @jenn_abrams (claiming to be a Virginian Trump supporter with 70,000 followers); @Pamela_Moore13 (claiming to be a Texan Trump supporter with 70,000 followers); and @America_1st_ (an anti-immigration persona with 24,000 followers). In May 2016, the IRA created the Twitter account @march_for_trump, which promoted IRA-organized rallies in support of the Trump Campaign.
>
> (Mueller 2019, 27)

The IRA also organised pro-Trump rallies (Mueller 2019, 29, 31, 32).

The highest peak of IRA Facebook ads was reached at the time of the first US presidential debate between Clinton and Trump on 26 September 2016 (Howard et al. 2018, 15). Some 1,087 (38.1 per cent) of a sample of 2,855 analysed targeted ads focused on African Americans (Howard et al. 2018, 23). The analysed ads reached a total of 3,136,946 ad clicks (Howard et al. 2018, 23) and 33,679,119 ad impressions (Howard et al. 2018, 23). These ads cost a total of RUB 4,911,680 (around US$75,000; Howard et al. 2018, 23). Facebook says "that fake accounts associated with the IRA spent approximately $100,000 on more than 3,000 Facebook and Instagram ads between June 2015 and August 2017" (Stretch 2018, 4). On Twitter, the IRA operated bots in order to intensify reactions to posts (Mueller 2019, 26; see also Isaac and Wakabayashi 2017).

Whereas the number of targeted ads and YouTube videos was comparatively low, the number of tweets and Facebook and Instagram posts was relatively high. It "is likely that the organic posts on Facebook, not the ads, had the most reach" (Howard et al. 2018, 13). The amounts the IRA invested into social media ads are rather low in comparison to the Trump campaign's investments. But the company's total investment of US$25 million into US operations is 29 per cent of the Trump campaign's estimated US$85.7 million investment into social media ads. Most of the Russian activity and investment seems not to have gone into algorithmic activities (such as targeted ads or bots), but into human troll labour that generates and spreads false and misleading content:

> At the height of the 2016 campaign, the effort employed more than 80 people, who used secure virtual private network connections to computer servers leased in the United States to hide the fact that they were in Russia. From there, they posed as American activists, emailing, advising and making payments to real Americans who were duped into believing that they were part of the same cause.
>
> (Shane and Mazzetti 2018)

> Dozens of IRA employees were responsible for operating accounts and personas on different U.S. social media platforms. [...] Initially, the IRA created social media accounts that pretended to be the personal accounts of U.S. persons. [...] By early 2015, the IRA began to create larger social media groups or public social media pages that claimed (falsely) to be affiliated with U.S. political and grass-roots organizations. In certain cases, the IRA created accounts that mimicked real U.S. organizations. [...] More commonly, the IRA created accounts in the names of fictitious U.S. organizations and grassroots groups and used these accounts to pose as anti-immigration groups, Tea Party activists, Black Lives Matter pro-testors, and other U.S. social and political activists.
>
> (Mueller 2019, 22)

The Implications of Cambridge Analytica and the Internet Research Agency

We can draw four lessons from the Cambridge Analytica data breach and the IRA's attempts to influence elections:

- *The political economy of online visibility.* The two cases show that creating visibility on social media is a question of political economy, i.e. a question of mobilising resources, especially money, labour-time, digital skills, people, investment possibilities into advertising, etc. There are different ways resources can be used for creating visibility on social media. In a capitalist society, money is the key resource because it can purchase labour-time and commodities. In the case of the Trump campaign, there were huge investments into targeted advertisements, especially Facebook-ads, whereas in the case of the IRA ad spend was much lower, but large investments were made into paying people who managed social media groups and created contacts to activists, who did not know that they were contacted by people working for the IRA. Both investments into labour-time and ads are important ways of achieving online visibility.
- *Unequal online visibility.* Right-wing authoritarian groups often have rich donors such as the US billionaire Robert Mercer, the CEO of the hedge fund Renaissance Technology, in the case of Cambridge Analytica, and Russian billionaire Yevgeny Prigozhin, who controls a range of companies, in the case of the IRA. For everyday users, who earn average salaries, garnering high online visibility is difficult. The capitalist Internet is divided and unequal.
- *Digital capitalism fails democracy.* Capitalist social media platforms are driven by the logic of capital accumulation, which makes them want to reduce labour-time and labour-costs and rely as much as possible on algorithms and artificial intelligence. The profit logic makes them to a certain degree blind to data breaches and far-right ideology that is spread in the form of false news. Targeted political ads are a matter of money. Those who have more money available can reach more users on social media. Democracy, elections, and campaigns thereby become an issue of money, not of arguments.
- *The need for an alternative Internet.* Given that the for-profit logic of these platforms has failed democracy, it is time to establish alternative social media platforms that are not-for-profit public services that foster the common good.

The proliferation of far-right ideology online, false news, political bots, and false accounts on social media has interacting political, economic, and ideological causes.

Political Causes of False News

We live in a politically highly polarised world that is shaped by constant political crises, in which the friend/enemy logic that does not advance engaging with, but harming political opponents proliferates. False news, political bots, and false accounts are political strategies indicative of a highly aggressive and polarised political context, in which political dialogue fails and forms of symbolic, ideological, cultural, structural, and direct violence flourish.

Economic Causes of False News

In the past decades, the news industry has experienced increasing commercialisation, monopolisation, financialisation, and the rising precariousness of labour. It has become more difficult to finance news by advertising, especially in an environment where digital advertising has accounted for a rising share of total advertising revenues and is controlled by Google and Facebook's duopoly (Kellner 2003; McChesney 2013, 2015). Given the increased competition about profits in the news media environment, funding the time and resources needed for investigative journalism has become difficult and the drive to automate news production has increased. These tendencies have in general advanced the tabloidisation and acceleration of news.

Dominant social media platforms are driven by the logic of algorithms, algorithmic automation, targeted advertising, and big data (Fuchs 2017b). Facebook, Twitter, and Google/YouTube achieve profits by selling targeted advertisements that are based on algorithms highly targeted to users' interests and behaviours, engaging in constant big data generating real-time surveillance of users, the commodification of users' online activities ("digital labour"), and the sale of ad space through algorithmic auctions (Fuchs 2017b). Targeted ad algorithms are blind to ethics, morals, and politics and are programmed to sell ads in order to achieve profits. On the dominant social media platforms, not humans but algorithms sell advertisements. News presented on newsfeeds, social media profiles, and walls are not checked by humans, but published based on algorithmic logic. Given that targeted advertising outsources value-generation to users' digital labour and uses algorithmic automation, it is no surprise that the number of social media companies' employees are relatively low: in 2016, Google had 72,053 employees, Facebook 17,048, and Twitter 3,583.

Not humans, but algorithms, decide which ads are featured and which contents presented on social media. The algorithm does not discern if an ad's content is about detergent or a false news story aimed at manipulating election results. It is blind to politics and morals because it is programmed to sell ads. As a consequence of algorithmic advertising, Alphabet/Google, in 2016, achieved profits of US$19.5 billion. Advertising accounted for 87.9 per cent of the search giant's total revenues. Facebook, in the same year, made profits of US$10.2 billion and advertising accounted for 97.3 per cent of its revenue. In 2016, 88.9 per cent of Twitter's revenue stemmed from selling advertisements. Facebook, Google, and Twitter are among the world's largest advertising agencies. According to estimations, Google and Facebook together control more than two-thirds of the worldwide online advertising revenues and thereby constitute a duopoly in the online ad market. The monopolistic market structure of social media and the Internet aggravates the false news problem because single platforms via their (non-transparent, secret) algorithms control vast amounts of users that can be targeted and profiled.

The profit logic of algorithmic, targeted advertising and algorithmic automation is the underlying economic factor that has enabled the emergence of false news, political bots, and false social media accounts.

Ideological Causes of False News

False news is an expression of a high degree of instrumental reason in society. Instrumental reason is an ideology that presents and aims at treating humans as things, resources, and instruments for advancing particularistic interests. The proliferation of instrumental reason has advanced social inequalities, fears of social decline, new nationalisms, the domination of the public sphere by tabloid media, the logic of advertising, branding and consumer culture, sensationalism, entertainment, and an accelerated and superficial news culture that leaves no time and does not foster adequate spaces for political engagement and political debate (Fuchs 2014, 2017b, 2018a). Social media news culture is a culture of acceleration, brevity, and superficiality that is prone to false news. The crisis of the public sphere expresses itself as the combination of the lack of time and space for political debate; the culture and politics of short sound bites; unreal reality TV; mediated spectacles; unsocial social media, short online attention span; personalised politics instead of issue-based politics; one-dimensional, superficial, tabloid, and "post-truth" politics; automated, algorithmic politics; and fragmented publics.

Problems and Impacts of False News, Political Bots, and False Accounts

There are a number of potential problems associated with false news, political bots, and false accounts that can limit and negatively impact the public sphere:

- *The undermining of human communication's validity claims*: In the age of false news, humans cannot trust that the news they receive is true; that the sources and producers are known, truthful, sincere, and credible; and that political communication follows rightful norms of behaviour and communication. False news, political bots, and false social media accounts violate what Jürgen Habermas (1984) calls the validity claims of communication (understandability, propositional truth, normative rightness, subjective truthfulness). As a consequence, it has become more difficult to discern what political communications, political communicators, and attentions given to political communication are factual or simulated.

- *Threats to democracy*: The logic of algorithms, big data, and targeted advertising threatens to undermine democracy. When false news, political bots, and false accounts proliferate because the profit interests of social media companies tolerate, are blind to, and cannot tackle powerful political interests that aim at manipulating political communication in the public sphere, then democracy is in danger.

- *One-dimensional, instrumental, highly polarised, and symbolically/communicatively violent politics*: Algorithms do not have feelings, sentiments, affects, morals, or ethics, and do not understand meanings. They are not human. They process the syntax of data but have no semantics and pragmatics. They do not understand jokes, sarcasm, humour, love, care, or empathy. They try to make a complex world one-dimensional and organised in the form of informatics' if-then-else logic. The trouble of big data analytics is that it approaches and assesses a contradictory world with statistical and mathematical models that are blind to the complexity and dialectics of society and human behaviour. When algorithms displace human decisions and human behaviour, we end up in a highly instrumental world. Given that algorithms disregard ethics, morals, and sentiments, there is a danger that they are programmed to polarise political communication and foster symbolic and communicative violence.

- *Spirals of intensifying political aggression and violence*: False news tends to be sensationalist and can spread at extremely high speed online. Combined with false news' often polarising character and the impossibility of fact-checking news in real time, there is a danger that in the age of false social media news, political communication between political opponents breaks down and that spirals of intensifying political aggression and violence emerge.

What Can Be Done against False News Culture?

In discussions about what can be done against false news culture, one should always bear in mind that the dominant social media companies (Facebook, Twitter, Google, etc.) profit from targeted advertising, algorithms that substitute human behaviour, and big data, and that they are therefore likely to come up with very limited suggestions that put the burden on users, suggest technological fixes to political problems that — because of the complex interaction of technology and society — can never work, or suggest to only intervene after the damage has already been done. Given that false news poses threats to democracy, superficial measures will not be sufficient to overcome the negative impacts on the public sphere that have emerged.

Twitter has, for example, recently said that it would no longer accept political ads from Russia Today and Sputnik. Social media companies confronted with false news often argue that they close false news accounts when the latter are reported. But given the global, complex, and dynamic character of the Internet, false news sources can easily be geographically and organisationally shifted and be multiplied (the so-called "Streisand effect", https://en.wikipedia.org/wiki/Streisand_effect). Banning certain organisations from political ads, banning accounts *ex post* after false news has been posted, purely relying on users reporting false news, etc. are superficial measures that will not overcome the threats to democracy that false news culture poses.

There are a number of feasible measures that can be taken in order to challenge false news culture:

- *Outlawing targeted and behavioural political online advertising* is a legal measure that any parliament can introduce. Practically speaking, this means that if such a ban is introduced, Facebook, Google, Twitter, etc. are no longer allowed to technically enable that users who access the Internet from the IP addresses associated with the specific country are targeted by political ads. Introducing such a measure is only effective if it is accompanied by penalties for violations of the political online ad ban. Such penalties can only be reasonably enforced if legislation does not define the advertising client, but the ad-selling online platform, as the offender. Ad clients can be located anywhere in the world, which makes enforcing penalties from one country difficult. If an online platform does not adequately disable targeted political online advertising and does not properly check whether a targeted online ad is political in nature, then a penalty should be due. In order to be effective, the penalty fare should be set at a significant share of the offending online company's worldwide annual revenue. Given that false news has become a global problem, it is likely that other countries will follow suit once one country starts outlawing targeted and behavioural political online advertising.

- *Substituting algorithmic activity by paid human work of fact-checkers and knowledge professionals* can help to reduce the dangers to democracy posed by false news. False news is not limited to political online ads, but also appears on social media newsfeeds, profiles, walls, and in other online spaces. Checking the facticity of news and content can only work if it is conducted by humans, not machines or algorithms. Fact-checking is a professional activity organised by independent organisations that specialise on conducting analyses of the truth, truthfulness, and rightness of claims.[7] Fact-checking is a complex, time-intensive, highly skilled work conducted by professionals who have a research background. Fact-checking does not work if it is simply crowd-sourced, but rather requires adequate funding for sustaining full-time jobs of fact-checkers.

- It makes sense that large social media companies are by law required to either, depending on their number of active monthly users, directly hire a specific number of fact-checkers or to cooperate with and pay for the services of a specific number of employees of independent, non-profit fact-checking organisations.

- If social media platforms are by law required to introduce a *false news alert button* that triggers a fact-check when a specified number of users click the button in respect to a specific content item, then progress could be achieved.

- False news culture can only be overcome if *alternative forms of political online communication* are actively fostered. This requires new types of online platforms and new formats that decelerate news and political communication and act as slow media. I have, in this context, suggested reviving the concept of the political debate format of *After Dark/Club 2* (for a detailed overview of this suggestion, see Fuchs 2017d). *After Dark* (see https://en.wikipedia.org/wiki/After_Dark_(TV_series) was an uncensored live discussion programme with open-ended debate broadcast on Channel 4 between 1987 and 1997 and on the BBC in 2003. The format originated in Austria, where the public service broadcaster ORF (Austrian Broadcasting Corporation) broadcast *Club 2* between 1976 and 1995. *Club 2.0* is a concept that updates this format by using social media (Fuchs 2017d). It aims at fostering political debate and providing adequate space and time for such discussions with the help of public service media and social media. Twitter, YouTube, and Facebook are manifestations of a fast media culture originating in Silicon Valley. Alternative social media are needed in order to challenge false news culture.

- In Europe, there is a long tradition of *public service media*. There is no European equivalent of Twitter, YouTube, and Facebook because in Europe there are different media traditions that are to a significant degree based on public service media. Regulatory changes that allow public service broadcasters to offer online formats and social media platforms (such as *Club 2.0* and other formats), aimed at advancing political communication and slow media that are advertising-free and adequately funding such activities, form a good way of establishing an alternative culture of political communication that weakens false news culture. Advancing public service Internet platforms is a step towards overcoming false news culture.

- Public service media can play an important role in advancing *public service Internet platforms* that foster advertising-free political debate that challenges false news.

- Advancing alternatives to false news culture requires *funding*. False news is the consequence of a media and political culture that is based on tabloidisation, for-profit culture, and advertising culture. An alternative logic should therefore be non-profit and advertising-free. Introducing an *online advertising tax* on all ads targeted at users accessing the Internet and a *digital services tax* on all digital services conducted for profit would provide a resource base for funding public service and alternative Internet platforms that foster a new culture of political debate capable of challenging false news culture. Such an online advertising tax could furthermore fund the strengthening and development of fact-checking as a new knowledge profession that actively works against false news culture.

False news is a serious and complex problem that has complex societal causes and threatens to undermine democracy. There are no technological fixes and superficial measures that can overcome false news culture. Challenging false news culture requires legal, political, economic, and media innovations that foster a culture of slow media, public service Internet platforms, fact-checking, and new forms of political engagement and debate.

8.4 Authoritarian Capitalism, Authoritarian Movements, Authoritarian Communication[8]

We live in times of rapid political and social change that are highly complex and unpredictable. The 2008 crisis of the capitalist economy constituted a societal watershed. Rebellions, uprisings, occupations, revolutions, and counter-revolutions have become more frequent in the years since the crisis. Austerity measures, as well as short-sighted, uncoordinated responses to the plight of refugees and to wars, have resulted in crises of national and transnational state power. In respect to ideologies and worldviews, socialism, nationalism, and right-wing radicalism have been strengthened. New technologies and popular culture have been embedded into these changes.

The far-right is successful in using social media for political communication. The far-right's use of the Internet has been much less studied than progressive movements' communication. W. Lance Bennett and Alexandra Segerberg's (2013) book *The Logic of Connective Action* mentions Occupy 70 times. It does not mention the Golden Dawn, Jobbik, the National Front, UKIP, Svoboda, Nigel Farage, the FPÖ, the Sweden Democrats, the Finns Party, Marine Le Pen, Geert Wilders, etc. a single time. The *Encyclopedia of Social Movement Media* (Downing 2011) presents 600 pages of analyses of "alternative media, citizens' media, community media, counterinformation media, grassroots media, independent media, nano-media, participatory media, social movement media, and underground media" (xxv). The focus is on all sorts of progressive, left-wing media, from the likes of the Adbusters Media Foundation to Zapatista media. The editor John Downing admits that "much less examination of media of extreme right movements occurs in this volume than there might be" (xxvi), but he does not explain why this might be the case, why it is problematic, and how it could be changed.

My argument is that we should not just study what we like, but also what we really dislike. Critical research is not a Facebook or Twitter "like" button, but must try to impart insights that can inform changes in the world. This does not simply require construction and positivism. It requires negative dialectics that hinders, and at the same time requires, determinate negations, positive negations of the negative.

Populism

I do not find the concept of populism theoretically meaningful. Its uses are too confused, meaning that the term requires constant explanation when employed in academic research. In the broadest sense, populism is the movement of making something popular, such as in popular culture. Etymologically, the term "popular" stems from the Latin word *popularis*, which designates that something is prevalent in the public (Williams 1983a, 236). In a more political understanding, populism means the movement of making something appealing to the people. The problem of this second meaning is that by "the people", one can refer to: (a) all humans; (b) all citizens; or (c) the nation and those belonging to it. There is a variety of meanings of the term "the people" as the *populace* that ranges from universalism on one end to nationalist particularism on the other end. Populism as a political movement goes back to revolutionary movements in nineteenth-century Russia (Labica 1987, 1026). But the term has also become associated with nationalist and right-wing extremist forces and ideology that try to appeal to prejudices, and conceive of the people as an "undifferentiated unity" so that classes and their antagonisms are "denied and downplayed" (Labica 1987, 1028). Populism is therefore often associated with *"demagogy*, which has moved from 'leading the people' to 'crude and simplifying agitation'" and with "rightist and fascist movements which exploit 'popular prejudices'" (Williams 1983a, 238). In addition, populism is also used as a term for a particular style of politics that uses tabloidisation, scandalisation, entertainment, ridicule, simplification, one-dimensionality, and banalisation. Using a term such as "left-wing populism" is confusing because it can have many meanings: it can mean a political strategy that aims at ownership and control of society by all (self-management), a left strategy that uses popular culture, one that denies the existence of classes in a class society, one that uses tabloid politics, or one that resorts to traditionalist, nationalist, or xenophobic rhetoric and prejudices.

Whereas for Gramsci (2000) the "national-popular" as populism has to do with popular culture, organic intellectuals, the cultural dimension of class struggle, the popular university, and the formation of a collective socialist will, Hitler (1988), in *Mein Kampf*, understands populism as the popularisation of the anti-Semitic Nazi movement:

Later on the National Socialist Movement presented the Jewish problem in a new light. Taking the question beyond the restricted circles of the upper classes and small bourgeoisie we succeeded in transforming it into the driving motive of a great popular movement.

That both Gramsci and Hitler embraced the notions of the popular and of populism shows that these are not well-suited terms for a socialist strategy. Populism is not a clearly delineated, but rather a politically confusing, term.

Authoritarianism

Instead, the notion of authoritarianism is a more suitable concept for explaining contemporary far-right practices. The critical theory of authoritarianism advanced by the Frankfurt School and related authors on fascism, Nazism, and the authoritarian personality is a helpful tool for understanding authoritarian capitalism. In this context, particularly works by Franz L. Neumann, Erich Fromm, Theodor W. Adorno, Herbert Marcuse, Leo Löwenthal, and Willhelm Reich matter (Fuchs 2018a). Seen as a totality, the body of works of these authors has the advantage that by combining political economy, ideology critique, and critical psychology, it enables an integrative analysis of society. Furthermore, it combines the social sciences and humanities, social analysis and philosophy, empirical social research, and sociological theory. These authors start from Karl Marx's notions of alienation and Georg Lukács' (1971) concept of reification. They see exploitation, domination, and ideological manipulation as types of instrumental reason, as forms of asymmetric power that instrumentalise labour power (exploitation), citizens (domination), and consciousness (ideology).

A first important insight of the Frankfurt School authors is that political economy and ideology critique are not enough to fully understand right-wing authoritarianism. The combination of both can explain why right-wing authoritarianism emerges in particular contexts, but not why individuals and groups follow it. Wilhelm Reich (1972) argued that the left and left analysis in the period form 1918 until 1933 only focused on "*objective* socio-economic processes at a time of crisis" and failed "to take into account the character structure" and the "social effect of mysticism" (5). In order to produce proper understandings, critical theory and critical empirical research need to combine political economy and ideology critique with critical psychology. The success of far-right authoritarian populism is not just a matter of political-economic crisis and nationalist ideology. A significant dimension is that it appeals to people's everyday affects, emotions, desires, instincts, and drives.

Franz L. Neumann is one of the rather forgotten thinkers of the Frankfurt School. His works managed to combine political economy, ideology critique, and critical psychology in the critical analysis of authoritarianism (see Fuchs 2018a, 2017c; Neumann 1944/2009, 1957/2017). Neumann (1957/2017) argues that destructive collective anxiety that generates large-scale support for far-right movements, groups, parties, institutions, and systems can emerge when six conditions coincide: (a) the alienation of labour; (b) destructive competition; (c) social alienation; (d) political alienation in respect to the political system; (e) the institutionalisation of anxiety; and (f) destructive psychological alienation and persecutory anxiety.

These categories can be applied to an analysis of the links between current forms of neoliberal capitalism and the rise of right-wing authoritarianism. Neoliberal capitalism has resulted in the intensification of labour's alienation, the destructiveness of competition, the great fear of social decline, political apathy, and a lack of trust in the political institutions of democracy and politicians. Neoliberalism has advanced wide socio-economic, political, and cultural alienation. Contemporary far-right politics stands in the context of alienation's economic, political, and cultural moments. Neoliberalism is a politics of social anxiety (precarious labour and precarious life) that can backfire and turn into fascist politics of political anxiety. In this political void, nationalist and xenophobic far-right movements and their authoritarian leaders have not only stoked fears by constructing scapegoats, but have also promised alternatives in the form of nationalism, strong leaders, and authoritarian rule. They advance persecutory anxiety by creating and supporting the unleashing of aggressions in collective forms, and direct these at scapegoats. Contemporary societies can come to tipping points where quantity turns into new qualities that may take on the form of authoritarian capitalism and the undermining of democracy. Neoliberal capitalism has experienced its own negative dialectic of the enlightenment and has increasingly been sublated into authoritarian capitalism (Fuchs 2018a).

However, authoritarianism is multi-layered. It can operate at the levels of: (a) an individual's psychology and behaviour; (b) groups/movements/parties; (c) institutions; or (d) society. We must distinguish between right-wing authoritarian personalities, groups, institutions, and society. These levels are nested, meaning that an upper level always contains and requires all necessary preceding levels. Each level is a necessity but not a sufficient condition for the next level. There is not deterministic or automatic development from one level to the next, only the possibility of emergence under specific conditions.

There are four elements of authoritarianism: (a) authoritarian leadership; (b) nationalism; (c) the friend/enemy scheme; and (d) patriarchy/law and order/militarism. Nationalism is the construction of fictive ethnicity that tries to unite people around the ideological belief in a commonality organised through elements such as blood, traditions, language, origin, and/or culture. Nationalism has a necessary outside from which it distinguishes itself. The friend/enemy scheme constructs scapegoats, typically minorities, that are presented as society's ills and as the causes of social problems. The inclusive form of the friend/enemy scheme argues for the inferiority of the enemy group in order to exploit it, and the exclusive form constructs the enemy as inferior for the purpose of deportation, imprisonment, or extermination. In authoritarianism, "[h]atred, resentment, dread, created by great upheavals, are concentrated on certain persons who are denounced as devilish conspirators". In such situations, the "fear of social degradation [...] creates for itself 'a target for the discharge of the resentments arising from damaged self-esteem'" (Neumann 1957/2017, 624).

Right-wing authoritarianism is a type of political fetishism that idolises the nation as a mythical collective that is directed against perceived outsiders who must be contained, purged, or eliminated in order to achieve greatness. Its ideological role is that it distracts attention from, and dissimulates, the complex structural causes of capitalism's social problems that have to do with class structures and social domination. Nationalism tries to construct an ideological unity of capital and labour in the form of the national collective that is said to share a national interest that is under threat by foreigners and foreignness. The world is presented as a struggle between nations, a view that fetishises and naturalises the nation and disregards the realities of class conflicts and power inequalities. There is a difference between right-wing authoritarianism, right-wing extremism, and fascism. Whereas right-wing authoritarianism violates democracy, opposition is still possible and to a certain extent tolerated, whereas right-wing extremism propagates and practices direct violence against opponents, and fascism institutionalises it in the form of a system of terror. Authoritarian capitalism is a form of capitalist political economy in which the principles of right-wing authoritarianism — authoritarian leadership, nationalism, the friend/enemy scheme, militarism, patriarchy, etc. — are, to a specific degree, practised by the state in order to organise capitalism and assert capitalist interests. In authoritarian capitalism, nationalism, political fetishism, and scapegoating are politically practised as ideology put into legal form in order to distract attention from class contradictions.

Authoritarianism involves the belief in, and the practice of, hierarchic social structures dominated by the leadership principle. Leadership is applied as a principle of totality that has no respect for individuality in the organisation of the political system, the capitalist economy, the army, the family, and the cultural organisation. Erich Fromm pioneered the study of the authoritarian personality. He describes the right-wing authoritarian leader and his followers as sadomasochistic personalities characterised by the simultaneous "striving for submission and domination" (Fromm 1942/2001, 122). A sadomasochistic individual "admires authority and tends to submit to it, but at the same time [...] wants to be an authority himself and have others submit to him" (141). Under the accumulated experience of particular conditions, the psychological striving for freedom and solidarity is suspended by negative dialectics of superiority/inferiority, love/hate, construction/destruction, and submission/aggression. One psychological dimension of authoritarianism is that it is a form of collective narcissism. The vision of the strong leader produces the psychological "enlargement of the subject: by making the leader his ideal he loves himself, as it were, but gets rid of the stains of frustration and discontent which mar his picture of his own empirical self" (Adorno 1951, 140). "The narcissistic *gain* provided by fascist propaganda is obvious" (145). An authoritarian leader presents himself as superman and ordinary, as a "great little man" (142). The image of the superman allows projection and submission – the sadomasochistic desire to be a superman and to be dominated by a superman.

Militarist patriarchy combines the gender division of social life with the fetishisation of the male soldier as the ideal human being. Competition, egoism, violence, and, in the final instance, physical destruction, war, and imperialism are seen as natural features of the human being and as appropriate solutions for social conflict. According to Klaus Theweleit (1987),"Under patriarchy, the productive force of women has been effectively excluded from participating in male public and social productions" (272). In patriarchy, leaders are typically male. The friend/enemy scheme in the final instance leads to wars. Patriarchy entails militarism, the glorification of the male soldier, surveillance, the police, imperialism, and warfare. The figures of the soldier and the policeman are also bound up with nationalist ideology. The soldier and the policeman are in nationalist ideology seen as the defenders of the nation against foreigners and enemies. Authoritarians "destroy others to create themselves; they destroy things in the alien object-world and metamorphose into killing-machines and their components: a 'baptism of fire.' *Wreaking revenge* is their way of becoming one with themselves" (Theweleit 1989, 382). Militarist ideology and practice aims at annihilating the perceived enemies.

Speaking of right-wing authoritarianism implies that there is also left-wing authoritarianism. Stalinism was the best example of left-wing authoritarianism. It employed a socialist rhetoric and language, but used the leadership principle, nationalism, militarism, patriarchy, and a repressive state apparatus for the organisation and defence of a state-capitalist regime (James 2013b). Only Stalinism's rhetoric was socialist. The Stalinist bureaucracy acted as a collective capitalist controlling the economy and exploiting waged and unwaged labour. In addition, the Stalinist economy was ideologically legitimated by a protestant ethic of toil, the idealisation of manual labour and abstinence (Marcuse 1958). Thus, the opposite of Stalinism is not "left populism", but democratic socialism.

Frankfurt School authors' analysis of right-wing authoritarianism remains crucial today for understanding phenomena such as Donald Trump and their use of digital media.

Authoritarian Social Media

Authoritarian populism appeals to emotions partly via public communications, including entertainment formats and social media. Among the reasons of the success of the authoritarian right is that the simplicity and aggressiveness of its ideology appeals to those who feel politically left alone, disenfranchised, disappointed, and anxious. Media-savvy right-wing leaders "instrumentalize such disenchantment in text, image and talk, via many discursive and material practices" (Wodak 2015, 182). Social media is, just like the beer tent, the pub, and the public assembly, a space in which right-wing authoritarianism is communicated. Right-wing authoritarianisation is based on the Haiderisation and the Berluconisation of politics (Wodak 2013) – two forms of far-right authoritarian politics using entertainment and media publicity that were pioneered by Jörg Haider in Austria and Silvio Berlusconi in Italy.

Right-wing authoritarian communication is a semiotic strategy that publicly communicates right-wing authoritarianism's four elements. Based on critical theory, we can study how right-wing authoritarianism is communicated in public, such as on social media.

Towards Chaplin 2.0, Brecht 2.0, Verfremdung 2.0, Critical Data Visualisation, Slow Media, and Critical Public Sociology

One of the problems of the left is that it has lost its appeal to blue-collar and other workers who fear or experience social degradation, and who are, despite automation, computerisation, and deindustrialisation, large enough in numbers to tip election results towards the right and the far-right. This is especially the case when voter turnouts are low, when the left is disorganised, factionalised, and weak, and when social democracy imitates neoliberalism and entrepreneurialism in an attempt to appeal to the new "middle class".[9] "It is only by offering that vision of expanded welfare provision and justice for all that the left will be able to break apart today's alliance of conservatives and those further to their right" (Renton 2019, 237).

Corporate media monopolies and the logic of the acceleration, spectacularisation, and tabloidisation of the media are part of the reason why we see a rise in right-wing authoritarianism. The left therefore needs to struggle for media reforms that advance slow media, non-commercial media, public interest media, a public service Internet, the digital and communicative commons, and platform cooperatives (Fuchs 2018a).

Part of the problem of the left is that it has more problems in appealing to the psyche, emotions, affects, and desires of those who feel politically anxious and disenfranchised than the right does. It would be wrong to imitate the communication strategies and elements of right-wing authoritarianism. But the left can also not leave political psychology entirely to the right. Those who feel politically anxious and disenfranchised need to express their desires for love and hate. The key question is then how the left can manage to turn a disenfranchised group's love for the authoritarian leader and nationalism into a love for participatory democracy and socialism, and its hatred of immigrants and foreigners into the hatred of capitalism and inequality. Part of the problem is that prejudices can often not be countered by rational arguments and citing statistical data, because they operate at the psychological level of hopes and fears that are the psychological material of post-truth politics. The solution, then, is not that the left gives up the use of well-thought-out arguments and debates. On the contrary, the point is to understand the complexity of the world and come up with proper responses that are supported by visual and argumentative strategies that bring the problem to the point.

Critical Data Visualisation

Critical visualisations of data, studies, and statistics can form one important element of how to popularise progressive thought so that it challenges right-wing authoritarianism's prejudices, nationalism, scapegoating, and leadership ideology. An interesting way of responding to right-wing authoritarianism's irrationality is by political humour, satire, and parody. Horkheimer and Adorno (2002) wrote about the "ambiguity of laughter":

> If laughter up to now has been a sign of violence, an outbreak of blind, obdurate nature, it nevertheless contains the opposite element, in that through laughter blind nature becomes aware of itself as such and thus abjures its destructive violence.
>
> (60)

Humour is part of oppression itself, but may also be turned into challenging oppression. Left critique can be simultaneously enlightening, humorous, and serious. There is much to learn in this respect from Charlie Chaplin and Bertolt Brecht. The left 2.0 requires Chaplin 2.0 and Brecht 2.0 for the age of social media and big data. The right-wing authoritarian spectacle staged via social media and reality TV needs to be challenged by the Brechtian epic and dialectical theatre 2.0, and the Boalian theatre of the oppressed 2.0.

Chaplin described the communicative approach of his movie *The Great Dictator* (1940):

> Pessimists say I may fail – that dictators aren't funny any more, that the evil is too serious. That is wrong. If there is one thing I know it is that power can always be made ridiculous. The bigger that fellow gets the harder my laughter will hit him.
>
> (Van Gelder 1940)

Brechtian Verfremdung

Brecht speaks of *Verfremdung* as opposed to *Entfremdung* (estrangement, alienation) as the principle of the dialectical theatre:

> Verfremdung estranges an incident or character simply by taking from the incident or character what is self-evident, familiar, obvious in order to produce wonder and curiosity. [...] The V-effect consists in turning the object of which it is to be made aware, to which one's attention is to be drawn,

from something ordinary, familiar, immediately accessible, into something
peculiar, striking and unexpected.

(Brecht 2015, 143, 192)

Verfremdung is a negation of the negation that creates feelings, emotions, and
affects of curiosity, surprise, and wonder. *Verfremdung* is the alienation of alienation
and the estrangement of estrangement. By *Verfremdung* 2.0, we mean equivalents
of the Brechtian dialectical principle in the digital age.

Semiotic Struggles

Ernst Bloch[10] suggests fighting the Nazis and fascism should also entail symbolic struggles
over words so that communists and socialists appropriate the words that fascists use and
give them a different meaning. He argued that the words home and homeland (*Heimat*)
should not be left to the fascists, but be used differently. Capitalism alienates humans
from society, nature, and themselves as their home. Socialism (or what today we could
call commonism or a commons-based democracy) is in contrast for Bloch a true homeland
that overcomes capitalism and the particularism of nationalist homeland ideology:

But the root of history is the working, creating human being who reshapes
and overhauls the given facts. Once he has grasped himself and established what is his, without expropriation and alienation, in real democracy,
there arises in the world something which shines into the childhood of all
and in which no one has yet been: homeland.

(Bloch 1995, 1375–1376)

Heimat (homeland) is an emotional category that appeals to humans' desire for
community, friendship, family, well-being, and stability. Trying to semiotically
recode the meaning of the category of the homeland as social security, social
justice, and solidarity that is opposed to exploitation and class structures can be
one of the strategies used for countering right-wing extremist homeland-ideology.
Hardt and Negri (2017) understand politics as not just taking place on the
streets, in factories, squares, and offices, but also in the realm of language and
communication. They argue that we must politically take and transform the
meaning of words and argue that "transforming words themselves, giving them
new meanings" (151) is part of political struggle. "Sometimes this involves coin-
ing new terms but more often it is a matter of taking back and giving new significance to existing ones" (151). "Indeed one of the central tasks of political

thought is to struggle over concepts, to clarify and transform their meaning" (xix). Semiotic guerrilla warfare needs to be part of the struggle against right-wing extremism:

> In an era in which mass communication often appears as the manifestation of a domination which makes sure of social control by planning the sending of messages, it remains possible (as in an ideal semiotic "guerilla warfare") to change the circumstances in the light of which the addressees will choose own ways of interpretation.
>
> (Eco 1976, 150)

The intellectual's task in the times we live in is to be a critical, public intellectual. The Jewish socialist intellectual Franz L. Neumann, who fled from Nazi-Germany to the USA, stressed the task of critical public social science in his essay *Anxiety and Politics*:

> Hence there remains for us as citizens of the university and of the state the dual offensive on anxiety and for liberty: that of education and that of politics. Politics, again, should be a dual thing for us: the penetration of the subject matter of our academic discipline with the problems of politics [...] and the taking of positions on political questions. If we are serious about the humanization of politics; if we wish to prevent a demagogue from using anxiety and apathy, then we – as teachers and students – must not be silent.
>
> (Neumann 1957/2017, 629)

8.5 From the Antagonism of the Empire and the Multitude Towards a Society of the Commons

Empire, Multitude, and the Commons

Hardt and Negri, in their tetralogy *Empire* (2000), *Multitude* (2004), *Commonwealth* (2009) and *Assembly* (2017), analyse the antagonism between capital and labour in contemporary capitalism as the antagonism between empire and multitude. Empire is a form of capitalism that is based on the cooperative labour of the social worker (the multitude) that creates social, cultural, educational, technological, and communicative commons:

> Production based on cooperation and communication makes perfectly clear how the common is both presupposition and result: there can be no

> cooperation without an existing commonality, and the result of cooperative production is the creation of a new commonality; similarly, communication cannot take place without a common basis, and the result of communication is a new common expression. The production of the multitude launches the common in an expanding, virtuous spiral.
>
> (Hardt and Negri 2004, 349–350)

Within the global capitalism that Hardt and Negri (2000) have termed empire, capital exploits the common that the multitude produces. In their book *Commonwealth*, Hardt and Negri (2009) envision an alternative to capitalism – the commonwealth. Commonwealth is "a world of common wealth" that expands "our capacities for collective and production and self-government" (xiii).

Hardt and Negri analyse capitalism as a contradictory open totality that in its development has become ever-more social and cooperative, but is subject to the dominant class' and political elites' control. A dialectic of crises and struggles drives the development of these contradictions.

The social production of the commons that are exploited by capital is a key feature of the contemporary economy and society:

> Today production is increasingly social in a double sense: on one hand, people produce ever more socially, in networks of cooperation and interaction; and, on the other, the result of production is not just commodities but social relations and ultimately society itself.
>
> (Hardt and Negri 2017, xv; see also 78)

The common consists, for Hardt and Negri (2017), of two main forms, the natural and the social commons (166), that are divided into five types: the earth and its ecosystems; the "immaterial" common of ideas, codes, images, and cultural products; "material" goods produced by cooperative work; metropolitan and rural spaces that are realms of communication, cultural interaction, and cooperation; and social institutions and services that organise housing, welfare, health, and education (166). Contemporary capitalism's class structure is, for Hardt and Negri (2017), based on the extraction of the commons, which includes the extraction of natural resources, data mining/data extraction, the extraction of the social from the urban spaces on real estate markets, and finance as extractive industry (166–171).

Hardt/Negri and David Harvey

Hardt and Negri (2017) analyse capitalism as having developed in three phases: the phase of primitive accumulation, the phase of manufacture and large-scale industry, and the phase of social production. In Chapter 11 of their book *Assembly*, they provide a typology of ten features of these three phases. In this analysis, a difference between Hardt/Negri's and David Harvey's approach becomes evident: whereas Harvey characterises capitalism's imperialistic and exploitative nature, based on Rosa Luxemburg, as ongoing primitive accumulation, primitive accumulation is, for Hardt and Negri, a stage of capitalist development. Hardt/Negri prefer Marx's notions of formal and real subsumption for characterising capitalism's processes of exploitation and commodification. In an interlude, Hardt and Negri explicitly discuss this difference of their approach to the one by David Harvey (Hardt and Negri 2017, 178–182).

David Harvey uses the notions of formal/real subsumption and primitive accumulation in a converse manner to Hardt/Negri: whereas primitive accumulation is, in his theory, an ongoing process of accumulation by dispossession, formal and real subsumption characterise two stages in the development of capitalism, one dominated by absolute surplus-value production, the other by relative surplus-value production. Harvey (2017), in his book *Marx, Capital and the Madness of Economic Reason*, says that Marx describes a "move from a formal (coordinations through market mechanisms) to a real (under the direct supervision of capital) subsumption of labour under capital" (117). "All the features of primitive accumulation that Marx mentions have remained powerfully present within capitalism's historical geography up until now" (Harvey 2003, 145).

Whereas there are commonalities of Harvey's and Hardt/Negri's analysis of the commons and urban space (see Harvey et al. 2009), it is evident that there are also differences. There is certainly not one correct or valid interpretation of Marx. The decisive circumstance is that Marx, 200 years after his birth, remains the key influence for understanding capitalism critically. Both Harvey's and Hardt/Negri's works are updates of Marx's theory under the conditions of twenty-first-century capitalism.

The Dialectic of Multitude and Empire

Hardt and Negri (2000, 51) consider Hegelian dialectics as deterministic and teleological. They use Spinoza's immanentism rather than Hegel's dialectics. But Hegelian dialectics has shaped Hardt's and Negri's works behind their back. Figure 8.1 visualises Hardt and Negri's concepts of empire (Hardt and Negri 2000), the multitude (Hardt and Negri 2004), and

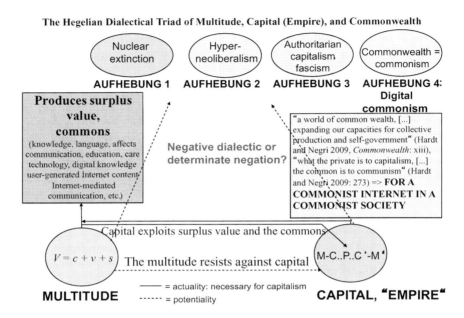

FIGURE 8.1 The antagonism between the capitalist empire and the multitude

commonwealth (Hardt and Negri 2009) as a dialectical triad. The multitude produces the commons. Capital organises itself as a global empire for exploiting the commons. There is an antagonism of capital and the multitude. Capital requires the multitude that produces the commons, but at the same time capital exploits and excludes the multitude. Commonwealth is a new self-managed form of the commons that emerges from the negation of the negative relation of capital and the multitude.

In *Empire, Multitude, Commonwealth*, and *Assembly*, Hardt and Negri (2000, 2004, 2009) describe a stage in capitalist development in which global capital (the empire) faces a new working class (the multitude). New common potentials emerge that could become the foundation of a society of the commons, the commonwealth. Commonwealth is, however, just one possible outcome of twenty-first-century society's development. There could also be negative developments such as a new fascism or the end of humanity. Which option prevails depends on how social struggles will develop. The truth of what Rosa Luxemburg wrote in 1918 has today again become very urgent: "In this hour, socialism is the only salvation for humanity" (Luxemburg 1971, 367).

Right-wing authoritarian movements advance particularistic politics of nature, of the social, and of communication. In respect to nature, they fetishise national identity, the family, and conservative traditions, and see immigrants and global identity as environmental problems disrupting the nation. Right-wing authoritarianism's social policies are a combination of neoliberal ideology that propagates survival of the fittest and a national "socialist" rhetoric that reserves welfare for the autochthonous, national population. In respect to communication, right-wing authoritarianism combines conservative techno-pessimism that sees traditional values under threat on the Internet and argues in favour of law and order control of the Internet, combined with a neoliberal techno-capitalist ideology that celebrates the corporate media and the corporate Internet.

Hardt and Negri (2017, Chapter 4) analyse contemporary far-right politics. The aim of contemporary right-wing movements is to "restore an imagined national identity that is primarily white, Christian, and heterosexual" (50). Hardt and Negri argue that contemporary far-right politics often imitates left-wing movements and are organised as leaderless and structureless movements so that they are different from classical right-wing movements. Donald Trump is arguably the most influential far-right politician today. Trump certainly undermines established party structures. But at the same time, he has used money, ideology, and popularity to build new structures. And he constitutes a new form of authoritarian right-wing leadership, in which the power of big politics and big capital are fused in one person, the authoritarian spectacle mobilises citizens via reality TV and social media, and a narcissistic self-branding machine engages in constant friend/enemy politics that takes symbolic political violence to a new level (see Fuchs 2018a). Trump is a non-trivial far-right phenomenon that is neither completely new nor completely old, but a development of the strategy and tactics of the far-right.

Progressive forces are today often split and fragmented. The commons consist of social, natural, and communicative commons. All of these commons have become increasingly commodified and privatised. Left-wing parties and movements predominantly struggle for the defence of the social commons, green movements for the defence of the natural commons, and tech movements for the defence of the communicative commons. In order to challenge right-wing authoritarianism, progressive forces should learn from the failures of the left in the 1920s when various factions, especially social democrats and communists, opposed each other and did not unite against the fascist threat. We need a united political front against right-wing authoritarianism where the defence of the social, natural, and communicative commons becomes one movement associated with one progressive party and an associated movement. Social democracy needs a renewal in the form of social democracy 2.0, a movement for socialist democracy and democratic socialism. To the convergence of capital and the convergence of the non-progressive political landscape, the only feasible answer is left-wing convergence into an internationalist progressive movement (see Figure 8.2).

The Appropriation of Fixed Digital Capital

In respect to communications, the perspective of the commons-based society stands for the advancement of the digital commons, platform cooperatives, and a public service Internet. Democratic communications shape and are shaped by "an association of free men, working with the means of production held in common, and expending their many different forms of labour-power in full self-awareness as one single social labour force" (Marx 1867, 171).

Digital technologies are ambivalent and through the contradictory development of the productive forces also advance the socialisation of work and increase the cooperative character of life and society. Hardt and Negri (2017) therefore oppose smashing digital machines. They argue for the "reappropriation of fixed capital, taking back control of the physical machines, intelligent machines, social machines, and scientific knowledges that were created by us in the first place, is one daring, powerful enterprise we could launch in that battle" (120). Appropriating fixed capital

FIGURE 8.2 Political convergence of movements for the commons

"is not a matter of struggling against or destroying machines or algorithms or any other forms in which our past production is accumulated, but rather wresting them back from capital, expropriating the expropriators, and opening that wealth to society" (287). Hardt and Negri stress the insight that given that technologies are made by humans, they shouldn't be left to capital and the state as tools of domination, but should be transformed into tools of emancipation.

In the age of algorithms, social media, big data, and digital machines, the relationship of fixed constant capital and variable capital has become more dynamic. Traditionally, engineers created machines that were used in the production process over a longer time period until they became physically or morally depreciated and had to be replaced. Digital machines operate on binary data. Digital capitalism has datafied our lives. Our online activities are to a significant degree digital labour that creates data that are both a commodity and become part of fixed capital. Data storage is an inherent element of the digital machine. Once created, data in digital capitalism become fixed constant capital. They are stored on servers as part of the digital machine that enables digital capital accumulation. But data are also the building blocks, the circulating constant capital, based on which digital labour creates new content and data. In the realm of big data, circulating constant capital and fixed constant capital show a tendency of convergence. Data are the objectification of digital labour, of human subjectivity that goes online. Data as constant capital is therefore an objectification of the general intellect. Datafication generalises human knowledge and fixes it in databases stored on servers.

When human subjects become political subjects, then commonist digital appropriation is the potential answer of political resistance they can give to digital capitalism. Hardt and Negri (2017) remind us that algorithms and digital machines are not intelligent. Only humans have intelligence. And it is their political intelligence that gives them the capacity to turn digital capital into digital commons, the capitalist digital machine into digital machines of commoning and social cooperation.

Are the big data commons the alternative to big data capitalism? On the one hand, amassing, leaking, and publishing big data about capitalist power and state power has become a strategy of resistance. On the other hand, one must see that big data generation and big data storage serves the interests of capital and the state. Big data has emerged from capitalist control (big data-based capital accumulation) and state control (state-surveillance of citizens because of the false surveillance ideology that not socialism, but surveillance and a police state, are the best means against political and social problems). In addition, big data capitalism requires massive amounts of energy that is predominantly based on non-renewable sources and it advances climate change. Big data commons therefore aim to reduce the amount of data stored to necessary data and to get rid of surplus data that today become surplus-value and surplus-power.

But how do you appropriate an algorithm, Google, YouTube, or Facebook? There are different strategies. The *first strategy* is capital taxation. Global Internet giants constantly avoid paying taxes, which is supported by the contradiction between the global Internet and regulation at the level of the nation-state. Taxing global corporations and online advertising can create state income that can be distributed to citizens via participatory budgeting. The participatory media fee taxes global corporations, and it gives everyone a citizens' communication income that is donated to non-profit media projects. Alternative media often lack resources. Via participatory budgeting and capital taxation, the alternative media sector could be strengthened in order to weaken the corporate character of the Internet and the media in general. Wages for Facebook is in general not a feasible strategy because it does not question the dominant character of digital monopoly capital. A universal basic income for universal labour, which includes unpaid digital labour and other unpaid reproductive labour, is in contrast a better political strategy.

Platform co-ops and peer-to-peer production are a *second strategy*. These are civil society projects that organise online platforms and digital machines as user-controlled and digital worker-controlled organisations that do not operate for-profit and for the interests of the few, but for the benefit of all and the common good. Resource precarity is one of the main problems alternative economy projects tend to face. Combining the first and the second strategies allows generating a resource base for platform co-ops and peer-to-peer projects. If they can expand, then they can create an economic realm that poses an alternative to digital capital and is in itself a form of digital class struggle against digital capitalism.

The left has traditionally been afraid of conquering state power. To a certain degree, the Stalinist experience justifies such scepticism. But the anarchist rejection of appropriating the state in order to transform and transcend it often leaves alternative projects powerless, marginalised, and confronted with a political economy of precarity (of voluntary labour and resources) that fosters sectarianism and anarchist versions of Stalinist orthodoxy and hierarchy. In the realm of communications, we should not forget that besides citizens' media, there is the realm of public service media (PSM). Especially in Europe, there is a strong PSM-tradition that operates to a significant degree outside of the logic of capital. Political clientelism is the problem that PSM faces. But just like there can be struggles for more autonomous realms from capital in the economy, there can be struggles for more autonomous realms from the state in the public sphere. PSM are today by legal frameworks kept from becoming public digital services and public service Internet platform providers. Monopoly media capital sees PSM as competitors and has influenced legislation that in the end helps advance the economic interests of digital monopoly capital (Google, Facebook, Amazon, Microsoft, Apple, etc.). I am not arguing in favour of a state-controlled Internet, as we already can find it where secret services implement a surveillance-industrial Internet complex (as revealed by Edward Snowden), but for independent, critical public service media that offer specific online services, such as *Club 2.0* (Fuchs 2017d) or a public service YouTube that offers all archived public service television and radio content to the public as common good (using Creative Commons licences) that can be appropriated and remixed.

What does the appropriation of the capitalist digital machine mean? It means the struggle for alternatives to digital capitalism, the de-commodification, de-capitalisation, and de-commercialisation of the digital and the Internet. Today, we often find private–public partnerships that foster commodification. Digital appropriation promises to be an effective form of digital struggle when organised as commons–public partnerships that negate the logic of digital capital and aim at a negation of digital capitalism's negativity in processes of struggles that, as determinate negations, advance the digital commons in order to transcend and abolish digital capitalism. The broader context of such digital struggles is the renewal of the left as dialectic of movement and party (Dean 2016).

We need a kind of Luxemburgism 2.0 in the age of the social production of the common. Rosa Luxemburg in her time argued against Eduard Bernstein's pure parliamentary social democratic reformism. She opposed anarchist individualism and propagated using the mass strike as political tactic. Luxemburg neither rejected nor fetishised parliamentary politics. She rejected Leninist vanguard party politics and argued for organising the spontaneity of protest. She opposed war, imperialism, and nationalism with internationalist politics. She saw that the limitation of democracy in post-revolutionary Russia was a serious shortcoming that would create major problems. Luxemburg argued for dialectics of party/movements, organisation/spontaneity, and leader/masses (see Luxemburg 2008). The point, where we need to transcend Luxemburg's politics today, is that she was very sceptical about the feasibility of autonomous projects, especially cooperatives. Self-management cannot begin from nothing in the creation of a novel society. It requires forms that develop within, against and beyond capitalism and produce commons that transcend capitalism.

Notes

1 Translation from German: „Die faschistischen und rechtsextremen Bewegungen sind die ‚Wundmale und die Narben einer Demokratie […], die ihrem eigenen Begriff eben doch bis heute noch nicht voll gerecht wird'."
2 www.collinsdictionary.com/dictionary/english/fake-news
3 Twitter, @RealDonaldTrump, 17 February 2017, https://twitter.com/realdonaldtrump/status/832708293516632065
4 Journalists first estimated that the data breach affected around 50 million Facebook users. A bit later, Facebook indicated that almost 90 million users' personal data may have been accessed and collected (Kang and Frenkel 2018).
5 BBC Stories, tweet from 21 March 2018, https://twitter.com/bbcstories/status/976415490993283073
6 2016 US Election: Donald J. Trump For President Inc., campaign finance data obtained and exported from: Federal Election Commission, www.fec.gov/data/candidate/P80001571, time period: all years (2013–2016).
7 See the International Fact-Checking Network Fact-Checkers' Code of Principles: www.poynter.org/international-fact-checking-network-fact-checkers-code-principles
8 A slightly longer version of this section has been published as a discussion piece in the journal *Media, Culture & Society*. Christian Fuchs. 2018. Authoritarian Capitalism, Authoritarian Movements and Authoritarian Communication. *Media, Culture & Society* 40 (5): 779–791. Reproduced with permission.
9 This paragraph as well as the following five paragraphs were first published in the article "Authoritarian Capitalism, Authoritarian Movements and Authoritarian Communication" in the journal *Media, Culture & Society*. Reproduced with permission.
10 Parts of the following paragraphs and the following section (8.5) were first published as part of the following article: Christian Fuchs. 2017. Reflections on Michael Hardt and Antonio Negri's Book "Assembly". *tripleC: Communication, Capitalism & Critique* 15 (2): 851–865. Reproduced with permission.

References

Adler, Max. 1932. *Lehrbuch der materialistischen Geschichtsauffassung (Soziologie des Marxismus). 2. Band: Die statischen und dynamischen Grundbegriffe. 1. Teil: Die statischen Grundbegriffe*. Berlin: E. Laubsche Verlagsbuchhandlung.

Adorno, Theodor. 1951. Freudian Theory and the Pattern of Fascist Propaganda. In *The Culture Industry*, 132–157. Abingdon: Routledge.

Adorno, Theodor W. 1967. *Aspekte des neuen Rechtsradikalismus*. Talk at the University of Vienna on 6 April 1967. www.youtube.com/watch?v=ECQOctFuw50

Adorno, Theodor W. 1985. On the Question "What Is German?". *New German Critique* 36: 121–131.

AfD. 2017. *Programm für Deutschland. Wahlprogramm der Alternative für Deutschland für die Wahl zum Deutschen Bundestag am 24. September 2017.* www.afd.de (accessed 8 October 2017).

Alexander, Anne. 2015. ISIS and Counter-Revolution: Towards a Marxist Analysis. *International Socialism* 145. http://isj.org.uk/isis-and-counter-revolution-towards-a-marxist-analysis/

Allcott, Hunt and Matthew Gentzkow. 2017. Social Media and Fake News in the 2016 Election. *Journal of Economic Perspectives* 31 (2): 211–236.

Allen, Theodor W. 2001. On Roediger's Wages of Whiteness. *Cultural Logic* 4 (2).

Al-Youssef, Muzayen. 2017. Facebook-Wahlkampf: Migration macht die meisten User "Angry". *Der Standard Online*. 21 May 2018. https://derstandard.at/2000064964789/Facebook-Wahlkampf-Migration-macht-die-meisten-User-angry

Al-Youssef, Muzayen. 2018. Facebook: Das Zusammenspiel von Strache und der "Kronen Zeitung". *Der Standard Online*. 4 October 2017. https://derstandard.at/2000079390789/Facebook-Das-Zusammenspiel-von-Strache-und-der-Kronen-Zeitung

AMECO. 2019. *AMECO Database*. http://ec.europa.eu/economy_finance/ameco (accessed 15 July 2019).

Anderson, Benedict. 2006. *Imagined Communities. Reflections on the Origin and Spread of Nationalism*. London: Verso. Revised edition.

Anderson, Kevin. 2014. Popular Movements and Their Contradictions: From the Arab Revolutions to Today. *The International Marxist-Humanist*. 26 July 2014. www.internationalmarxisthumanist.org/articles/popular-movements-contradictions-arab-revolutions-today-kevin-anderson

Anderson, Kevin B. 2016. *Marx at the Margins. On Nationalism, Ethnicity, and Non-Western Societies*. Chicago, IL: University of Chicago Press. Expanded edition.

Austria Press Agency. 2017. Facebook-Blase: FPÖ- und ÖVP-Fans bleiben unter sich. *Futurezone*. 21October 2017. https://futurezone.at/digital-life/facebook-blase-fpoe-und-oevp-fans-bleiben-unter-sich/293.380.892

Avineri, Shlomo. 1991. Marxism and Nationalism. *Journal of Contemporary History* 26 (3): 637–657.

Baier, Walter. 2008. Integraler Sozialismus und radikale Demokratie. In *Otto Bauer under der Austromarxismus*, eds. Walter Baier, Lisbeth N. Trallori, and Derek Weber, 17–31. Berlin: Dietz.

Baier, Walter. 2009. *Das kurze Jahrhundert. Kommunismus in Österreich. KPÖ 1918 bis 2008.* Wien: Edition Steinbauer.

Bailer-Galanda, Brigitte and Wolfgang Neugebauer. 1997. *Haider und die Freiheitlichen in Österreich.* Berlin: Elefanten Press.

Bakir, Vian and Andrew McStay. 2018. Fake News and the Economy of Emotions. *Digital Journalism* 6 (2): 154–175.

Balibar, Étienne and Immanuel Wallerstein. 1991. *Race, Nation, Class.* London: Verso.

Banks, Marcus and Andre Gingrich. 2006. Introduction: Neo-Nationalism in Europe and Beyond. In *Neo-Nationalism in Europe & Beyond*, eds. Andre Gingrich and Marcus Banks, 1–26. New York: Berghahn.

Barker, Martin. 1981. *The New Racism: Conservatives and the Ideology of the Tribe.* London: Junction Books.

Bauer, Otto. 1919/2017. *Der Weg zum Sozialismus.* Wien: Gimesi.

Bauer, Otto. 1923. *Die österreichische Revolution.* Wien: Wiener Volksbuchhandlung.

Bauer, Otto. 1924/2000. *The Question of Nationalities and Social Democracy.* Minneapolis, MN: University of Minnesota Press.

Bauer, Otto. 1936. *Zwischen zwei Weltkriegen? Die Krise der Weltwirtschaft, der Demokratie und des Sozialismus.* Bratislava: Eugen Prager.

Bauer, Otto. 1938a. Fascism. In *Austro-Marxism*, eds. Tom Bottomore and Patrick Goode, 167–186. Oxford: Clarendon Press.

Bauer, Otto. 1938b. Nach der Annexion. In *Werkausgabe Band 9*, 853–860. Wien: Europaverlag.

Bauer, Otto. 1938c. Österreichs Ende. In *Werkausgabe Band 9*, 834–844. Wien: Europaverlag.

BBC. 2002. Queen Offers Glimpse of Speech. *BBC Online.* 23December 2017. http://news.bbc.co.uk/1/hi/uk/2600177.stm

BBC. 2017. Christmas Day TV. *BBC Online.* 26 December 2017. www.bbc.co.uk/news/entertainment-arts-42484128

BBC. 2018. Far-Right Austria Minister's "Nazi Language" Causes Anger. *BBC Online.* 11 January 2018.

Benner, Erica. 1995. *Really Existing Nationalisms: A Post-Communist View from Marx and Engels.* Oxford: Clarendon Press.

Bennett, W. Lance and Alexandra Segerberg. 2013. *The Logic of Connective Action. Digital Media and the Personalization of Contentious Politics.* Cambridge: Cambridge University Press.

Bensmann, Marcus and Justus von Daniels. 2017. AfD-Meuthen und die Spende aus der Schweiz. *Correctiv – Recherchen für die Gesellschaft.* 29 August 2017. https://correctiv.org/aktuelles/neue-rechte/2017/08/29/afd-meuthen-und-die-spende-aus-der-schweiz

References **287**

Bernaschek, Richard. 1934. *Die Tragödie der österreichischen Sozialdemokratie*. www.antifa-info.at/archiv/Bernaschek.pdf

Billig, Michael. 1995. *Banal Nationalism*. Los Angeles, CA: Sage.

Bloch, Ernst. 1995. *The Principle of Hope. Volume Three*. Cambridge, MA: MIT Press.

Bobbio, Norberto. 1996. *Left and Right: The Significance of a Political Distinction*. Chicago, IL: University of Chicago Press.

Bourdieu, Pierre. 1984. *Distinction: A Social Critique of the Judgement of Taste*. Cambridge, MA: Harvard University Press.

Brecht, Bertolt. 2015. *Brecht on Theatre*, ed. Marc Silberman, Steve Giles, and Tom Kuhn. London: Bloomsbury Methuen Drama. Third edition.

Bronner, Stephen Eric. 2013a. Red Dreams and the New Millennium: Notes on the Legacy of Rosa Luxemburg. In *Rosa Luxemburg: Her Life and Legacy*, ed. Jason Schulman, 11–19. Basingstoke: Palgrave Macmillan.

Bronner, Stephen Eric. 2013b. Reflections on Red Rosa: An Interview with Stephen Eric Bronner. In *Rosa Luxemburg: Her Life and Legacy*, ed. Jason Schulman, 185–195. Basingstoke: Palgrave Macmillan.

Brown, Wendy. 2015. *Undoing the Demos. Neoliberalism's Stealth Revolution*. Cambridge, MA: MIT Press.

Bundesamt für Verfassungsschutz und Terrorismusbekämpfung. 2016. *"Europäisches Forum Linz" – "Kongress: Verteidiger Europas"*. 28 September 2016. www.land-oberoesterreich.gv.at/Mediendateien/LK/beilage-kongress.pdf

Bundeskriminalamt. 2016. *Sicherheit 2016: Kriminalitätsentwicklung in Österreich*. Wien: Bundeskriminalamt.

Bundeszentrale für politische Bildung. 2017. *Zahlen zu Asyl in Deutschland*. www.bpb.de/politik/innenpolitik/flucht/218788/zahlen-zu-asyl-in-deutschland#Antraege

Cadwalladr, Carole. 2018. "I Made Steve Bannon's Psychological Warfare Tool": Meet the Data War Whistleblower. *The Guardian Online*. 18 March 2018. www.theguardian.com/news/2018/mar/17/data-war-whistleblower-christopher-wylie-faceook-nix-bannon-trump

Cadwalladr, Carole and Emma Graham-Harrison. 2018. Revealed: 50 Million Facebook Profiles Harvested for Cambridge Analytica in Major Data Breach. *The Guardian Online*. 17 March 2018. www.theguardian.com/news/2018/mar/17/cambridge-analytica-facebook-influence-us-election

CBS. 2017. *CBS 60 Minutes*. Season 50, Episode 3. 8October 2017. Transcript. www.cbsnews.com/news/facebook-embeds-russia-and-the-trump-campaigns-secret-weapon/

CDU. 2017. *Für ein Deutschland, in dem wir gut und gerne leben. Regierungsprogramm 2017–2021*. www.cdu.de (accessed 7 October 2017).

Charim, Isolde. 2017. Der Körper des Politikers. *Wiener Zeitung Online*. 3 November 2017.

Chatterjee, Partha. 1986. *Nationalist Thought and the Colonial World: A Derivative Discourse*. London: Zed Books.

Chatterjee, Partha. 1993. *The Nation and its Fragments. Colonial and Postcolonial Histories.* Princeton, NJ: Princeton University Press.

Chatterjee, Partha. 2017. Subaltern Studies and Capital. In *The Debate on "Postcolonial Theory and the Specter of Capital"*, ed. Rosie Warren, 31–47. London: Verso.

Chibber, Vivek. 2013. *Postcolonial Theory and the Specter of Capital.* London: Verso.

Chibber, Vivek. 2017a. Does the Subaltern Speak? An Interview with Vivek Chibber. In *The Debate on "Postcolonial Theory and the Specter of Capital"*, ed. Rosie Warren, 15–28. London: Verso.

Chibber, Vivek. 2017b. Subaltern Studies Revisited. A Response to Partha Chatterjee. In *The Debate on "Postcolonial Theory and the Specter of Capital"*, ed. Rosie Warren, 49–69. London: Verso.

CSU. 2017. *Der Bayernplan. Klar für unser Land. Programm der CSU zur Bundestagswahl 2017.* www.csu.de (accessed 8 October 2017).

Curran, James. 1991. Rethinking the Media as a Public Sphere. In *Communication and Citizenship. Journalism and the Public Sphere*, eds. Peter Dahlgren and Colin Sparks, 27–57. London: Routledge.

Davis, Clayton A. et al. 2016. BotOrNot: A System to Evaluate Social Bots. In *WWW '16 Companion: Proceedings of the 25th International Conference Companion on World Wide Web*, 273–274. New York: ACM.

Davis, Horace B. 1978. *Toward A Marxist Theory of Nationalism.* New York: Monthly Review Press.

Davis, Mike. 2018. *Old Gods, New Enigmas. Marx's Lost Theory.* London: Verso.

Dean, Jodi. 2016. *Crowds and Party.* London: Verso.

Der Standard. 2017. TV-Duelle bescherten ORF und Puls 4 Traumquoten. *Der Standard Online.* 13October 2017.

Deutsch, Karl. 1966. *Nationalism and Social Communication. An Inquiry into the Foundations of Nationality.* Cambridge, MA: MIT Press.

Die Welt. 2017. Kurz hält Verteilung von Flüchtlingen in der EU nach Quoten für gescheitert. *Die Welt Online*, 24 December 2017.

Digital Forensic Lab. 2017. *#ElectionWatch: The Curious Case of the Far-right Feed in Germany.* https://medium.com/dfrlab/german-election-the-curious-case-of-the-far-right-feed-84cc7a8dabd9

Digital, Culture, Media and Sport Committee. 2019. *Disinformation and "Fake News": Final Report.* HC 1791. London: House of Commons.

Dossier. 2017. Die Lieblingszeitungen der Parteien. *Dossier.* 13October 2017. www.dossier.at/dossiers/inserate/vonpetersimundflorianskrabal/

Downing, John D. H., ed. 2011. *Encyclopedia of Social Movement Media.* Thousand Oaks, CA: Sage.

Du Bois, W.E.B. 1935. *Black Reconstruction: An Essay toward a History of the Part which Black Folk Played in the Attempt to Reconstruct Democracy in America, 1860–1880.* New York: Harcourt, Brace & Co.

Eckerstorfer, Paul et al. 2013. *Vermögen im Wandel.* https://media.arbeiterkammer.at/PDF/Ver moegen_in_Oesterreich.pdf

Eco, Umberto. 1976. *A Theory of Semiotics.* Bloomington, IN: Indiana University Press.

Eicken, Joachim and Ansgar Schmitz-Veltin. 2010. Die Entwicklung der Kirchenmitglieder in Deutschland. *Wirtschaft und Statistik* 6 (2010): 576–580.

European Commission. 2015. *Refugee Crisis – Q&A on Emergency Relocation.* http://europa.eu /rapid/press-release_MEMO-15-5698_en.htm (accessed 6 October 2017).

Eurostat. 2019. *Home – Eurostat.* https://ec.europa.eu/eurostat (accessed 15 July 2019).

Facebook Ireland. 2018. *Letter to the Electoral Commission.* 14May 2018. www.parliament.uk /documents/commons-committees/culture-media-and-sport/180514-Facebook-to-Electoral-Commission.pdf

Fairclough, Norman. 2015. *Language and Power.* London: Routledge. Third edition.

Fischer, Ernst. 1969. *Erinnerungen und Reflexionen.* Reinbek bei Hamburg: Rowohlt.

Forman, Michael. 1998. *Nationalism and the International Labor Movement. The Idea of the Nation in Socialist and Anrchist Theory.* University Park, PA: Pennsylvania State University Press.

Forschungsgruppe Ideologien und Politiken der Ungleichheit (FIPU). 2016. *Korporierte FPÖ-PolitikerInnen.* https://forschungsgruppefipu.wordpress.com/2016/01/21/korporierte-fpoe-funktionaeremandatare/

Forschungsgruppe Wahlen. 2017a. *Bundestagswahl.* www.forschungsgruppe.de/Aktuelles/Wah lanalyse_Bundestagswahl/Newsl_Bund_170928.pdf (accessed 6 October 2017).

Forschungsgruppe Wahlen. 2017b. *Umfrage zur Bundestagswahl 2017.* https://wahltool.zdf.de /wahlergebnisse/2017-09-24-BT-DE.html?i=23 (accessed 6 October 2017).

Forschungsgruppe Weltanschauungen in Deutschland. 2019. *fowid – Forschungsgruppe Weltan-schauungen in Deutschland.* https://fowid.de/frontpage (accessed 15 July 2019).

Fourney, Adam et al. 2017. Geographic and Temporal Trends in Fake News Consumption During the 2016 US Presidential Election. In *CIKM'17: Proceedings of the 2017 ACM Conference on Information and Knowledge Management,* 2071–2074. New York: ACM.

Freiheitliche Partei Österreichs (FPÖ). 2011. *Party programme.* English version. www.fpoe.at/ fileadmin/user_upload/www.fpoe.at/dokumente/2015/2011_graz_parteiprogramm_englisch_ web.pdf (accessed 1 January 2018).

Freiheitliche Partei Österreichs (FPÖ). 2013. *Handbuch freiheitlicher Politik.* Vienna: FPÖ- Bil-dungsinstitut. Fourth edition.

Freiheitliche Partei Österreichs (FPÖ). 2017. *Österreicher verdienen Fairness: Freiheitliches Wahlprogramm zur Nationalratswahl 2017.* www.fpoe.at/fileadmin/user_upload/Wahlpro gramm_8_9_low.pdf

Fromm, Erich. 1936. Sozialpsychologischer Teil. In *Studien über Autorität und Familie,* 77–135. Lüneburg: zu Klampen.

Fromm, Erich. 1942/2001. *The Fear of Freedom.* Abingdon: Routledge.

Fromm, Erich. 1956. *The Sane Society.* London: Routledge.

Fromm, Erich, ed. 1966. *Socialist Humanism. An International Symposium*. Garden City, NY: Doubleday.

Frontal21. 2017a. AfD-Sprecher Meuthen sagte Unwahrheit über Wahlkampfhilfen. *Frontal 21 Online*. 29August 2017.

Frontal21. 2017b. Fragwürdige Wahlwerbung. *Frontal 21 Online*. 16 May 2017. www.zdf.de/poli tik/frontal-21/das-diskrete-helfernetzwerk-der-afd-100.html

Fuchs, Christian. 2014. Social Media and the Public Sphere. *tripleC: Communication, Capitalism & Critique* 12 (1): 57–101.

Fuchs, Christian. 2016a. Racism, Nationalism and Right-Wing Extremism Online: The Austrian Presidential Election 2016 on Facebook. *Momentum Quarterly – Zeitschrift für sozialen Fortschritt (Journal for Societal Progress)* 5 (3): 172–196.

Fuchs, Christian. 2016b. *Reading Marx in the Information Age. A Media and Communication Studies Perspective on "Capital Volume I"*. New York: Routledge.

Fuchs, Christian. 2017a. Raymond Williams' Communicative Materialism. *European Journal of Cultural Studies* 20 (6): 744–762.

Fuchs, Christian. 2017b. *Social Media: A Critical Introduction*. London: Sage. Second edition.

Fuchs, Christian. 2017c. The Relevance of Franz L. Neumann's Critical Theory in 2017: "Anxiety and Politics" in the New Age of Authoritarian Capitalism. *tripleC: Communication, Capitalism & Critique* 15 (2): 637–650.

Fuchs, Christian. 2017d. Towards the Public Service Internet as Alternative to the Commercial Internet. In *ORF Texte No. 20 – Öffentlich-Rechtliche Qualität im Diskurs*, 43–50. Vienna: ORF. http://fuchs.uti.at/wp-content/ORFTexte.pdf

Fuchs, Christian. 2018a. *Digital Demagogue: Authoritarian Capitalism in the Age of Trump and Twitter*. London: Pluto.

Fuchs, Christian. 2018b. Propaganda 2.0: Herman and Chomsky's Propaganda Model in the Age of the Internet, Big Data and Social Media. In *The Propaganda Model Today: Filtering Perception and Awareness*, eds. Joan Pedro-Carañana, Daniel Broudy, and Jeffery Klaehn, 71–91. London: University of Westminster Press.

Gelfert, Axel. 2018. Fake News: A Definition. *Informal Logic* 38 (1): 84–117.

Gellner, Ernest. 2006. *Nations and Nationalism*. Malden, MA: Blackwell.

Geras, Norman. 1976/2015. *The Legacy of Rosa Luxemburg*. London: Verso.

Gilroy, Paul. 1987. *There Ain't No Black in the Union Jack. The Cultural Politics of Race and Nation*. London: Hutchinson.

Gramsci, Antonio. 2000. *The Gramsci Reader*, ed. David Forgacs. New York: New York University Press.

Grill, Markus, Sebastian Pittelkow, and Katja Riedel. 2018. Anonymer Hintermann unterstützte Weidel. *ARD Online*. 12 November 2018. www.tagesschau.de/inland/afd-parteispenden-109.html

Habermas, Jürgen. 1984. *The Theory of Communicative Action. Volume One*. Boston, MA: Beacon Press.

Habermas, Jürgen. 1991. *The Structural Transformation of the Public Sphere. An Inquiry into a Category of Bourgeois Society*. Cambridge, MA: MIT Press.

Habermas, Jürgen. 1998. *The Inclusion of the Other*. Cambridge, MA: MIT Press.

Hall, Stuart. 1988. *The Hard Road to Renewal. Thatcherism and the Crisis of the Left*. London: Lawrence & Wishart.

Hall, Stuart. 1993. Culture, Community, Nation. *Cultural Studies* 7 (3): 349–363.

Hall, Stuart. 1996. Cultural Studies and the Politics of Internationalization. An Interview with Stuart Hall by Kuan-Hsing Chen. In *Stuart Hall: Critical Dialogues in Cultural Studies*, eds. David Morley and Kuan-Hsing Chen, 392–408. London: Routledge.

Hans Böckler Stiftung. 2017. *Wer wählt Rechtspopulisten?* www.boeckler.de/pdf/pm_fo foe_2017_08_09.pdf

Hardt, Michael and Antonio Negri. 2000. *Empire*. Cambridge, MA: Harvard University Press.

Hardt, Michael and Antonio Negri. 2004. *Multitude, War and Democracy in the Age of Empire*. London: Penguin.

Hardt, Michael and Antonio Negri. 2009. *Commonwealth*. Cambridge, MA: Harvard University Press.

Hardt, Michael and Antonio Negri. 2017. *Assembly*. Oxford: Oxford University Press.

Harvey, David. 2003. *The New Imperialism*. Oxford: Oxford University Press.

Harvey, David. 2017. *Marx, Capital and the Madness of Economic Reason*. London: Profile Books.

Harvey, David, Michael Hardt, and Antonio Negri. 2009. *Commonwealth*: An Exchange. *Artforum* 48 (3): 210–221.

Häusler, Alexander. 2018. Die AfD: Partei des völkisch-autoritären Populismus. In *Völkisch-autoritärer Populismus*, ed. Alexander Häusler, 9–19. Hamburg: VSA.

Hegel, Georg Wilhelm Friedrich. 1820/2008. *Outlines of the Philosophy of Right*. Oxford: Oxford University Press.

Hegel, Georg Wilhelm Friedrich. 1991. *The Encyclopaedia Logic (with the Zusätze). Part I of the Encyclopaedia of Philosophical Sciences with the Zusätze*. Indianapolis, IN: Hackett.

Herman, Edward S. and Noam Chomsky. 1988. *Manufacturing Consent: The Political Economy of the Mass Media*. London: Vintage Books.

Heute. 2017. Wien: Mehr muslimische als katholische Schüler. *Heute Online*. 13 September 2017.

Higgins, John. 1999. *Raymond Williams: Literature, Marxism and Cultural Materialism*. London: Routledge.

Hitler, Adolf. 1988. *Mein Kampf*. Ahmedabad: Jaico.

Hobsbawm, Eric J. 1977. Some Reflections on "The Break-Up of Britain". *New Left Review* 105: 3–23.

Hobsbawm, Eric J. 1983a. Introduction: Inventing Traditions. In *The Invention of Tradition*, eds. Eric J. Hobsbawm and Terence Ranger, 1–14. Cambridge: Cambridge University Press.

Hobsbawm, Eric J. 1983b. Mass-Producing Traditions: Europe, 1870–1914. In *The Invention of Tradition*, eds. Eric J. Hobsbawm and Terence Ranger, 263–307. Cambridge: Cambridge University Press.

Hobsbawm, Eric J. 1989. *The Age of Empire 1875–1914*. New York: Vintage Books.

Hobsbawm, Eric J. 1992a. Ethnicity and Nationalism in Europe Today. *Anthropology Today* 8 (1): 3–8.

Hobsbawm, Eric J. 1992b. *Nations and Nationalism since 1780. Programme, Myth, Reality*. Cambridge: Cambridge University Press. Second edition.

Hobsbawm, Eric J. 1995. *The Age of Extremes. The Short Twentieth Century 1914–1991*. London: Abacus.

Hofer, Norbert. 2017. *Rede beim Neujahrstreffend der FPÖ*. Salzburg, 14January 2017. www.youtube.com/watch?v=4xmUU1H9CFA

Hoke, Rudolf and Ilse Reiter. 1993. *Quellensammlung zur österreichischen und deutschen Rechtsgeschichte*. Wien: Böhlau.

Holzkamp, Klaus. 2013. Racism and the Unconscious as Understood by Psychoanalysis and Critical Psychology. In *Psychology from the Standpoint of the Subject. Selected Writings of Klaus Holzkamp*, eds. Ernst Schraube and Ute Osterkamp, 172–209. Basingstoke: Palgrave Macmillan.

Holzkamp-Osterkamp, Ute. 1981. Faschistische Ideologie und Psychologie. *Forum Kritische Psychologie* 9: 155–170.

Horaczek, Nina. 2018. "Wir schaffen die siebte Million": Die Burschenschaft des FPÖ-Spitzenkandidaten Udo Landbauer treibt ihre "Späße" über die Schoah. *Der Falter* 4 (2018).

Horaczek, Nina and Barbara Tóth. 2017. *Sebasian Kurz: Österreichs neues Wunderkind?* Salzburg: Residenz Verlag.

Horkheimer, Max and Theodor W. Adorno. 2002. *Dialectic of Enlightenment*. Stanford, CA: Stanford University Press.

Howard, Philip N. et al. 2018. *The IRA, Social Media and Political Polarization in the United States, 2012–2018*. Oxford: University of Oxford.

Isaac, Mike and Daisuke Wakabayashi. 2017. Russian Influence Reached 126 Million Through Facebook Alone. *The New York Times Online*. 30 October 2017. www.nytimes.com/2017/10/30/technology/facebook-google-russia.html

James, Cyril Lionel Robert. 1943. *The Way Out for Europe*. www.marxists.org/archive/james-clr/works/1943/04/way-out-europe.htm, www.marxists.org/archive/james-clr/works/1943/05/way-out-europe.htm

James, Cyril Lionel Robert. 1971. Colonialism and National Liberation in Africa: The Gold Coast Revolution. In *National Liberation: Revolution in the Third World*, eds. Norman Miller and Roderick Aya, 102–137. New York: The Free Press.

James, Cyril Lionel Robert. 1973. *Reflections on Pan-Africanism*. www.marxists.org/archive/james-clr/works/1973/panafricanism.htm

James, Cyril Lionel Robert. 2009. *You Don't Play with Revolution. The Montreal Lectures of C.L. R. James*. Oakland, CA: AK Press.

James, Cyril Lionel Robert. 2012. *A History of Pan-African Revolt*. Oakland, CA: PM Press.

James, Cyril Lionel Robert. 2013a. *Modern Politics*. Oakland, CA: PM Press.

James, Cyril Lionel Robert. 2013b. *State Capitalism and World Revolution*. Oakland, CA: PM Press.

Jameson, Frederic. 1990. Modernism and Imperialism. In *Nationalism, Colonialism, and Literature*, 43–66. Minneapolis, MN: University of Minnesota Press.

Jikjareva, Anna, Jan Jirát and Kaspar Surber. 2018. Eine schrecklich rechte Familie. *WOZ Online*. 29 November 2018. www.woz.ch/1848/verdeckte-parteienfinanzierung/eine-schrecklich-rechte-familie

John, Gerald. 2016. Ausländer zahlen mehr ins Sozialsystem ein, als sie erhalten. *Der Standard Online*. 19 May 2016.

Kang, Cecilia and Sheera Frenkel. 2018. Facebook Says Cambridge Analytica Harvested Data of Up to 87 Million Users. *The New York Times Online*. 4April 2018. www.nytimes.com/2018/04/04/technology/mark-zuckerberg-testify-congress.html?rref=collection%2Fbyline%2Fmatthew-rosenberg

Kartheuser, Boris and Paul Middelhoff. 2017. Im Bett mit der Alternative. *Die Zeit Online*. 24May 2017. www.zeit.de/2017/22/afd-folkard-edler-parteienfinanzierung-parteispenden/komplettansicht

Katholische Kirche Österreich. 2017. *Statistik: Die Hälfte der Wiener Schüler bis 14 sind Christen*. www.katholisch.at/aktuelles/2017/09/21/statistik-die-haelfte-der-wiener-schueler-bis-14-sind-christen

Kautsky, Karl. 1908. Nationalität und Internationalität. *Ergänzungshefte zur Neuen Zeit* 1: 1–36.

Kellner, Douglas. 2003. *Media Spectacle*. London: Routledge.

Khomenko, Sofia. 2018. Facebook: 8900 User bestimmten Wahlkampf-Diskurs. *Mokant.at*. 2 January 2018.

Klahr, Alfred. 1937. *Zur nationalen Frage in Österreich*. www.antifa-info.at/archiv/KLAHR.PDF

Kleine Zeitung. 2015. FPÖ absolvierte Wahlkampfauftakt. *Kleine Zeitung Online*. 4 September 2015.

Kollanyi, Bence, Philip N. Howard, and Samuel C. Woolley. 2016. *Bots and Automation over Twitter during the Third U.S. Presidential Debate*. http://comprop.oii.ox.ac.uk/wp-content/uploads/sites/89/2016/10/Data-Memo-Third-Presidential-Debate.pdf

Kristeva, Julia. 1977. *About Chinese Women*. London: Marion Boyars.

Kronen Zeitung. 2017. Mehr Muslime als Katholiken in Wien. *Kronen Zeitung Online*. 13 September 2017.

Krzyżanowski, Michał. 2013. From Anti-Immigration and Nationalist Revisionism to Islamophobia: Continuities and Shifts in Recent Discourses and Patterns of Political Communication of the Freedom Party of Austria (FPÖ). In *Right-Wing Populism in Europe: Politics and Discourse*, eds. Ruth Wodak, Majid KhosraviNik and Brigitte Mral, 135–148. London: Bloomsbury Academic.

Kurier. 2017. So national wird der neue Nationalrat. *Kurier Online.* 25 October 2017.

Kurz, Sebastian. 2017a. *Auftaktrede zum ÖVP-Wahlkampf.* 25 September 2017. www .youtube.com/watch?v=8qU1Teouq5s

Kurz, Sebastian. 2017b. *Regierungserklärung im Nationalrat. Rede von Bundeskanzler Sebastian Kurz im Wortlaut.* www.oevp.at/Download/Regierungserklaerung_Nationalrat.pdf

Labica, Georges. 1987. Populismus. In *Kritisches Wörterbuch des Marxismus Band 6*, 1026–1029. Hamburg: Argument.

Lagler, Claudia. 2008. Strache: "Du musst nur ein Kopftuch tragen". *Die Presse Online.* 7 February 2008.

Lapavitsas, Costas. 2012. *Crisis in the Eurozone.* London: Verso.

Laskos, Christos and Euclid Tsakalotos. 2013. *Crucible of Resistance: Greece, the Eurozone & the World Economic Crisis.* London: Pluto.

Lazer, David M. J. et al. 2018. The Science of Fake News. Addressing Fake News Requires A Multidisciplinary Effort. *Science* 6380: 1094–1096.

Lenin, Vladimir I. 1914. The Right of Nations to Self-Determination. In *Lenin Collected Works Volume 20*, 393–454. Moscow: Progress.

Liebknecht, Karl et al. 1918. *To the Proletarians of All Countries.* www.rosalux.de/stiftung/histor isches-zentrum/rosa-luxemburg/100-tage-dokumente/englisch/artikel-rl/by-manuela-koelke /to-the-proletarians-of-all-countries/ (accessed 2 May 2019).

Löwy, Michael. 1998. *Fatherland or Motherland. Essays on the National Question.* London: Pluto.

Lukács, Georg. 1971. *History and Class Consciousness. Studies in Marxist Dialectics.* Cambridge, MA: MIT Press.

Luxemburg, Rosa. 1913/2003. *The Accumulation of Capital.* London: Routledge.

Luxemburg, Rosa. 1914a. Militarismus und Arbeiterklassen. In *Rosa Luxemburg Gesammelte Werke, Band 7.2*, 845–850. Berlin: Dietz.

Luxemburg, Rosa. 1914b. Über Militarismus und Arbeiterklasse. In *Rosa Luxemburg Gesammelte Werke, Band 3*, 443–445. Berlin: Dietz.

Luxemburg, Rosa. 1918. Fragment über Krieg, nationale Frage und Revolution. In *Rosa Luxemburg Gesammelte Werke, Band 4*, 366–373. Berlin: Dietz.

Luxemburg, Rosa. 1970. *Rosa Luxemburg Speaks.* New York: Pathfinder.

Luxemburg, Rosa. 1971. *Selected Political Writings of Rosa Luxemburg.* New York: Monthly Review Press.

Luxemburg, Rosa. 1976. *The National Question: Selected Writings.* New York: Monthly Review Press.

Luxemburg, Rosa. 2008. *The Essential Rosa Luxemburg.* Chicago, IL: Haymarket Books.

Luxemburg, Rosa. 2013. *The Letters of Rosa Luxemburg*, ed. Georg Adler, Peter Hudis, and Annelies Laschitza. London: Verso.

Marcuse, Herbert. 1941/1955. *Reason and Revolution: Hegel and the Rise of Social Theory.* London: Routledge.

Marcuse, Herbert. 1958. *Soviet Marxism*. New York: Columbia University Press.

Marx, Anthony W. 2003. *Faith in Nation. Exclusionary Origins of Nationalism*. Oxford: Oxford University Press.

Marx, Karl. 1844a. Contribution to the Critique of Hegel's Philosophy of Law. In *MECW Volume 3*, 175–187. London: Lawrence & Wishart.

Marx, Karl. 1844b. Economic and Philosophic Manuscripts of 1844. In *Marx & Engels Collected Works (MECW) Volume 3*, 229–346. London: Lawrence & Wishart.

Marx, Karl. 1845. Theses on Feuerbach. In *Marx-Engels-Collected-Works Volume 5*, 3–5. London: Lawrence & Wishart.

Marx, Karl. 1852. The Eighteenth Brumaire of Louis Bonaparte. In *Marx & Engels Collected Works (MECW), Volume 11*, 99–197. New York: International Publishers.

Marx, Karl. 1853. Works on India published in the "New-York Daily Tribune". In *Marx Engels Collected Works Volume 12*, 125–133, 157–162, 174–184, 192–200, 209–216, 217–222. London: Lawrence & Wishart.

Marx, Karl. 1857/1858. *Grundrisse*. London: Penguin.

Marx, Karl. 1864. Inaugural Address of the Working Men's International Association. In *MECW, Volume 20*, 5–13. London: Lawrence & Wishart.

Marx, Karl. 1867. *Capital: A Critique of Political Economy, Volume 1*. London: Penguin.

Marx, Karl. 1869. The General Council to the Federal Council of Romance Switzerland. In *Marx Engels Collected Works Volume 21*, 84–91. London: Lawrence & Wishart.

Marx, Karl. 1870. Letter of Marx to Sigfrid Meyer and August Vogt, 9 April 1870. In *Marx Engels Collected Works Volume 43*, 471–476. London: Lawrence & Wishart.

Marx, Karl. 1871. The Civil War in France. In *Marx & Engels Collected Works (MECW), Volume 22*, 307–359. New York: International Publishers.

Marx, Karl and Friedrich Engels. 1845/1846a. Die deutsche Ideologie. In *Marx Engels Werke (MEW), Band 3*, 5–530. Berlin: Dietz.

Marx, Karl and Friedrich Engels. 1845/1846b. The German Ideology. In *MECW Volume 5*, 19–539. London: Lawrence & Wishart.

Marx, Karl and Friedrich Engels. 1848. Manifesto of the Communist Party. In *Marx-Engels-Collected Works (MECW), Volume 6*, 477–517. London: Lawrence & Wishart.

McChesney, Robert. 2013. *Digital Disconnect. How Capitalism is Turning the Internet against Democracy*. New York: The New Press.

McChesney, Robert. 2015. *Rich Media, Poor Democracy. Communication Politics in Dubious Times*. New York: The New Press.

McLuhan, Marshall. 1997. *Essential McLuhan*, ed. Eric McLuhan and Frank Zingrone. London: Routledge.

Mueller, Robert S. 2019. *Report on the Investigation into Russian Interference in the 2016 Presidential Election*. Washington, DC: US Department of Justice.

Munck, Ronaldo. 2000. *Marxism @ 2000. Late Marxist Perspectives*. Basingstoke: Macmillan.

Nairn, Tom. 1977/2015. *The Break-Up of Britain. Crisis and Neo-Nationalism*. Champaign, IL: Common Ground.

Nairn, Tom. 1997. *Faces of Nationalism. Janus Revisited*. London: Verso.

Negt, Oskar and Alexander Kluge. 1993. *Public Sphere and Experience. Toward an Analysis of the Bourgeois and Proletarian Public Sphere*. Minneapolis, MN: University of Minnesota Press.

Neudert, Lisa-Maria N. 2019. Germany: A Cautionary Tale. In *Computational Propaganda: Political Parties, Politicians, and Political Manipulation on Social Media*, eds. Samuel C. Woolley and Philip N. Howard, 153–184. Oxford: Oxford University Press.

Neumann, Franz. 1944/2009. *Behemoth: The Structure and Practice of National Socialism, 1933-1944*. Chicago, IL: Ivan R. Dee.

Neumann, Franz. 1957/2017. Anxiety and Politics. *tripleC: Communication, Capitalism & Critique* 15 (2): 612–636.

Nevradakis, Michael. 2014. *Germany's Unpaid Debt to Greece: Economist Albrecht Ritschl on WWII Reparations that Never Were*. www.truth-out.org/news/item/27261-germany-s-unpaid-debt-to-greece-albrecht-ritschl-on-germany-s-war-debts-and-reparations (accessed 12 April 2015).

New Knowledge. 2018. *The Tactics & Tropes of the Internet Research Agency*. https://disinformationreport.blob.core.windows.net/disinformation-report/NewKnowledge-Disinformation-Report-Whitepaper.pdf

New York Times/Reuters. 2018. Austria's Jews Boycott Holocaust Commemoration Over Rise of Far Right. *New York Times Online*. 25 January 2018.

Nimni, Ephraim. 1991. *Marxism and Nationalism. Theoretical Origins of a Political Crisis*. London: Pluto.

Österreich. 2017. Wiener Schulen: Mehr Muslime als Katholiken. *OE24.at*. 13 September 2017.

Österreichischer Integrationsfonds (ÖIF). 2017. *Demographie und Religion in Österreich. Szenarien 2016 bis 2046. Deutsche Zusammenfassung und englischer Gesamtbericht*. Wien: ÖIF.

ÖVP/FPÖ. 2017. *Zusammen. Für unser Österreich. Regierungsprogramm 2017–2022*. www.oevp.at/download/Regierungsprogramm.pdf

Özkirimli, Umut. 2010. *Theories of Nationalism. A Critical Introduction*. Basingstoke: Palgrave Macmillan. Second edition.

Pariser, Eli. 2011. *The Filter Bubble: What the Internet Is Hiding from You*. London: Penguin.

Pedro-Carañana, Joan, Daniel Broudy, and Jeffery Klaehn, eds. 2018. *The Propaganda Model Today: Filtering Perception and Awareness*. London: University of Westminster Press.

Peham, Andi. 2008. Parteimarxismus und Antisemitismus. Anmerkungen zu einem historischen Versagen. In *Otto Bauer under der Austromarxismus*, eds. Walter Baier, Lisbeth N. Trallori, and Derek Weber, 95–111. Berlin: Dietz.

Pink, Oliver and Norbert Rief. 2017. Interview mit Finanzminister Hartwig Löger: "Wir haben einen Schuldenstand, der überbordend ist". *Die Presse Online*. 27 December 2017.

References

Pittelkow, Sebastian and Katja Riedel. 2018. AfD nahm offenbar illegal Großspenden an. *Süddeutsche Zeitung Online*. 11 November 2018. www.sueddeutsche.de/politik/parteienfinanzierung-afd-nahm-offenbar-illegale-grossspende-an-1.4206221

Plunkett, John. 2011. Queen's Christmas Message to Be Produced by Sky for First Time. *The Guardian Online*. 19 January 2011.

Puri, Jyoti. 2004. *Encountering Nationalism*. Malden, MA: Blackwell.

Williams Raymond. 1980/2005. *Culture and Materialism*. London: Verso.

Williams Raymond. 1981. *Culture*. Glasgow: Fontana-Collins.

Reich, Wilhelm. 1972. *The Mass Psychology of Fascism*. London: Souvenir Press.

Reich, Wilhelm. 1975. *Listen, Little Man!*. New York: Penguin.

Reisigl, Martin. 2018. The Discourse-Historical Approach. In *The Routledge Handbook of Critical Discourse Studies*, eds. John Flowerdew and John E. Richardson, 44–58. Abingdon: Routledge.

Reisigl, Martin and Ruth Wodak. 2001. *Discourse and Discrimination. Rhetorics of Racism and Antisemitism*. London: Routledge.

Renner, Karl. 1899. State and National: A Constitutional Investigation of the Possible Principles of a Solution and the Juridical Prerequisistes of a Law of Nationalities. In *Austro-Marxism: The Ideology of Unity. Volume I: Austro-Marxist Theory and Strategy*, eds. Mark E. Blum andWilliam Smaldone, 369–402. Chicago, IL: Haymarket Books.

Renner, Karl. 1938. Interview. *Neues Wiener Tagblatt*. 3 April 1938.

Renner, Karl. 1952. *Mensch und Gesellschaft. Grundriß einer Soziologie*. Wien: Verlag der Wiener Volksbuchhandlung.

Renton, David. 2019. *The New Authoritarians*. London: Pluto.

Riedel, Katja and Sebastian Pittelkow. 2017. Die Hayek-Gesellschaft – "Misbeet der AfD"? *Süddeutsche Zeitung Online*. 14 July 2017. www.sueddeutsche.de/wirtschaft/hayek-gesellschaft-mistbeet-der-afd-1.3589049

Roediger, David. 2017. *Class, Race, and Marxism*. London: Verso.

Roediger, David R. 2007. *The Wages of Whiteness: Race and the Making of the American Working Class*. London: Verso. Revised edition.

Rosenberg, Matthew, Nicholas Confessore, and Carole Cadwalladr. 2018. How Trump Consultants Exploited the Facebook Data of Millions. *The New York Times Online*. 17 March 2018. www.nytimes.com/2018/03/17/us/politics/cambridge-analytica-trump-campaign.html

RTL Extra. 2017. *Undercover bei Unzensuriert.at*. www.youtube.com/watch?v=CzALZjiURWs

Said, Edward W. 1979. *Orientalism*. New York: Vintage Books.

Sandoval, Marisol. 2014. *From Corporate to Social Media. Critical Perspectives on Corporate Social Responsibility in Media and Communication Industries*. Abingdon: Routledge.

Sängerlaub, Alexander, Miriam Meier, and Wolf-Dieter Rühl. 2018. *Fakten statt Fakes: Verursacher, Verbreitungswege und Wirkungen von Fake News im Bundestagswahlkampf 2017*. Berlin: Stiftung Neue Verantwortung.

Scharsach, Hans-Henning. 2017. *Stille Machtergreifung: Hofer, Strache und die Burschenschaften.* Wien: Kremayr & Scheriau.

Schiedel, Heribert. 2007. *Der rechte Rand: Extremistische Gesinnungen in unserer Gesellschaft.* Wien: Edition Steinbauer.

Schmitt, Carl. 1932/1996. *The Concept of the Political.* Chicago, IL: University of Chicago Press.

SDAP (Sozialdemokratische Arbeiterpartei Deutschösterreichs). 1926. Programm der Sozialdemokratischen Arbeiterpartei Deutschösterreichs. Beschlossen vom Parteitag zu Linz am 3. November 1926. In *Austromarxismus: Texte zu "Ideologie und Klassenkampf"*, eds. Hans-Jörg Sandkühler and Rafael de la Vega, 378–402. Frankfurt: Europäische Verlagsanstalt.

Segger, Marie, Christoph Sydow, and Caroline Wiemann. 2018. Daten-Auswertung zum TV-Duell: 31 Prozent Abschiebung, 9 Prozent Diesel – 0 Prozent Bildung. *Spiegel Online.* 4 September 2017.

Shane, Scott and Mark Mazzetti. 2018. Inside a 3-Year Russian Campaign to Influence U.S. Voters. *The New York Times Online.* 16 February 2018. www.nytimes.com/2018/02/16/us/politics/russia-mueller-election.html

Shao, Chengcheng et al. 2018. *The Spread of Low-Credibility Content by Social Bots.* https://arxiv.org/pdf/1707.07592.pdf

Silverman, Craig. 2016. This Analysis Shows How Viral Fake Election News Stories Outperformed Real News on Facebook. *BuzzFeed.* 16 November 2016.

Silverman, Craig and Jeremy Singer-Vine. 2016. Most Americans Who See Fake News Believe It, New Survey Says. *BuzzFeed.* 7 December 2016.

Smith, Anthony D. 1998. *Nationalism and Modernism. A Critical Survey of Recent Theories of Nations and Nationalism.* London: Routledge.

SORA. 2013. *Wahlanalyse Nationalratswahl 2013.* www.sora.at/fileadmin/downloads/wahlen/2013_NRW_Wahlanalyse.pdf

SORA. 2016. *Wahlanalyse Bundespräsidentschaftsswahl 2016.* www.sora.at/fileadmin/downloads/wahlen/2016_BP-Wahl_Wahlanalyse.pdf, www.sora.at/fileadmin/downloads/wahlen/2016_BP-Stichwahl_Wahlanalyse.pdf

SORA. 2017. *Wahlanalyse Nationalratswahl 2017.* www.sora.at/fileadmin/downloads/wahlen/2017_NRW_Wahlanalyse.pdf

SPD. 2017. *Zeit für mehr Gerechtigkeit. Unser Regierungsprogramm für Deutschland.* www.spd.de (accessed 7 October 2017).

Spiegel. 2018. August von Finck: Wer ist der mysteriöse Millardär, der die AfD unterstützt haben soll? *Spiegel Online.* 24 November 2018. www.spiegel.de/politik/deutschland/august-von-finck-junior-wer-ist-der-mysterioese-milliardaer-a-1240268.html

Spivak, Gayatri Chakravorty. 1981. French Feminism in an International Frame. *Yale French Studies* 62: 154–184.

Spivak, Gayatri Chakravorty. 1988. Can the Subaltern Speak? In *Marxism and the Interpretation of Culture*, eds. Cary Nelson and Lawrence Grossberg, 271–313. Urbana, IL: University of Illinois Press.

Spivak, Gayatri Chakravorty. 2005. Scattered Speculations on the Subaltern and the Popular. *Postcolonial Studies* 8 (4): 475–486.

Spivak, Gayatri Chakravorty. 2009. Nationalism and the Imagination. *Lectora* 15: 75–98.

Stalin, Joseph. 1913. Marxism and the National Question. In *Stalin Works 2*, 300–381. Moscow: Foreign Languages Publishing House.

Stalin, Joseph. 1936. *Constitution (Fundamental Law) of the Union of Soviet Socialist Republics.* www.marxists.org/reference/archive/stalin/works/1936/12/05.htm

Statistik Austria. 2019. *Statistiken.* www.statistik.at(accessed 15 July 2019).

Statistische Ämter des Bundes und der Länder. 2014. *Zensus 2011.* Bad Ems: Statistisches Landesamt des Bundes und der Länder.

Statistisches Bundesamt. 2015. *Bevölkerung Deutschlands bis 2060.* Wiesbaden: Statistisches Bundesamt.

Steingress, Gerhard. 2008. Zur Aktualität der ‚nationalen Frage' im Zeitalter der Globalisierung. Betrachtungen zum Austromarxismus. In *Otto Bauer under der Austromarxismus*, eds. Walter Baier, Lisbeth N. Trallori, and Derek Weber, 209–220. Berlin: Dietz.

Stichs, Anja. 2016. *Wie viele Muslime leben in Deutschland?* Nürnberg: Bundesamt für Migration und Flüchtlinge.

Strasser, Josef. 1982. *Der Arbeiter und die Nation. Anhang: Schriften zum Austromarxismus.* Wien: Junius.

Stretch, Colin. 2018. *Written Submission to the US Senate Select Committee on Intelligence.* 8 January 2018. www.intelligence.senate.gov/sites/default/files/documents/Facebook%20Response%20to%20Committee%20QFRs.pdf

Taguieff, Pierre-André. 2001. *The Force of Prejudice. On Racism and Its Doubles.* Minneaplois, MN: University of Minnesota Press.

Tandoc, Edson C., Zheng Wei Lim, and Richard Ling. 2018. Defining "Fake News". A Typology of Scholarly Definitions. *Digital Journalism* 6 (2): 137–153.

Theweleit, Klaus. 1987. *Male Fantasies. Volume 1: Women, Floods, Bodies, History.* Minneapolis, MN: University of Minnesota Press.

Theweleit, Klaus. 1989. *Male Fantasies. Volume 2: Male Bodies: Psychoanalyzing the White Terror.* Minneapolis, MN: University of Minnesota Press.

Thompson, Edward B. 1963. *The Making of the English Working Class.* New York: Vintage Books.

Thompson, Edward P. 1978. *The Poverty of Theory & Other Essays.* London: Merlin.

Thompson, Edward P. 1993. *Customs in Common.* London: Penguin.

Townsend, Leanne and Claire Wallace2016. *Social Media Research: A Guide to Ethics.* Output from the ESRC project "Social Media, Privacy and Risk: Towards More Ethical Research Methodologies". www.gla.ac.uk/media/media_487729_en.pdf

Trallori, Lisbeth N. 2008. Körperpolitische Diskurse im Austromarxismus. In *Otto Bauer under der Austromarxismus*, eds. Walter Baier, Lisbeth N. Trallori, and Derek Weber, 113–125. Berlin: Dietz.

Trump, Donald J. 2016. *Contract for the American Voter: 100-Day Plan to Make America Great Again – For Everyone.* https://assets.donaldjtrump.com/_landings/contract/O-TRU-102316-Contractv02.pdf

United Nations. 1955. State Treaty (with Annexes and Maps) for the Re-Establishment of an Independent and Democratic Austria. Signed at Vienna, on 15 May 1955. In *United Nations Treaty Series*, 217, 223–381.

US Senate Select Committee on Intelligence. 2017. *Hearing on November 1, 2017.* www.intelligence.senate.gov/hearings/open-hearing-social-media-influence-2016-us-elections#

Van Biezen, Ingrid, Peter Mair, and Thomas Poguntke. 2012. Going, Going, … Gone? The Decline of Party Membership in Contemporary Europe. *European Journal of Political Research* 51 (1): 24–56.

van Dijk, Teun. 1987. *Communicating Racism. Ethnic Prejudice in Thought and Talk.* Newbury Park, CA: Sage.

van Dijk, Teun. 2011. Discourse and Ideology. In *Discourse Studies. A Multidisciplinary Introduction*, ed. Teun van Dijk, 379–407. London: Sage.

van Dijk, Teun. 2018. Socio-Cognitive Discourse Studies. In *The Routledge Handbook of Critical Discourse Studies*, eds. John Flowerdew and John E. Richardson, 26–43. Abingdon: Routledge.

Van Gelder, Robert. 1940. Chaplin Draws a Keen Weapon. *New York Times.* 8 September 1940.

Varoufakis, Yanis. 2015. *And the Weak Suffer What They Must? Europe, Austerity and the Threat to Global Stability.* London: Bodley Head.

Volkshilfe Österreich. 2015. *Armut, Bildung und Aufstiegschancen. Daten und Fakten.* www.volkshilfe.at/images/content/files/Fakten%20Bildung%20und%20Armut%20August%202015.pdf

Wardle, Claire. 2017. Fake News. It's Complicated. *First Draft.* 16 February 2017. https://medium.com/1st-draft/fake-news-its-complicated-d0f773766c79

Wehner, Markus and Eckart Lohse. 2016. "Nicht als Nachbarn": Gauland beleidigt Boateng. *FAZ Online.* 29 May 2016.

Weidinger, Bernhard. 2015. *"Im nationalen Abwehrkampf der Grenzlanddeutschen". Akademische Burschenschaften und Politik in Österreich nach 1945.* Wien: Böhlau.

Williams, Raymond, ed. 1968. *May Day Manifesto 1968.* Harmondsworth: Penguin.

Williams, Raymond. 1974/2003. *Television, Technology and Cultural Form.* London: Routledge.

Williams, Raymond. 1977. *Marxism and Literature.* Oxford: Oxford University Press.

Williams, Raymond. 1983a. *Keywords: A Vocabulary of Culture and Society.* New York: Oxford University Press. Revised edition.

Williams, Raymond. 1983b. *Towards 2000.* London: Chatto & Windus.

Williams, Raymond. 2003a. *Television: Technology and Cultural Form.* London: Routledge.

Williams, Raymond. 2003b. *Who Speaks for Wales? Nation, Culture, Identity*, ed. Daniel Williams. Cardiff: University of Wales Press.

Winter, Jakob and Ingrid Brodnig. 2016. unzensuriert.at: Wie die FPÖ-nahe Site systematisch Stimmung macht. *Profil Online.* 30 November 2016.

Wodak, Ruth. 2002. Discourse and Politics: The Rhetoric of Exclusion. In *The Haider Phenomenon in Austria*, eds. Ruth Wodak and Anton Pelinka, 33–60. New Brunswick, NJ: Transaction.

Wodak, Ruth. 2013. "Anything Goes!" – The Haiderization of Europe. In *Right-Wing Populism in Europe: Politics and Discourse*, eds. Ruth Wodak, Majid KosraviNik, and Brigitte Mral, 23–37. London: Bloomsburg.

Wodak, Ruth. 2015. *The Politics of Fear. What Right-Wing Populist Discourses Mean.* London: Sage.

Wodak, Ruth. 2017. Interview: „Die Medien haben Kurz mitgemacht". *Der Falter* 2017 (51–52).

Wodak, Ruth and Brigitta Busch. 2004. Approaches to Media Texts. In *The Sage Handbook of Media Studies*, eds. John Downing, Denis McQuail, Philip Schlesinger, and Ellen Wartella, 105–123. London: Sage.

Wodak, Ruth and Michael Meyer, eds. 2016. *Methods of Critical Discourse Studies*. London: Sage. Third edition.

Woolley, Samuel C. and Douglas Guilbeault. 2019. United States: Manufacturing Consensus Online. In *Computational Propaganda: Political Parties, Politicians, and Political Manipulation on Social Media*, eds. Samuel C. Woolley and Philip N. Howard, 185–211. Oxford: Oxford University Press.

Žižek, Slavoj. 2014. ISIS is a Disgrace to True Fundamentalism. *New York Times Online.* 3 September 2014.

Index

Locators in *italics* refer to figures, those in **bold** refer to tables

accounts: false 261–262; social media 160, 164

accumulation 13, 15, 159, 276, 281

actors 15, 250

Adler, Max 54–55

Adorno, Theodor W. 143–144, 267, 273

advertising (ads) 213, 250–253, 255–264, 282

AfD (Alternative für Deutschland, Alternative for Germany) 6, 127–129, 142–143, 149–150, 153–156, 159–161; social media opposition to AfD 164–166

Afghanistan 222

After Dark 264

AggregateIQ (AIQ) 253

algorithms 250, 253, 255, 258–262, 281, 282

alienation 15–16, 28, 102, 205, 221

alternative economy projects 282

Alternative for Germany/Alternative für Deutschland (AfD) *see* AfD

alternative media sector 282

Anderson, Benedict 27–31, 30–31

Anderson, Kevin B. 33, 40, 41–42

annihilation 4, 271; *see also* killings

anonymity 24, 248

Anschluss 53–55, 56, 62–63, 68, 216; *see also* unification

antagonism 10, 129

anthroponyms 215

anti-Semitism 22, 28, 57

Anxiety and Politics (Franz L. Neumann) 275

appearance 36, 188

Arbeiter-Zeitung 60, 64

Aryans 9, 57

Assembly (Michael Hardt and Antonio Negri) 275, 276

asylum applications 125–126, 147, 158, 222, 223

asylum seekers 126, 147, 149, 153, 158

attacks, terror 157–158

audiences 196, 250–251; *see also* users; viewers

austerity 125–126, 265

Austria 126, 179–183; education and Hauptschule 193–195; incomplete denazification 189–191; *Kronen Zeitung*'s role in Austria 191–193; Kurz and ÖVP in Austria 188–189; law and order politics in Austria 225–230; leadership discourse in the Austrian case study 214–216; methodology of the Austrian case study 196–201; nationalism in Austria 217–218; Proporz 195; social media analysis of the Austrian case study 210–214

Austrian Press Agency 210

Austro-Marxism 61–63

authoritarianism 213, **214**, 265–266, 267–271; challenging 232–234; populism and authoritarianism 266–267; right-wing authoritarianism 109, 159–161, 166, 247–248, 254, 279; semiotic struggles in the context of authoritarianism 274–275; social media and authoritarianism 271–272

Balibar, Étienne 28, 247

banalisation 127, 266

Bauer, Otto 9, 43–44, 55, **71**, 72, 246; 1919 peace treaty 56; Alfred Klahr on Bauer 46–47; *Anschluss* 53–55, 56–57; Austro-Marxism and Nazi-Fascism 61–63; Bauer and Luxemburg 45–47, 49, 53–57, 56, 61–63, 63–64, 68; culture 51; European Union (EU) 70; Hitler 57–58; Josef Strasser on Bauer 58; Karl Kautsky on Bauer 50–51; language 51–52; Marxism 44–45; nationalism 52–53; nationality 47–48; nations 44–45; non-historical nations 48–50; political pragmatism of Bauer 59–60; Schutzbund and Heimwehr 59; servitude and submission 63–64

belonging 7, 45

benefit scroungers *see* scroungers, benefit

biases 250, 256

big data 259, 261, 281–282

Bonapartism 39

borders 145, 158, 216, 231

bots 6, 137–139, 160, 210; political 261–262

boundaries 4, 24, 27, 67, 130, 132

breaches, data 253, 258

Brecht, Bertolt 273

Benner, Erica 34, 35

Brexit 9, 10, 68, 69

Britain *see* United Kingdom (UK)

British Broadcasting Corporation (BBC) 118–120, 229, 253, 264

broadcasters 181, 196, 234; *see also* public services

budgeting, participatory 282

budgets 147, **148**, 149, 162

Bündnis Zukunft Österreich (BZÖ) 185

burdening, ideological discourse of 147, 149, 150, 162, 210, 220, 221

bureaucracy 24, 26

Burschenschaften 186–188

Cambridge Analytica 252–255

campaigns, election 140–142, 149–150, 161, 198, 258; USA 257

camps, concentration (internment) 229, 231

capital 10, 15, 144; Austria 193, 208–210, 232; Bauer and Luxemburg 52, 66

capital, global 11, 278

capitalism 9–13, 16; Austria 232, 234; Bauer and Luxemburg on capitalism 52, 66, 69, 72; contemporary Marxist theories 101–102; Germany 126, 129, 143, 159, 162; Marx 36–37, 41–42; nationalism theories 25, 27–30, 28–30; *see also* authoritarianism; digital capitalism

capitalism, global 15, 82, 85, 90

Charter of Fundamental Rights of the European Union 222

Chatterjee, Partha 81–86, 247

Chibber, Vivek 84–88, 247

children (kids) 129, 204, 205, 220, 221, 231

Christian Democratic Union (CDU) 127

Christian Social Union (CSU) 151, 153

Christianity 206, 231

citizens 4, 15; Austria 191, 193, 216, 224, 230; Germany 138, 142, 153, 156–158, 161

citizenship 11, 23, 52, 127, 182

class 9, 21, 23; Austria 194–195, 234; Bauer and Luxemburg on class 55, 65; Germany 164; Marx on class 36–37; theories of nationalism 28–29

class conflicts 11, 42, 66, 127; Austria 209–210, 232

class contradictions 23, 37, 39, 129, 270

class, social 65, 143, 194

class structures 66, 129, 207; theories of nationalism 25, 28–31

class struggles 7, 9, 11, 31; containment in Austria 193; Germany 164; Marx 38, 40–41

clientelism 195, 283

climate change 282

Cold War 193

colonialism 5, 9, 10, 25, 35, 41; Nigeria and Rwanda 89–90

colonialism (anti-colonialism) 28

commercialisation 259, 283

commodification 245, 259, 276, 279, 283

commodities 21–22, 37, 52, 258

commons 275–276, 276, 279–280

commonwealth 276, 278

Commonwealth (Michael Hardt and Antonio Negri) 275

communication 4, 6–7, 12; types and structures of nationalist communication 113–120

communication, political 3–5, 12

communism 42, 46, 94

Communist Party of Austria (KPÖ) 46, 60, 62

consciousness 143, 267; Bauer and Luxemburg 45, 50–51, 55; Marx 38, 40; theories of nationalism 21, 23–24

consciousness, false 38, 93, 164, 250

consciousness, national 24, 52–53, 55, 62, 107, 247

consent 130, 199

conspiracy theories 138–139, 212

consumers 15, 28, 37, 260

consumption 12, 27, 48, 114–115, 153, 248

convergence 12–13

cooperation 24, 275–276, 280, 281

cooperatives 282, 284

corporations 15, 24

corruption 234, 235

crime 3, 129, 160; Austria 192, 197, 208, 212, 224

criminals 5, 23, 221, 224, 231

criminonyms 208

crises 11–12, 15–16; Austria 185, 195, 209; Bauer and Luxemburg 67, 69; Germany 125–126, 132, 159

critical theory 8

culture 16; Bauer and Luxemburg 46–49, 51, 54–55, 57, 66; Germany 151, 155; online 139, 160; theories of nationalism 23–25

data, big 6, 13

Davis, Mike 33

democracy 11–12, 16, 63–64; Austria 231, 234–235; Germany 127

demographic development 224, **227**

denazification 189–191

deportation 132, 182, 228, 231, 269

deregulation 189, 245

development 141; demographic 152

dialects 49–50, 270

dialogues 259

dictatorships 3, 10

Die Linke 128, 131, 134, 166, 175

differences 9, 25, 59; cultural 47–48; radical cultural 47–48

digital capitalism 5–6, 245, 250, 254, 258, 281–283

Digital Forensic Lab 137–138

digital media 13, 27, 132, 248, 271

discourses, nationalist 83, 113, 129, 200, 248

discourses, online 130, 160, 196

disenfranchisement 271, 272

dispossession 159, 231, 276

diversity 6, 47, 69

Dollfuss, Engelbert 60, 62, 64

domination 5, 37, 66; Germany 143, 164; theories of nationalism 21, 25, 28
donors 161–162, 189, 235, 258
Du Bois, W.E.B. 105–106

education 24–25, 276; Austria 183, 193–195, 221, 225; Germany 132, 141, 149, 162
election campaigns 247, 253; *see also* Austria; Germany
election programmes 140–143, 151, 154, 208
election results 127, **128**, 260, 272
elections 162, 179–180, 184, 235, 253–255, 258, 272
elites 15, 210
elites, political 81, 107–108, 248
emancipation 40, 281
emotions 166, 274
empire 275–276, 277–280
Empire (Michael Hardt and Antonio Negri) 275
employability 24
employment policies 184–185
employment (unemployment) 125–126, 182–183, 185, 231
enemies 4–5, 9, 37, 66; Austria 213, 218, 220, 225; Germany 129, 133, 163; theories of nationalism 22, 25, 28; *see also* friend/enemy scheme
engagement 138, 160, 164, 215, 254, 256; political 260, 265
Engels, Friedrich 34, 36, 58
Enlightenment 155
entertainment 127, 251, 260, 266
entrepreneurs (entrepreneurial spirits) 24, 98, 182–183, 188, 215, 245, 272
equality 4, 15, 91, 93, 141, 209, 272; *see also* inequality
Erdoğan, Recep Tayyip 5, 233, 245
ethics 130, 259, 261; research 199

ethnicity 28, 41–42
ethno-symbolism 23, 246
ethnonyms 142
eugenics 57
European Central Bank 125
European South 144–146
European Union (EU) 11, 69–70; Austria 185, 212, 222, 224; Germany 125–127, 132, 134–135, 144–146, 160
events, media 130, 248
evidence 161, 165
exclusion 29, 53
experiences 21, 55
exploitation 5, 10, 65; Marx 35, 37; theories of nationalism 25, 28
extermination 269; *see also* killings
extremism 4, 126, 269

Facebook 12; Germany 127, 130, 132, 138, 154
fact-checking 263, 264
fake news 6, 137–139, 161, 207, 212, 249–252; Cambridge Analytica 252–255; causes 259–260; implications 257–258; Internet Research Agency 255–257; problems and impacts 261–262; what can be done? 262–265
Falter, Der 234
families 30; Austria 182, 194, 203–204, 218; Germany 147, 149, 165, 174
fascism 4; Austrian 60, 64; Nazi- 6, 13, 61–63, 93–94, 157
feelings 261, 274
fetishism 9–10; Bauer and Luxemburg 66, 70, 72; Germany 129, 143, 246; Marx 37–38; theories of nationalism 21–23
filter bubbles 135, 211, 250
finances (financial situation) 129, 147, 150

financialisation 15, 245, 259
First International 35, 39
First World War 9, 43, 50, 56, 66–67, 246
Fischer, Ernst 60, 62
foreigners 10, 271; Austria 184–185, 197, 203–205, 216; Germany 128, 142–143; theories of nationalism 25, 28
FPÖ (Freiheitliche Partei Österreichs) *see* Freedom Party of Austria
France 125
Frankfurt School 267–268, 271
freedom 229, 234, 270
Freedom Party of Austria (FPÖ) 6, 47, 183–186; FPÖ and Burschenschaften 186–188; *see also* Gudenus, Johann; Haider, Jörg; Kickl, Herbert; Hofer, Norbert; Strache, Heinz-Christian
friend/enemy scheme: Austria 200, 213, 217–225, 230, 232; Germany 127, 142–144, 162, **163**; society of the commons 248, 259, 269–270, 279; *see also* enemies
Fromm, Erich 63, 101–102, 247, 267, 270

Gauland, Alexander 149–150, 159
Gellner, Ernest 24–27, 68
gender 25, 270
genderonyms 216
generalisation 208; inductive 157–159
Geneva Convention 222
genocide 53
German Ideology, The (Karl Marx and Friedrich Engels) 36
Germany 43, 45–47, 53–55, 57, 61–62, 72
Germany, elections 125–126, 129–133, 159–166; AfD 127–129, 135–137, 139; bots and fake news 137–139; European Union (EU) 126–127, 144–146; Islam 153–159; nationalism 140–144; refugees and migration 146–153; Twitter 134–135
Global Science Research (GSR) 252
globalisation 6, 12, 15, 47, 185, 245, 254
Google 253, 254, 259, 260
governments 126, 185
governments, coalition 179, 183, 213, 235
Gramsci, Antonio 266–267
Greece 125, 144–146
Green Party: Austria 173, 179, 194, 196, 210; Germany 134, 152–153
Guardian, The 252
Gudenus, Johann 229, 234, 235

Habermas, Jürgen 7, 68–69, 261
Haider, Jörg 183, 184, 185, 198, 271
Hardt, Michael 274, 275, 280–281
#IbizaGate 234–235
hatred 4, 9, 66, 143, 216, 272
Hauptschule 193–195
Hayek Gesellschaft 162
headlines 192, 251
healthcare 276; Austria 183, 231; Germany 132, 147, 149, 163
Heimat (homeland) 274
Heimwehr 59
hierarchies 127, 270
history 7, 21, 22, 46, 143–144, 186
Hitler, Adolf 57–58, 61
Hobsbawm, Eric J. 6, 6–7, 9, 28, 245, 246, 247; critique of Nairn's theory 94–95; history of nationalism 96–99; Nairn 92–94; Nairn's response 95–96; nationalism as invented tradition 106–107
Hofer, Norbert 185, 186, 194–195, 206, 212
Holzkamp, Klaus 102–103, 247
homicides, intentional 224, **226**
housing 220, 231, 276
humour (comedy) 233, 251, 273

identity 4–5, 8, 28, 37, 68, 129, 217; global 279; inner 213; national 191, 206, 278, 279; political 132–133

ideology 36, 50, 248

images 188, 276

Imagined Communities: Reflections on the Origin and Spread of Nationalism (Benedict Anderson) 27–31

immigrants 5, 10–11, 16, 25, 37, 127, 132, 146–153, 279

immigration (anti-immigration) 47, 68, 128, 138, 145, 184–185, 205

imperialism (anti-imperialist) 5, 9, 11–12, 28; Bauer and Luxemburg 43, 52, 65; theories of nationalism 25–26

in-groups 205, 217

income 141, 282; *see also* wages

India 35, 40–41

indicators 125, **126**

individualisation 15, 248

industrialism 24, 25

industries 189, 276

inequality 4, 15, 23, 37, 69, 141, 209–210; society of the commons 245, 254, 260, 272

information 13, 250, 251, 254

Instagram 154, 188, 255, 256, 257

institutions 28, 52

International Monetary Fund (IMF) 125

International Workingmen's Association 35

internationalism 11, 12, 34–35, 64, 72, 79–81, 132; intransigent 58

Internet Research Agency 255–257

intruders 23, 37, 129, 217

invasion 145, 146

investment 254, 257, 258

Iraq 222

Iraq War 147

Ireland 38, 164

Islam: Austria 181, 196–198, 205, 208; Germany 132–135, 153–160

Islamic State of Iraq and Syria (ISIS) 16, 147, 149, 156–157, 222

Islamophobia 185

James, C.L.R. 9, 10, 90–92, 247

journalism 212, 259

journalists 210, 212, 234

Junge Freiheit 138

Kautsky, Karl 50–51

Kern, Christian 179, 210

keywords 130, 131

Kickl, Herbert 197, 215–216, 229

killings 59, 229, 231

Klahr, Alfred 46–47

knowledge 280, 281

Kristeva, Julia 87

Kronen Zeitung 191–193, 197, 212, 234

Kurz, Sebastian 6, 179, 231; #IbizaGate 235; debates excerpts 201–203, 208; FPÖ 184; friend/enemy scheme 224; leadership 215; ÖVP 188–189; social media 210–211

labour 4, 10, 15, 24–25, 161; Austria 193, 208–209; Bauer and Luxemburg 52, 66

languages 269; Austria 206, 220, 231; Bauer and Luxemburg 46–49, 51–52, 54; Germany 140, 146, 151; theories of nationalism 24, 26–29

law and order policies/politics 182, 200, 213, 216–217, 225–232, 248, 269

Le Pen, Marine 5, 245

leadership 2, 4, 16, 160, 271; Austria 179, 181, 200, 213, 215–216, 231–232; Germany 127, 147, 159

leadership discourse 214–216

legislation 252, 262–263

Lenin, Vladimir I. 9, 67–68
Liebknecht, Karl 11–12, 43
likes (social media) 71, 119, 138, 197, 210, 251–252, 256
Lithuania 64
lobbying 250
Löwenthal, Leo 267
Löwy, Michael 44
Lukás, Georg 267
Luxemburg, Rosa 6, 9, 11–12, 22, 43–44, **71**, 72; European Union (EU) 69–70; First World War 66–67; Germany 143; Habermas 68–69; internationalism 64; by Lenin 67–68; self-determination 65–66; society of the commons 245–247, 276, 278, 283

machines 280–281
manipulation 127, 235, 254, 267
Marcuse, Herbert 8, 267
markets 52, 66, 140
Marx at the Margins: On Nationalism, Ethnicity, and Non-Western Societies (Kevin B. Anderson) 33
Marx, Karl 6–9, 13, 21, 33–34, 39–40, 58, 164; Bonapartism 39; Edward Said 40–41; fetishism 37; ideology 36; internationalism 34–35; Kevin B. Anderson 41–42; nationalism 38–39; society of the commons 245–247, 267, 276
McLuhan, Marshall 26, 30
media 12, 26–27, 42, 127, 154, 206, 211; *see also* digital media; slow media; social media
Merkel, Angela 130, 140, 216, 218
Mia san Mia 191
Middle East 16
migrants 10; criminal 228; Germany 126, 133, 135, 142, 145; *see also* Austria

migration 181, 225; Germany 128, 132, 134, 146–153, 160
militarionyms 145, 157
militarism 2, 4, 23, 66, 146, 149; Austria 213, 225; Germany 127, 16
minorities 10, 16, 25, 185, 269; Bauer and Luxemburg 47, 69
modernization 35, 156
money 161, 204, 258, 279
morals 151, 259, 260, 261
multiculturalism 11, 47, 151, 153, 186, 218
multitude 275–276, 277–280
Multitude, War and Democracy in the Age of Empire (Michael Hardt and Antonio Negri) 275
Muslims 5, 16, 132, 205, 206, 212, 221, 232
Mutbürger 150

Nairn, Tom 92–96; *see also* Hobsbawm, Eric J.
nation-states 5, 34, 52–53, 143; *see also* nation
National Question and Autonomy, The (Rosa Luxemburg) 64
nationalism 52–53, 66, 67–68; 2.0 12–13; Benedict Anderson 27–31; communication theory 112–113; Ernest Gellner 24–27; forms of **110–111**; general features 107–109, 111–112; Jürgen Habermas 68–69; Karl Marx 34–40; new 70–72; new nationalisms 13–16; society of the commons as alternative to nationalism 269, 270, 273, 283; studying 6–12; surplus 104–105; today 1–5; types and structures 112–120; types of theories 21–24; *see also* Bauer, Otto; Luxemburg, Rosa
nationalism, Austrian 191, 199–200, 217–218, 231, 233

nationalism, contemporary 120–122; anti-
colonial and internationalism 79–92; Eric
J. Hobsbawm 92–112; national
communication theory 112–120
nationalism, German 140–144, 157; AfD and
authoritarianism 159–161; AfD (Alternative
for Germany) dominance on social media
135–137; AfD social media strategy 139;
background 125–129; bots and fake news
137–139; capitalist donors and supporters
161–162; empirical ideology critique
129–133; European Union 144–146; Islam
153–159; logic of nationalism and racism
162–164; opposition to AfD on social
media 164–166; refugees and migration
146–153; Twitter 134–135
nationality 45, 47–48
Nations and Nationalism (Ernest Gellner)
24–27
nation (nation-states) 5, 9, 11, 22–23, 37, 247;
Austria 186, 208, 217, 231–232; community
of character 45–46; Germany 127; Karl
Renner 45; *see also* Bauer, Otto; Luxemburg, Rosa; nation-states; nationalism,
German
nationyms 142
nature 247, 274, 278
Nazi-Fascism 6, 61–63
Nazi-Germany 9
Nazism 165
negationyms 204
Negri, Antonio 274, 275, 280–281
neoliberalism 162, 268, 272; Austria 191,
215, 234
Nestbeschmutzer 191
networks 13, 27, 251
Neumann, Franz L. 267–268, 275
New York Sun, The 249
New York Times, The 229, 252

news 154
news, fake *see* fake news
news media 259
newspapers 12, 27, 29, 154, 161, 191, 250;
online articles 197, **198**
Nigeria 89–90
9/11 16
North Atlantic Treaty Organization (NATO) 147
numbers, large 205, 220

Obergrenze 133
old age 129, 215; *see also* pensioners
Orbán, Viktor 5, 245
origionyms 204
outsiders 8, 9, 22–23, 37, 71, 247, 269
outsourcing 15, 245, 259
over-foreignerisation (Überfremdung) 149–153
ÖVP (Österreichische Volkspartei) 6; *see also*
Austria; Kurz, Sebastian
Özdemir, Cem 130–131
Özkirimli, Umut 21–24, 129

parasites 205, 220, 221
parody 251, 273
Parscale, Brad 253
participation 15, 160, 222, 270
patriarchy 2, 127, 269, 270
patronage system, Austrian 195
peace (peace treaties) 56, 140
peasants 48, 53
peers (peer-to-peer production) 282
penalties 262–263
pensioners 152–153, 180, 225
pensions 182, 204–205; Germany 128, 141,
147, 149, 153, 162–163
perenialism 23, 246
petitions 182, 184
Petry, Frauke 138, 153–154, 155
Philosophia Perennis 138, 212

philosophy 7, 8

Philosophy of Right (Georg Wilhelm Friedrich Hegel) 8

Pilz, Peter 179, 210

platforms 211–212; *see also* society of the commons

Poland 64

police (policemen) 59, 270

politicians 215, 235, 248, 268

politics 215, 259–260, 283; algorithmic 6, 50; right-wing 2–3

populations 189, 225, 232; aging 224; Germany 126, 138, 152–153

postings (posts) on social media 134, 192, 198, *199*, *200*, *201*, 211, 213, 256

postmodernism 246

poverty 38, 141, 202

power 8–9, 37, 129; Bauer and Luxemburg 63, 65–66; state 282; theories of nationalism 23, 28; *see also* Austria

practices 21, 248

prejudices 38, 49, 149, 158

presentation styles (presentations) 203, 251

press 30, 191, 234, 250; *see also* newspapers

primordialism 23, 246

print capitalism 27, 29–30

privatisation 15, 245, 279

problems, social 25, 164; *see also* social problems

production 4, 37, 49

professionyms 204

profiles, social media 13, **14**, 199, 232

profits 248, 254, 255, 259

programmes, election 151, 154, 186, 208

programmes, government 218, 225

Project Alamo 253

propaganda 143, 162, 193, 224, 250

Proporz 195

prosperity 140, 141

Provisional Irish Republican Army *see* Irish Republican Army (IRA)

public attention 129, 215

public expenditures 182–183

public interest media 272

public relations (PR) 118, 161, 251

public service media (PSM) and public service Internet 49, 250, 264, 282–283

public services 183, 235, 258, 264, 272, 280

public spheres 12, 15, 29, 69, 235; Germany 129, 161; society of the commons 254, 260–262, 283

public visibility *see* visibility

purity 5, 28

quarters, mass 229

Question of Nationalities and Social Democracy, The (Otto Bauer) 43, 44, 57

racism 8–10, 22, 28, 41, 233, 247; Germany 138, 143, 155, 157, 162–165

racism (new) 111, 161, 200, 217

reactions 210, 211, 212, 257

reality 21, 36

refugees 5, 10, 16, 37, 265; Bauer and Luxemburg 69, 71–72; Germany 126–128, 132–135, 138, 145–153, 158–160, 162; *see also* Austria

regulation 252, 253, 282

Reich, Wilhelm 100–101, 247, 267

relationships 4, 44, 144, 194; social 22

religion 36, 46, 151–152; Austria 205, 207, 220; theories of nationalism 27, 29

Renner, Karl 45, 61

repression 3, 213, 225

reputations 193, 248

resistance 60, 63

resources 66, 254, 258, 276, 282
retirement age 141
retweets 135–137
revenues 260, 263
revolution 41, 57, 57–58
rhetoric, political 4
rights 183
Roediger, David R. 103–104, 247
Royal Christmas message 118–120
Russia 212; *see also* Soviet Union
Rwanda 89–90

Said, Edward 40–42
Saint-Germain-en-Laye 56
Sandoval, Marisol 113–115, 114–115, 247
satire 233, 251, 273
scandalisation 127, 266
scapegoats (scapegoating) 2, 4, 10, 16, 28, 72; Austria 183, 191–193, 232; Germany 127, 132, 149, 159, 164; society of the commons 268–270, 273; *see also* Greece
Scharsach, Hans-Henning 186, 212
schools 141, 194, 206–207
Schulz, Martin 130, 135
Schutzbund 59, 60
scroungers, benefit 193, 210
secularism (secularisation) 152, 161, 207, 221
security 24, 156, 216, 229, 231; financial 129; inner 132; national 25–26, 220; social 274
self-determination 57, 68, 246; national 65–66
self-regulation 254, 255
sentiments 24, 137, 149, 261
servitude 63–64
shares (sharing) 138–139, 192–193, 211, 256
simplification 127, 266
skills 225, 258
slavery 40, 41, 156
slogans 184, 185
slow media 263–265, 272

Smith, Anthony, D. 21–24
social burdens 146–153
social decline: Austria 180, 185, 191, 193; Bauer and Luxemburg 69, 72; Germany 140, 160
social democracy 2.0 279
Social Democratic Party of Austria (SPÖ) 180
Social Democratic Party of Germany (SDP) 134–135, 141, 165, 170, 175; *see also* Schulz, Martin
social justice 91, 128, 141, 165, 180, 274
social media 5–6, 8, 12–13, 16; Bauer and Luxemburg 70–72; Germany 162, 164–166; *see also* nationalism, Austria; nationalism, German; society of the commons
social problems 3, 10, 25, 42, 66; Austria 204, 234; Germany 126, 142–143, 149, 164
social services 147, 149, 183, 220
social systems 10, 12, 115; Austria 203, 205, 213, 231
socialism 10–12, 143; Marx 39–40; society of the commons 246, 265, 271–272, 274, 278–279, 281; theories of nationalism 26; *see also* Bauer, Otto; Luxemburg, Rosa
society 3–4, 8–10, 15–16; Marx 35–37, 40–41; society of the commons 281–282, 284; theories of nationalism 21–26, 28; *see also* Austria; Bauer, Otto; Germany; Luxemburg, Rosa; nationalism, contemporary
society, ageing 152; *see also* pensioners
society, class 4, 25–26, 250, 266
society of the commons 245–247, 275–284; authoritarianism 265–275; fake news 249–265; nationalism and social media 247–249
solidarity 11, 39–41, 188; Germany 140, 147, 159; society of the commons 246, 270, 274
songs (songbooks) 187–188, 235
sovereignty 84, 189

Soviet Union 26; *see also* Russia
spaces 23; advertising (ads) 213, 259; Austria 230, 234; Germany 129; online 130, 263; society of the commons 260, 264, 271, 276, 276–277
Spartacus League 43
Spiegel, Der 162, 234
Spivak, Gayatri Chakravorty 86–88
stability 59, 140, 274
standpoints 180–181
states *see* nation-states
status 194, 216
stereotypes 49, 158–159, 163
storage, data 281
Strache, Heinz-Christian 4, 6, 179, 231, 234–235; debates 201–203, 208; law and order 228–229; political context 185, 192; social media 210–212
Strasser, Josef 58, 63–64
strategies 127; political 259
strikes 60, 193
struggles 30; Bauer and Luxemburg 49, 60; Marx 34, 38; society of the commons 246, 276, 283
struggles, class 7, 9, 11; Austria 193; Bauer and Luxemburg 59; Marx 40, 52, 59
struggles, social 8, 40, 80–81, 91, 254, 278
subhumans 23, 129
submission 63–64, 270
Süddeutsche Zeitung 161, 234
superiority 26, 230
support 194, 212
supporters **137**, 192, 231, 234; *see also* Germany
surveillance 3, 259, 270, 281, 283
Sweden 125
symbols 10, 71, 140, 141, 245, 248
synecdoches 157, 163
Syria 222

tabloidization, tabloids 127, 250, 259, 266
taxes 182, 183, 189, 205, 264; corporate 234
technologies 13, 28–29, 138, 156; society of the commons 248, 251–252, 280–281
television 12, 279; *see also* debates, TV
terror (terrorism) 3–4, 16, 269; Austria 181, 208, 222; Germany 132, 142, 147, 157, 160
terrorists 23, 142, 156, 158, 163, 192, 231
Theweleit, Klaus 230, 270
thought, bourgeois (theories) 21–24, 36; Benedict Anderson 27–31; Gellner 24–27
thought, political 274–275
threats 142, 143, 220, 221, 225
time 23, 161, 260, 264
topics, discourse 199–200, **202**
topics, election 128, 181
traditions 46, 231, 269, 279, 281
trolls 255, 257
Trump, Donald 4, 70–72, 157, 212
trust 15, 138, 261, 268
Turkey 132
tweets 132, 134, **135**, 256, 257; automated 138
Twitter 12; Austria 188, 234; Germany 127, 130, 132, 134–135, 141, 154

Überfremdung *see* over-foreignerisation
UKIP (UK Independence Party) 10
understanding 126
unification 45, 46, 53, 56, 57; *see also* Anschluss
United Kingdom (UK) 40–41, 125
United States of America (USA) 40, 72, 158, 189, 253, 255
unity 25, 29, 140, 247
universal basic income 282
Universal Declaration of Human Rights 208
Unzensuriert.at 211
uprisings 59, 60

users: Austria 193, 199, 210, 216, 234; Germany 130, 137–139, 150, 153, 160, 165; *see also* audiences; content, user-generated; society of the commons; viewers

Verfremdung 273–274
Vernaderer 191
victimonyms 155, 204
victims 129, 155, 189, 204
videos 140, 141, 149–150, 152, 234, 256
viewers 118, 196; *see also* audiences; users
violence 4, 25, 52; Austria 192, 221; Germany 129, 157, 163; society of the commons 261–262, 269, 279
Visegrád Group 125
visibility 13, 138, 159, 252, 258; public 130
voters: Austria 180, 189, 194; Germany 127–129, 159, 161; society of the commons 252, 256, 272
votes (voting) 128, 184, 195

wages 15, 282; Austria 182, 193, 209, 231; Germany 141, 153; *see also* incomes
Wales 79–81
walls, building of 145
wars (warfare) 5, 7, 12, 35, 53, 66–67; Austria 195, 222; Germany 126, 147, 150, 156, 163; society of the commons 265, 270, 283; theories of nationalism 23, 25–26, 29

Weidel, Alice 70–72, 131, 135; bots and fake news 138; donors and supporters 161–162; refugees and migration 149–150, 159
welfare 162, 218, 272, 276, 279
welfare states 147, 149, 215, 218
Welt, Die 154
Williams, Raymond 30, 113–115, 247
Wodak, Ruth 127, 188
women 156, 194, 221, 231, 270
words 274; *see also* language
workers (workforce) 10–11, 28, 163; Austria 180, 193, 225; Bauer and Luxemburg 48, 53–55, 59–60; Marx 38, 40; society of the commons 272, 275
working classes 9, 34, 65
working conditions (time) 182, 189, 193
worldviews 194, 265
WOZ 162

xenonyms 204
xenophobia 8, 38, 268; Austria 192, 212, 233; Bauer and Luxemburg 47, 71; Germany 126, 128, 138, 159

YouTube 12; Austria 188, 212, 234; Germany 127, 130, 132, 138, 141, 154; society of the commons 247, 255, 257, 259

Zeit, Die 162

Printed in the United States
by Baker & Taylor Publisher Services